THE SOLDIER'S TRUTH

THE
SOLDIER'S
TRUTH

Ernie Pyle and the
Story of World War II

DAVID CHRISINGER

PENGUIN PRESS NEW YORK 2023

PENGUIN PRESS
An imprint of Penguin Random House LLC
penguinrandomhouse.com

Excerpts from Ernie Pyle's dispatches courtesy of the Lilly Library,
Indiana University, Bloomington, Indiana.

LIBRARY OF CONGRESS CATALOGING-IN-PUBLICATION DATA
Names: Chrisinger, David, 1986– author.
Title: The soldier's truth : Ernie Pyle and the story of World War II /David Chrisinger.
Other titles: Ernie Pyle and the story of World War II
Description: New York : Penguin, 2023. | Includes bibliographical references and index.
Identifiers: LCCN 2022041989 (print) | LCCN 2022041990 (ebook) |
ISBN 9781984881311 (hardcover) | ISBN 9781984881328 (ebook)
Subjects: LCSH: Pyle, Ernie, 1900–1945. | World War, 1939–1945—Journalists—Biography. |
World War, 1939–1945—Europe. |World War, 1939–1945—Pacific Area. |
War correspondents—United States—Biography.
Classification: LCC D799.U6 P953 2023 (print) | LCC D799.U6 (ebook) |
DDC 940.54/8173092 [B]—dc23/eng/20230103
LC record available at https://lccn.loc.gov/2022041989
LC ebook record available at https://lccn.loc.gov/2022041990

Printed in the United States of America
1st Printing

Book design by Daniel Lagin

To Ashley, George, Henry, and Stella

To a foot-soldier, war is almost entirely physical. That is why some men, when they think about war, fall silent. Language seems a betrayal of physical life and a betrayal of those who have experienced it absolutely—the dead.

LOUIS SIMPSON, *AIR WITH ARMED MEN*

The following pages include details of suicide attempts and may upset some readers.

If you find yourself in distress, call the 988 National Suicide & Crisis Lifeline by dialing 988, and if you fear that you may hurt yourself, please seek help from a medical or mental health professional. You can also text HOME to 741741 to speak with a trained listener and receive emotional support through the Crisis Text Line.

CONTENTS

THE SOLDIER'S TRUTH

CHAPTER 1

WARHORSING AROUND

▪▪▪▪▪▪▪▪▪▪▪▪▪▪▪▪▪▪

This is the last of these columns from Europe. By the time you read this, the old man will be on his way back to America. After that will come a long, long rest. And after the rest—well, you never can tell.

ERNIE PYLE, "FAREWELL TO EUROPE," SEPTEMBER 5, 1944[1]

1

A warm summer rain soaked the men as they mounted muddy tanks and stuffed themselves into half-tracks or jeeps pointed east.[2] The smell of soggy gear and idling engines overpowered the sweet scent of the honeysuckle that climbed the gray siding of a nearby three-story inn.[3] In a darkened shed out behind the inn, a forty-three-year-old pipe cleaner of a man sat hunched over his portable typewriter, ankle deep in straw, his back curved like a cashew. "This morning we are sort of stymied as far as moving is concerned," he pecked out with his index fingers to his wife back home in New Mexico, "so in order not to waste the day I dug up a white metal table out of a nearby garden."[4]

After nearly three months of hellish fighting through the hedgerow country of France, the Americans and their allies were thirty miles from the center of Nazi-occupied Paris.[5] Capturing Paris had never been part of the Allies' plan,[6] which involved a strike through to the Low Countries, across the industrial heartland of Germany, and straight to the heart of

Berlin.[7] The supreme commander of the Allied forces in Europe, General Dwight D. Eisenhower, had grave concerns that if he marched his men into Paris, they would likely bog themselves down in brutal street-by-street combat with seasoned enemy troops and reduce one of the world's most magnificent cities to a charred graveyard.[8] Not even an impassioned plea from the French commander, General Charles de Gaulle, had been able to dissuade him.

On August 22, 1944, the French Resistance's chief of staff, Roger Gallois, slipped through German lines on the outskirts of Paris and found his way to General George S. Patton's headquarters. The situation on the ground was not what the Americans thought, Gallois told General Omar Bradley's chief intelligence officer.[9] The Resistance movement in the capital city had infiltrated the police force, and the week before, fifteen thousand Parisian policemen had gone on strike.[10] More than that, the tens of thousands of Resistance fighters had risen up to attack and harass their Nazi occupiers, even though they were armed with not much more than antique rifles and Molotov cocktails.[11] In the days following the police strike, many more Parisians of all ages and abilities dug up paving stones, collected piles of furniture and other odds and ends, and felled trees to construct an elaborate network of more than four hundred street blockades.[12] Even though they were outnumbered and now outmaneuvered, the Germans were nowhere near outgunned and would eventually crush the insurrection and inflict untold amounts of suffering and destruction as they retreated east— unless the Allies came to the rescue. This new intelligence quickly reached Eisenhower, who dispatched the Free French forces under his command to liberate their capital with American and British backup while the rest of his forces pushed east and north toward the Belgian border.[13]

On August 25, 1944—Liberation Day—after a brilliant sun burned away the morning mist, Ernest Taylor Pyle, better known as Ernie to his millions of readers back home in America, stuffed his typewriter into its case, slung his musette bag over his shoulder, and hopped into a jeep with a couple of fellow combat newspapermen.[14] Through most of the early part of the day, they felt their way through gardenlike country toward the out-

skirts of Paris, far behind the lead tanks and the more daring Allied correspondents, such as Robert Capa, Ernest Hemingway, and Don Whitehead.
The outer rings of the city hadn't been bombed much, Ernie was heartened
to find, and most of the bridges were still safe to cross.[15] Not at all desperate to be the first to secure that coveted "Liberated Paris" dateline under
their bylines, Ernie and his companions entered the city from the south,
along the Rue d'Orléans, where they discovered "a pandemonium of surely
the greatest mass joy that has ever happened."[16]

Women in brightly colored blouses and skirts lined the wide city streets
in a carnival-like frenzy, leaving only a narrow corridor of pavement for
the hulking military vehicles to navigate. Aging veterans of the Franco-
Prussian War stood at attention, saluting their liberators.[17] Excited children
bounced and waved. Some ran along jeeps with their hands extended,
hoping for a shake but settling for slaps on the back or pats on the shoulder.
The demented choir of shrieking shells and zipping machine-gun tracers
the Allies had expected to encounter that day had mostly been replaced by
cheers of *Vive la France!* and *Vive l'Amerique!*—even as pockets of German
resistance in the city remained.[18] "They tossed flowers and friendly toma-
toes into your jeep," Ernie later reported. "One little girl even threw a bottle
of cider into ours."[19]

"Once when the jeep was simply swamped in human traffic and had to
stop," he wrote, "we were swarmed over and hugged and kissed and torn at.
Everybody, even beautiful girls, insisted on kissing you on both cheeks." At
least one ecstatic woman, with full pompadour and flashy earrings, reached
out to grab Ernie by the slack in his collar. Before he could protest, she
pulled his gray-bearded face, smudged with dust and lipstick, to her wine-
colored lips. *Thank you, oh thank you,* she squealed between kisses. *Thank
you for coming.* "We all got kissed until we were literally red in the face," he
later recalled, "and I must say we enjoyed it."[20] At long last, Ernie's ability
to relish in the beauty of the world at war, something he feared might have
atrophied inside his chest, suddenly flickered back to life.

After inching through so much gratitude and joy for about an hour,
Ernie had the driver pull over in front of a hotel near the Luxembourg Palace,

across the river from the Louvre.[21] They'd heard scuttlebutt that there were any number of desperate Germans holed up in the palace, firing indiscriminately at anything wearing green. While others fought, Ernie and two United Press correspondents wrote their first dispatches from Paris in a room overlooking the street below. "I had thought for me there could never again be any elation in war," Ernie wrote of that joyous day. "But I had reckoned without the liberation of Paris—I had reckoned without remembering that I might be a part of this richly historic day."[22]

The day after the city was liberated, Ernie and crew puttered over the Seine and past the Place de la Concorde and the gardens of the Champs-Élysées. From there, they meandered their way to the gilt-edged Grand Hôtel, across the street from the Allied press camp taking shape inside the Hôtel Scribe. Like Mary and Joseph, when Ernie and his companions arrived at the Scribe, they were told there was no room at the inn. Not long after the Nazi propaganda officers who had occupied the hotel had fled, some two hundred Allied correspondents "under an emotional tension, a pent-up semi-delirium," moved in and set up shop.[23]

Through the gilded lobby of the Grand Hôtel, up a set of marble stairs, and down the carpeted hallway all the way to the corner, Ernie found a room with clean sheets but no electricity. From the balcony three floors above the street, he grinned down in the afternoon sun at the joyous abandon below.[24] After so much darkness, grateful Parisians had found the light. Standing there with several other correspondents, in as genteel a way as his tongue could muster, Ernie quipped, "Any GI who doesn't get laid tonight is a sissy."[25] In fact, as one military study later showed, eight out of ten unmarried American soldiers had liaisons at some point during the war in Europe. About half of married soldiers did, too.[26] But not Ernie.

As the sun began to set, Ernie and his buddies made their way back across to the Scribe and claimed a table near the bar on the far side of the room. The booze did what Ernie wanted it to; it dissolved him. Soon a couple of dozen war correspondents had him encircled, eager to hear a tale or two from the little man everyone loved so much.[27]

At one point, the other famous Ernie—Hemingway—bellied up to the opposite end of the bar with the swagger of a lonely warlord, seemingly resentful of Pyle's command of his hangers-on. *SLAP!* Hemingway stung the air with a heavy hand on the bar top. A grenade he carried with him "just in case" pulled on the inside pocket of his field jacket.[28] "Let's have a drink here," he spat from the corner of his bearded mouth. The bartender baby-sitting Ernie and his buddies turned. Hemingway motioned for him. "I'm Ernest Hemorrhoid," he roared across the room, "the rich man's Ernie Pyle!"[29]

Around eleven o'clock, in between rounds of cocktails, air-raid sirens wailed, snapping everyone back to reality. In a raid of vicious retaliation, German bombers flew low over the rejoicing city, dropping their payloads and strafing anything that moved. Back suddenly was the "little knot of fear" in Ernie's stomach. Back was the "animal-like alertness for the meaning of every distant sound." Back was the "perpetual weight" on his spirit that comes with "death and dirt and noise and anguish."[30]

Gin-saddened, Ernie Pyle realized he had reached his limit. What should have felt like a gigantic relief—celebrating the beginning of the end for Nazi Germany—had become another opportunity to die. The German air raid killed as many as two hundred people who probably thought their war was over.[31] Another nine hundred were wounded.[32]

The next morning, Ernie sent a telegram to his longtime editor, dear friend, and amateur business manager, Lee G. Miller.[33] "About done up," he started. Physically, everything was fine, Ernie added, "but dogged clear down inside and can barely keep columns going." That final German raid had brought home the truth. Ernie was wrung out. There was nothing left to give. It was time to come home.[34]

2

A ren't you Ernie Pyle?" the young man asked.[35] After sending the telegram, Ernie headed back to the Scribe to surround himself with buddies and booze. Ernie didn't recognize the young man, though the red cross on his shoulder told him he was a medic, and the insignia on his collar meant he was an officer. Helmet in his hands, the captain waited for a reply from the pink-cheeked man with boots and fatigues grimy with war.

Even though Ernie never courted fame, in the late summer of 1944 he *was* famous, perhaps the most famous and most loved American war correspondent before or since. In the spring of 1944, he had been awarded the Pulitzer Prize for foreign correspondence. The column that earned him that honor ran in about four hundred daily newspapers and three hundred weeklies at the peak of its popularity. Two published collections of his best wartime columns, *Here Is Your War* (1943) and *Brave Men* (1944), were huge commercial successes that stayed at the top of bestseller lists for months. While he was reporting from France during the Normandy campaign, *Time* magazine put him on its cover. At the same time, a well-known Hollywood producer was making a movie, *The Story of G.I. Joe*, based on Ernie's European columns. In an age before celebrity journalists, Ernie was *the* celebrity journalist.

"Yes, I am," Ernie replied in his flat Indiana drawl. This sort of thing happened wherever he went. "G.I.s and generals recognize him where he goes, seek him out, confide in him," a writer for *The Saturday Evening Post* once explained. "The War Department and the high command in the field, rating him a top morale-builder, scan his column for hints."[36] The "folks back home," as he called them, adored Ernie even more. Thousands of them wrote letters asking him to check in on their boy or to find out the details of how their sons or husbands had gotten killed.[37] Ernie's readers saw his columns as vivid letters from someone they loved and cared about. Ernie saw his work the same way. "That's what I did," Pyle once told an interviewer, "traveled for other people and wrote their letters home. I'm really a letter writer."[38]

"I just want to thank you," the medic said, earnestly. "You've done some great things for us in your column. I read it whenever I can."

Despite the twenty-odd years he had on most of the troops he embedded with, Ernie had a knack for blending in wherever he went. He listened a great deal more than he talked, and he excelled at stating things simply that weren't simple to state. From the front lines of North Africa, Sicily, mainland Italy, and France, he dedicated himself to describing the everyday realities of America's fighting men in an accessible and personal way—without upsetting the military's capricious censors. In the hands of a less talented writer, the subjects of Ernie's columns could have come across as hopelessly trivial. Instead, his keen attention to detail gave his columns a granularity and an immersive feel that was easy for many readers to connect with.

"You won't be reading it much longer," Ernie huffed, perhaps expecting the medic to disapprove. "I'm going back to the States in a couple of days." I imagine his face. It's etched with weariness and grief and a twinge of shame. I imagine him looking back down at his drink, with an air of failure and self-hatred as he gently rotates his champagne flute on the table.

"Are you?" the medic replied. He looked relieved. "By God, I'm glad," he said. "You've seen enough of it."

Decades before expressing vulnerability came to be seen as the primary ingredient in meaningful connection, the struggles Ernie detailed for his readers helped to humanize him, and to convince a generation of Americans that he'd always give them what they needed—the truth. As when he told them, "Even after a winter of living with wholesale death and vile destruction, it is only spasmodically that I seem capable of realizing how real and how awful this war is. My emotions seem dead and crusty when presented with the tangibles of war. I find I can look on rows of fresh graves without a lump in my throat. Somehow I can look on mutilated bodies without flinching or feeling deeply."[39]

Granted, he quipped in his column a few days later, it was a "funny time for a fellow to be quitting the war." But he wasn't leaving on a whim—or "even especially because I'm homesick." The reason was much simpler than that. If he didn't stop, he confessed, he'd crumble. "All of a sudden," Ernie wrote, "it seemed to me that if I heard one more shot or saw one more dead man, I would go off my nut. And if I had to write one more column I'd collapse. So I'm on my way."[40]

Ernie's particular brand of truth-telling earned him an enormous and loyal fan base. But after twenty-nine months of living in war zones, nearly a year of that at the front lines, and after writing nearly seven hundred thousand words about the war, Ernie had grown tired of stitching it all into some orderly narration. The truth was that he had no more stories to relate, no more anecdotes. His spirit was wobbly, his mind confused.[41]

The average GI in Europe, it was later estimated by the American government, was capable of lasting between 200 and 240 days of combat before becoming a "psychiatric casualty," though only about 7 percent of all frontline troops lasted that long without being wounded or killed.[42] There was no such thing as "getting used to war."

Ernie didn't end his column on that note. As with much of what Ernie wrote to deliver hard truths, in his final dispatch from the European theater he sprinkled in enough reassurance to keep the overall tone more optimistic than it might have otherwise been.

"It may be that a few months of peace will restore some vim to my spirit," he speculated, "and I can go war-horsing off to the Pacific."[43]

3

The first time I remember coming across the name Ernie Pyle was during a war-related trip across the Pacific of my own. I cannot tell you personally what it is like to go to war. I've never been to war. What I can tell you is this: I know what it looks like when a man comes home from war and never finds that path that could lead him to a life of peace. I know about the alcohol and the rage, the depression, and the thoughts of suicide. I know what it feels like when trauma reverberates throughout the generations of a family. I know how the ripples eventually fade with time, but not before they do their damage. I know about bitterness and hopelessness. I know about silence. And lies. I know about the great gate that is the truth and what it feels like to have it slam shut on silent hinges. I know all of this because my grandfather, fresh from the family farm in Wisconsin, served his country during World War II by "mopping up" Japanese resistance and guarding "enemy civilians" during the Battle of Okinawa, the longest and bloodiest battle in the Pacific theater.

It was Memorial Day weekend in 2016, and my wife, Ashley, and I had three days to uncover as much as we could about what my grandfather had witnessed and endured. With the help of a local amateur battlefield historian, we retraced the battle from the records my grandfather's tank battalion had kept. To put the battle's bloody impact into stark relief, our guide, an American expat named Jack Letscher, drove us in his small baby-blue four-cylinder to the Cornerstone of Peace monument, near the southernmost end of Okinawa, atop steep cliffs overlooking the azure Philippine Sea.

The names of over 240,000 thousand people who lost their lives during the Battle of Okinawa are inscribed on wavelike concentric arcs of black granite slabs. Ernie's name, along with those of 14,008 other Americans who were killed, is no more prominently displayed than those of the nearly 150,000 Okinawans—close to half of the island's prewar population—or the 110,000 Japanese soldiers who lost their lives. Military and civilian. Allied and Axis. It doesn't matter. Everyone who lost their lives is treated equally. It's the only war memorial I've ever visited where all sides of the conflict are represented, without judgment, side by side. The Cornerstone of Peace, not unlike the Vietnam Veterans Memorial wall in Washington, DC, does not speak to the righteousness of the cause or to the courage of the sacrifice it required. The 116 slabs of stone speak to something simpler. They say: *This* is what it cost.

Because my grandfather destroyed all the letters he sent home from the war, and because he rarely spoke of his experiences, I didn't know the names of anyone he might have lost. When our guide Jack asked me whether I wanted to use paper and charcoal to make a rubbing, I froze in the blazing Okinawan sun. "That's OK," he assured me. "Let me show you one you might recognize."

At that time, the name Ernest Taylor Pyle didn't mean much to me. Jack jogged my memory—even read a passage about it from the battle's official military history. I remembered coming across it in my own reading—every book on the Battle of Okinawa dedicates at least a couple of paragraphs to the story of Ernie's death at the hands of a Japanese machine gunner during an ambush on Ie Shima, a tiny island off the northwest coast of Okinawa.

When I returned home from my pilgrimage to the Pacific, I bought a used copy of Pyle's book *Brave Men*. Its blue cover felt smooth in my hands. The old pages, smelling of vanilla, looked thumbed through, and lines throughout were underlined in pencil. Reading his stories made me feel as if I had been walking with him every step of the way.

In the months after I first read the book, whenever I came across something that tried too hard to make a point, that lost itself in purple prose, there in the back of my mind was the Pyle of *Brave Men*, looking askance at that untrue thing, waiting for me to see the untruth in it, too. In his voice I heard evidence of humility. War really was hell, no matter who told you different. But sometimes it was necessary, especially when some purported great power felt that its proper place in the world was to invade, conquer, and subjugate its sovereign neighbors because it had the power to do so, and because of some intoxicating ahistorical claim to greatness that helped salve the humiliations wrought the last time the world went to war. Make no mistake, though. The hell that war brings, he showed me, is the place, real or imagined, where whatever you normally count on is taken from you, absolutely.

4

Ernie jiggled the doorknob. It wouldn't turn. He pounded on the door. No answer. With one hand he yanked at the knob once more, hoping somehow to jar the bolt out of its latch. With the other, he pounded the wood until his hand stung. He dropped his hands and stepped back. At five-foot-nothing, one-hundred-and-nothing, Ernie wasn't the door-ramming type, but he took a running lunge. The door wouldn't budge. Out on the front lawn, Jerry's nurse, Mrs. Ella Streger, wept into her hands.[44]

Another running lunge.[45] The door banged open as the latch bolt gave way.[46] He pinned the door against the wall with his thin forearm and stepped inside. It took a moment before he registered what his wife had done to herself. It was her linen suit—that's what he noticed first. From her neck and chest, blood flowed in rivulets from deep puncture wounds, crimson streams down her frail figure.[47] Jerry turned to him, face expressionless and numb. Ernie trained his eyes on hers, expecting to see fear. He'd seen fear in the eyes of so many young men recently that it was all he could do *not* to see them whenever he closed his eyes.[48] But fear was not what he saw in his wife's awful stare that morning in the fall of 1944. What he saw was hopelessness.

A familiar jolt of adrenaline surged through him, though he felt calm, even detached. He registered his fear but didn't freeze. For years Ernie had feared that this was how things were likely to end.[49]

Taking her hands in his, Ernie led Jerry—better known to his readers as "That Girl"—out of the bathroom the way one might help an ice-skating toddler. He sat her down on the edge of the bed in his room and held her close. "At first glance," Ernie wrote to a friend the next day, "you would have thought she would be dead in a few minutes. But after a minute or so I realized her face wasn't getting the death pallor, and that the blood was clotting and not flowing very fast."[50]

Ernie and Mrs. Streger sat on the edge of the bed, Jerry between them, until Jerry's doctor arrived. He took a quick look at her, determined she'd somehow missed every vital area in her neck, and assured Ernie that she'd pull through. A few minutes later, another doctor—a surgeon—arrived with all his gear. After sewing up Jerry's twenty or so wounds, he sprinkled them with sulfa powder. Then her doctor, a man by the name of William Randolph Lovelace,[51] jabbed Jerry with shots of morphine, tetanus vaccine, and anti–gas gangrene serum.[52] "As the doctor said," Ernie told his best friend from college, Paige Cavanaugh, "thanks to her ignorance of anatomy, she missed every vital point."[53] Even without an anesthetic, Jerry never uttered a sound while the surgeon patched her up. She stared blankly.[54]

Jerry's doctor called out to Nazareth Sanitarium,[55] about eight miles north of town, to see if they had a bed for her. There was nothing else to do except to keep a watchful eye on her and clean up the bloody mess, which is what they did until about four o'clock that afternoon. The only words Jerry spoke between being sewn up and when the ambulance arrived to take her away were to ask Ernie for a cigarette.

"Darling," Ernie said, "we're going to the hospital now."

Jerry stood up straight, walked into the front room, and laid herself down on the stretcher.[56]

On a hill outside of town, the Spanish-style sanitarium was two stories tall, with a red tile roof. The locked ward on the top floor was reserved for patients who might be a danger to themselves or others.[57] Ernie and Mrs. Streger followed Jerry down the antiseptic hallway to her room. Jerry sat down on the lonely hospital bed.

"You can't do this to me," she said to Ernie. "I don't deserve this."

"But, Jerry," Ernie pleaded, "this is where you asked to come."

Jerry couldn't remember having told Ernie to take her to Nazareth instead of St. Joseph's. She lay down, resigned to what she believed was a death sentence. Ernie sat down beside her.

"May I ask you something?" she asked in a whisper. Ernie leaned his face in close, the hot breath of Jerry's mouth close to his ear.

"Are you Ernie Pyle?"

"I most certainly am," Ernie replied, stunned.

"I don't believe it."[58]

5

Who really was Ernie Pyle? Today, almost eight decades after his death, he remains an enigmatic figure. Despite his fame, he was a supremely private man. And because he left behind such a large body of writing, both published and not, and the views he expressed publicly did not always match what he wrote privately, it's entirely possible to cherry-pick either a confirmation or a rebuttal to almost every accolade and every accusation.

Beyond being simply a morale booster among the troops, Ernie was what the writer who knew him best, Lee Miller, called a bridge builder. "He bridged a gap in our knowledge," Miller wrote, "of the great war and of the men who were waging it—a gap of which we were not actively conscious until his reporting began to span it."[59] For millions of American troops overseas, Ernie was their scribe, their translator, and their champion. And he did it all, as his friend Miller put it, without the public or his fellow correspondents suspecting that at the exact time that "Ernie was making his reputation as the outstanding and best-loved correspondent of the war," his difficult marriage had "reached its tragic climax."[60]

Unlike most of his peers, Ernie tended to ignore the war's big picture.[61] With only a superficial grasp of military strategy and geopolitics, he chose to immerse himself in frontline living so he could tell stories from what he called the soldiers' "worm's eye view."[62] He first honed this approach during his early days as America's first aviation columnist for *The Washington Daily News* and later during his six years crisscrossing the country as a roving correspondent toward the end of the Great Depression, building a strong reader base by telling stories about the people and places most other reporters took little interest in. Little did he know that some of the pilots he befriended after work at Bolling Field outside Washington, DC, would one day swap nighttime mail runs for firebombing missions over German cities. Or that many of the desperate farmers he met in the Dust Bowl, and the lumberjacks in the Pacific Northwest, and the bellhops and bartenders from all over would end up as privates digging slit trenches in the Algerian desert, as sergeants leading their men up heavily defended mountain passes in central Italy, as pilots steering landing craft full of trapped troops onto hostile beaches.

It was his familiarity and kinship with "unimportant small people and small things," as a writer for *Time* put it in the summer of 1944,[63] that would suddenly become enormously important to millions of readers when the American involvement in the war began. Instead of writing exclusively about heroes and high drama, he made ordinary readers feel they understood what the people they knew were going through, so far away—small parts of an almost unimaginably complex war effort. He wrote of "tired and dirty soldiers who are alive and don't want to die; of long darkened convoys in the middle of the night, of shocked silent men wandering back down the hill from battle."[64] Ernie's reporting on the desperate struggle American soldiers endured would endear him to a generation of readers who came to see the war the way Ernie described it to them, not the mode of strategic overview but that of moral intuition.

Even as Ernie set the tone for his time, later reception of his work also mirrored the changes in American sentiment. One of Pyle's biographers, the journalist and historian James Tobin, portrayed Ernie in his 1997 book, *Ernie Pyle's War,* as a mythmaker—not because what Ernie wrote was a myth or because it was ever intended to be, but because after his death, Ernie's version of the war became as sanctified as he was. In essence, Ernie's war became the version America chose to remember. Ernie and the troops he wrote about became, in Tobin's words, "the heroic symbols of what the soldiers and their children would remember as 'the Good War.'"[65]

The less generous among Ernie's chroniclers have argued that his style of storytelling made him less of a journalist and more of a propagandist. They say he was nothing more, really, than a public relations man, that he sold a story about the war that omitted more truth than it espoused. The journalist and critic H. L. Mencken, for example, once described Ernie's work as mere sentimental fluff about the common soldier and said that what Pyle wrote couldn't possibly be described as "factual reporting of the war."[66] While there's some truth to what Mencken believed, it's also clear that Mencken had ideological ends of his own. Mencken never supported America's participation in the war, nor was he bothered much by the National Socialist worldview.[67]

But Mencken wasn't the only one to make such claims. Another journalist, Charles Lynch—very much not a Nazi sympathizer—described feeling similarly in an interview he gave Phillip Knightley for Knightley's now-classic 1975 history of war reporting, *The First Casualty*. He was humili-ated, he told Knightley thirty years after reporting for Reuters during the war, at what he and other correspondents, including Pyle, had done. "It was crap," he said. "We were a propaganda arm of our governments. At the start the censors enforced that, but by the end we were our own censors." He ac-knowledged that there wasn't much of an alternative considering the grave stakes of the war, "But, for God's sake," he said, "let's not glorify our role. It wasn't good journalism. It wasn't journalism at all."[68]

A dear friend of Ernie's, the famed novelist John Steinbeck, who defied his own wife's wishes and shipped off to Europe to cover the war for the *New York Herald Tribune* for a spell,[69] made sense of experiences like those faced by Pyle, himself, and other correspondents this way: "We were all part of the war effort. We went along with it, and not only that, we abetted it. Gradually it became a part of us that the truth about anything was au-tomatically secret and that to trifle with it was to interfere with the war effort. By this I don't mean that the correspondents were liars. We were not." Instead, Steinbeck decided, "It is in the things not mentioned that the untruth lies."[70]

These somewhat tiresome debates about whether Ernie was a great journalist or an accomplished cheerleader obscure the biggest riddle of Pyle's story: How did he do it? How did a middle-aged travel writer with-out any experience covering combat, the military, or foreign affairs become the most widely read war correspondent of all time?

6

On December 31, 1944, Henry Holt and Company released *Brave Men*, an edited collection of Ernie's best columns from the campaigns in Sicily, Italy, and France. By the beginning of October that year, only a few weeks after Ernie had returned to America, the publisher had already received over 100,000 advance orders—four times more advance orders than the previous collection, *Here Is Your War*, published the year before.[71] At first, Holt secured enough paper to print 170,000 copies,[72] but after those incredible advance sales numbers rolled in, they commandeered extra paper from their textbook department to print nearly 200,000 copies.[73] This success was even more impressive when we remember that relatively few Americans at the time could afford the three dollars for a book like *Brave Men*, and only a third of the country had access to a local bookstore.[74]

Between the royalties Ernie received each time a newspaper syndicated his column, his cut of book sales, and the 10 percent of the earnings from *The Story of G.I. Joe* once it premiered,[75] Ernie was projected to earn about $275,000 in 1945—twenty-five times what he was making as a roving columnist before the war. It's always tricky to calculate the purchasing power of money at different points in history, though it's safe to assume that in 2022 dollars, Ernie would have taken home more than $4.3 million that year alone.[76] With all his success and all that came with it, the conditions for a certain kind of happiness were present, though not for him.

There was no part of Ernie that felt fulfilled by the glowing attention his writing received. His fame, rather than freeing him to pursue the quiet life of reflection and friendship he ultimately desired, had made him "afraid to go into a restaurant because people whisper and stare." This fame had "taken away that saving gift of serenity of mind and soul," he confessed. "My life now, day and night, is a frenzy. There is no mental leisure in it; never the freedom to sit down and let your mind go blank."[77]

As if guilty about his "magnificent privilege" of being able to step away from the war for several months, Ernie wrote Lee Miller that he took on "more duties and worked harder" at home while he was on "vacation" than he did at the front. "There has been no rest," he told his readers. "There has been no time for composure. No day has been long enough to finish the things required in that day."[78]

"Sometimes," Ernie confided in Lee, "I wish I'd never been born."[79]

7

During his few short years as a war correspondent, Ernie Pyle was embraced by enlisted troops, commissioned officers, and a huge civilian public as a voice for the common soldier. After sharing so much of their experience, he understood how gravely war can alter the people who have to fight it. He knew that the survivors often come home with damage that is profound, painful, and long-lasting. It was a truth that he found difficult, sometimes even impossible, to communicate to his readers back home.

A couple of months before he was killed, Ernie received a short note of praise from General Eisenhower, thanking him for promoting "an understanding of what the infantry soldier endures."[80]

Ernie wrote a longer letter in reply. "I've found that no matter how much we talk, or write, or show pictures," he said, "people who have not actually been in war are incapable of having any real conception of it. I don't really blame the people. Some of them try hard to understand. But the world of the infantryman is a world so far removed from anything normal, that it can be no more than academic to the average person.

"I think I have helped make America conscious of, and sympathetic toward him," Pyle continued, "but haven't made them feel what he goes through. I believe it's impossible."[81]

When I read those words for the first time, I couldn't help but think about my grandfather. I'll never know exactly why he never told anyone his whole story. Perhaps he felt ashamed of something he had done or hadn't done. Or maybe, I started to think, he had felt the same sort of hopelessness Ernie came to feel at the end of his life.

What could I find, I wondered, if I left the view out my office window, roused the hibernating nomad buried deep inside me, and retraced Ernie's steps through the war? Was there some truth I could uncover if I followed the cartography he mapped out in his columns? What might be there for me to discover in the dry plains of central Tunisia, or in the steep mountain trails of Italy, or on the pancake-flat beaches of Normandy? Part of me also wondered what I might learn—or at least better understand—about my grandfather's wartime experiences. There was only one way to find out.

The primary goal I laid out for myself at the beginning of this project was to uncover the stories beneath the stories Ernie told his readers. I told as much to Yomna, the daughter of a Tunisian diplomat, over WhatsApp in the weeks leading up to my trip to North Africa. Fluent in English, Arabic, and French, Yomna had agreed to serve as my translator and guide for about a week in December 2019 after a professor of hers, my good friend Jennifer Orth-Veillon, asked Yomna if she had any advice to pass along to me about navigating Tunisia. What could the places I planned to visit, I asked Yomna, tell me that they didn't tell Ernie? What had we learned in the decades since the war ended that could help us better understand not only Ernie's life story, but also the story he told America? Yomna was intrigued, though she also expressed a fair bit of skepticism that American readers would want to know anything about her and her people. We'll see, I told her.

Staring out the plane window into the dark night sky on my connecting flight from Lyon, where Yomna attended university, to Tunis, I pondered the end of the living memory of the Greatest Generation and whether, along with the sadness of its passing, there might not also be an opening for a new, more honest account. Turning to my green reporter's notebook, I jotted down a flurry of questions I was hoping to answer, then I put down my pen and took a deep breath. As the plane banked to the east, it flew parallel to the coastline of North Africa. Dull orange lights close to the shore blurred into a mass of life; the desert beyond the coast was as black and lifeless as the sea below. Over the plane's intercom, the pilot spoke in Arabic, then in French, and finally in English. We would be touching down within the next twenty minutes, he said. The time for questions was over. Ernie was waiting for me.

CHAPTER 2

AT LAST THEY ARE IN THE FIGHTING

They poured around us, charging forward. They weren't close together—probably a couple of hundred yards apart. There weren't lines or any specific formation. They were just everywhere. They covered the desert to the right and left, ahead and behind as far as we could see, trailing their eager dust tails behind. It was almost as though some official starter had fired his blank pistol. The battle was on.

ERNIE PYLE, "TANK BATTLE AT SIDI-BOU-ZID," MARCH 1, 1943[1]

1

Yomna cinched the belt on her coat as a run-down pickup loaded with sheep blew past us. A blazing sun high in the clear December sky warmed my face and the top of my head. Once she was ready, we darted across the two-lane highway, hopped a concrete water pipe that ran the highway's length, and landed in a ditch. The ground beneath our feet was spongy and uneven where the earth had healed over discarded plastic shopping bags, crinkled water bottles, and paper espresso cups. A stiff wind kicked up sand from the west, stirring the smells of modern life in rural Tunisia into an odd bouquet of damp earth, truck exhaust, and the sweet smell of barbecued camel. "We will *not* be eating that," Yomna told me when I asked about the food served up by the roadside eatery we passed a few hundred yards down the highway from where we parked. On the other side of the ditch, a small field with neatly cultivated rows sprawled out before us. In the far corner of that field, two farmers Yomna had spotted, a man and a woman, were picking onions with their two mangy dogs.

We were there to climb Djebel Hamra, the Red Mountain—a jagged, steep-sloped escarpment that juts out of the desert valley a short distance from the farmers' field. On February 15, 1942, Ernie scaled Djebel Hamra after he and several other correspondents were assured its summit would provide an unobstructed view of the Americans' planned counterattack on the ancient camel-trading city of Sidi Bou Zid,[2] which had fallen easily to the two German Panzer tank divisions the day before.

Despite the devastating losses sustained at Sidi Bou Zid, an impenetrable sense of denial blanketed the Allied high command over the border in Algeria. Rather than withdraw and regroup, the order was issued to counterattack more than two hundred German tanks, half-tracks, and big guns[3] with what little was left of the American force—a tank battalion, a tank destroyer company, an infantry battalion, and some artillery pieces.[4] "We are going to kick the hell out of them today," an army officer told Ernie, "and we've got the stuff to do it with."[5]

"Unfortunately," Ernie would report, "we didn't kick hell out of them. In fact, the boot was on the other foot."[6]

When Yomna had picked me up from the hotel in Kasserine that morning, she told me that she wasn't going to let me climb any mountain in Tunisia until she first talked with a local who knew the area well. Since the winter of 2012, Islamist terrorists had used the cave-rich mountains in central and western Tunisia to hide from the military and stage attacks. "I don't want you to end up on some ISIS propaganda video," she told me from the back seat of our rental car as she queued up a playlist of her favorite Frank Sinatra tunes on her phone.

We met the farmer's dogs first. Yomna stayed behind me, using me as a shield. The mixed-breeds seemed friendly enough. They jumped up at me and nipped at the bottom of my jacket until the man whistled for them. We met and shook hands in the middle of the field, between rows of onions that looked ready to be picked. The man wore a dingy white scarf wrapped loosely around his head and a baggy black suit jacket and pants. Earth had worked into his pores and under his nails, and his hand felt cool and hard in mine. His wife stood behind him, squinting in the sun. Her colorful scarf looked handmade and much too nice to be worn while laboring in the dirt. Their faces were as wrinkled and weathered as their clothes, their eyes kind and watery from the wind.

Once I had exhausted my conversational French, which didn't take long, Yomna spoke in the Tunisian dialect of Arabic—a mix of Berber, Arabic, and a little French—about my project, how I was there to write a book about a man who had watched a tank battle between the Americans and the Germans from the Red Mountain.

"You mean 'Black Mountain'?" the woman said, pointing to it in the distance behind us.

I looked down at the map I had brought with me titled "Central Tunisia, 1943: Battle of Kasserine Pass." Allied movements were marked in blue dotted lines. The Germans were red. With my finger I found Fäid Pass, where the Germans had launched their offensive. Halfway between Sidi Bou Zid and Sbeïtla, I looked for the mountain. It wasn't there. I flipped to another map. "Here," I said looking to Yomna for confirmation. "This map calls it 'Dj Hamra.' Are we in the right place?"[7]

"She says everyone always called it 'Black Mountain,'" Yomna said with a shrug. "Maybe because it isn't red?"

The man spoke to me in French. I nodded politely and waited for him to finish.

"He wants to know what Ernie looked like," Yomna interjected.

He was a small man, I said, holding my hand flat against my sternum. About 110 pounds. When he was here, he was forty-two years old, I continued. Thinning white hair on the top of his head. He had a big nose, too. People said he looked frail, like he was sick all the time.

Yomna translated. The man nodded. He looked down at the ground, then back up at me. His lips tightened. His brow furrowed. When he spoke, it seemed he was trying to comfort me, as if he were a doctor gently explaining the inoperable nature of a lump I had found.

I looked to Yomna as I folded my maps and slid them back into the inside pocket of my jacket. She took off her sunglasses and smiled. "He says your friend is not there anymore."

After thanking the couple for giving us the go-ahead to climb the mountain, Yomna and I hurried back to the car, where we found her cousin, Zakariya—our chauffeur for the week—leaned against the front fender, scrolling on his phone and finishing a cigarette. About a thousand yards up the highway we crossed a bridge and turned left down a dirt road that followed the edge of an olive grove. The road dissolved into more of a trail, with ruts so deep Zakariya had to stick his head out the window to navigate them. As we crawled along, Yomna cranked up the volume on Sinatra's "You Make Me Feel So Young." At the end of the trail stood a small stucco building, ten feet by ten feet and fifteen feet tall. There was enough shade on the eastern side of the building for Zakariya to park and continue checking his text messages while Yomna and I hiked the rest of the way to the base of the two-thousand-foot mountain.

2

Ernie had thought he was ready for war. "Personally, I'm just about to bust I want to get over there as a war correspondent or something so bad," he wrote to his old friend Paige Cavanaugh,[8] eight days after the British and French declared war on Germany in the fall of 1939. "Pacifism is fine as long as there ain't no war around," he continued. "But when they start shooting I want to get close enough just a couple of times to get good and scared."[9]

In 1932, when Ernie was asked to drop his widely read aviation column to lead The Washington Daily News as managing editor, he didn't think it right to turn down the promotion.[10] A few years later, Pyle convinced his bosses that he'd make a far better roving columnist than a deskbound manager.[11] The truth was he'd always preferred writing to the routines of office life. His bosses were no doubt at least partly persuaded to finally cut him loose from his management duties by the reception Ernie received in 1934, when he wrote a short series of travel articles about a freighter trip he took from Los Angeles down around the tip of South America and back up to Philadelphia.[12] The series, according to the editor in chief of Scripps-Howard Newspapers, had a "Mark Twain quality that knocked my eyes out."[13]

With twenty-four papers in the Scripps-Howard chain committed to printing his column six days a week,[14] Ernie and his wife, Geraldine "Jerry" Siebolds,[15] gave up their apartment in Washington, DC, pawned their few bits of furniture off on Ernie's editor,[16] and hopped into their beloved Dodge convertible coupe to begin an epic tour of the Americas. Most spouses in America circa 1935 likely would have balked at such a lifestyle, but Jerry embraced it.[17]

Reporter by profession, out on the road Ernie would be a poet in spirit and a nomad by necessity. "I've had a good stroke of luck," he wrote a friend about the new gig. "I've finally been transferred from this man-killing job" to "the kind of job I've always wanted."[18] By the time the British and French were being evacuated from Dunkirk in the spring of 1940, the Pyles had crossed the lower continental United States thirty-five times[19] and visited twenty-one countries in Central and South America. Three cars and three typewriters later, Pyle had pecked out some 2.5 million words,[20] enough to fill thirty-one average-length books.

The stories Pyle wrote during his half a decade on the road weren't hard-news articles by any means; they were human-interest stories that highlighted ordinary Americans doing extraordinary things to make it through the Great Depression. There was the one he wrote about the married couple in Yuma, Arizona, who made a living by selling to zoos the twenty thousand snakes they had captured in the desert outside of town.[21] There was the short-order cook in Nashville who had once been enslaved by President

Andrew Johnson.[22] He profiled a national champion ice-cream-soda maker,[23] a genuine frontier woman living in what Pyle called a "disappearing America," and a family that built a boat themselves and sailed from Washington State to Alaska and back. In Montana, he wrote nostalgically about a farmer turned hitchhiker he picked up named Roy Meehan. "Young Mr. Meehan is as fine a fellow as I've ever met," Pyle wrote. "He's about 25, nice-looking and very tanned, and he rolls his own cigarettes. You could put him on Long Island in flannel pants and blue coat some evening, and he would be very quiet and everybody would like him."[24]

Ernie did much of his prospecting for stories in the smoky newsrooms of small-town papers in each of the places he and Jerry visited.[25] He found that fellow reporters and editors were reliable sources for unreported stories that needed a bit of the Pyle treatment. With his one suit, one of his three neckties, and his Borsalino felt hat cocked to the side,[26] Ernie followed up on his leads, reported for a few days, and then bunked down with Jerry in a hotel they found in the AAA directory. With the material he had collected, Ernie usually had enough to write for a couple of days and build for himself what he called his "cushion." On one trip, he and Jerry spent seven days in Monument Valley and the Four Corners region, and then, sunburned and nursing a cold, he spent the next week in an Arizona tourist cabin writing twenty thousand words—enough for three weeks of columns.

Part of the Pyle treatment included weaving in vivid descriptions to create an immersive experience. Of a Dust Bowl sandstorm—part of a series on the drought-stricken upper plains that Ernie's editor nominated for a Pulitzer Prize[27]—Ernie wrote, "The wind howled. It came at least 40 miles an hour, across the prairie from the north. It was hard to steer the car. The roar of the wind was louder than your voice . . . on the rises the sand-laden wind cut across the highway like a horizontal waterfall. The sand was not drifting, or floating, or hanging in the air—it was shooting south, in thick veins, like air full of thrown baseballs."[28] In Seattle, a city Ernie called a "bewitching thing," he told his readers it was good to "hear the foghorns on the Sound, and the deep bellow of departing steamers; to feel the creeping fog all around you, the fog that softens things and makes a velvet trance out of nighttime."[29] Of Bryce Canyon in southern Utah, Pyle wrote that the forest of stone spires looked like "a solar pipe organ," "10,000 pink flagpoles," and "what you see if somebody hits you on the head with a mallet."[30]

Ernie rarely mentioned any of the problems that weighed heavily on the minds of Americans during the Great Depression. When he did write about such things, he tended to restrain himself. When he wrote about drought, for example, he said it was not a spectacular thing. "Crops are gone. Farmers are gone. The heat is terrific. The whole thing is awful. And yet I feel sure that a city-bred man, who had heard about the drought and who came out to see the devastation, would be disappointed." Perhaps, Pyle speculated, some of his readers had been led to believe a drought was something far more dramatic. Desperate people gasping for water. Shabby houses burning to the arid ground. Carcasses of desiccated cattle littering the highways. "We think of farmers standing around in groups," he wrote, "making desperate decisions." But that wasn't the America Ernie knew.[31]

Perhaps what Pyle's readers appreciated most about him was that the Depression and all that came with it was a mere backdrop to the stories he told. Unlike some of his contemporaries, like Walter Winchell, who used his platform to attack appeasers of Nazism, Pyle focused on telling wholesome stories of people readers could admire. Instead of more devastating stories of bank failures, labor strife, and the down-and-out, Ernie's readers counted on being transported to someplace fascinating, whether it be among fishermen in Cape Cod, icebreakers on the Great Lakes, or prospectors in Alaska.

By the end of 1940, the next place Ernie wanted to take his readers was London. He wanted to see with his own eyes what it was like to stand alone against Hitler. France had fallen to the Germans by then, and the Vichy government dictated life in the parts of the country not occupied by the Germans. If Pyle was going to get a break from writing "silly dull columns about Mt. Hood and hop ranches" and get close enough to the shooting to "get good and scared,"[32] London might be his only chance.[33]

3

When Ernie and Jerry married, back in the summer of 1925, she had been working as a civil service employee in postwar Washington, DC, for nearly seven years, five of those on her own before she even heard of Ernie Pyle.[34] Subtle, penetrating, and sometimes mischievous, Jerry was inclined to love, though her determined self-sufficiency made it hard for her to admit that. A stubborn nonconformist,[35] she claimed she did not believe in marriage, finally agreeing to wed Ernie only after he wrung his hands about what his parents back on the farm in Indiana would say about their relaxed relationship.[36] For years afterward, Jerry insisted to her friends in Washington that she and Ernie were not actually married.[37]

The details of Jerry's life were not well-known while she was alive, and what is known about her is somewhat difficult to parse. A few months after Ernie was killed, an obscure magazine published a long feature article about "'That Girl' of Ernie Pyle's," in which the author wrote that despite Jerry's independent streak, she gladly "shrugged aside her personal ambitions to assume the role of Pyle critic," that "her confidence in his ability was steadfast long before he became America's most acclaimed columnist," and that whenever he grew discouraged, "it was Jerry who kept him at it."[38] Though few knew it, it was true that behind Ernie's outwardly easygoing manner, he was laceratingly critical of himself and his writing. He was also prone to fits of temper, barking insults as directions. And Ernie was almost constantly sick and in need of Jerry's care.

Two years after Ernie died, a writer named Esther Chapman Robb wrote a piece for another magazine that described Jerry's role in Ernie's life this way: "'That girl' devoted . . . twenty years to cherishing, like a votive priestess, the often wavering flame of her husband's special talent for writing about unimportant people so understandingly that both the important and the unimportant wanted to read about them." Moreover, she continued, Jerry "believed passionately in Ernie's great gift, even when he did not;

she guarded his uncertain health with maternal vigilance; she sacrificed her own personal life, and very possibly, a literary career of her own."[39]

In the years after that article about Jerry was published, after the first biography of Pyle appeared, some of the more haunting details surrounding her marriage to Ernie came to light. With nearly eight decades of perspective, it's plain to see that Jerry was anything but glad that she "shrugged aside her personal ambitions." In giving herself to him fully and supporting him in his sensitivities and resentments[40]—and his drinking[41]—Jerry felt forced to abandon her own needs and had to commit herself fully to Ernie's interests and desires, without a defined, long-term role aside from being Ernie's assistant.[42]

Even if Jerry initially accepted the limitations of such a life, after half a decade of being "that girl"[43] she had reached a breaking point.[44] Her contentment was replaced with exhaustion that morphed into a desperation that felt like carrying a heavy backpack, which pulled at her shoulders and wore her down.

On her best days, Jerry could brighten a room with a sudden smile or leave everyone speechless with a bit of improvisation on the piano. "She loved to play the good old favorites, with a sob in them," a family friend recalled. "And when she was in the mood to improvise, she was amazing. Then we all stopped singing, drew in our breath, and listened."[45]

Ernie's need for her could not have been an easy burden. He needed her acceptance and her love. He needed her protection. He needed her sparkle.[46] When the roving life ground her down and Ernie began to feel robbed of her silent assuring presence, his resentment festered.

Even to an untrained eye, it seems clear that by 1937, Jerry was demonstrating signs of what the French psychiatrist Jean-Pierre Falret called *la folie circulaire*, what we call bipolar disorder.[47] Jerry broke down again and again, especially after heavy stretches of drinking—in 1936, while Ernie was covering the drought in the Dakotas;[48] in 1937,[49] when Ernie left her home alone again, this time for four months to roam around in Alaska;[50] in 1938;[51] and again in 1940—landing her in hospitals for unhelpful examinations or in sanitariums for expensive stays. No treatment she ever received seemed to help for long.

4

I scanned the ground, searching for any signs of the battle. Slit trenches or rusty C-ration cans, maybe a rifle cartridge or shrapnel if I was lucky. Many American soldiers treated bits of shrapnel like good-luck amulets.[52] In the half hour it took Yomna and me to hike from the base of Djebel Hamra, there was nothing to be found but sand and shale and flecks of mica that glittered in the sun. The side of the mountain was steeper than it looked from a distance. With Yomna trailing behind me, I switchbacked across the south-facing slope. The sun baked the back of my neck. Dressed in tight black jeans and pearly white Adidas sneakers, Yomna kept pace with me until we hit a stretch made up of flat, loose stones. It was like try-ing to walk on dinner plates spilled all over the kitchen floor; Yomna slipped every few steps. She fell down hard on her side about three quarters of the way to the top. I heard her break her fall with her elbow and hip. She winced in pain as I trotted back to where she had fallen and helped her re-gain her footing. Her right side was dusted with powdery soil, like flour.

"Is that a cave?" she asked as she dusted herself off.

"Where?"

"There!" She pointed up and to the left. "Right there! That's a cave. That's definitely a cave."

A few hundred feet above us, a black hole big enough for a person to climb through stuck out among the light brown stones and green shrubbery.

"We need to turn back," Yomna said. "We need to get off this mountain."

For the first time in Tunisia, I was occupying the exact ground Pyle had. We were so close, yet Pyle suddenly seemed to be drawing back, like a desert mirage. I took a deep breath. The cool breeze dried the sweat on the back of my neck.

"What if we hiked this way?" I said, pointing to the far side of the mountain, away from the cave opening. "Then if someone comes out of there, we'd have more time to go down."

"But what if they have a gun?" Yomna asked. Her arms were crossed.

"We'll be fine," I tried to assure her.

5

In the early fall of 1940, Ernie and Jerry bought a small corner lot on the outskirts of Albuquerque where you could stand and look westward eighty miles.[53] "We're building a regular little boxed-up mass production shack," Ernie wrote to his old friend Paige. They paid $3,848 for the lot and the house—a little more than they originally thought they were going to spend, but then they were convinced by their contractors to have a real fireplace installed and to upgrade from stucco on the exterior to horizontal planking instead.[54] After so many years living like vagabonds, with clothes and books cached away at homes of friends around the country,[55] Ernie wanted to believe building a home together with Jerry and laying down some roots would help them mend whatever was wearing out between them. "It's foolish and an utter luxury," he wrote to Paige, "and yet I have a feeling it is gravely important for us."[56]

Before the green-roofed house[57] was completed, Ernie accepted an assignment to cover the German bombing campaign against England. Jerry put on a brave face when Ernie broke the news to her, but there was no denying the truth.[58] He was abandoning her right after he promised to stay put for a while. Jerry was "really grieving and feels awfully alone and pointless," Ernie said of his decision at the end of October, "and I feel like an absolute sonovabitch to go under the circumstances; and yet I've just lately had a feeling I had to be in London, and if I didn't go now with the opportunity there, I would regret it the rest of my life."[59]

Once Ernie decided to leave against her wishes, Jerry lost all interest in their little house and whatever contentment she thought she could find in it. "To pretend that I give one single solitary good goddamn about a shack or a palace or any other material consideration in this world," she wrote to her best friend in Albuquerque, "would be to foist upon everybody at all interested the greatest gold-brick insult a low mind could conceive." Ernie's plan to leave her to finish and furnish the house on her own, she continued, "seems to me as diabolically ironical as any ever devised."[60]

On November 16, while Jerry was waiting for their furniture to arrive from Washington[61] and double-hemming the window curtains,[62] Ernie took a steamship from New York to Lisbon.[63] A couple of hours before the ship docked, he pecked out a letter on his portable typewriter. He wanted Jerry to know how much he missed her and how it seemed to him "sheer insanity that we haven't always been happy." Perhaps in an attempt to justify the trip, he wrote that "after the terrific emotional experiences we've been through this fall we can appreciate ourselves more now, and be better off in the future."[64]

In Lisbon, Pyle caught a British government plane that flew him across the Bay of Biscay and the English Channel to London, where he would report on the German aerial offensive still underway there.[65] Pyle's editors had wanted him to go to France back in May, but Ernie was afraid that his not knowing any European languages along with stringent censorship and everybody being "too damn busy fighting a war to monkey around with a nosey feature writer" was a recipe for failure.[66]

Ultimately, Ernie changed his mind and told his editors he did want to go. By that time, however, the situation on the ground had changed. "Europe is OUT," his editor in Washington, DC, wrote to Pyle as the German blitzkrieg raced across France. "Good God, there won't be any Europe in a week or two. The War Department here has given the Allies up for lost."[67]

A month after he arrived in England,[68] Ernie caught what turned out to be his biggest story of the trip when he witnessed an incendiary bombing from a hotel balcony in London. Hurrying from his cold and blacked-out room at the first low groan of the air-raid siren, he was high above the city streets when the fire burst up all around him. It was an incredible sight, he told Jerry. "The English say the most spectacular night they've had, even including the September blitz."[69] The horizon that Sunday night was red, he reported, and billows of dirty pink smoke choked the lungs. On nearby roofs, antiaircraft guns thudded at the German Luftwaffe while volunteer firemen on the ground extinguished one fire after another.[70]

Ernie wrote two pieces about that night. When the New York correspondent of the London *Telegraph* cabled him to say the last third of the first article offered the most vivid description of the bombings that any American correspondent had yet written, Ernie was shocked. He had thought both articles were terrible.[71] A week later, the chairman of Scripps-Howard Newspapers, Roy W. Howard, cabled Ernie in London, congratulating him on the "marvelous stuff" he had written, which was "without doubt best so far on war and building tremendous following." Ernie was tickled, he wrote to Jerry, quoting directly from the telegram: "And then this masterpiece right out of a clear sky from Roy," he wrote. "'Your stuff not only greatest your career but most illuminating human and appealing descriptive matter printed America since outbreak battle Britain.'"[72] Jerry agreed. In a letter to a friend, she wrote that she thought "Ernie's column about the burning of London is the most terrible and beautiful I have ever read."[73]

In the subsequent columns he wrote from London that winter, Pyle never mentioned the number of planes shot down, buildings destroyed, or people killed. Instead, he focused on the ways the bombings had affected the British people, how life carried on. In many ways, he wrote about the British the same way he had written about the Americans he met during his years living on the road. They were the courageous underdogs with indefatigable spirits, democracy's David squaring off against fascism's Goliath in an epic tragedy whose ending had yet to be written.

By simply detailing what he saw and humanizing the ways in which the people themselves resolved to withstand the German offensive, no matter the cost, Pyle answered a tremendously important question for the American people: Was the Nazi war machine strong enough to break the will of the British people? "They have tough years ahead," Ernie knew, "but I don't believe they will ever crack."[74]

6

Ernie returned to the United States in March 1941[75] without having had "the obscenity" scared out him[76] and went straight to his hometown of Dana, Indiana, to visit his mother's grave. Maria Pyle had suffered a series of strokes and died while Ernie was still in London. "I went alone yesterday to the graveyard," he later wrote in his column, "and stood in the sharp wind over my mother's grave, with its flowers put there on a recent day when I was across the ocean." As he stood there, unable to fully grasp his loss, it seemed to Ernie that he and his mother were all alone in the world—and that he could speak to her. "It was brief," he continued. "I could not bear it. I got into the car and put on my dark glasses and drove to town and got a loaf of bread for supper, and drove home with it as though I had not been anywhere special and nothing had happened."[77] He was empty but at peace.

From there he drove in a car packed with family straight east from the farm in Dana to Indianapolis to catch a flight back to Albuquerque.[78] Before he climbed aboard his plane, Ernie stood and chatted for a short while with a woman by the name of Mabel Calvin,[79] whom he'd met the summer before while vacationing at a cabin about an hour south of Indianapolis owned by a journalist friend of his.[80] The particulars of how they met and how they spent their time together that last week in July 1940 can only be inferred. Soon after arriving, Ernie wrote a letter to the cabin's owner, admonishing him for not giving it to him straight about Mabel. "You deliberately drew me a distorted picture," he wrote. "Hell, I thought she was hare-lipped and 50 and 200 lb and wore a fascinator and said 'shit' in polite company."

A little over a week later, Ernie wrote another note to his friend, thanking him for the lovely gift. "I broke one canvas chair," he confessed. "Mabel broke the other." In case his friend was curious, Ernie continued, "Mabel can—if she will—give you a report on many things, including the fact that I am practically insane about her."[81]

Later that fall, during a brief stop in Indianapolis, Ernie and Mabel met up again. "I wish I were mystic or all-seeing and could give you some fine, wise advice to cure what hurts you," Ernie wrote to her the day after they met up. "But hell if I knew I'd apply it to myself. I'm selfish enough to want you to love me always, but it kills me to think of you being unhappy.

"I wonder if we will ever again relive our perfect days at the cabin," he continued. "It seems almost too much to hope for, and yet that's almost all I do hope for, or could ever ask of whoever runs this world, and us dopes in it."[82]

On November 6, 1940, shortly before his planned departure for London, Ernie described the status of his relationship with Jerry, clarifying how he saw Mabel fitting into his life after he returned. "I cannot disavow my loyalty to Jerry; to her I have never denied or belittled my great feeling for you," he said. "We shall," he continued, "if Fate is willing, be together again. And then we will talk and drink and talk and have our beautiful times again."

"No one in my adult life has ever given me the feeling I have for you," he added, "and I will take it with me."[83]

Jerry, for her part, was supportive—at least at first. In her own letter to Mabel, she explained that she loved anyone who loved Ernie and that there was so much she couldn't be for him. "The best I can do," she wrote, "and it's a poor best, is to say to you that your attachment interferes in no way with my regard for either of you. I say that from my heart. What is my share in him, no one can take away from me; for so far as our minds are concerned, neither of us knows where the one leaves off and the other begins."

"I have lived long enough to know," she concluded, "that sufficient as two people may be basically, each to the other, there are doldrums periods, when new and stimulating association is necessary."[84]

7

With the Blitz behind him and the spark of a new flame to buoy him in his grief, Ernie took some much-needed rest at the behest of Roy W. Howard, the chairman of Scripps-Howard Newspapers. On May 26, Ernie sent an airmail invitation to Mabel. "For some time I had had the idea of having you come out while we were here on vacation," he wrote. "But this morning Jerry suggested it, and we've been talking about it, and we both want you to come so much we can almost see you here right now." He enclosed a note Jerry had written for Mabel's eyes only: "Don't fail us— we want you so much—Ernie will need help with his fence," she wrote. "I need help with the dishes!—Maybe we can all help one another—You *must* come."[85]

What exactly happened during the week Mabel stayed with the Pyles at their home in Albuquerque may never be known. Photographs snapped during her visit show, among other things, Jerry and Mabel sitting together out in the sun, or visiting with neighbors. Mabel told her family the story, impossible now to corroborate, that one night during her stay she woke to find Jerry at the end of the bed, holding a knife in her hand. The day after Mabel left for home back in Indiana, Jerry wrote her a cryptically worded letter to apologize for something. "Since you came here at my wish, desire and suggestion I am doubly sorry your visit was so short of pleasant," she apologized. "Had I realized how close to the breaking point I was, I'd have waited until our next visit here to invite you."

"Everything is much too complicated and involved for my feeble mind to try to fathom it at the moment," she continued. "I hope with all my heart you can continue to regard me with compassion."[86]

On the first sunny Saturday in June, sans Mabel, Ernie dug post holes in the shadeless yard by hand for a white picket fence Jerry said she wanted built alongside the driveway. He set all thirty posts himself, his work boots stamping down the sandy clay to help keep them rooted. Ernie had always loved to tinker, especially when the labor was methodical and there were matters concerning Jerry's mental health that he hoped would resolve themselves in his absence.[87]

After a few more days of hammering, Ernie had finished tacking up two sets of two-by-fours to support the top and bottom of the fence's pickets. He thought briefly about extending the fence around the south end of the lot. More time to think, to process. More time for Jerry to fix herself.[88]

One of the contractors who built the Pyles' home, Earl Mount,[89] lived right next door. Over time, the Pyles and the Mounts became quite close. Ernie wrote a few columns about Earl's daughter, Shirley, including one about her helping Ernie build that white picket fence.[90] "We worked out a sort of speed-up system," Ernie told his readers. "While I nailed one picket, Shirley would measure and mark where the next picket should go, then hand me the picket and the four nails to put in it." He and Shirley put up between nine hundred and a thousand pickets "so fast that we picketed seven feet beyond the end of the fence before realizing we had finished." And he never hit his thumb.[91]

Two letters Ernie sent Mabel hint that Jerry might have had a brief affair with Earl, which may help explain her enthusiasm for an open marriage.[92]

For an article Ernie had coming out in *New Mexico Magazine* titled "Why Albuquerque?," a photographer came out to the Pyle home to snap some photos of Ernie nailing on the final white picket. In one, Ernie is crouched low at the end of the fence, near the opening to the gravel driveway. Curly-haired Shirley is on the other side with her hands grasping the top of a picket. She's looking down at Ernie, whose head is lost in a ten-gallon hat. Ernie is holding a cigarette with his left hand and pointing at something in the distance behind the photographer. The house behind him beams bright white, and the sun casts dark fence-shaped shadows along the length of the driveway. In another photo, Ernie is standing, holding Shirley around the waist as she leans up over the fence. Shirley's right arm drapes around Ernie's narrow shoulders. With his free hand, Ernie clutches his hat against his chest. The final nail has been set.

In a letter to Mabel dated June 24, Ernie told her that he had found Jerry one morning sitting on her bed, "looking like death, and shaking so bad she could hardly stay on the bed." It seemed to Ernie that "the full re-alization of what she had done" to Mabel during her visit "came upon her for the first time, and it horrified her."[93]

One night in late June that summer, soon after Ernie and Shirley had finished the fence, Jerry tried to kill herself for the first time. "Went completely screwball," Ernie later wrote to Paige about it. "She tried the gas. Had to have a doctor. Had to phone Poe."[94] That was Jerry's sister, a former nurse who lived with her husband in Denver. For ten days after her failed attempt, Jerry stayed at the Presbyterian Hospital up near there,[95] until her doctor felt confident she was no longer suicidal.

Three months later, at the beginning of September, Jerry passed out in the middle of the night after an ulcer in her stomach ate its way into a blood vessel.[96] Ernie was in Canada then, touring a string of new military airfields, trying to rekindle some of the excitement he had felt in London. His work, he was discovering, could not be balanced easily with his marriage to a sick woman. From Ottawa, Ernie wrote Liz Shaffer, a friend of his and Jerry's, asking her to check in on Jerry while he was away. "I get so little out of her," he wrote, "that I've just got to have some word of how she is."[97]

When Liz went to check in on Jerry, the early evening sun shone on closed curtains. She was fine, Jerry tried to convince Liz through the dead-bolted door. No need to worry. But Liz did worry. And after a while, she convinced Jerry to open the door. Inside, Liz found a dear friend who was lost to herself, who couldn't come to the surface. Liz refused to leave when Jerry begged her to. No way, she said. She was going to at least spend the night.[98] Several times during the early hours that night Jerry woke with a fright and bolted to the bathroom, waking Liz each time. At about four o'clock in the morning, with the moon high in the sky above the Pyles' dream home, Liz followed Jerry into the bathroom and found her cough-ing blood into the sink, which was half full of half-dried and viscous clots Jerry had barked out during her previous dashes to the bathroom. The fam-ily doctor arrived twenty minutes after Liz had rung him. Forty minutes after he arrived, Jerry was in a hospital bed being prepped for surgery.

Five days and two thousand miles later, Ernie was back in Albuquerque. The doctor told him Jerry had suffered a gastric hemorrhage brought on by heavy drinking.[99] "If Liz hadn't stayed," Pyle said, "they would simply have found her dead the next day when they came to the house. The doctor says that he has never seen anyone so nearly dead and come through it."[100]

For four miserable days after Ernie arrived, Dr. Lovelace, one of the "finest men in the Southwest" in Ernie's estimation,[101] and a doctor named Richards from Denver tried to convince Jerry that enough was enough. She needed to commit herself. Six months at least. Maybe a year.[102] Jerry flatly refused.[103] "And in that dogmatic, autocratic way in which she has ruled ever since I've known her," Ernie later explained, "she simply refused to go. It was as though she had said 'I will not go, you are now all dismissed.'"[104]

"The doctor, who is good and a bit of a psychologist," Ernie wrote to friends back in Albuquerque, "says (and I agree) that it would be futile and possibly dangerous to put her in the hands of a psychoanalyst." Jerry was too smart for psychoanalysis, her doctor told him. When the doctor tried to get inside her personality, to "find out what made her the way she is," Ernie once explained, "she turned on the old armor of gayety and charm, and he never got anywhere."[105] The cure, if there was one, had to "come out of her own desires and will," he continued, "and I don't know whether it's too late or not."[106]

With no legal recourse to have her committed, Ernie resigned himself to staying home with Jerry, who told Ernie this was her second chance—"that because of the fact that she has been scared for the first time in her life, she will be allright from now on.

"I know she means it," Ernie continued, "but I also know she meant it all the other hundreds of times she said it. She has the most dominant will-power of anyone I've ever known over everybody but herself. And even if she is kept from drinking, that isn't the fundamental; the fundamental is her mind and spirit and approach to life."[107]

So that he could help Jerry recover from home, Ernie asked his bosses back in Washington for a three-month leave of absence.[108] He was spent, he said, in mind, body, and spirit, and couldn't see how he would possibly be able to get back to writing. He had to either take a break or quit his job as a roving correspondent. "Whichever I do is up to you," he told them.[109] "I either have to stick with her now or else abandon her," he wrote, "and obviously I couldn't and wouldn't do that.

"If I am to leave Scripps-Howard after 17 years of mighty fine association," he continued, "I think it is only fair to give you the whole story, as much as I hate to."[110]

"For more than ten years," he recounted to Lee Miller and Walker Stone, the editor in chief of Scripps-Howard Newspapers, in a highly revealing letter, "Jerry has been a psychopathic case." Over the past few months, since Mabel's visit to Albuquerque, her illness had "reached a stage in which you would have to turn your back to call it anything less than a form of insanity." Although Ernie was no stranger to depression himself, the catastrophic gloom Jerry battled had overflowed past the level of his own relatively manageable doldrums. "She is a dual personality," he continued, "you might say a triple personality—one side of utter charm and captivation for people she cares nothing about; one side of cruelty and dishonesty toward the few people she does care about; and another side of almost insane melancholy and futility and cynicism when she is alone, which is her true personality."[111]

Ernie's bosses granted him his request without hesitation, offering him not only three months of leave but also full pay as a bonus.[112] It was not only the right thing to do, but it was also plain "good business," they told him.[113] Ernie balked at becoming the "highest-paid housemaid in the world" and said he would take the leave, but not the pay.[114] His bosses wouldn't hear of it. They insisted, and in early January 1942, they deposited what Ernie would have made during his time off into his account. "It makes me ashamed," he later told Jerry, "but there's apparently nothing I can do about it."[115] In a letter to Lee, he was more compassionate with himself, more practical in his thinking, too. "As much as I hate the idea of taking it," he explained, "it does put a little security back under me again." Over the course of that previous summer, Jerry's medical bills ran into the thousands, and truth be told, Ernie confessed to Lee, he and Jerry were "skating pretty thin."

"And although I don't mind that," he continued, "I'll never be awfully surprised if Jerry goes invalid again at any time, and that requires dough. Even $30 a week for a nurse all winter ain't chicken feed."[116]

Part of Ernie wanted to push away from Jerry and all her expenses, as if pushing himself back from a string of bad luck at a poker table. But he didn't. He resisted that urge. He knew that if nothing else, he owed it to Jerry to stay. So he stayed. "If I ever had any thoughts of breaking off and changing my life into a new pattern," he broke it to Mabel, "they have to be gone now, for you can't abandon someone who is desperately in need." More than that, he continued, his "old, deep feelings" had finally frizzled. "What it will be like in the future I have no idea; probably constant misery for her, and for me a perpetual shifting of emotions between annoyance and a ghastly guilty feeling that maybe I never gave her enough."[117]

Each day he was home with Jerry in Albuquerque that fall, Ernie went to bed early and got up early. From the front window of the house he would spy the shoulders of Mount Taylor in the distance and listen for the early-morning songs of the meadowlarks that lived in the sagebrush across the road.[118] He found Albuquerque's desert dawns violently beautiful, and each evening the fireplace glowed and crackled, the smoke curling between heavy pieces of wood, until it was time to watch the sun set and head off to bed.[119] When he wasn't helping tend to Jerry or tackling maintenance projects around the house, Ernie read the books that had stacked up in his office and wrote letters to friends he had not had time to write when he was constantly on the road. In such a simple existence, there was time for everything.

But Ernie also worried. To the point of bewilderment, he fretted about Jerry's health, the fate of the world, and his career. Getting loose with tumblers of gin was all he could do to slow the flywheel, heavy with momentum, that churned in the back of his mind. After only six weeks, he had reached the end of the line. Jerry had made some progress at the beginning of his leave, but then, he said, she had "cracked up again."[120] "She's so off balance," he told Paige, "I have run out of possible ideas for approaching it. Nobody can help her but her, and she won't, or can't. Everything looks blue."[121]

It was time to plot his escape. *What about a three-month tour,* he pitched to his editors, *of the Philippines, Hong Kong, Chungking, the Burma Road, Rangoon, Singapore, and the East Indies?*[122] He could check out Australia and New Zealand, too.[123] "I don't know what I'll do this winter if I don't go there," he explained to Lee, "and if Russia should still be holding by the time the Russian fall weather sets in, I don't believe there'll be much danger from Japan till spring. And even so, what? There was a war on when I went to England."[124] Plus Jerry didn't seem like she really needed Ernie that much anymore, at least in his estimation. "The reason for my leave of absence—to try to help Jerry over the hump—has either been done or hasn't been done, I don't know yet," he wrote to his editor and the bosses at Scripps-Howard. "But regardless, I feel there is no necessity or possibility of gain by me staying on more than another month."[125]

"I feel like I've just got to make this Orient trip," he pleaded with Lee at the end of October. "The trip honestly seems perfectly logical to me, and I can't conceive of there being any real danger to it," which was evidently what worried Ernie's bosses most.[126]

"I think if we don't start doing something tangible in the war," Ernie continued, and if the president didn't start telling the American people the truth of what was going on "now and then," he feared morale among the American people was going "to go the way of Army morale." At least Ernie's was.[127]

"Honestly," he confided in Lee, "I don't go back to work with any relish at all. If it could just be under different circumstances, I'd love to stay here a year, just pissing around at nothing."[128]

On his way back from Washington, DC, where he secured visas and permits and received the inoculations required for travel to the Far East, Ernie stopped in Indianapolis briefly to say goodbye to Mabel. "It's almost like a dream that I saw you at all," he later wrote to her. "The next time we're together maybe I can be spared the flu and a dog. Maybe it'll be summer and a log cabin." He signed the letter, "Lots of love." Ernie and Mabel never saw each other again.[129]

Two weeks later, on December 7, 1941, the Imperial Japanese Navy Air Service laid waste to the American fleet at Pearl Harbor. On that day of infamy, Ernie was resting up at home in Albuquerque in preparation for his big trip,[130] which he hoped would help rejuvenate his column and lead to more income from syndication.[131] The next night after the attack, while the rumor circulated that the Japanese had positioned two aircraft carriers off the coast of San Francisco, Ernie bought a seat on the first flight there.[132] If he could get someone to drive his car up to him, he could cruise along the coast, writing what he called "semi-war columns" for at least a month.[133] He ended up spending the rest of 1941 and the first two months of 1942 working his way down the coast to Los Angeles. In late February, he had dinner with Paige, and another night the two best friends from Indiana University, along with Paige's wife, Edna, met for drinks in Ernie's room at the Mayfair Hotel, getting loose and talking late into the night. During the day, as always, Ernie gathered material for the column or poked at his typewriter, trying to build himself a cushion so when he eventually returned to Albuquerque, he could spend more time with Jerry and less time stressing about money and his deadlines.[134]

The demands of a daily column had always been hard on him, but by then it seemed the work was so tough he couldn't find a rhythm.[135] "I still don't know what my plans are," he wrote to Jerry about the rest of 1942. "Lee and I have been writing back and forth about it, and we can't seem to fish out any kind of a trip that would be feasible. So I guess it'll be just the same old traipse across the continent, till my tires give out."[136]

By the middle of March, Ernie learned from friends in Albuquerque that Jerry was back on the bottle. "Fooling everybody in the daytime," he told Paige, "and drinking all night, apparently. The nurse told me she carried from her room ten empty quart bottles at the end of one week!"[137] Ernie was still on the road then, almost eight hundred miles away in San Diego. Jerry apparently couldn't sleep without him home, so she drank, and her nurse had been doping her with opiates whenever she needed to be "put under."[138] All day she was besieged by a multiplicity of worries and a resigned sense that she had been relegated to less than a supporting role. She wasn't even on the cast list anymore. Her separation from Ernie made her as resentful as he was feeling about her illness.

"I know you went through a soul-searching while I was in England," Ernie told Jerry, "and I think you felt exactly this way when I came back, and I think the fact that I didn't feel that way and couldn't respond is what sent you down the last toboggan. I believe you had gone to the depths of yourself and had come out on top during the time you felt that you might never see me again. The tragedy of our lives is that I did come back alive from England, the same person, while you had remade yourself."[139]

After about a month of torturous life on the road, struggling to maintain his cushion of columns, Ernie started to wonder whether he might be better off quitting and maybe finding a job in the booming defense industry growing up around Albuquerque. Or perhaps he and Jerry could open up a home-decorating business. They could "charge rich bastards $1,000 a home and do about six a year," he pitched to Jerry. "You could furnish the taste and imagination."[140]

On January 14, 1942, he wrote to Lee saying that he was in a slump and that he had received a nice letter from one of the bosses at Scripps-Howard telling him to follow his nose. "But if I do," he quipped to Lee, "I'll probably just follow it to the bottom of a lake somewhere. I simply can't hit my stride. I'm almost desperate. Have been thinking very seriously of quitting." Ernie couldn't seem to find interest in anything. He'd go a mile out of his way to avoid collecting material for his column. "Can't make anything light-hearted enough to make it readable," he fretted.[141]

"I've been gravely concerned about the war lately," Ernie also confided in Jerry. "I really can't feel positive any more that we're going to win the damn war. But regardless, life is going to be tough, and plenty, starting about a year from now. We'll be denied most everything that is pleasant to have, and most of our jobs won't last, and we'll be back again to our 'poor' days of the early '20s. It gives me the creeps. And if we should lose, God knows what our state would be."[142]

Jerry was back in the hospital. She was there to receive a blood transfusion. Her red blood cell count was down to 30 percent of normal, Ernie later learned. "She wrote me about it," he told Lee, "and made it sound so matter-of-fact that I wasn't worried about it very much. But early this morning I had a call from Albuquerque—and the reason for this set-back is that she's been doping and drinking to excess again."[143] More than that, "the goddam nurse, put there purposefully to regiment and taper her off on her dope, has apparently been conniving with her in getting it in large quantities. I don't know how much longer I can take it."[144]

After a week in the hospital, Jerry returned home. On February 5, she wrote to Ernie. She understood his thoughts and fears and how his sense of duty was telling him he had to do something else. "But for once," she wrote, "I know I'm right." He should stay on, doing what he was doing, until his hand was forced. All the distressing war news coming out of Europe and the Pacific "boils down to the point where everyone is thinking about himself" and "your column gets them away from that."

"And furthermore," she continued, "what with an invalid woman on your hands, and god knows how many dogs, well, you just have to go on supporting us in the style to which you've accustomed us."[145]

She was tired of hearing about money, too, and how Ernie used it as an excuse to leave her behind. "You've mentioned several times that we need it," she wrote to Ernie. "You left me well provided for. I'm sorry as the devil that I've had to make such inroads into that amount." She had tried, she said, to be as little burden to Ernie and his wallet as she could. "As far as I know," she continued, "we're still solvent, and better off than we would have been had we stayed on in Washington, and tried to keep with the various Jones families."

"I guess I'm just trying to defend myself," she concluded, "where I know there's no defense. I should have done better, and I know it."[146]

"I've looked and searched in a million directions," Ernie later replied to Jerry in exasperation, "and I can see nothing but that we're trapped. I can't see any way out for us."

"The only thing I could see for our future," he explained to Jerry, "was an endless continuation of what we are doing now—you lonely and wildly introspective and miserable, and running a perpetual cycle from hope to hospital to sanitarium to back home again; and me lonely and growing increasingly desperate and cynical until I finally cracked up and would have to quit the columns, and then down the chute I'd go."[147]

One way Jerry saw to break that cycle was for her and Ernie to have a child. Jerry had been pregnant once before, early in their marriage, but for whatever reason Jerry chose to end that pregnancy. She didn't tell Ernie about the pregnancy or about the abortion until long afterward. It's not clear how much, if at all, they ever talked about it.

"It seems to me unfair to a child to be born of parents our age," Ernie told her. Plus, they were both a little neurotic, he knew. More than that, he continued, "I can't give you a child, as you know." He wasn't lying, he reminded her, "when I've told you that the power of sex had gone from me."[148] The previous month, in fact, while Ernie was roving in and around San Diego, he elected to undergo six weeks of agonizing treatments designed to cure his erectile dysfunction.[149] "I doubt that I have the courage to continue them much longer," he confessed to Jerry. "And there seems little hope that they'll be successful anyway."[150]

Ernie knew that if he quit his column, if he settled down and took up normal office hours, he'd grow despondent from the drudgery in six months or less, "which would destroy us both," he wrote to Jerry.[151]

8

Once Yomna and I reached the summit of Djebel Hamra, I sat down on a flat rock next to a low shrub. When Ernie sat and took in the same sight back on February 15, 1943, he was reminded of the high plains of the American Southwest. "The whole vast scene was treeless,"[152] he wrote, with semi-irrigated vegetable fields broken up by patches of wild growth.[153] There were also "shoulder-high cactus of the prickly-pear variety" and the occasional stucco house, tiny and square.[154] Through a pair of binoculars, Pyle could see the smear of Sidi Bou Zid, thirteen miles away,[155] which

Ernie described as "a great oasis whose green trees stood out against the bare brown of the desert."[156]

The vista Yomna and I spied from atop Djebel Hamra nearly eight decades later closely matched Ernie's description. The dips and folds of the tan-brown plain below the mountain undulated like waves in the ocean. The sun was high in the sky, shining brightly over a monotonous landscape of sand, gullies, and dry washes, broken up only occasionally by patches of dark prickly pears and geometric patterns of olive orchards and irrigated farm fields planted by hand. Sidi Bou Zid, thirteen miles to the southeast, was a tiny spot of dark-hued greenery and cream-colored houses. Beyond the city, the purple ridges of Djebel Ksaira stood above an arid haze. To our left, rising majestically from inhospitable soil, was Djebel Lessouda. Other than the semi-trucks barreling down the highway in the distance, the panorama seemed little changed since Pyle had been there to watch the Americans' disastrous tank battle.

Looking out over the land, I tried to picture Ernie in his knit cap

The view from the top of Djebel Hamra, with Sidi Bou Zid, Tunisia, in the background, December 2019

and brown army coveralls fading into white from exposure and too many washings.[157] I tried to picture his overshoes and the weariness of his features, his body bundled tightly in his double-breasted coat. I tried to picture him squinting into the sun, taking mental snapshots, waiting for the action to begin.

All I could envision was a young man, wavy haired and silhouetted in a rising sun. It wasn't Ernie; it was my grandpa Hod. During my reading into what his tank company endured during the Battle of Okinawa, I learned the details of a tank battle that had been as devastating as the one Ernie had watched from atop Djebel Hamra. On April 19, 1945—the day after Ernie was killed—twenty-two of thirty American tanks from my grandfather's company were disabled or destroyed while attacking a village called Kakazu. It was, according to one historian of the battle, the greatest loss of American armor in a single engagement during the entire Pacific war.[158]

I thought about the last time I spoke to my grandfather. It was in the summer, August I think, the year before I started eighth grade. The battered shell of a rusted-out 1927 John Deere B tractor rotted in the front yard, overgrown with weeds. Crumbling concrete steps and a rusty pipe for a handrail led to the front door. My father went inside first, leaving me, my mother, and my younger brother in the yard. There was a hollowness in the air, a dark unspeakable silence as we waited for my father to return to the steps and give us the go-ahead to enter.

We filed into the tiny kitchen and lined up, tallest to shortest. With only a single kitchen chair to his name, my grandfather was the only one who could sit, not that I would have wanted to. The stained linoleum floor and the windowsill above the table were layered with dust and dead flies. The soles of my shoes stuck to the floor. His old stove and the week's old dishes piled up in the crusty kitchen sink mixed into a faint stench that seemed to hang in the air above our heads,

I remembered standing there before him, wondering to myself how long it had been since he'd handled the greasy wrenches piled up in front of where a guest might have joined him for coffee and a chat. It had been decades since he'd retired from the tractor-repair shop he'd once owned with his father, and still, I remember the calluses and the fingernails lined with grease. I remember his eyes, a deep blue, like mine. I remember his face, rough and broken in a way that could have been handsome. I remember the sweet-and-sour smell of brandy on his breath and fixating on the way he dug the bloated knuckles of his left hand into the top of his thigh to keep himself propped up in his chair. He was almost like an exhibit in a museum. "The Lasting Effects of Unaddressed Combat Trauma," his display placard would have read. Only there wasn't any signage to explain what I was seeing and what it all meant.

My father did most of the talking. The weather was nice, he said. Perfect for cutting hay. He seemed so different while in his father's presence. Diminished, somehow, hiding behind a carefree demeanor, as if what had become of his father was normal or acceptable. Then he talked about me and my brother, how we were playing football again that fall. Grandpa smiled with his toothless farmer's grin. Were we practicing our war cries? he asked. My father laughed. I tried to follow his lead. Then my father patted me on the back. He smiled at me through clenched teeth. There was nothing left to talk about. We had been there only fifteen minutes, and I felt exhausted by all the tension, by everything left unsaid between my father and his.

9

On April 14, 1942, Ernie and Jerry divorced in municipal court. The end of their tenure together came all of a sudden, at Jerry's suggestion, after Ernie had abandoned the idea altogether for lack of courage.[159] She had to say the words.

Though they both claimed to be devastated,[160] Ernie was also hopeful that the shock of the divorce would be "just the medicine" Jerry needed.[161] "A last-hope form of psychological surgery," is how he put it.[162] Jerry's doctors and her family were hopeful, too. Her biggest problem, Ernie believed, was that she refused to "face life like other people."[163]

If the separation forced her to cure herself in that way, Ernie was more than willing to remarry.[164] "My life is purposeless and tortured," he told her. "There must be something definite soon; a drastic change; a recapturing of the lightheartedness; a contentment through companionship, something."[165]

Jerry committed herself to quit drinking, dismissed the nurse who had been doping her at night, and told Ernie she planned to get a job to occupy her time while he was gone.[166] "All of which is exactly what we hoped would come out of the divorce," he later said. "I don't know whether she has the willpower to stick to a job or not, but even if she tries that's the first progress that has been made for years."[167] And even if she never did find a job, Jerry would be taken care of financially—that much Ernie had promised. The house on Girard Boulevard would stay in her name, they decided. And their savings were evenly divided, too; each would receive a little over twenty-two thousand dollars.[168] Ernie also established a trust for Jerry that would pay her a weekly stipend.[169]

"Now and then I get myself around to a decision to resume the columns," he wrote to Lee a week and a half after the divorce was finalized, "but most of the time I know I'm absolutely incapable of resuming them any time soon."[170]

What did it matter, anyway? The country was at war, and Ernie was convinced that he would eventually be drafted, especially now that he was single as well as childless. Perhaps it would be best for him, he thought, to leave Albuquerque, loaf around somewhere peaceful for a couple of months. That way he could have time and space to rest his mind, build up his strength, and add some pounds to his frame. He'd already tried to enlist in the navy by that point, but he couldn't pass their minimum weight requirements. Plus, they said, they weren't yet taking anyone over the age of thirty-five unless they had a high-demand skill or knew a trade—writing, editing, driving, and drinking weren't on the list.[171]

"Maybe once I'm gone for good," he confided in Lee, "she can brace herself and start facing things." If she didn't, though, Jerry's sister, Poe, would be there to implement the next step, which for Jerry was commitment to a sanitarium. There was a nice one in Colorado Springs, in a state where it was still legal to commit someone against their will. They never told Jerry about it, "for she has a horror that amounts to mania against going into a sanitarium," as he wrote to Lee.[172]

"It's simply so hard (so almost impossible) to leave Jerry in her tragic lonely feeling about our parting," Ernie went on, "that I just haven't so far had the moral courage to make a decision on going." But if he did go, he also wrote, it had better be back to England, especially if there was "any possibility that the Allies might feint toward a continental invasion this summer."[173]

Ernie traveled east to Washington, DC, in early May to meet with the director of the Bureau of Public Relations for the War Department, Major General Alexander Day Surles. Ernie's hunch was correct, the general confirmed. England was the place to be. The army would be glad to have him, Surles told Ernie. They could put him on the next convoy headed east across the Atlantic. "It all sounded too easy to be true," he later told Jerry.[174] The next day he met with one of his bosses and talked through a few options. They settled on a plan that would send Ernie to England for a few months before touring Central Africa, for about a six-month trip altogether.[175] He thought that would be plenty of time away before the army could gobble him up.[176]

Until the next day, when he learned from his draft board that they were planning to draft his forty-two-year-old Class 1-A self[177] later that summer.[178] One of Ernie's bosses, Walker Stone, wanted Ernie to drop the column for good if he had only a few months before he'd have to drop it *again* to complete his obligations to the army. He pointed out that three newspapers owned by Jack Knight[179] had canceled their syndication of Ernie's column already. Ernie didn't give a damn about that. In the meantime, Walker told him, Ernie could do straight news reporting if he liked. Ernie did not. His other boss, George B. "Deac" Parker, still thought it best to send Ernie abroad somewhere, preferably England. Ernie was torn. "I feel that my capacity ever to produce the column again has died," he confessed to Jerry. "I don't truly want either to go to England, resume the column, nor go into the Army."

"Everything is confused in my mind," he continued. "I feel that if I could just run back to Albuquerque and start a life of utter simplicity I would be happy. But I guess I can't, and I have determined not to come back until you have won your great fight." He expressed confidence Jerry could do it, too. "Otherwise," he wrote, "I would be utterly insane with despair."[180]

He was low in spirit and feeling rudderless and lost, and the thought of leaving the States was a dreadful one. "I wish I had more enthusiasm over the trip to England," he said at the time. "But actually I still look with horror on starting the columns again." What he'd much rather do, more than anything on earth, he said, was return home to Albuquerque for the summer to putter in the yard and play with his dog, Cheetah. "But the office is insistent," he said, "and unless I take this trip and get the columns started right away, I'll have to quit Scripps-Howard forever."[181]

In a letter dated May 16, five weeks after the Pyles finalized their divorce, Ernie explained to Mabel why he hadn't written or called. "I hardly know how to start or what to say," he began. "For I had felt that our understanding about each other was clear and accepted, but now somehow I feel that you have let your deep feeling for me grow into a hope for things that can never be. And somehow, for me now to talk as we used to and say that our friendship can never be more than a friendship, seems cruel and hard, when actually it shouldn't be, for that was always our understanding."[182]

If there was any romantic feeling for him in her heart, Ernie commanded, she must "kill it," even if that meant making herself detest him. "Now, even more than ever," he continued, "my future is in Jerry's hands. If she recovers, I want my life to be with her. If she doesn't, then god knows what will happen, but you must not be hanging through the years on any future hope for us."[183] His one goal in life, he pledged to Jerry, was to be together with her again—and happy.

Three days after sending his "Dear John" letter to Mabel, Ernie decided his best course of action was to report from England for as long as he could before getting drafted, perhaps until October or November.[184] Ernie's draft board gave him permission to remain overseas until mid-November at the latest, though the length of his trip would depend mostly on how much

Scripps-Howard was willing to spend to keep him over there.[185] When he returned to America in the fall, Ernie planned to accept a commission with Army Air Corps intelligence. Ernie had friends from his days as an aviation columnist who said they could hook him up if Ernie was interested. "It isn't public relations work," he explained to Jerry. "You go to school in Miami for six weeks, then to school in Harrisburg, PA, for six weeks, then are attached directly to an air fighting unit, sort of wet-nursing the pilots and working information out of them when they get back from raids."[186] The work sounded interesting to Ernie, and at least it wasn't too far a departure from what he did as a roving correspondent. There seemed to be no other better option. He was all out of moves. Trapped, even. That was one way to look at it. Another way Ernie could look at it would be to say the war could serve as a form of abduction—one that offered a kind of relief from the imprisoning forces of his failed marriage and the duties and responsibilities that surrounded him.

On May 25, Jerry's sister and her husband, Bill, drove south from Denver through the Rockies to Albuquerque. They were worried about Jerry. Her mind had ground to a halt, and she would wake each day with a profound sense of dread that she was going to have to somehow make it through another entire day. Dying, she had convinced herself, was the only way to release herself from the overwhelming sense of inadequacy and blackness that surrounded her.

The day after they arrived, Bill turned around and headed back to Denver while Poe escorted Jerry on the train up to Pueblo, Colorado. There, Poe and Jerry's doctor committed her to the Woodcroft Sanitarium for a six-month stay.[187] First constructed in 1879 on forty donated acres northeast of the city's limits, by the 1940s, the main hospital, dormitories, and several other buildings that were constructed by the Public Works Administration on its sprawling 306-acre property housed, in overcrowded conditions, upward of five thousand residents who were living with mental illness, physical and developmental disabilities, neurological disorders, severe venereal disease, or substance-abuse issues.[188]

Ernie turned control of Jerry's trust over to Poe so that she could pay for Jerry's care while he was overseas. "We all feel pretty hopeful," Ernie wrote to his father and aunt, "that a few months in the sanitarium will fix Jerry up."[189] It was better, he later tried to convince Jerry, for her to be somewhere she could work on herself, even if it meant being in a miserable place. That was better, in Ernie's mind, than Jerry being miserable in her own way of freedom which "only leads down to deeper and deeper and endless misery."[190]

"It should have been done long ago," Ernie later confided in Paige, "but I never had the heart or the will-power over Jerry."[191]

Ernie had regrets—or knew he would before too long. He missed Jerry, the familiarity of her, the constancy of her, even though he hadn't felt that way in he couldn't remember how long.

"Things are tough for me too," he reminded her. "I've wanted to die. I've lost interest, and almost given up hope that I had any will power left. I've found myself frighteningly close to the very state of mind that has caused you to take the down-route."[192]

Ernie left the United States on a Pan American Clipper flight[193] for Ireland on June 18, 1942, vowing to remain overseas until he was drafted, the war ended, or Jerry was "so far along the road of cheerfulness and normal outlook and usefulness" that there could be no doubt about their future together—and not until then.[194] "That isn't meant as a threat," he promised Jerry. "It's our goal. Anything short of that would be only tragedy and misery for us again."[195]

10

At the beginning of August, Ernie traveled to London, where he planned to get caught up on his columns[196] and recuperate from a nasty cold he caught covering the troop buildup in the rainy bitterness of Belfast.[197] While he had been back in America, the Hotel Savoy—Ernie's favorite haunt during the Blitz—had upped its rate for a room and a meal to $8.00 per day, which was too much for a frugal Indiana farm boy on Scripps-Howard's shoestring budget. Instead, he set up his base camp[198] at the Mount Royal Hotel, about a twenty-minute walk north, near the British Museum, for $3.20.[199]

For the next several weeks, Ernie shuttled back and forth between London and any number of soldiers' camps, where he'd stay for a few days with the enlisted Americans before returning to his quiet room full of sunshine[200] at the Mount Royal to write up what he'd seen. "I wander among the tents, picking up new friends here and there," he wrote. "Even in the dark the presence of a stranger draws soldiers as molasses draws flies, for an outsider in camp is a curiosity and anything that breaks the monotony is welcome."[201] After living with them in tents and freezing to death at night and waking bright and early with them at five o'clock each morning,[202] Ernie knew how "our boys" felt, what they longed for, and how they blew off steam. He longed for the same things. And he blew off steam like them, too. Ernie found this simple existence out in the field served his constitution well. "When I'm out like that," he wrote to Jerry, "the knot in my head and my 'out of focus' eyes completely disappear."[203]

When fall rolled around, Ernie learned he would not be drafted and trucked off to basic training after all. His draft board back in DC, at the behest of his bosses at Scripps-Howard, granted Ernie a series of six-month "non-deferment" draft deferments. The growing popularity of his column proved to the draft board—and his bosses, too—that he was far more valuable to the Allied war effort as an overseas correspondent than he ever would be as a lowly private running a typewriter at some army camp in North Dakota or synthesizing intelligence reports for some general at a bomber base in northern England. Ernie agreed.

Even though he never even pretended to have any actual plans to become a frontline war correspondent,[204] "as things now stand," he wrote to Jerry at the end of September, "I believe it wisest for me to stay on this side indefinitely. As much as I would like to come home, I don't see any point in getting home for a few days and then spending the rest of the war as a private[205] when I can do more good—if any at all—by sticking to what I'm doing. The way it looks now, I don't see how I can return to the States until just about a year from now."[206]

"Of course nobody knows a damn bit more about it than I do," Ernie told Paige in a letter. No matter. He was ready regardless of what happened next, a suitcase at the ready stuffed with a tin hat, a gas mask, Marine Corps shirts, a navy sweater, army pants, a gray fedora, overshoes, and a carton of Hershey bars. Air, land, or sea, Ernest Taylor Pyle was ready.[207]

11

Yomna's family owned much of Kasserine Pass, the site of America's first major defeat at the hands of German field marshal Erwin Rommel. Her great-grandfather had built a compound made of stone and mortar, large enough to house his entire extended family, in the southern half of the pass near the base of Djebel Chambi, a five-thousand-foot limestone mountain with six deep cuts along its face. A few miles to the north, on the other side of the pass, is Djebel Semmama, a rounded hump of a mountain, forty-three hundred feet tall at its summit, that rises straight up from a blacktopped highway, a narrow-gauge railroad that's no longer in use, and a stretch of the steep-banked Hatab River, which meanders through the pass toward the border with Algeria.

"When Zakariya and I were kids," Yomna told me as we passed the city limits of Kasserine on our way to visit her uncle, "we would climb Mount Chambi every time we visited Kasserine. It was so thick with trees; the smell was amazing." Yomna inhaled deeply as if she were trying to capture some long-forgotten scent. We had just finished a breakfast of eggs, chocolate croissants, and yogurt at a café called the Baltimore Club, and my own sense of smell was still overpowered by all the secondhand smoke from the men who had gathered that morning to watch Tunisia take on Qatar in a soccer match. "But then the terrorists came," she continued, leaning in between me and Zakariya from the back seat, "and the Tunisian military bulldozed a dirt barricade on the trail. Then they set fire to the trees in 2014, I think. So now it's just a big burnt mountain. It's so sad."

With the sun at our backs, the exposed strata beneath new-growth pines on Djebel Chambi glowed orange. "That's why we cannot climb this one," Yomna said. "There are still terrorists hiding there. The military has forbidden anyone from being on the mountain. If they see someone up there, they shoot. They don't even try to see if you're a terrorist or not; they just kill you."

Before we could enter the pass, Zakariya told Yomna that I needed to register with the national police at a checkpoint along the highway. Zakariya had studied mechanical engineering in college, though he'd been unemployed for several years. There wasn't much work to be had in Tunisia, where the unemployment rate in December 2019 hovered around 15 percent. When I asked Yomna why Zakariya doesn't move to France or somewhere else, she said that getting a visa to work abroad was incredibly difficult for Tunisian men. "There's so much prejudice against Arabs in Europe," she said. The money I'd pay him to be my driver for a week was more than he'd made in a long time.

Through the bug-splattered windshield, I could see Zakariya speaking to one of the police officers in front of a two-story concrete tower surrounded by concrete barriers taller than a man, with gun ports carved out at eye level. Zakariya motioned to me to get out of the car. With Yomna at my side, we walked past mobile barricades made of steel Xs, painted red with white tips, strung together with strands of razor wire. The officer spoke to Zakariya, Zakariya spoke to Yomna, and I stood there feeling totally out of place and grateful I had a guide.

"They want to see your passport and your international driver's license—and the rental-car agreement, too," Yomna said to me. I handed my documents to the officer. He was dressed in a dark green camouflage uniform and a black leather jacket. He smiled, pushed the submachine gun slung around his shoulder behind his back, and tipped his white peaked cap. As he walked back to the concrete tower, a few other officers, two men and a woman with a bright pink lipstick, came out. Zakariya and Yomna chatted with them for a moment. The gravel around the tower was littered with cigarette butts and small chunks of orange rind. Yomna tipped her sunglasses at me and said, "They've been waiting for us. Since the other day, when we checked in with the police in Sbeïtla. Word traveled fast that there was a tall white man from America here in Kasserine."

Zakariya took a long drag on his cigarette and blew the smoke out of the corner of his mouth into the wind. He said something to Yomna under his breath and then stepped away to answer his cell.

"They want to know what you are doing here," Yomna said. I thought maybe it was part of their check-in process, like when the customs agent at the airport asks you whether your trip abroad was for business or pleasure and if you'd brought anything with you that needed to be declared. "They haven't seen an American in a very long time," Yomna continued. "They probably think you're in the CIA or something."

I turned to the three officers and opened my left hand, mimicking writing into a journal with my right hand. "J'écris un livre . . ." I said in my best French accent. "I'm writing a book." But for whatever reason, I couldn't remember how to say "about," and I wasn't sure whether Tunisie was a masculine or feminine noun. "J'écris un livre . . ." I said again and then pointed all around me. "Kasserine. Tunisie. Guerre." Yomna corrected me. I wasn't there to write about the Tunisian war against the terrorists. "Ce n'est pas un journaliste," she assured them. "He is not a journalist." I was there to write about World War II, she said. The woman with the pink lipstick smiled and nodded. The other two officers stared at me with blank windburned faces.

"Don't worry," Yomna said to me after my papers were returned. "They just don't want an American tourist to get killed here."

12

Ernie landed in Oran, Algeria, a few days before Thanksgiving 1942.[208] Three weeks before he arrived, the first waves of Allied troops stormed the coastlines of French Morocco and Algeria intent on cutting off the escape route of Rommel's Afrika Korps, which at that moment was fleeing west across Libya after being run out of Egypt by the British Eighth Army.[209] Despite their bitter conviction that an American-led attack in North Africa was a "defeatist sideshow" that would provide only an "indirect contribution to the defeat of the Nazis,"[210] President Franklin D. Roosevelt's military planners devised a daring operation they called Torch. Rather than lunge straight for the Nazi jugular, the Allies would take a few windmill swings at the enemy's extremities by landing about a hundred thousand troops in Casablanca, Oran, and Algiers.[211] From there, the Allies predicted they'd be able to pivot ninety degrees and swiftly cut east along the Mediterranean coast to seize the Tunisian port cities of Bizerte and Tunis, effectively cutting Rommel off from reinforcements from Sicily and mainland Italy.[212] If the Allies were able to annihilate Rommel's forces and take control of North Africa, they'd have a sturdy platform from which they could then invade southern Europe.

Ernie was more than twice as old as many of the fresh combat replacements aboard his ship, the *Rangitiki*, a converted British passenger liner named after a New Zealand river, which was drafted into service soon after Great Britain declared war on Germany in 1939. When Pyle boarded in the late hours of a chilly night in November, he had no idea where the ship was headed. It was only after four days at sea that he and the men in the holds below his cabin learned they would soon be landing in Algeria to square off against the battle-hardened German Wehrmacht.

"There were times when the trip was tremendously moving and beautiful," Ernie wrote to Jerry after the ship docked in Oran. "The weather was grand after the first few days, and I didn't even get seasick." He did catch a cold, though, a cold so miserable he barely got out of his bunk for nearly a week. "The ship was lousy with Army doctors," he said, "so they took good care of me." To keep him company, Pyle had roommates, Will Lang of *Time-Life* and two lieutenants in press censorship—"both nice fellows"—as well as Aldous Huxley's dystopian novel, *Brave New World*. When he wasn't gabbing through curled cigarette smoke or reading by dim light, Ernie was dreaming lonely dreams of Jerry, wondering where she was and when he would hear from her next. In a Thanksgiving Day letter to her, Ernie suggested they remarry via proxy, as long as she was amenable to the idea. "If I only knew how you felt and what your wishes were," he wrote, "I'd try to see if it could be done." Remarrying wouldn't bring him home any faster, he confessed, but it would make him happy.[213]

By the time the *Rangitiki* docked in Oran on November 22, 1942, the shooting had been over for nearly two weeks. The First Infantry soldiers, including my great-great-uncle Robert Mullikin, had splashed ashore in green herringbone twill and creaky rucksacks for two days of house-to-house fighting against what one historian later described as "halfhearted opposition."[214] While the enemy commanders were mostly French and well trained, the soldiers the Allies fought were mostly native North Africans who were not well trained and fought with ancient weapons ill-suited for modern combat.[215] Halfhearted opposition, however, is still opposition, and according to the soldiers Pyle talked to, the hardest fighting in all of North Africa had taken place right there in Oran. "Many of my friends whom I knew in England went through it, and they have told me all about it," he told his readers. "Without exception, they admit they were scared stiff."[216]

Once the ink on the armistice with the Vichy French was dry, the Allies, under the command of an uncharismatic and opinionated[217] fifty-eight-year-old major general named Lloyd R. Fredendall,[218] set out converting the narrow port of Oran, once the greatest seaport on the old "Pirate Coast,"[219] from one of the most heavily defended in the Mediterranean to a super-highway for men and material. A beachhead seventy miles wide and fifteen miles deep soon resembled a giant ant farm, with thirty-seven thousand busy men moving day and night up and down gangplanks to bring ashore all that was needed[220] to slam the Afrika Korps into the jaws of a giant pincer movement.[221]

Even as Pyle wrote that the war was beginning to look "rather good for a change," fresh German troops and equipment were pouring into northern Tunisia. By the end of November, seventeen thousand German and eleven thousand Italian troops were dug in around Bizerte and Tunis.[222] The thousands of Germans who had flooded into Tunisia included battle-hardened paratroopers and panzer grenadiers, and they would soon be followed by the tanks of the Tenth Panzer Division.[223] "The African situation isn't cleaned up yet but surely will be within a few weeks," Pyle wrote, apparently unaware of the Axis buildup waiting for the Allies. His fellow war correspondents, he assured Jerry, "can visualize the European end of the war being over this time next year."[224] Soon enough, Ernie and his fellow correspondents would learn that can-do zeal untempered by battlefield experience can exact a heavy toll on the soldiers who do the fighting.

13

Instead of embedding with the frontline troops straightaway, Ernie checked into the seaside Grand Hotel with A. J. Liebling, a columnist for *The New Yorker*. At first, the weather at the end of November along the Mediterranean reminded Ernie of autumn in Albuquerque—bright in the daytime and a little chilly after the sun went down. Their room had two French doors overlooking the turquoise water, and when the sun came up, its rays beamed in all day long, warming the tile floor. The sun warmed Ernie's spirits, too.[225]

Outside the hotel, the Moorish city reminded Ernie of his travels to Latin America. The streets near the harbor and fancy waterfront hotels were lined with palm trees, broad sidewalks, outdoor cafés warmed with the murmur of conversation, and restaurants with soft-colored lighting where the "French, Spanish, and Jewish" people ate their dinners.[226] Of the two hundred thousand residents of Oran, three quarters were of European descent.[227] The streets farther away from the water were choked with garbage, and had far more horses than automobiles.[228]

The Arab men who called Oran home were "dressed in ragged sheets," and their wives were veiled. Their children wore dirty kaftans and shouted "Hi yo, Silver!" to their American liberators before flinging stiff-armed Fascist salutes to passing convoys.[229] "The Arabs are strange people," Ernie wrote. "They are poor, and they look as tight-lipped and unfriendly as the

Indians in some of the Latin countries, yet they're friendly and happy when you get close to them."[230] Another correspondent described the locals as "scrofulous," "unpicturesque," and "lamentable."[231] Whatever the case, Ernie concluded that Oran was not a "bad place" at all, "but most of the Americans here would trade the whole layout for the worst town in the United States, and throw in a hundred dollars to boot."[232]

Within a few weeks of Ernie's arrival in Oran, the rainy season arrived, cold and miserable. By Christmas Eve—his third in a row away from Jerry—Ernie was sidelined by what he called, rather proudly, the "African flu," a heavy cold with a vicious sore throat and a little influenza sprinkled on top.[233] Sick or not, Ernie had committed himself to providing a steady flow of stories for the folks at home. He fell into his usual working routine, spending half his time in the field, gathering enough material for a cushion of several columns, and the other half writing them from the comfort of his hotel room.[234]

"Most of the press association guys and the newspaper people were interested in the daily news," Ernie's friend and fellow correspondent Ralph Martin remembered after the war. Martin wrote for the military magazine Stars and Stripes and got to know Ernie well while they were both in Algeria. "They'd want a byline of the town that was just captured. They were interested in the hot news." Pyle wasn't. "That was the root of his whole marvelous success," Martin continued, "because he worked up a relationship with these fellows and they would talk to him, as they would not talk to the ordinary correspondent who wanted a quick quote on something."[235] The executive editor of Scripps-Howard, John Sorrells, agreed. "Folks with 'boys' over there are a damned sight more interested in reading the homely, every day, what do they eat and how do they live sort of stuff," he said, "than they are in reading the heavy strategic, as-I-predicted-in-my-analysis-back-in-1920 sort of stuff."[236]

In the first four weeks he was in Africa, Ernie sent forty-five columns back to his editor in Washington.[237] He was focused at that time on the fringes of the war[238] and on setting the scene for readers who had likely never heard of places like Oran or Algiers. In addition to commentary on

Ernie Pyle interviewing Sergeant Ralph Gower of Sacramento, Private Raymond Astrackon (left) of New York City, and Second Lieutenant Annette Heaton, ANC, of Detroit, in North Africa, December 2, 1942

soldiers' living conditions, he wrote about them being foolishly generous to the "pitiful-looking Arab children" they encountered around Oran[239] and about the confidence and enthusiasm they felt after defeating the Vichy forces so quickly. "They were impatient to get started and get it over," he wrote in one column, "and now that they've started and feel sort of like veterans, they are eager to sweep on through."[240]

As always, the scenery and the weather were easy for Ernie to describe. "Boys from New Mexico and Arizona were amazed at how much the country around here resembles their own desert Southwest," he said of the land. Of the temperature, Pyle noted, "It got hot in the daytime, so hot that the advancing soldiers kept stripping and abandoning their clothes until some were down to their undershirts." But when the sun set in the west and the moon lit up the rolling, treeless hills, the temperature dropped sharply, and the men looked out across a sky that seemed larger than the one back home,[241] wishing they'd held on to the warmer parts of their uniform.[242]

After he'd exhausted the limits of such scene-setting—and finished reassuring his readers that the "American soldier is quick in adapting himself to a new mode of living"[243]—Ernie abruptly changed gears: "At last we are in it up to our necks, and everything is changed, even your outlook on life," he wrote. "Swinging first and swinging to kill is all that matters now."[244]

14

On Christmas Eve 1942, General Eisenhower met with a group of his officers and admitted to them that the "pell-mell race for Tunisia" had been lost. To one of the men there that night, Eisenhower, with his modest, wide-set eyes and square shoulders, had come across as "uninspiring."[245] The reason for the loss, the general explained, his face and hands in perpetual movement,[246] was a lack of supplies. There weren't enough trucks or forward air bases. The railroads were too congested. The steady stream of munitions, spare vehicle parts, and fresh replacement troops needed to capture Tunis had been reduced to a trickle.[247] Even though nearly 180,000 American troops were then in North Africa, fewer than 12,000 could be found at the Tunisian front.[248]

Then there was the weather—rain and more rain.[249] The normally arid ground became a sea of mud. Without adequate supplies and agreeable weather, Eisenhower continued, he felt forced to postpone the offensive he had planned to capture Tunis by the end of the year. Irritable and depressed,[250] Eisenhower confessed in a cable to the Joint Chiefs of Staff two days later that the abandonment of the drive on Tunis "has been the severest disappointment I have suffered to date."[251] His focus would turn instead toward the border region between Tébessa in Algeria and Kasserine in Tunisia, a gateway through the Atlas Mountains where he expected to confront Rommel and his Afrika Korps.[252]

When Ernie learned the dash to Tunis had been indefinitely postponed, he was relieved. After the war ended, A. J. Liebling recalled a conversation he had with Pyle about it. "Fellows like Will Lang (a *Life* correspondent who had been on the *Rangitiki*) and you," Liebling remembered Ernie explaining, "who have roots in Europe, can work up a real hate about this thing, but I can't. When you figure how many boys are going to get killed, what's the use of it anyway?"[253]

On December 30, Ernie received a letter from Sister Margaret Jane, the Mother Superior at St. Joseph's Hospital in Albuquerque.[254] She said that she had talked with Jerry about remarrying him and that Jerry had declined. The sun was beginning to set when Ernie read those crushing words. Bundled up against the cold, he sat on a stump and read and reread the letter. It was the first news he'd received from his adopted hometown since leaving months earlier, and in that faraway place in the middle of a world war, Ernie was so disappointed he almost felt like crying.[255] "You must know one thing," he later told Jerry. He didn't send his remarriage proposal solely for her benefit. It was "wholly for my own," he confessed.[256]

Some of that self-pity—which Ernie described as his "chronic depression of spirit"[257]—found its way into his columns in the form of a kind of pity for the men on the front lines.[258] Other times it may have manifested itself in a need to chasten the folks at home who didn't have an accurate impression of the North African campaign. In a column titled "Snakes in Our Midst" that was published on January 4, 1943, Pyle said that the men who bring in convoys from America told him those still at home thought the war in North Africa would be over quickly without many losses and that the French were in love with the United States Army. "If you think that," Pyle wrote, "it is because we newspapermen here have failed at getting the finer points over to you."[259] That and the fact that Allied commanders had their censors actively suppress any news on how tenaciously Vichy forces had fought in North Africa so the French would not "remain embittered against us for having to fight them into submission."[260]

While the army was "doing wonderfully," America's fighting men were also clumsy amateurs compared to the Germans, and it was going to take some time to gain the necessary experience. Men were dying as a result.

Not at an "appalling" rate, Ernie reassured his readers, but the numbers were much higher than were being reported.[261] "The other day an American ship brought the first newspaper home I had seen since the occupation," Pyle wrote, "and it said only twelve men were lost taking Oran. The losses, in fact, were not great, but they were a good many twelve times twelve."[262]

There were three things, according to Ernie, that the troops wanted their folks at home to know. First, the going was going to be tough, and it was going to be some time before the Allies would be ready to move to bigger fronts. Second, most of the French in North Africa were fundamentally behind the Allies, though there was a "strange, illogical stratum" that was still aligned with the Axis. And because of that, the third thing people at home needed to know was that "our fundamental policy still is one of soft-gloving snakes in our midst" who "being without any deep love of the country, favor whichever side appears most likely to feather their nest."[263] As the British prime minister Winston Churchill so famously put it: "This is not the end. It is not even the beginning of the end. But it is, perhaps, the end of the beginning."[264]

CHAPTER 3

DISAPPOINTING THE FOLKS AT HOME

▪ ▪ ▪ ▪ ▬▬▬▬ ▪ ▪ ▪ ▪

Correspondents are not now permitted to write anything critical
concerning the Tunisian situation, or to tell what we think was
wrong. The powers that be feel that this would be bad for "home
morale." So you just have to trust that our forces are learning to
do better next time.

ERNIE PYLE, "A HUMILIATING PREDICAMENT," FEBRUARY 23, 1943[1]

1

Before sunrise on Sunday morning, February 14, 1943, Ernie was asleep
inside an igloo tent[2] at General Fredendall's II Corps' headquarters[3] on
the Algerian side of the border with Tunisia.[4] For nearly a month, the frigid
tent pitched at the bottom of a sunless valley[5] had served as Ernie's personal
base camp.[6] When he wasn't poking at his typewriter perched atop a wooden
crate he begged off a supply sergeant, he was jetting up and over mountains
and across barren stretches of frozen mud in an open-air jeep, the wind
burning his face. During most of January, the frontline units had been preparing for Operation Satin, which was designed to knock the Germans in
North Africa out of the war by trapping them between a rock and a hard
place.[7] The rock was General Bernard Montgomery's Eighth Army coming
up on Rommel from the south; the hard place was Fredendall's green-as-
grass II Corps.[8] Right before the operation was set to begin at the end of
January, however, Eisenhower scuttled it because the Eighth Army had yet

to arrive in Tunisia from Libya. The rock in the equation was missing. Rather than push east toward the Tunisian coast, Fredendall's troops were split and scattered across hundreds of miles into a "bits and pieces war"[9] aimed at keeping the Germans off-balance[10] until better weather afforded the Allies ideal conditions for a coordinated offensive.

Once Ernie reached the front dressed in his army coveralls, a private's mackinaw, knit cap, and overshoes, he would catch up with a unit and do his best to blend in. After setting up his pup tent and laying out a heavy canvas bedroll stuffed with blankets,[11] he visited foxholes and hung out by the mess tent, talking to soldiers and mentally recording the details of their everyday lives. Most of his colleagues in North Africa weren't doing that. They were mostly press association reporters tethered to Eisenhower's head-quarters staff back in Algiers. From the safe confines of seaside hotels, they attended press briefings, reviewed dry military communiqués,[12] and churned out articles liberally sprinkled with vivid verbs like "smash" and "pound" that failed to impress on the folks at home any of the harsh realities of war. Ernie, on the other hand, was free to revel in the "magnificent simplicity" and "perpetual discomfort"[13] of life on the front lines, where he learned firsthand that the easy war Americans had come to expect, bolstered by ar-ticles that gave the impression that this place or that German division could simply be bombed out of the war, bore little resemblance to the terrifying reality on the ground.

Once he'd gathered enough material,[14] Ernie would strap on a pair of race-track goggles,[15] bundle himself in a heavy army blanket,[16] and travel back to his base camp in the valley with the windshield down so the glare wouldn't attract the attention of a German dive bomber.[17] But even with hot food in his belly, an endless supply of cigarettes, and a wonderfully warm combat suit Fredendall had gifted him,[18] Ernie struggled to type with numb fingers in the bitter Algerian cold.[19] As the icy wind drummed on his tent, snapping its flaps, Ernie's head froze as cold as his fingers. How could he possibly convey to the folks at home the disturbing duality of life at the front?[20]

On the one hand, the front could be characterized by the loneliness and the danger and the never-ending fear that combined to create an ugly imitation of life there. "You just sort of exist, either standing up working or lying down asleep," Ernie wrote after realizing the best path forward for him might be to simply describe what he had seen and felt, even if it didn't necessarily speak to the bigger political questions about the war. "There is no pleasant in-between," he continued. "The velvet is all gone from the living."[21]

On the other hand, there was also an electric excitement and an addictive sense of purpose and awe inherent in life at the front, something Ernie had never quite felt before.[22] "A big military convoy moving at night across the mountains and deserts of Tunisia is something that nobody who has been in one can ever forget," he wrote.[23] With the sounds of tanks clanking and trucks groaning in low gear running through his mind on repeat,[24] and the images of his friends' faces painted white by the moonlight, Ernie continued: "I couldn't help feeling the immensity of the catastrophe that has put men all over the world, millions of us, to moving in machinelike precision throughout long foreign nights—men who should be comfortably asleep in their own warm beds at home."[25]

2

Word came to us about noon that the Germans were advancing upon Sbeïtla,"[26] Pyle wrote of the remote, sun-parched city eighty-five miles east of Fredendall's secluded headquarters.[27] February 14, 1943, was "a bright day and everything seemed peaceful,"[28] Ernie noted as he raced toward the sounds of battle on that fateful Valentine's Day. "The Germans just overran our troops that afternoon," he continued, swarming out from behind the mountains around Faïd Pass on their way to the sleepy village of Sidi Bou Zid, about a dozen miles west.[29] "They used tanks, artillery, infantry, and planes divebombing our troops continuously" in a blitzkrieg reminiscent of Germany's armored offensives in the spring of 1940.

Characterizing the attack as a "German surprise"[30] that swamped, scattered, and consumed the Americans, Ernie made it seem like Fredendall and his commanders had simply been outfoxed by Rommel. The ugly truth was much more complicated than that. Two weeks before the Germans began their five-day mauling, shortly after Eisenhower canceled Operation Satin, around a thousand French troops defending[31] Faïd Pass were killed or captured by a three-pronged attack spearheaded by thirty tanks from the Twenty-first Panzer Division.[32] During the worst of the fighting, French officers begged General Fredendall to rescue their two battalions. The general refused. Instead, because he was unwilling to weaken the defenses he had established around Sbeïtla, Fredendall ordered only a dozen Sherman tanks and two battalions of infantrymen from the First Armored Division to counterattack the pass first thing the next morning.[33] Fredendall, it seemed, was far less concerned with the fate of the French than he was with the defenses being built at his command post in Algeria. For weeks before the Germans attacked Faïd Pass, Fredendall had a desperately needed regiment of engineers working around the clock to construct a pair of enormous underground shelters for him and his staff at the bottom of the valley.[34]

With the French out of the way, and the Americans slow to react, the Germans had plenty of time during the night of January 30 to fortify their defenses in and around the pass. The next morning, when the American tank crews that had never been in combat before came roaring straight into the narrow pass, blinded by the rising sun, interlocking fields of machine guns and mortars—along with a few 88 mm antiaircraft guns—would be waiting for them.[35]

From the razorback ridges on three sides, the Germans whipcracked round after round from their 88s straight down upon the vulnerable Shermans. Confusion and error, valor and misdeed—the tanks had stuck their necks straight into a German noose. "The velocity of the enemy shells was so great that the suction created by the passing projectiles pulled the dirt, sand, and dust from the desert floor and formed a wall that traced the course of each shell," an officer who was there later recalled.[36] Within ten minutes, half of the American tanks had been transformed into metal funeral pyres. The few that hadn't yet been knocked out hauled out of the pass in reverse as quickly as they could, careful to keep their heavily armored fronts pointed toward the thundering German muzzle flashes.

Tankless survivors stumbled through the mud and over the corrugated vegetable fields west toward Sidi Bou Zid with the devilish hammering of the German's new MG 42 machine gun[37] all around them. My great-great-uncle Robert was among the First Armored Division infantrymen who tried several times to stop the German advance. Each defensive position they tried to occupy, however, had already been overrun, and their attacks against the Germans resulted in nothing but heavy losses.[38]

The next day, the Americans counterattacked one last time. Two infantry battalions hiked up the ridgeline three miles south of the pass in the hopes that they could outflank the German positions that had torn the Shermans apart the day before. As one officer later wrote, the Germans "held their fire until we were practically at the foot of the objective. The men got a terrific raking over by the enemy as they fell back."[39] One commander signaled the general in charge of the attack, Raymond McQuillin, that there was "too much tank and gun fire. . . . Infantry cannot go on without great loss." Not long after, fifteen panzers swung out from the pass and fired along the length of American infantrymen with their long-barreled 75 mm cannons from the left until they were checked by countercharging Shermans. "They shook us like we had been dragged over a plowed field," one sergeant later wrote.[40] The failed defense of Faïd Pass and the foolhardy American counterattack cost the French and the Americans dearly. More than nine hundred French soldiers were dead or missing. The American First Armored Division alone sustained 210 casualties.[41] Faïd Pass was lost.

"We could not help wondering," wrote an officer in his company's war diary, "whether the officers directing the American effort knew what they were doing."[42]

3

Soon after he arrived in Sbeïtla, as the sun was dying down on February 14, Ernie pitched his pup tent, ate supper, and went to bed. The next morning he caught a ride with two officers who were headed to a forward command post. "Occasionally we stopped the jeep and got far off the road behind some cactus hedges," Ernie wrote, "but the German dive bombers were interested only in our troop concentration ahead." When they finally reached the command post, Ernie found two acres of random vehicles and a few light tanks, along with only half of the troops who would normally staff a command post. "Half their comrades were missing," Pyle told his readers. "There was nothing left for them to work with, nothing to do."[43]

For the next few hours, Ernie sat with the men who "had been away—far along on the road that doesn't come back" and listened to their stories of near misses and miraculous survival.[44] "Not one of them had ever thought he'd see this dawn," Pyle later wrote, "and now that he had seen it his emotions had to pour out. And since I was the only newcomer to show up since their escape, I made a perfect sounding board."[45] Ernie listened without saying a word until the stories finally became merged into a generalized blur, "overlapping and paralleling and contradicting until the whole adventure became a composite."[46]

In the early hours of February 14, Pyle learned from the men, two weeks after the first battle at Faïd Pass, more than a hundred German tanks, including a dozen Tigers, had come across a small squad of American soldiers who were supposed to be on the lookout for a German attack through the pass. At the first sign, they were to fire rockets into the air, which would alert the artillerymen near Djebel Lessouda who had registered their guns on known features around Faïd.[47] Fredendall believed that his men could use accurate artillery fire like a wall to keep the Germans from spilling out of the pass and into the desert below. By the time the artillerymen heard the rumbling of German armor and smelled the scent of diesel coughing from the back of at least a hundred infantry lorries and half-tracks,[48] every member of the squad was dead, their rockets still in the boxes.

From there, the Germans came across a company from the First Armored Division. Most of the crews, unaware an attack was headed their way, were outside their idle tanks cooking Valentine's Day breakfast. In less than an hour, sixteen of the company's tanks had been reduced to burning hulks of steel. Emboldened by such quick and decisive victories, one group of about eighty German tanks and trucks then went north toward Djebel Lessouda while the rest headed south to envelop Sidi Bou Zid in a pincer movement, aiming to divide their forces and attack both flanks of the Allied defenses there.[49]

In an order entitled "Defense of Faïd Position," Fredandall explicitly dictated the positioning of units down to individual companies. Two prominent hills within sight of the pass were to be occupied, Fredendall wrote: "Djebel Ksaira on the south and Djebel Lessouda on the north are the key terrain features in the defense of Faïd. These two features must be strongly held, with a mobile reserve in the vicinity of Sid Bou Zid."[50] When Colonel Peter C. Hains III of the First Armored Division saw Fredendall's plan, he was disgusted. The only words he could mutter were: "Good God." He knew that any troops placed on the two hills would be marooned if a fast-moving attack swept around them. While the hills were mutually visible ten miles across the desert, they were not close enough for defenders on one to help their comrades on the other. Fredendall's orders resembled a defensive plan that might have worked during the First World War, without an appreciation for the speed and power of modern tank divisions.[51]

American units fell like tenpins. East of Sidi Bou Zid, the Second Battalion of the Seventeenth Field Artillery—armed with a dozen and a half antique 155 mm howitzers—was erased; the Germans got "every gun and most of the men," a staff officer later reported.[52] Trying to avoid a similar fate after their forward observers were all killed or wounded, Battery A of the Ninety-first Field Artillery dragged their dead to an empty trailer, tossed them in, and retreated to the west. "We didn't know exactly where to fire," one platoon leader said. "There was artillery fire, machine gun fire, armor-piercing tank shells whizzing through the town."[53] A captain in a jeep sped through the olive groves that sheltered the American supply trains. "Take off, men!" he roared over the noise of battle. "You are on your own."[54]

What happened next reminded an artillery lieutenant of the Oklahoma land rush, except that "the air was full of whistles" from enemy projectiles.[55] Of the fifty-two American tanks that took on the Germans that day, only six survived past lunchtime. At 1:45 p.m., half a dozen German Tigers bulled through the rubble on the outskirts of Sidi Bou Zid. About three hours after that, tanks from the Twenty-first Panzer Division in the south and those from the Tenth in the north met two miles east of town. The double envelopment had taken less than twelve hours to complete.[56]

4

At quarter to three on February 15, the battalion commander's voice crackled to life over the radio, snapping Ernie to attention. "We're on the edge of Sidi Bou Zid and have struck no opposition yet," the commander reported. Across the parched plain before them, forty American tanks and a dozen tank destroyers roared and poured blue smoke into the sand-dusted sky.[57] Following in their dust plumes were trucks and half-tracks shepherding a battalion's worth of infantrymen. Behind them followed a dozen artillery pieces.[58] "The peaceful report from our tank charge brought no comment from anyone around the command truck," Pyle wrote. "Faces were grave: it wasn't right—this business of no opposition at all; there must be a trick in it somewhere." The Germans must either be much smaller than they thought—or they were biding their time, sucking the Americans into a trap.

As the outnumbered and outgunned American tanks reached the outskirts of the blown-apart village,[59] a flare arced over Sidi Bou Zid, "like a diamond in the afternoon sun," A. D. Divine reported from Djebel Hamra.[60] Ernie and the other correspondents glued their eyes to their binoculars. Muzzle flashes blinked like Christmas lights near the town. "Then, from far off," Ernie continued, "came the sound of explosions." German artillery airbursts ripped to shreds the artillerymen and their tubes pulling up the rear of the American attack. "Brown geysers of earth and smoke began to spout."[61]

Fredendall's plan to counterattack two battle-hardened tank divisions with the reserve elements of a battalion that had never seen combat[62] was doomed from the moment it was drawn out in grease pen on some map board back in Speedy Valley.[63] The Germans held nothing back. Stukas dived and strafed. Panzers fired hundreds of armor-piercing rounds with a deafening report. Most of the dead had been killed in a small onion field two miles west of town. The bodies were twisted and bent into cruel angles. Maroon blood pooled atop the sand, and black smoke blotted out the sky.[64] "One of our half-tracks, full of ammunition, was livid red, with flames leaping and swaying," Pyle wrote of the peculiar sights and sounds of battle. "Every few seconds one of its shells would go off, and the projectile would tear into the sky with a weird whanging sort of noise."[65]

"As dusk began to settle," General McQuillin later reported, "the sunset showed red on the dust of the Sidi Bou Zid area. There was no wind, and the frequent black smoke pillars scattered over the terrain marked locations of burning tanks." He counted twenty-seven American tanks aflame, but "the heavier dust cloud near Sidi Bou Zid no doubt obscured more that were afire. It was easy to recognize a burning tank due to the vertical shaft of smoke." Once the attack was aborted, four Sherman tanks rallied below Djebel Hamra. They were all that remained after the slaughter. All through the night, diesel-blackened tankers who had managed to escape their burning coffins stumbled back to the American lines in Sbeïtla exhausted and dazed. "I found myself all alone wandering amongst the dead and wreckage," said one. "The night had a dead silence except for a few howling dogs."[66]

By the next morning, it was estimated that the previous two days of fighting had cost the Americans at least sixteen hundred men, nearly a hundred tanks, and plenty of half-tracks and artillery pieces. Also lost that day, after so many had been led so ineptly, was confidence. Soldiers lost confidence in themselves and in their commanders; commanders in each other. The "awful nights of fleeing, crawling, and hiding from death," in Ernie's words, had begun.[67]

5

Yomna's uncle Rabeh was waiting for us outside the main house, a flat-roofed duplex made from terra-cotta bricks, reinforced with rebar, and slathered with a thin layer of cement. Piled in front was a pallet's worth of hollow bricks and a small mound of stiff bags of unmixed concrete. Strung on a drooping wire between the porch's main support beams were a few dozen bundles of desiccated red chili peppers swaying in the stiff breeze.

Rabeh kept his hands in the pockets of his blue jeans until I reached mine out to greet him. "Comment ça va?" he asked as the wind kicked dust up into our faces. "Salut, ça va, et vous?" I replied. He nodded back, his dark eyes like the bottom of the ocean. I wanted to thank him for taking a break from his work to show me his land, but the conversational French I'd studied before the trip suddenly felt locked inside my head. With our muted pleasantries exhausted, Rabeh stuffed his hands back in his pockets and turned to Yomna and Zakariya. He said something in Arabic and cut across the yard down a short hill. The puffy sleeves of his dusty canvas coat fluttered against the wind. The three of us followed him down the hill, crossed the blacktop road that splits Rabeh's property in half, and climbed up to a large mound of earth littered with stones and tall clumps of prickly pears. Small red fruits covered in sharp spines sprouted from the ends of each Ping-Pong-paddle-shaped pad. Beneath a blanket of pewter clouds, Rabeh began to speak, waving his arms from side to side. Then he pointed down at the ground and across the land to Mount Chambi.

"This is where my great-grandfather's castle was," Yomna said, referring to the large compound that once housed her extended family. Strands of her short walnut-colored hair blew across her face and stuck to her deep red lipstick. "Until it was bombed and turned to rubble, it was the most magnificent castle. He built it with his own hands."

"How big was it?" I asked.

"As big as this hill," she said. "Everywhere you see stones. Maybe two acres?"

"Are there any pictures of it? Do you know what it looked like?"

"My great-grandfather knew, but he died a couple years ago. There was probably a large courtyard in the middle—a 'hoch'—surrounded by lots of little rooms for all the different families."

"All we know for sure," Yomna continued, "is that it was big and that my great-grandfather liked to show how rich he was, so he mixed the cement with olive oil. Kasserine has the very best olive oil."

"Does Rabeh know who bombed it? Was it the Germans or the Americans?"

"He does not know for sure," Yomna said after asking her uncle. "We can't prove who did it, so we don't know which country to ask for damages."

"He also says this is where my other uncle's cousin's mother was killed when she stepped on a land mine. She is buried across the pass, below Semmama."

The blasted and overgrown ruins of Yomna's family's compound, Kasserine Pass, Tunisia, December 2019

Whichever side destroyed the castle spared no expense. The once-flat hill was pocked with bomb craters, some shallow and others at least a dozen feet deep and twenty or thirty feet wide. I asked Yomna why her family never tried to rebuild the castle or at least reuse the stones. "Lack of funds," she said. "My great-grandfather lost everything."

My intuition tells me that it must have been the Germans who destroyed Yomna's family's castle. My guess is that it was destroyed the morning of February 19 or shortly thereafter. On February 17, two days after the Americans' disastrous counterattack at Sidi Bou Zid, twelve hundred combat engineers who never completed rifle training formed a three-mile skirmish line across the opening of the pass.[68] Yomna's family's castle would have been behind that line. In the fog and drizzle, the engineers waited with their anxious fingers on their triggers for the Germans to storm across the wet and spongy Sbeïtla plain,[69] through the badlands around the village of Kasserine, and straight down their throats. But the Germans did not come that day. After three days of relentlessly hammering the Americans, they had slowed to a crawl.[70]

On February 18, Rommel submitted a proposal[71] that he be allowed to resume his push against the disordered and panicky Americans and attack straight through Kasserine Pass all the way to the Allied nerve center at Tébessa,[72] where he could eliminate the Americans' ability to attack the coastal corridor linking Tunis to central Tunisia and threaten the southern flank of the American First Army.[73] To Rommel's shocked amazement, his proposal was disregarded, and he was ordered to divide his forces so that he could send half of his men and armor west through Kasserine Pass and the other half north along Djebel Semmama, through a mountain pass at Sbiba, and on to the city of Le Kef. Doing so, Rommel feared, would not only water down the strength of his forces, but also needlessly expose his flanks.[74]

While Rommel and the Axis high command took two days to decide what to do next, the combat engineers turned infantrymen, reinforced by a battalion from the First Division,[75] built up their defenses of Kasserine Pass. They dumped[76] close to three thousand mines along both sides of the main road between the village of Kasserine and the pass[77] and positioned two batteries of 105 mm howitzers and a four-gun French battery of horse-drawn 75s.[78] Behind them in the plain of Feriana, on the other side of the pass, behind Yomna's family's castle, was the last line of Allied defense between the Pass and Tébessa—a single battalion of tank destroyers.

With all this hurried reinforcing and repositioning, the Americans had somehow failed to secure the high ground around the pass. Rather than dig in on the summit and along the sides of Chambi and Semmama, the vast majority of the two thousand soldiers defending the pass entrenched themselves under heavy low clouds[79] in too-shallow foxholes on the floor of the pass. As one officer later said, much of the American campaign in Tunisia involved "trying to draw a line between what we knew and what we did."[80]

Back in Speedy Valley, General Fredendall was begging for more reinforcements. "I am holding a lot of mountain passes against armor with three and a half battalions of infantry," he told General Lucian K. Truscott around two o'clock in the afternoon on February 17. If the Germans concentrate their forces on any one pass, he continued, "they might smoke me out." Even though Eisenhower was shipping roughly a battalion's worth of soldiers east from Casablanca every day, few would get all the way to Tunisia before the end of February. It was Truscott who broke the bad news. "There isn't any hope of getting a combat team up here for a number of days," he told Fredendall.[81]

In the early hours of February 19, Rommel finally issued his orders. His Afrika Korps was to drive west from Sbeïtla to capture Kasserine Pass while the Twenty-first Panzer Division headed north toward Le Kef, seventy miles north of the village of Kasserine. Back in Sbeïtla, the Tenth Panzer Division would lie in wait, ready to exploit whichever route was less heavily defended.[82]

In the late morning of February 19, the sky was cloudy, the ground soggy. The sounds of a battalion's worth of ghosts in field-gray trench coats snaking toward the narrows of Kasserine Pass mingled with those of water rushing through streambeds overflowing with the runoff from the winter rains.[83] Once they realized the heights of Chambi were mostly undefended, the Germans scrambled up its rocky inclines, through the middle of the deep gulches that scarred the mountain's eastern face. Behind them followed panzers and a new weapon that had never been deployed before—the Nebelwerfer.[84]

"The Germans used this weapon called the Nebelwerfer," I explained to Yomna from the bottom of one of the largest bomb craters on the hill. "It had six barrels and could fire these huge mortars. They weighed seventy-five pounds each. The Americans called them 'screaming meemies' because while they were flying through the air, they sounded like a woman crying.

"I wonder whether that's what was used to destroy the castle. If the Germans held the high ground on Chambi and the ridgeline below Sem-mama, and if the Americans were all dug in over there," I said, waving east toward the village of Kasserine, "it would make sense for them to destroy the castle so the Americans couldn't use it in their defenses." I paused. "I can't think of a good reason why the Americans would want to destroy it," I continued, "unless they bombed it later, once the Germans were retreating back through the pass?"

6

No one gave the order to retreat. As three columns of German tanks approached the windswept city of Sbeïtla on a frigid night three days into Rommel's thrust toward Tébessa, several smaller vehicles out ahead of the tanks scouting the American positions opened fire on a group of engineers laying mines. A stray burst of German machine-gun fire that had been directed at the engineers tore through the gnarled olive grove near General McQuillin's command post. Convinced that the western side of Sbeïtla, near its ancient Roman ruins, would offer better protection from the advancing Germans, McQuillin ordered that his command center be moved.[85]

When the soldiers saw their commander's headquarters staff moving east to west across Sbeïtla, many misinterpreted their movement—mixed with the distant sounds of clanking tank treads and artillery shells barking into the blackness—as a signal for them to withdraw. Most needed little encouragement. Exhausted and terrified, and without clear direction from their leaders, some of the soldiers struck their tents and had their trucks loaded before their chain of command knew what was happening.[86]

To deny the Germans easy access to Sbeïtla, American engineers demolished a railroad trestle east of the city, as well as road culverts and an aqueduct. When they lit up their own ammunition dump, many of the more steadfast soldiers who hadn't yet begun to "pack and run" assumed that German infiltrators must have caused the thunderous yellow roar.[87] What had started out as isolated pockets of soldiers acting out of confusion and miscommunication became a full-blown panic. Before long, a dense mass of trucks and jeeps, bumper to bumper and sometimes three abreast, choked the arrow-straight road heading west.[88] "There was indescribable confusion," wrote one officer. With clouds red from the burning ammunition dumps,[89] "the road was jammed as far as one could see [with] remnants of a beaten force hurrying to the rear."[90]

Back in Speedy Valley, the echoes of tunneling were replaced by the sounds of retreat. Fredendall's corps was in tatters, already thrown back fifty miles with twenty-five hundred casualties and no end in sight. His career seemed over; surely Eisenhower would need a scapegoat.[91]

"Never were so few commanded so badly by so many," Ernie wrote of the debacle in the first draft of a column.[92] Thanks to the military censors, that sentence never made it back home.[93] If a story about an American defeat had anything in it that could negatively affect the troops' morale or the perceptions of readers at home, the censors and their superior officers could kill the story or cut or revise it. Once the censors did whatever they needed to do, remembered Walter Cronkite, who covered the war for United Press, "they sent it back out to you, whether you wanted to file it that way or not. Sometimes, if you didn't care how they censored it but just wanted it to move as quickly as possible, you could mark it, 'Read and File.' This meant for them to censor it and then send it to your office in the censored form."[94]

To avoid upsetting the censors and to reduce delays to publication, many war correspondents policed themselves. They avoided sensitive topics and anything controversial.[95] Absentee leadership went unmentioned. So did poor planning and slipshod communications. The friction that existed in North Africa between the United States and its British and French allies was mostly off-limits. So was the racial tension within the American ranks. Despite plenty of examples to pull from, there wasn't a single story published during the entirety of the war about atrocities committed by the Allies.[96]

Reflecting on his brief time as a correspondent for the *New York Herald Tribune*, the novelist John Steinbeck confessed, "We edited ourselves much more than we were edited. We felt responsible to what was called the home front. There was a general feeling that unless the home front was carefully protected from the whole account of what war was like, it might panic." Censoring himself was not only patriotic, but also practical, Steinbeck claimed, for any correspondent who was foolish enough to push the limits set by the censors "would be put out of the theater by the command, and a correspondent with no theater has no job."[97]

"The withdrawal of our American forces from the vast Sbeïtla Valley, back through Kasserine Pass, was a majestic thing in a way," Ernie wrote of the panicked retreat in the column that ultimately passed the censor's blue pencil. The retreat, he continued, didn't actually look like a retreat, though Ernie had never seen a retreat to which he could compare it. "It was carried out so calmly and methodically," he said. "It differed in no way, except size, from the normal daily convoys of troops and supplies."[98] Being in the thick of it himself, shoulder to shoulder with America's fighting men, my great-great-uncle among them, Pyle had an aura of credibility and authenticity that wasn't easily replicated in articles transmitted by correspondents who relied mostly on military communiqués. "As for our soldiers," Ernie assured the readers at home, "you need feel no shame nor concern about their ability. I have seen them in battle and afterwards and there is nothing wrong with the common American soldier. His fighting spirit is good. His morale is okay. The deeper he gets into a fight the more of a fighting man he becomes."[99]

Even though the Americans had "lost a great deal of equipment, many American lives, and valuable time and territory—to say nothing of face,"[100] Ernie felt compelled to explain, the fight against the Germans in Tunisia was mainly a "British show"; America's role in it was small. The defeat, therefore, may have been "damned humiliating,"[101] but it wasn't nearly as disastrous as it may have seemed. There was a whole big war left to fight, and one little setback in North Africa was just that—a setback. Such artful narratives, which reassured his disappointed readers that "no one over here has the slightest doubt that the Germans will be thrown out of Tunisia,"[102] lent a certain dignity and purpose to defeat, transforming it into a signpost to eventual victory.

7

Where was Ernie during all of this?" Yomna asked as I climbed back out of the bomb crater in the middle of where her family's ancestral home had been.

"He retreated with the rest of the Americans all the way from Sbeïtla to here," I said. "And then I'd have to assume he kept going through the pass, probably right past the castle on the road, back to Tébessa. He didn't write anything about having witnessed the fighting here."[103]

At the base of Djebel Chambi, five German panzers had their treads knocked off[104] by the land mines the American engineers had sprinkled a couple days before. Others bogged down in the mud.[105] The tanks heading north to Sbiba didn't fare much better. About six miles below the village, the Twenty-first Panzer Division ran into a narrow line of mines. After clearing a path, the Germans continued their march only to stumble into a field of American mines also covered by artillery. When Rommel learned that his forces had lost around a dozen tanks to the presighted guns, he called off the attack[106] and focused his attention on exploiting the comparatively weak defenses in Kasserine Pass.[107]

As darkness descended across the battlefield on February 19, so too did uncontrollable fear among the surviving American engineers. "A considerable number of men left their positions and went to the rear," an engineer officer later reported. Some were rounded up and marched back to the line. Many more disappeared into the night. Some had their clothes and weapons stolen from them by enterprising Arabs who had scrounged M-1s and '03 rifles from the dead hands of American soldiers.[108] "My main anxiety is the poor fighting value of the Americans," British general Harold Alexander wrote. "They simply do not know their job as soldiers and this is the case from the highest to the lowest."

"Perhaps the weakest link of all is the junior leader," the general continued, "who just does not lead, with the result that their men don't really fight."[109]

By lunchtime the next day, while Ernie was in a jeep on the way back to Oran, Kasserine Pass was lost. Colonel A. T. W. Moore, the commander of the engineers dug in across the mouth of the pass, radioed that German infantry and tanks were forcing their way through. Rommel had finally committed two battalions from the Tenth Panzer Division. There was no way to stop them. An American officer roared over the noise of battle for his men to abandon their equipment. "Just save your life!" he ordered. Companies fragmented into platoons, platoons into squads, squads into lone survivors. Casualties among infantrymen totaled nearly five hundred dead, wounded, and missing. Italian tanks from the Centauro Division drove five miles toward Tébessa without encountering a hint of resistance. There was nothing but burning American wreckage and the footprints of fleeing men across the soggy, shell-plowed terrain.[110]

Twenty miles west of Kasserine Pass, a jagged escarpment runs north to south. German scouts reported back to Rommel that there were no Allied forces east of the escarpment, and Rommel ordered the Tenth Panzer Division to continue north toward Thala while the Afrika Korps pushed west. They were to take the escarpment and seal off any mountain passes to protect the Tenth Panzer's flank.[111]

The scouts had been wrong. The escarpment's high ground was crawling with Americans who had fled from Kasserine, and their blood was finally up. Twenty-three miles from Tébessa, the Afrika Korps ground to a halt.[112] They were overextended, running low on supplies, and pinned down by Allied artillery.[113] The next night, Rommel conceded defeat and ordered the Afrika Korps to abandon their foxholes and withdraw back through Kasserine Pass.[114] He had lost a thousand men, but his troops had killed, wounded, or captured six times that many[115] and driven the Americans back eighty-five miles.[116] "The proud and cocky Americans stand humiliated by one of the greatest defeats in our history," Harry C. Butcher, an aide to General Eisenhower, scribbled in his diary. "There is a definite hangheadedness."[117]

8

American and British soldiers returned to Kasserine Pass on the morning of February 25. A light snow had covered the detritus of battle. Yomna's family's land was cluttered with wrecked German and American airplanes, burned-out vehicles, abandoned tanks, and scattered shell cases. To discourage a hot pursuit, Rommel ordered his engineers to demolish thirteen bridges around Kasserine and nine bridges between Sbiba and Sbeïtla. They also planted more than forty-three thousand mines. Because their detectors tended to short out in damp weather, American engineers resorted to probing for mines with their bayonets, "spread out like caddies and golfers looking for a lost ball," as one historian noted.[118]

After we had finished touring the hill that had once been home to Yomna's family's castle, Rabeh led us to a wheat field and a small olive grove. Green and blue tarps had been stretched out and pinned to the ground beneath a handful of the short, wide-canopied trees. Middle-aged women

standing on stepladders or perched on some of the thicker limbs were claw-
ing at the trees' branches with plastic cultivators. As we got closer, I could
hear the plunking of ripe olives falling onto the tarps. The women's children, all elementary school aged, were sweeping the fallen fruits into piles
and tying them up in bindles of the sort you might find at the end of a ho-
bo's stick. Most of them wore Nike and Adidas sweatshirts and track pants.
When they saw me, they huddled together, pointing toward me and whis-
pering. "You're probably the first American they've ever seen," Yomna said.

In one tree on the edge of the grove, two women had climbed up into
the center mass of limbs while two other women, their heads and necks
wrapped in colorful scarves, raked the lower branches. While I watched,
the woman in the center of the tree climbed out on her limb as far as she
could. She was dressed in all black, except for the dark blue scarf tied
around her head and neck. She yelled out to Yomna.

"What is she saying?" I asked. "Does she not want me to watch her
work?"

"Actually," Yomna said, "she wants you to know she hates America."
Yomna laughed. "You can't really blame her, can you?"

I figured her feelings toward America had something to do with its relationship with Israel. It wouldn't be the first time on my trip that someone,
after finding out I was American, felt the need to tell me what a despicable
act it was for President Trump to recognize Jerusalem as Israel's capital back
in 2017.

That was part of it, Yomna told me, but the main reason she hated the
United States was because it was America's fault Saddam Hussein was dead.
If it wasn't for us, Iraq's infamous dictator would never have been over-
thrown. If it wasn't for America, he'd never have had to hide in hole like an
animal, and he never would have been executed. I was confused. Saddam
was tried and convicted of heinous crimes, including genocide. Many Tunisians, Zakariya explained through Yomna, never believed any of America's propaganda about Saddam. He was a good man, Zakariya said, who
had done more for the Sunni Muslims in Tunisia than anyone else he could
think of. Most Tunisians, including Zakariya, are Sunni—as was Saddam—

and most of the universities in Tunisia, including the one Zakariya gradu-ated from, were either built by or maintained by Saddam and his riches.

I tried to explain that I was a writer and that I had nothing to do with American foreign policy. I was not proud of what we had done in Iraq. It was, in so many ways, a colossal mistake. Yomna translated. The woman smiled, seemingly satisfied at having had her views validated.

"Would it be OK," I asked, holding up my black iPhone, "if I took your picture?"

After Yomna translated my request, the woman smiled wide and in broken English shouted, "For Facebook?"

9

On Sunday, February 21, 1943, as Rommel planned his withdrawal through Kasserine, Ernie was back in Oran at the Aletti Hotel, over-looking the Mediterranean, after an eighteen-hour solo drive from the front. After spending so many weeks hopping from unit to unit, freezing in the snow and the rain with only his army bedroll to keep him warm at night, he felt it odd to be "living half-way normal again," he wrote to Jerry in a letter home. While at the front, Ernie had slept in chicken houses, under wagons, in cactus patches, and among fir trees on the sides of moun-tains with nothing but stars for a roof.[119] In Oran, which he described elsewhere as a "minor Washington, only not so minor" because it was so overcrowded with backbiting correspondents,[120] Ernie had a sun-drenched hotel room and a double bed all to himself. "It's mighty good in a way," he continued to Jerry, "and yet in another way you feel a strange sort of rest-lessness and keep halfway wishing you were back there shivering and sleep-ing on the ground and never taking your clothes off. Which must be proof that I have reached the final stages of insanity."[121]

Ernie had also mostly given up on writing while he was at the front. He was supposed to have about two dozen columns ready to send to Lee when he returned to Oran, but he had managed only seven. On the sun-drenched balcony outside his hotel room, Ernie sat staring at the blank sheet of paper wound up in his typewriter. Smoke from his cigarette blanketed the idle keys with every exhale. After a hacking cough, he rubbed the bridge of his windburned nose, unable to untangle the jumble of sights and sounds knotted in his brain.[122]

After he signed his letter to Jerry, Ernie, defeated by the blank page, moved his typewriter back into the room. Chilled to the bone after a thick cloud had maneuvered across the sky, blocking the warmth from the sun, he went for lunch across the street from the hotel to where the army had set up an officers' mess hall.[123] When Ernie returned to his room, he turned his attention back to the Herculean task of writing a balanced account of the American defeat that was accurate and insightful and also in compliance with the military authorities, who viewed correspondents as quasi–staff officers there to help win the war.[124] What had he really *seen*, after all? There was dust and there was noise and there was confusion. There was desperate radio chatter from the frontline units outnumbered and outgunned. There was what he thought happened and what the reports from Fredendall's headquarters staff said happened.[125] And then there were the soldiers and their stories, their grimy faces and their vacant stares.[126]

"Is war dramatic, or isn't it?" he typed, a Bull Durham[127] cigarette hanging from his lips. "Certainly there are great tragedies, unbelievable heroics, even a constant undertone of comedy. It is the job of us writers to transfer all that drama back to you folks at home. Most of the other correspondents have the ability to do it. But when I sit down to write, here is what I see instead:

"Men at the front suffering and wishing they were somewhere else, men in routine jobs just behind the lines bellyaching because they can't get to the front, all of them desperately hungry for somebody to talk to besides themselves, no women to be heroes in front of, damn little wine to drink, precious little song, cold and fairly dirty, just toiling from day to day in a world full of insecurity, discomfort, homesickness and a dulled sense of danger."[128]

If he couldn't speak truth to power, Ernie could instead hold up hope for those who had none by painting a human face on the abstraction of war. Rather than add to the mountain of sketchy details emerging from Kasserine, Ernie could tell a different story, one that disguised bad news as promising and transformed "our boys" into the heroes America needed—heroes who slogged and suffered without glamour or glory, who wanted nothing more than to finish the fight and return home to their families.

At the end of a ten-day writing binge, Ernie looked back on the stack of copy he'd churned out and couldn't help but feel disappointment. "They are the ones I wanted to do especially good on," he told Jerry, "but they are especially bad." He had waited too long to write, and the subjects were too big to cover in only a few columns. Plus, he was sick with another cold. "But I'm not discouraged," he continued, "for it isn't important."[129]

Despite Ernie's disappointment, the folks at home devoured his columns, making Ernie an overnight sensation.[130] Every week dozens of papers added his column to their pages.[131] In the *Detroit Free Press*, Malcolm W. Bingay wrote that Ernie was "doing the best job of war correspondence that has come out of this conflict."[132]

It's not clear whether Ernie was simply being modest in his letter to Jerry or if he had exhausted himself into an apathetic melancholy. What is clear is that the Battle of Kasserine Pass had set its hooks in him. Even though war had revealed itself to be more unalleviated misery than romantic adventure, Ernie knew he couldn't escape it. "I too hate and detest the war and the tragedy and insanity of it," he told Jerry, but "I truly believe the only thing left to do is to be in it to the hilt."[133] Instead of embarking on reporting trips to India and China, followed by a ticket home, as he had originally planned, Ernie decided to stay on so he could see the "African thing" through to the end.[134] The front had gotten into his blood. He needed it. "Life up there is very simple," he wrote, "very uncomplicated, devoid of all the jealousy and meanness that floats around a headquarters city, very healthful despite the cold, and time passes so damned fast it's just unbelievable."[135]

Ernie's purpose was now clear. Americans at home needed him to explain the war to them, and what life for their sons and husbands was really like. If those who made it home were ever going to find some semblance of peace, Pyle realized, the American people needed to be able to understand why their boys froze at the sound of trucks backfiring, why the smell of diesel or copper transported them back to some shell-pocked battlefield, why they were coarsened and reluctant to talk about all they endured.[136] It was the least they could do.

10

A fter we finished our tour of Rabeh's farm, Yomna and Zakariya took me for green olive and tuna pizza near the base of Djebel Chambi. The terra-cotta-roofed restaurant was one of several buildings on the property that Yomna's family had sold to a doctor friend of theirs. In addition to a restaurant, he had also built a large spa with several steam rooms and a medical treatment area, as well as a stable and corral for horseback riding and equine therapy.

We were the only ones eating inside that night. Yomna picked a table against the wall under an open window and sat down. We ordered Cokes and watched as the chef made each of our pizzas and slid them with a long wooden paddle into a large stone oven on the far side of the restaurant. I took out my pocket notebook. Zakariyah pulled out his phone. Yomna watched as I jotted a few notes.

"What are you writing now?" she asked.

"Just little details I see," I said. "Like how I can see the base of Mount Chambi through the open front door and how I can smell the faint smell of a horse barn."

She grabbed my notebook from me, midnote, and flipped to the first page. She smiled at me with a look that said, *Don't mind if I do.*

"'Was taken advantage by taxi driver, just like my seatmate on the plane warned me about. Man approached me outside baggage claim, took my bag,'" she read aloud. "'Wait . . . you paid your driver ninety dinar?" she asked incredulously. That got Zakariyah's attention. Even with his limited

English, he knew enough to know I'd been taken to the cleaners. He chuck-led. "You should have paid him twenty or thirty at the most. He played you for a total fool," Yomna said as she flipped several pages.

"'So far Tunis has been quite overwhelming. Very windy today. Traffic is horrendous,'" she continued to read. "'No lanes in the roads, very few traf-fic signs or lights. Cars weave in and out, cut off oncoming traffic, bunch up and surge.'" She nodded. "That is why we have Zakariyah," she said. A few more pages. "'Young single women walk in pairs and threesomes,'" she read. "'Most women I saw were wearing the hijab.'" She closed my notebook and handed it back to me. "That is why I went to school in France," she said with a sigh. "I cannot let the old ways here rule my life like that."

Zakariyah put away his phone and checked the time on his large-faced watch. Then he pushed the sleeves up on the sweater he'd worn the past few days and ran his palms along the sides of his head, smoothing out his closely cropped black hair. The silence at our table made me feel a bit awk-ward, as if it were my job to liven up our time together. It was then that a strange memory zapped into my brain of the time my wife and I saw David Sedaris read from a new book of his in a large auditorium in central Wis-consin. His essays are both immaturely humorous and profanely human-izing, and there was one he read that night that was especially so. In it, Sedaris recounted all the many times he had asked people from different countries what cuss words they yelled out their car windows when they were angry with another driver. I remembered that it was a Romanian woman who made the most lasting impression on him. When he posed the question to her, she said the most popular curse in Romanian roughly trans-lated to "I shit in your mother's mouth." Anything terrible having to do with mothers—those were the absolute worst curses they could muster.[137]

"What's the worst thing you can call someone in Arabic?" I asked Yomna, hoping to spark as lively discussion as Sedaris described. Zakari-yah smiled at me. He understood more than he let on.

"I cannot tell you," Yomna said. She was blushing.

I turned my gaze to Zakariyah. He snapped his fingers and motioned to my notebook. He couldn't stop himself from snickering as he wrote out four Arabic cuss words in large block letters. He passed the notebook across the table to Yomna. She looked shocked.

"I would *never* say any of these out loud," she implored.

The first was *massakh*, which Yomna translated in writing in my notebook as "pig." *Kahba* meant "slut," and *miboun*, which Yomna said meant "gay," was a word she detested. "I do not agree it is OK to ever call someone that," she protested with her nose turned down in a show of disgust. The final word, *baranayek*, was what you would say when someone cut you off in traffic. It meant "fuck off." The absolute worst thing someone could say, Yomna told me, was anything bad about someone's mother.

"These are the words the Tunisians had for the French after the Battle of Kasserine Pass," Yomna said.

"What do you mean?"

"After the battle ended and the Americans moved on," she explained, "the French were still in power here. Our farmland was destroyed, and our olive trees, too. Our animals were killed or stolen from us. We had no home. And then the French rounded up and murdered anyone they thought had helped the Germans. The Americans did nothing to stop them."

"I had no idea," I said. "Honestly."

"My father's cousin—his name was Hafnaoui Monsori—was executed by the French in Kasserine alongside fifteen others. They shot him. They said he had collaborated with the Germans, but then three days later, it was in the paper that he had been falsely accused. They killed him for nothing."

Yomna's father's cousin and the others who were executed alongside him were far from the only Tunisians to suffer great injustice under French rule once the Germans were expelled. At least eight thousand Tunisians were rounded up, almost all without being charged or standing trial. Most suffered for months in makeshift concentration camps, where they were beaten, tortured, and starved. Hundreds of others were summarily killed.

American observers reported at the time that they believed the French were not as interested in curbing lawlessness as they were in rewriting the history of their own collaboration with the Nazis. The French were also acutely aware of the need to cripple the nascent Tunisian nationalist movement led by Habib Bourguiba, a stern-faced man who returned to Tunisia in April 1943 after serving five years in prison, first in Tunisia and later in France, for conspiring against the state and inciting civil war. In 1952, Bourguiba led an armed struggle against French colonial authorities in Tunisia, was arrested and imprisoned again, and then, to end the violence, negotiated agreements with the French prime minister to give Tunisians more internal autonomy. In 1957, once his country finally gained its independence, Bourguiba became Tunisia's first president, a position he kept for three decades. "He is our country's most important historical figure," Yomna told me. "I aspire to be like him and live up to what he gained for us every day."

Soon after our pizzas arrived, we heard what sounded like a muffled explosion. Then another, this one closer. A third explosion rattled the open window at the end of our table. I stopped chewing, put down my slice, and looked to Yomna for an explanation.

"That's the army," Yomna said as Zakariyah walked to the door to look out at Mount Chambi, now a beautiful shade of greenish purple in the fleeting light. "They must have spotted a terrorist."

CHAPTER 4

DRIFTING WITH THE WAR

It's the perpetual, choking dust, the muscle-racking hard ground, the snatched food sitting ill on the stomach, the heat and the flies and dirty feet and the constant roar of engines and the perpetual moving and the never settling down and the go, go, go, night and day, and on through the night again. Eventually it all works itself into an emotional tapestry of one dull, dead pattern—yesterday is tomorrow and Troina is Randazzo and when will we ever stop and, God, I'm so tired.

ERNIE PYLE, "IT IS TRUE WE DON'T FIGHT ON," AUGUST 25, 1943[1]

1

On May 14, 1943, a couple of days before the North African campaign officially ended, Ernie and his bunkmate from the voyage to North Africa, Will Lang, commandeered a jeep and set out on what they figured would be a five-day journey west from the Tunisian coast to Allied headquarters back in Algiers. The drive itself would take half that time, Ernie thought, but they both wanted to stop at several airfields along the way to help break up the monotony of driving so far.[2]

Ernie and Will had heard that back in Algiers the army's public relations department had set up a tent camp on the beach, about half an hour outside of the city.[3] "I'll have a tent alone and daily courier service to the city and it should be ideal for a couple or three weeks of constant writing,"

Ernie told Jerry in a letter. "Having lived outdoors for so long now," he continued, "my feeling against cities has grown worse than ever, and I can hardly bear the thought of being cooped up in one among all the people."[4]

Ernie was tired, and the tent camp sounded like a perfect place to finish up a few columns, catch up on his letters, and churn out a conclusion for his forthcoming book, *Here Is Your War.* The thought of doing anything else seemed impossible. Other than sleeping, rereading Jerry's letters for the dozenth time, and poking at his typewriter, he could hardly make himself do anything. Nearly two weeks of nonstop action at the end of the campaign, paired with the excitement of victory, had drained out into the desert sands whatever energy Ernie had left.[5]

One of Ernie's bosses at Scripps-Howard told Lee Miller to tell Ernie it was time to come home for a rest. Another boss thought that maybe if Ernie came home he could build a nice cushion for himself reporting on life in wartime America—it could make powerful reading to have a combat veteran like Ernie weigh in on how the "folks at home" were faring. "Of course," Ernie explained to Jerry, "they're both wrong." That wasn't Ernie's style. "If I'm put to experting the home front I'm completely out of character," he continued; "and as we know from our yearly returns to Washington even in peacetime, a visit 'home' doesn't rest you but destroys you. I really don't think I could stand crossing the ocean twice on a hurry trip and the madness of two or three weeks in the states."[6]

The one consideration that complicated his decision to stay was the thought that he might see Jerry again. She had found a steady routine in his absence. By day, she filed all technical orders, memos, and regulations as a file clerk in the sub-depot supply shop out at nearby Kirtland Field, an Army Air Corps base.[7] She enjoyed the job, at least at first, until she grew tired of the "repulsive nest of intrigue and backbiting."[8] In the evening she took Spanish lessons[9] and cared for the family pet, a border collie named Cheetah. Plus there was all the sprucing up at the house, which a friend had written to Ernie was looking like a "little show-place—perfect in every detail."[10]

"I'm terribly proud of you," Ernie wrote. "I know how hard it has been for you to establish yourself in your new routine, and I think it might be wrong to interrupt it."[11] Plus there was that "vague and probably false" sense of duty Ernie felt tugging at him like a hook. What he felt was more particular and disciplined than simple patriotism—less a matter of idealism or morality than a kind of counterintuitive self-preservation.

"I hope you won't feel I've done wrong if I don't come home yet," he wrote.[12] "I think I'll just drift with the war, and let events make my decisions for me."[13] At the same time, however, Ernie was beginning to worry about what he called the "slowing down" period—that "terrible readjustment to make to normal life." Ernie knew that he, along with millions of others, might get caught in a never-ending cycle of not wanting to stop—not really, anyway. "Even though my only goal and dream is to slow down to a complete stop," he told Jerry of his stint as a war correspondent, "I know it will be difficult."[14]

2

Ernie was behind the wheel, headed west along the Mediterranean coast. The jeep's engine hummed. The gears ground. Clouds of dust billowed out from under the tires. Few words were spoken over the sounds of driving.[15] Back then there wasn't anything that could have been described as a highway that connected Tunis to Algiers, so Ernie puttered along at about twenty miles per hour, enjoying the Sunday-stroll pace in the blindingly bright sun of North Africa.[16] To Ernie the Mediterranean looked much like the coast of Oregon, which he loved, and "inland there are scenes which are really lovelier than anything I ever remember seeing at home anywhere."[17]

At some point in one of Ernie's two-hour driving shifts, "one of the uncountable flea-like Arab kids that infest the roads," as Ernie described the boy, "almost literally jumped from the roadside into our radiator."[18] Ernie pressed down on the brake with all his might, and the jeep skidded to a stop. He'd struck a small boy. It was Ernie's first accident in twenty-five years.

After checking for a pulse and realizing there still might be time to save the boy, Ernie and Will scooped him up and laid him down across the back seat of the jeep. Ernie drove to a nearby French hospital while Will tried to keep the boy from jostling. At the hospital a French doctor was there when the boy regained consciousness. There didn't appear to be anything seriously the matter with him. Probably just shock. Ernie and Will thanked the doctor. Will took his shift behind the wheel, and Ernie sat in the passenger's seat, silent.[19]

A short while later, Will pulled up to the gate of an American air base, and he and Ernie quicky found the mess hall. While they sat at a long wooden table eating their lunch, scores of old Army Air Corps friends Ernie had made while still back in England came by to give their regards. "It was one of those chaotic periods with too much talk and too many people that I never could stand," he wrote to Jerry, "even though enjoying it."[20]

About an hour after lunch, Ernie's stomach stabbed him with a pain so intense he pleaded to be taken to see a doctor. Later, Ernie chalked the pain up to nervous tension and "over-tautness," and when the doctor couldn't find anything medically wrong with him, he prescribed Ernie some stomach-settling pills that did the trick. The next morning, Ernie was too weak to get out of bed, but by the day after that he was feeling fine once again.[21]

Ernie stayed in the bustling headquarters city only long enough to bathe for the first time in a month and a half.[22] After thirty minutes on the coastal road, he pulled up to the Allies' beachfront tent camp, where he found what he was looking for.[23] On a sand dune punctuated with scrub pine growing improbably right up out of the sand, a tent fixed up like home with a low wicker chair parked outside was waiting for him. In a tent all to himself, with grass mats for rugs, Ernie sat from breakfast to bedtime[24] on a folding cot with his typewriter perched on a small table.[25] The only light hung above his cot, which was shrouded in a mosquito net that was perfect for keeping the flies at bay.[26] In a little under a week, in the graveyard quiet of the homey camp,[27] Ernie pecked out nearly fifteen thousand words—nine columns, an article for *Stars and Stripes*, and a five-thousand-word ending for his forthcoming book. He figured he had another week or so of column and letter writing to do, but after that he planned to let the column drop for a week or two so he could finally rest his weary mind. It had been nearly a year since he'd taken anything resembling a break, and, as he explained to Jerry, "the future will be tough so I think it wise for me to get a little rest while I can."[28]

During this respite from the war, the only time Ernie traveled back to Algiers for anything more involved than picking up his rations of cigarettes was to attend a small, very select dinner hosted by the Red Cross.[29] After having mostly abstained from alcohol for so long while living at the front, Ernie found his tolerance for brown liquor had deteriorated precipitously. A couple of drinks before dinner made him lose his appetite, and a few drinks more went straight to his head. With a faintly upset stomach, eyes out of focus, and a tense pain in the back of his skull,[30] the only recourse left was to close his eyes and wish for relief. Once the other dinner guests noticed Ernie nodding off in front of his barely touched plate, some men took him to a nearby apartment and tucked him into bed with his knit cap still on. At the crack of dawn the next day, Ernie was found wrapped up in a rug, asleep on the hard stone floor of the hallway outside the apartment.[31]

"But I enjoyed it," he wrote to Lee, "think it was probably good for me, and for once had a hangover and didn't regret it."[32]

Back at his beachfront tent,[33] Ernie found sacks full of mail that had finally caught up to him. Most were from fans of the column, letters that he appreciated but also felt bad about not always being able to answer. "I'm completely over my head," he confided in Jerry, "and won't be able to answer even the few that almost have to be answered."[34] There were also flattering cables from Lee and letters full of congratulations and accolades from newspaper editors from around the country.[35] Ben McKelway, the managing editor of *The Washington Star*, wrote to Ernie to tell him that a general by the name of Devers told a thousand army officers at Fort Leavenworth in Kansas that if they wanted a sense for what the war was really like, they should read Pyle. "That's something from a General," Ernie wrote to Jerry.[36] In a letter from Lee, Ernie learned that Walter Leckrone, an editor at *The Indianapolis Times*, believed Ernie's column was the "hottest feature" they had. "Best criticism I've heard of his," Leckrone wrote, "came from our maid (black), who said: 'He writes so I can understand it.'"[37]

Then there were the letters from friends that included details of the new and improved Jerry back home in Albuquerque. Ernie's secretary, Roz Goodman, wrote in mid-May after visiting Jerry that "I have never seen Jerry looking so lovely. She is much thinner in the face and her profile was exquisite."[38] Even Walker Stone, the editor in chief of Scripps-Howard Newspapers, after visiting Jerry at home, wrote to Ernie that Jerry was looking better and "seemed to feel better than at any time in the last 16 years."[39]

"I'm jealous," Ernie wrote to Jerry, "that everybody is seeing you and I can't."[40] It had been over a year since he last saw her. "You're all that matters to me," he wrote to her, "and I only exist for the day I can get home."[41]

But something wasn't right. By mid-June, Ernie was starting to worry again. It had been nearly two months since he'd received a letter from Jerry—even though she had promised she would write at least twice a week.[42] He found it hard to believe that everyone else's letters were getting through to him while all her letters were lost. "I get mail from a lot of people," he confided in Paige, "but am gradually sinking into my oldtime funk (from which I've been free for several months) about Jerry." If his intuition was correct, something bad had happened again. And if it had, he wrote Paige, "I don't know what to do."[43]

He could come home, of course. But if he did, if he came home and gave up everything he'd been building since heading overseas with six months of runway to get his column off the ground, what would he be giving it up for?[44]

Four days later, word finally came, via a cable from Lee. Jerry had been promoted at her job at the airfield. Ernie's spirits, so vulnerable to lack of mail from Jerry, were equally flexible, for they rose as fast as they had plummeted. "I still have never got any of your letters at the time you started work," Ernie replied in another letter, "so I don't know just what you're doing." As for him, "I can assure you that I will be in very little danger."

Whatever the next phase of the war required of him, Ernie continued, he'd be "only on the edges rather than in the thick of things."[45]

On June 21, 1943, Ernie received a most flattering cable from Lee.[46] The First Lady of the United States, Eleanor Roosevelt, mentioned Ernie's work in her own daily syndicated column, My Day. "The column which to me stands out as the most human and vivid story of the men in the African Theatre is Ernie Pyle's," she proclaimed. "I would not miss that column every day if I possibly could help it, and I am sure that many people feel just as I do."[47] Five months later, once Here Is Your War was published, Mrs. Roosevelt dedicated a column to it. "He has told a story of our Army as it is, of its life, day by day," she wrote. "It will give a vivid picture to anyone who has never been near a front. In the future, it will be one of the books to which historians will turn to explain the kind of men who fought this war."[48] She also invited Ernie to her apartment overlooking Washington Square Park in Greenwich Village for an evening cocktail. "I followed your articles with great interest and admiration," she wrote on October 1, 1943, "and look forward to the pleasure of meeting you."[49]

When he finally got to take his vacation from writing, Ernie buried himself in books. He read James Hilton's We Are Not Alone, which he loved; Thornton Wilder's play Our Town; Henry James's The Turn of the Screw, which he found fascinating but ultimately too "windy" for his taste; a travel book written in 1912 about Gafsa, Tunisia; several W. Somerset Maugham short stories; a novelette by Joseph Conrad called "Youth";[50] and Sinclair Lewis's novel Arrowsmith, which Ernie was very moved by. In a long letter to Jerry, he explained that he identified strongly with the lead character, a precocious and principled boy wonder from the Midwest named Martin Arrowsmith. Throughout most of the book, Arrowsmith struggles to find his place in the world, bouncing from one serious relationship to another, one seemingly perfect job to another, until he abandons the last people on earth who loved him and resigns himself to the life of a hermit scientist in the backwoods of Vermont. "In so many ways it is so much you and so much me," he wrote to Jerry, "that it sort of haunts me." In all of Arrowsmith's faults, he explained, he recognized his own: "his one-trackedness, his shallow wanderings from it, his self-centeredness, his neglects." And in Arrowsmith's wife, Leora, Ernie saw Jerry. "There is so much of you," he wrote, "the seeing beyond all sham, the patience with my childishnesses, that acute and automatic understanding of absolutely everything."[51]

While experimenting with viruses that could be used to combat bacterial infections at an elite research institute in New York City, Arrowsmith is summoned to a Caribbean island to test whether his latest discovery can be used to combat an outbreak of bubonic plague. Arrowsmith's man-of-science principles prevent him from offering the treatment widely, not until it can be properly tested—never mind how many may die before the data can be analyzed. Only after Leora and every other member of his team succumb to the plague does Arrowsmith administer his treatment to everyone on the island.

"Somehow I knew that Lewis would have her die in the book," Ernie continued in his letter to Jerry, "and the book ended there for me. I finished it, but I wasn't interested after that. Possibly because I felt it might picture my own pathetic and wretched flounderings if you were ever gone. Which seems romantic, considering that I'm still alive after two and a half years without you—but the point is, of course, that I haven't been without you."[52]

When he wasn't reading or writing letters, Ernie was dreaming about what the future might hold for him and Jerry. "I hope you will help me have the courage to give up this devastating job," he wrote to her. He knew he'd never be one to sit around and putter away the rest of his life, that much covering the war had taught him. Covering the war had also revealed something to him, something Jerry had understood from the moment she met him—that he'd "got to be hacking away at something." He didn't know why exactly, but without having something to accomplish, Ernie didn't know what he would do. It didn't even necessarily have to be writing, he explained, "but since I do like to write and do know my way around in that world, perhaps it may as well be that as anything else. But not this all-consuming every day thing, which exalts a little and destroys completely, unless I should find happiness in being devoured by it."[53]

3

For the invasion of Sicily, Ernie was given his pick of what he wanted to cover. His options were to trudge through the surf with the assault forces, hang back on a ship tasked with supporting the invasion fleet, or remain at headquarters in Algeria. Since he hadn't yet had the opportunity to embed with the navy, Ernie chose to hang back on a ship. "It is grand to be with the Navy,"[54] he wrote to Jerry about his week aboard a headquarters ship called the *Biscayne*.[55] For his readers back home, he added, "It was wonderful to get with the Navy for a change, to sink into the blessedness of a world that was orderly and civilized by comparison with that animal-like existence in the field."[56]

Ernie's coverage of the prelude to invasion contained some subtle—and not-so-subtle—digs at the navy. With showers and bunks with real mattresses, ice cream and Coca-Cola, hot coffee all day and movies after supper,[57] the sailors Ernie came to see as his family started to resemble the spoiled rich kids in town compared to the working-class rabble in the infantry who did the real fighting. "The sailors weren't hardened and toughened as much as the soldiers." It was understandable, Ernie explained. "The front-line soldier I knew lived for months like an animal, and was a veteran in the cruel, fierce world of death. Everything was abnormal and unstable in his life. He was filthy dirty, ate if and when, slept on hard ground without cover. His clothes were greasy and he lived in a constant haze of dust, pestered by flies and heat, moving constantly, deprived of all the things that once meant stability—things such as walls, chairs, floors, windows, faucets, shelves, Coca-Colas, and the little matter of knowing that he would go to bed at night in the same place he had left in the morning."[58]

The main difference, however, between sailors and soldiers, according to Pyle, was that the frontline soldier had to "harden his inside as well as his outside or he would crack under the strain."[59] The sailors Ernie met, in his estimation, couldn't cut that mustard.[60] And some of the sailors knew it, too. One night while Ernie was talking with a bunch of sailors at the far end of the stern, one of them gave credit where credit was due: "Believe me, after seeing these soldiers aboard, my hat's off to the Army, the poor bastards. They really take it and they don't complain about anything. Why, it's pitiful to see how grateful they are just to have a hard deck to sleep on."[61]

Of course, when sailors died in war, "death for them is just as horrible," Ernie reminded his readers, "and sometimes they die in greater masses than soldiers. But until the enemy comes over the horizon a sailor doesn't have to fight. A front-line soldier has to fight everything all the time. It makes a difference in a man's character."[62]

4

By the time the *Biscayne* set sail across an "ageless and indifferent sea" to the invasion beaches of Sicily, Ernie was sick of war and worried that his columns were sounding redundant and lifeless. He pressed on partly out of a sense of obligation and partly because he felt inspired by the young sailors all around him aboard ship who he saw were willing to do everything they could to win the war.

Ernie had originally planned to focus his reporting on the seaborne aspect of the invasion, but then the enemy surprised everyone and barely contested the landing beaches near the coastal city of Licata.[63] "A few preliminary shots gave us our range," Ernie wrote of his ship firing its big guns the morning of the invasion, "and then we started pouring shells into the town and into the gun positions in the hills. The whole vessel shook with every salvo, and scorched wadding came raining down on the deck."[64]

While the big ships kept firing, small assault craft floated up close all along the shore, dropped their heavy metal ramps into the relatively calm surf, and spewed out their human cargo before dashing off again.[65] "Before long," Ernie told his readers, "we could see the tanks let go at the town. They had to fire only a couple of salvos before the town surrendered. That was the end of the beach fighting in our sector of the American front."[66]

"Our portion of the assault," Ernie concluded, seemingly disappointed, "was far less spectacular than the practice landings I'd seen our troops make back in Algeria."[67]

With the seaborne portion of the invasion pretty much finished, aside from ferrying supplies to shore and wounded men back to hospital ships, there wasn't much more for Ernie to see. Unable to resist the chance to tangle up with his "god-damned infantry," Ernie climbed down a cargo net onto an assault barge and went ashore about six hours after the first Americans had landed. "The enemy defenses throughout our special sector were almost childish," Ernie later reported. "They didn't bother to mess up their harbor or to blow out the two river bridges which would have cut our forces in half. They had only a few mines on the beaches and practically no barbed wire."[68] Down near the docks along the shore, some soldiers discovered land mines still in their unopened boxes. Instead of being pleased with their good fortune at having caught the enemy by surprise, the soldiers Ernie talked to, soldiers who had been trained to expect, adapt to, and overcome the worst the enemy could throw at them, were shocked and even a little annoyed by the Italians' piss-poor performance.[69]

"The local people said the reason their army put up such a poor show in our sector," Ernie wrote, "was that the soldiers didn't want to fight." All of Sicily, they said, was "sick of being browbeaten and starved by the Germans, who had lots of wheat locked in granaries. The natives hoped we would unlock the buildings and give them some of it."[70]

Ernie wasn't impressed. "On the whole," he wrote of the "natives," the Sicilian people he encountered in Licata seemed "a pretty third-rate lot." The land in Sicily was wonderfully fertile, Ernie reasoned, but the Sicilian people were poor and starving because they were not "capable of organizing and using their land to its fullest." Describing them further as "absurd" and "pathetic" in how they threshed grain ("by tying three mules together and running them around in a small circle all day long while another fellow keeps throwing grain under their hoofs with a wooden pitchfork"),[71] Ernie painted the Sicilians as "poorly dressed" wretches with expressionless faces who were good for nothing except disrupting traffic.[72]

"By nightfall," he continued, "most of our invading soldiers summed up their impressions of the newly acquired soil and its inhabitants by saying, 'Hell, this is just as bad as Africa.'"[73]

The frustration didn't end with the Sicilian people, either. Their countryside was also a supreme disappointment.[74] "I for one had always romanticized it in my mind," Ernie wrote in his column, "as a lush green picturesque island." Wondering if perhaps he had been thinking of the isle of Capri, Ernie wrote that what he had encountered in Sicily was a "drab light-brown country" devoid of trees and dotted with pale gray villages that were "indistinguishable at a distance from the rest of the country."[75]

"By sunset of the first day," Ernie told his readers, "the Army had taken everything we had hoped to get during the first five days."[76] In a letter home to Jerry he wrote the next day, Ernie showed he wasn't fooled by the Allies' initial successes. "It isn't over yet by any means," he wrote, "as counterattacks are developing and their air is getting heavier. It's noon now and we've had 11 raids since dawn."[77]

One day into the campaign, and Ernie was already more exhausted than he'd ever been in his life. He told Jerry it was likely due to several days and nights without much sleep, paired with the climax of the landings and "all day barging around on the island and dodging raids." It all had left Ernie so "worn out and dopey" that he was having a hell of a time getting started on his columns. "I'm getting awfully tired of war and writing about it," he confessed. "It seems like I can't think of anything new to say—each time it's like going to the same movie again."[78]

Ernie stayed aboard the *Biscayne* with his new navy family for almost a week.[79] He did his writing in the chief engineer's cabin,[80] which afforded him plenty of distraction-free time to peck out nineteen columns on his time with the navy, more than enough to keep the folks at home satiated until the Sicilian campaign was over. When he was too tired to write, Ernie played gin rummy with the ship's captain, who had too much time on his hands after his ship's phase in the battle had ended. The break in the action was a welcome change of pace.[81] For a little while, at least. Once they started

sending sailors ashore for sightseeing tours, Ernie knew it was time to return to life with the dogfaces from the First Infantry Division. Ernie had
gotten word that they'd been asking about him, wondering if he had deserted them to turn sailor.[82] "So I shouldered my barracks bag," he wrote,
"and trundled myself ashore in Sicily for good."[83]

<h1 style="text-align:center">5</h1>

My first stop in Sicily after picking up my black rental car from the airport outside Palermo was Licata, about three hours south along the
coast. During my drive through the same countryside Ernie had traversed
seventy-five years before, I too noticed the lack of trees and the pale gray
villages, though what I saw was quite lush and even more picturesque than
I had hoped. The drive itself was hypnotic in a way. Mountains and steep
cliff faces morphed into rolling hills and luscious valley gorges. In 1943,
Ernie later learned, Sicily was having one of its driest summers in years,[84]
making everything look "naked and dusty."[85] Not until he reached the
north of the island did Ernie's opinion of it evolve. "Sicily is really a beautiful country," he wrote. "Up here in the north it is all mountainous, and all
but the most rugged of the mountains are covered with fields or orchards."[86]

After parking on the narrow street outside the Chiesa San Salvatore, a
gray-stone Catholic church with tall black doors, I walked toward the smell
of the shore, past the city's main municipal building, and up a steep hill
Ernie had spied from the *Biscayne* soon after the invasion began. "We could
see the American flag flying from the top of a sort of fort on a hill," Ernie
wrote. "Although the city itself had not yet surrendered, some Rangers had
climbed up there and hoisted the flag."[87] On my own hike up, I noticed a
graffito on a stucco wall that read VIVA IL DUCE—a phrase used to honor
the fascist dictator Benito Mussolini. A little farther up the hill, I saw another spot where a swastika had been tagged, though someone had tried to
scrub it off, leaving only a faint remnant.

Licata is a small city of thirty-seven thousand souls, only a tiny bit larger than it was in the summer of 1943. From the top of the hill, I could see the small river that runs through the town. I could see the wide main street and small harbor. Most of the buildings still around from the prewar era are made of local stone, which gives much of the city its substantial and heavy essence. The city had largely survived the American invasion unscathed, as Ernie had reported. While there was some damage, "on the whole," Ernie wrote, "Licata had got off pretty nicely."[88]

After a short stroll through downtown Licata, I headed back to my car and headed north, back to Palermo. From there, the next morning, I drove east and south to the ancient port city of Catania, which sits at the foot of Mount Etna. There I toured the Historic Museum of the Landing in Sicily 1943, the largest World War II museum in Italy. After I watched a brief introductory video on the history of the Allied invasion through Italian eyes, my tour guide led me into a replica of a Sicilian town square, which she told me was a close approximation of how things looked before the Allied bombings began. We then turned a corner and walked through a dark doorway flanked by stacks of sandbags into a long, skinny bomb shelter. The tour guide closed the door behind me, and for several minutes I got to experience what it might have sounded and felt like to live through a bombing raid. Once the all-clear sign was given, I exited through a door on the far end of the shelter and emerged into a large room full of half-standing facades, piles of rubble, and other evidence of destruction. "If you'll notice," my guide said, "this is the same town square that you first entered, only now it is no more."

I spent the most time in the museum learning more about the weeklong battle for Troina, a mountaintop town of around twelve thousand people the Germans had converted into a fortress.[89] In 1943, only four roads led to Messina, where the Germans were evacuating the bulk of their forces across the narrow strait to the toe of Italy. Before their work was completed, the Germans were able to evacuate some sixty thousand troops (including almost five thousand wounded men), ten thousand vehicles, one hundred artillery pieces, more than one thousand tons of ammunition, and another thousand tons of fuel.[90] One of those roads passed through Troina.

6

O ne recent sunny afternoon," Ernie's copy for the Treasury Department's war-bond drive read, "I sat on a Sicilian slope and watched our artillery turn the German hillside across the valley into an insufferable _____ of dirt, crock, smoke, explosions and flame. Our troops sat waiting until this appalling barrage finally _____. We had plenty of skills, and we used them in masses until the enemy was a pitiful thing. In the midst of it the commanding colonel walked up and sort of grinning said, 'We're letting the taxpayers back home take the kill this afternoon.'"[91] The blank spots were for Lee, Ernie's editor, to fill in with whatever he thought best. Sometimes when Ernie couldn't get the rhythm of a sentence to flow, he'd tee it up for Lee to take a crack at. No one could edit Ernie like Lee,[92] except for maybe Jerry.

"The bond you buy has by now become a direct thing which actually does save some Americans lives," the Treasury's ad continued. "And just as real and direct is the extra toil you put into every manufacture of every kind."[93]

Thanks to the folks at home who worked hard, sacrificed, scrimped pennies, and then, naturally, bought war bonds, "we no longer must chant our bitter refrain of 'too little and too late.' We're getting the stuff, and fighting spirit is high."

"If you could see just one man die on the battlefield," Ernie's copy concluded, "you would know how right it is to 'let the taxpayers take' every hill possible. More bonds and sweat at home mean less blood and tears."[94]

Ernie knew what he was doing. All those years cleaning up other people's copy back at The Washington Daily News had afforded him the opportunity to learn what sticks and then replicate it on demand. That crescendo

of an ending to make you want to give a little extra, to put your own relatively petty feelings aside and dedicate yourself to a cause greater than your
own, was vintage Pyle. For millions of Americans in 1943, it worked. That's
why the Treasury Department had reached out to Ernie in the first place.
Only he could so poetically portray the "ceaseless agony of the men at the
front" while also pumping up the people back home to show them they
weren't "part of the war effort"—they *were* the war effort. Their hard work
and generous pockets didn't "help" the troops—it *saved* them. And it tied
together the entire supply chain of war the United States needed to maintain to defeat the Nazis. As Ernie added, "The long disheartening gap between effort and achievement has been bridged, and we see that American
production can overwhelm our enemies."[95] For Pyle, these were not hollow
words. He really did mean what he wrote, as evidenced by his own prodi-
gious purchases of war bonds with the huge sums of money his royalties
would bring him.

One such battlefield in which the "taxpayers back home" took their
kills was the fortified ridgetop town of Troina, which intelligence officers
had determined was lightly defended by exhausted German soldiers low on
ammo and morale. What the Americans found instead was the hinge of the
German's defensive line, made up of six fortified hills that controlled the
approaching highway. A full week of attacks and counterattacks turned
Troina into the bloodiest battle of the campaign.

Finally, on August 4, the Americans threw eighteen battalions' worth
of artillery and a sortie of seventy-two dive bombers at the redoubt. When
the bombardment began, Ernie recounted for his readers, "planes by the
score roared over and dropped their deadly loads, and as they left our artillery put down the most devastating barrage we'd ever used against a single point, even outdoing any shooting we did in Tunisia."[96] The horizon was
soon choked with "great clouds of dust and black smoke." The noise and the
concussion were terrific. "Our artillery," Ernie wrote, "in a great semicircle
crashed and roared like some gigantic inhuman beast that had broken
loose and was out to destroy the world."[97]

Ernie had figured hundreds of Germans were dead or about to die. "All over the mountainous horizon," he began, "the world seemed to be ending." And yet, from their safe distance, Ernie and the American officers he'd befriended "sat there in easy chairs under a tree—sipping cool drinks, relaxed and peaceful at the end of the day's work."

"After a while," he continued, "we walked up to the officers' mess in a big tent under a tree and ate captured German steak which tasted very good indeed."[98]

"But by then," Ralph Martin wrote after the war to correct the record, "we were mostly killing civilians because the Germans had pulled out."[99] All told, 116 Troinians were killed during the weeklong battle, part of the price of breaking the back of the German defenses and opening the way to Messina.

On the day the battle finally ended, August 6, 1943, Troina was an utter ruin. In the torn and rubble-strewn streets, Ernie found horror, grief, and pain in the form of what one historian described as "weeping, hysterical men, women and children who had stayed there through two terrible days of bombing and shelling."[100]

Like Ernie, I too noticed the "feeling of far greater antiquity" in Sicily than "you get even from looking at the Roman ruins in North Africa." Troina, for example, rests on the top of a needle-point mountain ridge. It was built there and in that way in the "old days for protection," as Ernie explained. The buildings were "cement-colored stone" that blended into the mountainous surroundings, and the town's narrow streets and right-angle turns made it impossible to navigate by car to the town center, where a feudal tower loomed over the steep and rugged approach from the canyons below. "All of it," one correspondent later wrote, "a demolition engineer's dream."

By the time the Americans came to Troina in the summer of 1943, it was a former capital city that had been in decline since the end of the eighteenth century. Its highest ground, the city's center, was, until the Americans arrived, dominated by a towering fortress. Mostly what remains today is a weathered stone church, unassuming municipal office buildings, and darkened stucco apartments with shallow balconies overlooking narrow cobblestone streets.

Church of St. Mary in Troina, Sicily, December 2019

The day I parked my rental car on a steep backstreet a couple of blocks from the city center, the weather was gray and foggy. I had read that it was possible to spy breathtaking views of the surrounding valleys from every alley in town, but when I looked out over the edge of a low stone wall on the edge of the city's deserted main square, all I saw was a row of clay-tiled roofs, the orange, smoke, and ocher of the tiles disappearing into a thick expanse of pewter-colored clouds that blocked my view to the valley below.

Near the steep stone stairs that lead to the tall dark wood doors of the Church of St. Mary, a parish cathedral of neoclassical design that somehow survived the worst of the fighting, I found a marker displaying a black-and-white image of a line of weaponless Germans with their arms out and hands up, marching out of the church. The second, third, and fourth men in the line of six surrendering soldiers are looking at the photographer, smiling wide with mouths full of white teeth.

7

Near the end of my stay in Sicily, I found something I hadn't been sure still existed—the bridge that was "hung in the sky." In northeastern Sicily, near the coast, where the mountains are close together and the valleys are steep and narrow, the Sicilians had constructed hundreds of bridges since the 1693 earthquake destroyed many bridges originally built by the ancient Romans. They were graceful and ancient-looking arches of stone. During their retreat east to the port city of Messina, the Germans destroyed nearly every one of them along Sicily's limited network of roads. Moreover, their demolition crews blew nearly every span of nearly every bridge, from abutment to abutment. "Shattering them so completely," Ernie told his readers, "was something like chopping down a shade tree or defacing a church."[101] Before the 38-day-long battle for Sicily was over, the Germans had blown 138 bridges and cratered 40 roads. The pure waste of the whole mess outraged the American combat engineers. Knocking down a span or two would have delayed the American advance as much as destroying an entire bridge.[102]

"Scores of times during the Sicilian fighting," Ernie wrote, "I heard everybody from generals to privates remark that 'This is certainly an engineers' war.' And indeed it was. Every foot of our advance upon the gradually withdrawing enemy was measured by the speed with which our engineers could open the highways, clear the mines, and bypass the blown bridges."[103]

One of the most badly damaged areas was a 150-foot section of a cliff-side road at the end of a long tunnel that the Germans blew right into the sea at Point Calavà. As Pyle looked on in amazement, American engineers took only twenty-four hours to hang a wooden bridge safe enough for a general to cross on the way to Messina.

The main highway that travels closest to the northern shore, SS113, is studded with bridges and pokes through so many mountains, I started to lose count after thirty bridges. The map on my phone showed it to be the only main road that went anywhere near Point Calavà, but somehow none of the dozens of bridges and tunnels I saw even reminded me of the grainy black-and-white photos I found of the bridge being built—the same view Ernie would have had. Perhaps the tunnel was bulldozed shut after the battle, the road diverted?

On my last day in Sicily, I plugged "Point Calavà" into the GPS on my phone one last time and followed the directions that took me along SS113, as it had the past several days as I voyaged back and forth from Palermo to all four corners of Sicily, searching for signs of Ernie. Zooming in close to the line between gray and blue, I saw a public beach called Spiaggia del Bue. If I couldn't find the bridge, I reasoned, I could at least sit with my toes in the sand and jot down thoughts in my notebook as the waves massaged the shoreline until it was time for me to return my rental car and fly on to Rome.

The beach was big, dull gray, and totally barren—not another soul in sight. I parked the car and walked out onto the beach, which was more pebble and seashell than sand so far away from the water's edge. As I strolled, the wind came up strong and plastered my wavy hair to my forehead. Icy white froth swirled with the ebb and flow of the water.

I sat with my legs crossed and my back against the wind, hunched over my notebook, when I caught the movement of a man out of the corner of my eye. He was an older gentleman dressed in a dark windbreaker with white trim. His dark sunglasses glinted in the sun. I waved to him, and he waved back. Then he took out one of his earbuds and shouted something into the wind. I cupped my ear. Not that it would have made any difference if whatever he shouted wasn't in English. Luckily, the retired beachcomber was an expert in deciphering my hand motions and knew enough English words to make sense of my questions. "Bridge," I said. My hands bracketed the space between us to show a span. Then I waved one hand back and forth in a slight arc. "A bridge." He nodded. Then I made my hands into a circle and pumped back and forth. "Tunnel." One more nod. Then he took off his sunglasses. Through squinted eyes he watched me slice my hand up and down, trying to show him this bridge and tunnel were built on a steep cliff.

"Sì, è laggiù," he nodded one last time. Then he turned and pointed with both hands. "Yes, it's there."

Point Calavà, as Ernie described it to his readers, "is a great stub of rock that sticks out into the sea, forming a high ridge running back into the interior. The coast highway is tunneled through this big rock, and on either side of the tunnel the road sticks out like a shelf on the sheer rock wall." The Germans could have simply blasted the tunnel's entrance, sealing it up and blocking the Americans from advancing for as long as it took to bulldoze it back out. "But they didn't," Ernie explained. "They had an even better idea. They picked out a spot about fifty feet beyond the tunnel mouth and blew a hole 150 feet long in the road shelf. They blew it so deeply and thoroughly that a stone dropped into it would never have stopped rolling until it bounced into the sea a couple of hundred feet below."

"We were beautifully bottlenecked," Ernie continued. "We couldn't bypass around the rock, for it dropped sheer into the sea. We couldn't bypass over the mountain; that would have taken weeks. We couldn't fill the hole, for the fill would keep sliding off into the water."[104]

On Ernie's first day with the engineers of the Third Division,[105] he tagged along with a few engineering officers and hiked four miles or so, all uphill, with a battalion of infantrymen nipping at the retreating Germans' heels. After navigating safely through the heavily mined tunnel, they came upon "the vast hole beyond." Ernie stood on achy legs,[106] chain-smoked, and bullshitted with the infantrymen in the early afternoon sunshine while the engineering officers measured this and that and scribbled out calculations in handheld notebooks with grease pencils.

"As they did so," Ernie continued, "the regiments of infantry crawled across the chasm, one man at a time. A man could just barely make it on foot by holding on to the rock juttings and practically crawling. Then another regiment, with only what weapons and provisions they could carry on their backs, went up over the ridge and took out after the evacuating enemy. Before another twenty-four hours, the two regiments would be twenty miles ahead of us and in contact with the enemy, so getting that hole bridged and supplies and supporting guns to them was indeed a matter of life and death."[107]

Once a plan was formulated, the enlisted men in the engineering outfit dragged up three big air compressors. Soon hoses snaked under and across one another, leaving the mouth of the crater looking more like the scene of a five-alarm fire. The jackhammers plugged into the end of the hoses, mixed with the "erratically deliberate manner of air compressors," combined into a "nerve shattering" clatter that bounced off the rock face and skipped across the face of the turquoise sea below.[108]

Then the bulldozers arrived to clear off the highway at the edge of the crater. Long diesel-smoking trucks hauling long railroad irons and thick timber deposited their loads to the platoon of men working down in the hole. All sorts and sizes of crowbars and sledges and huge thimbles of steel cable and kegs of spikes rounded out the scene. When one platoon had worked itself to the point of exhaustion, a fresh platoon of diggers and riggers moved in while the retiring platoon scarfed down hot food—a "military necessity," if there ever was one, Pyle remarked.[109]

The work didn't end when the sun went down. Fortunately for the Americans, the half-moon that night reflected off the high-flying clouds and bought them an extra hour of work time before the clouds sank to cover the light, engulfing the men with a "blinding nightlong darkness."[110]

That night, around half past ten o'clock, the commander of the Third Division, General Lucian K. Truscott, visited the work site to see how much progress had been made. "Bridging that hole," Ernie told his readers, "was his main interest in life right then. He couldn't help any, of course, but somehow he couldn't bear to leave." The general, who distinguished himself in Sicily and again in mainland Italy as one of America's most gifted combat commanders, stood talking to his officers, his voice gravelly, as the engineers drilled holes far down the jagged slope to hold heavy uprights and stop them from sliding down the hill once the weight of military vehicles was applied.[111] After a while, Truscott walked off to the side of the crater, sat down on its edge, and lit a cigarette in the darkness. Around his neck he wore a white scarf from an airman's escape kit that featured a map of the fighting area. He lay down in his battered brown leather jacket, his .45-caliber pistol strapped to his waist, and drifted off to sleep, never mind the noise. "One of the working engineers came past," Ernie recounted, "dragging some air hose" that got caught up in the general's knee-high cavalry boots. "The tired soldier was annoyed," Ernie continued, "and he said crossly to the dark, anonymous figure on the ground, 'If you're not working, get the hell out of the way.'" The general got up and moved farther back without saying a word.[112]

The next morning, Ernie returned to the crater to find the uprights being slid down the bank, where they were caught by a small group of soldiers who helped maneuver the huge timbers into the holes drilled the night before. Soldiers with ropes tied to the end of the timbers helped as well. On each side of the crater, the engineers had leveled off the ground and bolted timbers to small ledges of rock to form an abutment. Deep in the rock, steel hooks had been embedded, which would be used to hold wire cables. To span the hole, long timbers, two feet square, had been bolted together and were lying in wait at the end of the tunnel.

At Nettuno, Italy, Ernie Pyle and Major General Lucian Truscott stand in front of Corps Headquarters, March 26, 1944

"A half-naked soldier," Ernie recounted, "doing practically a wire-walking act, edged out over the timber and with an air-driven bit bored a long hole down through two timbers. Then he hammered a steel rod into it, tying them together. Others added more bracing, nailing the parts together with huge spikes driven in by sledge hammers. Then the engineers slung steel cable from one end of the crater to the other, wrapped it around the upright stanchions and drew it tight with a winch mounted on a truck."[113]

Ernie was still worn out from the hike the day before. He felt old as hell. Half the time, he had to lie down on the ground. He felt sleepy the whole day. "It's disgusting because I know it's nothing but just the all-over cell collapse that comes with too many years," he recounted to Jerry. "For I'm actually healthy and there's nothing wrong with me in the medical line."[114]

Once the spliced timbers had been laid across the chasm, resting on two wooden spans, they sagged under all that weight. "But still the cable beneath took most of the strain," Ernie wrote. "They laid ten of the big timbers across and the bridge began to take shape. Big stringers were bolted down, heavy flooring was carried on and nailed to the stringers. Men built up the approaches with stones. The bridge was almost ready."[115]

About an hour before noon, jeeps began lining up at the far end of the tunnel. The first jeep to attempt a crossing, at exactly noon that day, contained Truscott and his driver. If the bridge gave way, they would tumble two hundred feet into the sea below. "The engineers had insisted they send a test jeep across first," Ernie wrote. But when Truscott saw that the bridge was finally ready, he went for it. "It wasn't done dramatically," Ernie continued, "but it was a dramatic thing. It showed that the Old Man had complete faith in his engineers. I heard soldiers speak of it appreciatively for an hour."[116]

It wasn't pretty. The bridge squeaked and bent as jeeps and trucks crawled across it. But it held. The engineers had built a "jerry bridge, a comical bridge, a proud bridge," Ernie wrote, "but above all the kind of bridge that wins wars. And they had built it in one night and half a day. The general was mighty pleased."[117]

A rusty metal guardrail ran the length of the seaside road that led to the bridge and tunnel. The sky that last day for me in Sicily was a beautiful

The site where American combat engineers constructed the bridge "hung in the sky" near Point Calavà, Sicily, December 2019

baby blue, the sea a rich mixture of all manner of blues and greens, with hints of purple. On the mountainside above the road, the cliffs were so steep and rocky that several sections were draped with heavy-duty wire mesh to help prevent tumbling boulders from breaking away and sliding down onto the blacktop. The rusty metal guardrail transformed into a low stone wall. A triangular sign depicting falling rocks, framed in fire-engine red, cautioned motorists of what lay ahead. My heart rate picked up as I drove on. Closer still, the metal guardrails were back, built atop the low stone wall, effectively obscuring my view of the sea. After several curves in the mountain-hugging road, I saw it—the tunnel and the bridge, which had clearly been rebuilt with impossibly thick concrete footings and other signs of modern infrastructure.

Before I reached the bridge itself, I drove through a 305-meter-long man-made concrete tunnel with narrow slits cut out along the side facing the sea. On the other side of the tunnel, the heavy wire screens were back. They crawled at least forty feet up from the road, where long metal poles jutted out and up from the rock, forming a metal basket of sorts to catch falling rocks. A small black car and a short white van drove slowly in front of me. After I watched them disappear into yet another tunnel, I pressed my foot on the brake so that I could stop long enough to take a few pictures. Only a few seconds later, another car appeared in my rearview mirror, and because there was no place to safely pull over, I sped up and through the tunnel, feeling a bit giddy that I had again found somewhere I knew Ernie had been.

8

The empty bottle of blood plasma hung next to the dying man's body. A mustachioed young doctor with a stethoscope around his neck circulated among the wounded men stranded on nearby litters. There were no field nurses in the small tent hospital hidden in an olive grove back behind the front lines. In the silence between the man's dying breaths, Ernie swallowed hard. He could do nothing.[118]

When he first saw the dying man being brought into the tent, Ernie was recuperating among wounded soldiers with what the doctor called "battlefield fever."[119] "A man with this ailment aches all over and has a high temperature," Ernie reported. "The doctors thought it was caused by a combination of too much dust, bad eating, not enough sleep, exhaustion, and the unconscious nerve tension that comes to everybody in a front-line area."

"A man doesn't die of battlefield fever," Ernie reassured his readers, "but he thinks he's going to.[120]

To treat his fever, the doctor gave Ernie soup and tomato juice to rehydrate him, a cot for him to rest, an opiate-based solution to plug up his insides, an aspirin and some codeine, and, for good measure, a little morphine. "The surgeons believed in using lots of morphine," Ernie wrote. "It spares a man so much pain and consequently relieves the general shock to his system."[121]

"The only thing I can say on behalf of my treatment," he reported, "is that I became well and hearty again."[122]

Others were not so lucky, including the dying man with the gauze over his face, whom the orderlies had placed on the earthen ground in the middle of the main aisle. The same day they set the dying man down, the chaplain ran in to issue him his last rites. The dying man's name was John.

"John, I'm going to say a prayer for you," the chaplain whispered into the man's ear. The chaplain was kneeling. He made the sign of the cross and held John's hand as he recited the Act of Contrition:

My God, I am heartily sorry for having offended Thee,

And I detest all my sins, because I dread the loss of heaven and the pains of hell,

But most of all because they offend Thee, my God, Who art all good and deserving of all my love.

John gasped for breath through the thin gauze covering his face as he tried in vain to repeat the prayers. When the chaplain had finished his last refrain, he told John he was doing fine. A moment later, the chaplain rose to his feet and walked out of the tent. There were other dying men who needed him. With the tent flaps opened, a steady breeze brushed against the men in their bloody uniforms. As John's last breath passed from his lips, Ernie, watching him, felt a rush of hot blood flow from his stomach down through his leaden limbs. His breath came so heavy he could feel it in his ears. A sort of helplessness wrapped in anger welled up deep inside him, driving him close to tears.

"Of course it couldn't be otherwise," Ernie later told his readers, "but the aloneness of that man as he went through the last few minutes of his life was what tormented me. I felt like going over and at least holding his hand while he died, but it would have been out of order and I didn't do it. I wish now I had."[123]

9

By the time the campaign for Sicily ended in mid-August, Ernie had grown even more exhausted than he had been when he was first diagnosed with "battlefield fever." Ernie would write that the outstanding trait of the battle for Sicily was the terrible weariness that gradually devoured everyone who experienced it, no matter how hardened or resilient.

More than that, Ernie was simply weary of the war. He'd been at it too long. There was nothing new to say about a campaign like the one in Sicily, which was like the last one, as far as all the fundamentals were concerned. His perspective was wrung dry.[124] "The result is that all of us who have been with the thing for more than a year have finally grown befogged," Ernie continued. "We are grimy, mentally as well as physically. We've drained our emotions until they cringe from being called out from hiding. We look at bravery and death and battlefield waste and new countries almost as blind men, seeing only faintly and not really wanting to see at all."[125]

"I haven't been under fire very much during the Sicilian campaign," he confided in Jerry in a letter dated August 15. After using up half his time during the campaign with the navy recuperating in the hospital, Ernie found himself "more and more reluctant to repeat and repeat the old process of getting shot at." He tried to fool himself by bulldozing ahead with work and making believe that it was at all important to the war effort. "But it's hard for me to convince myself," he wrote, "when I see daily how easy my lot is compared to all the kids in there taking it constantly; and me making so much money out of it to boot. The only justification I can find for myself is that at least I'm making it the hard way, and not by sitting in New York or Washington pontificating over a typewriter."[126]

The war was so complicated, so confusing, that on especially sad days it was "almost impossible for me to believe that anything is worth such mass slaughter and misery; and the after-war outlook seems to me so gloomy and pathetic for everybody."[127]

A few days later, Ernie was back in Palermo to, as he put it, "get in touch with what we jokingly called 'civilization.'" His dungeon-like room over-looked an alley stuffed full of "Sicilians who screamed constantly and never cleaned up anything." Worse than that, the mosquitoes were thick as smoke, and his "lovely white sheets" were home to three bedbugs and a baby scor-pion. "Civilization," he quipped, "she is wonderful."[128]

Time to go home. Time for a rest.

"I've reached a state of mental dullness," he wrote to Lee on August 20, "where I've decided it absolutely necessary for me to get freshened up be-fore bogging down completely, so have decided to come home for a month or more as soon as possible."[129] He needed at least a month, he thought, to sit blankly with nothing to do. Only then could he imagine discussing what his future might hold. "Perhaps," he continued, "the time is ripe for a jaunt into the Pacific. We'll see."[130]

From Palermo, Ernie traveled back to Algiers, where he found himself a room at the Aletti. There he learned that a writer he greatly admired, John Steinbeck, was staying in Algiers as well, steeling himself to tag along for the planned Allied landings at Salerno, on the mainland of Italy. Even though Ernie thought Steinbeck's Pulitzer Prize–winning novel, *The Grapes of Wrath*, was a "very important book," he'd also written in his column that he felt Steinbeck had gone out of his way to be "vulgar."[131]

Convinced that Steinbeck wouldn't have even heard of Ernie Pyle, he gave his room a ring anyhow. Steinbeck, it turned out, not only knew Er-nie's work but was a great admirer and was anxious about meeting him. The two writers took to each other immediately. According to fellow corre-spondent Quentin Reynolds, who made introductions, they were soon "talking nineteen to a dozen, and exchanging praise of each other's work."

At dinner one night at a country villa occupied by a British official out-side the headquarters city, Ernie and Steinbeck met up again. As Reynolds recalled, Pyle and Steinbeck talked through a cloud of cigarette smoke out on a terrace until almost dawn and "acted like a couple of lovebirds courting each other." Ernie was excited, above all else, that a man with Steinbeck's writing chops could carry to the front lines "a delicate sympathy of moral man's transient nobility and beastliness" that he believed "no other writer possesses."[132]

On September 7, 1943, four days after the costly but successful landings at Salerno, Ernie flew from Rabat, Morocco, by clipper to New York City. "Perhaps you who have read this column wonder why I came home just at this special time, when events are boiling over in Italy," he began his first stateside column in fifteen months. "Well, I might as well tell you truthfully," he continued. "I knew, of course, that the Italian invasion was coming up, but I chose to skip it. I made that decision because I realized, in the middle of Sicily, that I had been too close to the war for too long."

He was fed up, he said. Bogged down. He wasn't alone in that, he knew. He also knew that when "our boys" at the front lines were feeling fed up, they had to keep going. "But if your job is to write about the war," Ernie wrote in his defense, "you're very apt to begin writing unconscious distortions and unwarranted pessimisms when you get too tired.

"I had come to despise and be revolted by war clear out of any logical proportion. I couldn't find the Four Freedoms among dead men," referring to President Roosevelt's 1941 State of the Union address, in which he proposed that people "everywhere in the world" ought to enjoy the freedom of speech and worship, as well as freedom from want and fear. "Personal weariness became a forest that shut off my view of events about me," he continued. "I was no longer seeing the little things that you at home want to know about the soldiers."[133]

After fifteen months living in war zones overseas, Ernie had "worn clear down to the nub" his tools of description, summation, and reflection, and because there was "still a lot of war to be written about," he decided a short rest at home would benefit both "you who read and I who write."

"To put it bluntly," he concluded, "I just got too tired in the head. So here I am."[134]

10

The weather in Albuquerque at the end of September was wonderful. Exactly what Ernie needed. After a week of running errands, catching up on correspondence, and tying up other loose ends, Ernie settled down enough to get some "real puttering" accomplished. "The south lot has grown up in weeds," he wrote to Lee, "and I have a lot of cutting and slashing to do there. Also the shed is bulging with debris, and it'll take me a couple of days to go through it, sorting and burning. That, on top of my house-work, a daily trip downtown, and an hour or so on new letters, will keep the days full."[135]

When he wasn't puttering, Ernie was turning down requests to speak to this group or that or record a "patriotic-type" piece for a newsreel. The requests came at all hours of the day, from long-distance calls, letters, and telegrams. He turned down the commercial ones without hesitation. "But some of them," he complained to Lee, "get pretty close to the borderline on things you damn near have to do."[136] General Orlando Ward, the former commander of the First Armored Division, whom Ernie met during the Tunisian campaign, asked him to visit the antitank training center he'd set up in Texas. Ernie was tempted but still said no.[137] An army hospital in Albuquerque called Ernie daily for nearly a week, trying to persuade him to visit with the wounded men for a couple of hours. They told him their wards were filled with wounded men from North Africa—"a kind of thing you just can't turn down," he wrote to Lee. But when Ernie arrived, he found "there isn't a soul in it from overseas, never has been, and that it's merely the camp hospital for the Air Depot Training Station here. What people won't do."[138]

Lester Cowan, a Hollywood producer who wanted to make a movie based on Ernie's columns from North Africa, had hired a twenty-eight-year-old up-and-coming "boy-writer" by the name of Arthur Miller, who was on his way to Albuquerque for half a week to get started on the first draft of the screenplay. Twice rejected for military service, Miller had not yet reached any sort of fame, having at that point written only rather unsuccessful plays and a few radio dramas. Cowan needed Ernie to make himself available to Miller for an hour or two each day so that Miller could have a little time to really pick Ernie's brain about matters big and small, all with the goal of ensuring whatever narrative he fleshed out was as true as possible. Despite Miller's mostly lackluster previous work, Cowan saw great promise in him and figured all he needed was the right project to break through. Cowan gave Miller a copy of *Here Is Your War* and sent him off on a cross-country tour of army training camps, where he met, befriended, and interviewed young men who were on their way to war, as Ernie had done in England before the Allied invasion of North Africa.[139]

The day after Ernie wrote to Lee to complain about having to entertain Cowan's wunderkind, an extensive "diary" Miller had kept while touring the training camps arrived in the mail. Ernie had been planning on undertaking an "eight-day program of literary creation that would take mortal men a month," including a five-thousand-word article for *Life* magazine,[140] ten or so columns on "nothing heavy or profound,"[141] and thirty or forty belated letters to dear friends and family. Well, he confessed to Lee, he hadn't finished anything but a dozen or so letters. "What happened is this," he explained. "I leaped upon Cowan's writer's camp 'diary' early Monday morning (a little tome of some 65,000 words) and read steadily at it until he came in by plane late Monday afternoon."[142] Ernie was impressed with Miller's instincts and his "manner of thinking"—they were like Ernie's, he told Lee, if not more so. "He is keenly intelligent and has an acute sensitiveness to the 'humanities' of people and soldiers. I believe he will turn out a script that would make a really great movie, and I believe Lester is all for it and will stick with it."[143]

"When I walked up to the little wooden house at the edge of the Albuquerque mesa, I was afraid," Miller later wrote of his first meeting with Ernie. "I was afraid of what he would say when he read what I had come to call my diary. For it was true, after all, that I had merely brushed shoulders with the men who were going to fight this war, and he had lived with them and seen them die. And the meanings I was seeking in their lives never seemed to penetrate his columns."[144]

After a moment, the front door opened, and "a skinny man with a gray stubble of beard and a smile as round as the arc of a saucer" welcomed Miller inside. Dressed in a blue woolen shirt, a black vest, and an old pair of trousers, Ernie reminded Miller of a "nightwatchman at a deserted track crossing."[145] Because, as Miller put it, he was "too tired to impress" Ernie "with the fact that I was also uncomfortable in pressed suits," he offered to call it a day and start fresh the following morning.

"Ernie, I want to tell you about a scene I have in mind for the picture," Miller began their first substantive conversation.

"Sure," Ernie replied. "Go ahead."

The movie, Miller outlined, would center on a platoon of soldiers fighting in the mountains of central Italy. One of the soldiers, a cynical Italian American, deserts and hides out with a local family, pretending to be Italian, after seeing two of his best friends killed in what would likely come across as pointless bloodshed. Meanwhile, another soldier in the platoon, a college boy who understands fascism and its frightening realities, would join forces with Italians living in a small village to overthrow their fascist mayor and vote for a more liberal-minded representative. Then, as the villagers celebrated their liberation with the help of America's best, that first soldier, the one who broke and abandoned his platoon, would realize the pointlessness of his cynicism and redeem himself by rejoining his buddies up on the front lines. Above all else, Miller wanted to help illuminate the meaning of the war, which he saw as an epic struggle between democracy and fascism, good and evil.

"I want to give a piece of meaning to all the bloodshed we have shown on the screen," Miller explained. "What do you think?"

"Well, I'll be darned," Ernie replied. Then he paused. Cheetah was there, sitting on his lap. Ernie petted him once, twice, three times. "It's pretty good," he finally said, after "trying to find facts that would make the scene all right with his aching for the truth," Miller wrote. "It could happen, I guess," he said.[146]

"Because I don't believe this war has no meaning," Miller said.

"Sure," Pyle replied once again. "You put that in."

"The war is about something," Miller insisted. For Miller, the truth was a "larger thing than what man feels or knows at any particular time in his life," he later wrote. "This war is not merely about a lot of guys, as Ernie knows. It is about a lot of guys who are doing something which will have significance when their uniforms are moth eaten and don't fit anymore."[147]

"What do you think it's about, Ernie?"

"Well," he said, still petting Cheetah, deep in thought, "I don't know. I know what it could be about, but I don't know what it is about." Try as he might, Miller couldn't persuade Ernie that the war had any meaning beyond the boys who make homes in foxholes. "The endless complex shadings of the war had him rocking," Miller figured, so Ernie simply told what he saw, not what he thought about "the ideas of men." As a result of this aversion to abstraction, Ernie had been "universally credited with having written the truth," Miller wrote, when in fact, "he had told as much of what he saw as people could read without vomiting."[148]

"He tried to tell me that you couldn't really tell it in words," Miller remembered. "Not war, you couldn't. He tried in many ways to make it clear to me. The need to tell the truth seemed like an ache he was always feeling."[149]

Later that night, after Ernie dropped Miller off at his hotel, he drove Jerry back to St. Joseph's Hospital once again. "She just went to pieces from too much of the usual," he later told Lee. "She says, and I believe her, that it isn't the result of too much chaos around here; actually it's emotional over our time being so short and my getting ready to go and her working all the time I was here and of her job being so damned hard that just too much work piled up on her and she couldn't take it."[150]

"She volunteered to go herself," he told Paige, "and has recovered rapidly." Ernie believed she'd eventually get herself well enough, again, and that "her will to control herself is really so much more sincere than it used to be that I can't help but have hope in spite of the facts."[151]

Ernie and Miller spent the whole next day again talking about the war, as well as the writing life and even matters of the heart. After Ernie confessed, cryptically, that he was impotent, Miller surprised himself by telling Ernie about a woman he was interested in back in Washington. Miller and this other woman were both married to other people, though the woman Miller had fallen for had recently learned her husband had been lost at sea. Before he could get into any details, Ernie cut him off.

"Don't do anything like that, ever," he said, suddenly turning quite serious. "The marriage is everything," he continued. "That sex stuff is no good, it won't get you a thing." Miller was amazed by the depth of Ernie's innocence and caring. "You think you have to," Ernie said, shaking his head, "but you don't. Your wife sounds like a wonderful woman."

At the end of the March 1944, Ernie learned that Arthur Miller had resigned from the project. The screenplay Cowan hired him to write was too challenging for someone with so little relevant experience, Miller claimed.[152] Ernie was disappointed but understood. He had liked Miller, believed he had what it took, and especially appreciated Miller's "naïve idealism," which Ernie thought "might be a good-balance wheel for Lester's natural hokum complex."[153]

The day after Ernie sent Miller off to New York by plane, he and his longtime friend Edward "Shafe" Shaffer, the editor of *The Albuquerque Tribune*, had invites for lunch with the governor of New Mexico.[154] Shafe was a combat veteran who had seen extensive action and been wounded in France during the First World War, and by 1943, he had developed a deathly serious addiction to strong liquor. Like Jerry, Shafe had also been hospitalized after hemorrhaging, only his hemorrhage was in his esophagus. "They say he really looked like a corpse," Ernie told Lee, "but he and Jerry are both freaks on quick recoveries, and he looks quite normal now." Aside from his many missing teeth, that is. "All of his upper teeth are out now," he reported to Lee, "and he just has ten lower ones to go. He feels rotten during this ordeal but his 'attitude' seems to be fine."[155]

Ernie also had to squeeze in another visit from Lester Cowan to talk through the finer points of their contract. Cowan agreed to pay Ernie ten thousand dollars for the rights to *Here Is Your War* and to share 10 percent of the movie's profits, up to $100,000—totaling close to $1.85 million in 2022 terms.[156] For two days he'd also have a few photographers from *Life* following him around, "shootin' 'home' pictures" to show the back-home version of America's favorite war correspondent. Paige was going to be around, and the comedian Jackie Gleason, too. Once everyone finally left town, it would be Ernie's turn. "Wish I had another month here," he later wrote, "but I ain't. Suppose I wouldn't rest if I did, so might as well get going."[157] Ernie figured he'd need at least a couple of weeks back East before he'd be ready to head off to the war raging in Italy.

Jerry left the hospital after a few days and took off from work until Ernie headed home to Indiana for a few days to check in on his father, who was immobile in the hospital while recuperating after injuring his hip.[158] Jerry was in "pretty good shape now," he told Lee, "and I believe has herself in hand where she can get over the hump of my going."[159] For a going-away present, Jerry forked over thirty-five dollars at a local hunting store for a "dandy sleeping bag" to help keep Ernie warm during the long winter that lay ahead for him. The zipper went clear around and it was padded with wool. It weighed only thirteen pounds, and there was even a little canopy Ernie could pull over his head if it ever got *really* cold.

From his hotel room in Washington, Ernie wrote to Jerry on November 1, 1943: "This is a blue Monday—not that everything isn't allright, but just because I feel sort of gloomy at being here instead of there. Also, I have to start work today in earnest, and the prospect of indulging in toil somewhat shatters me." Work, for Ernie, mostly consisted of meetings with bosses and people from the War Department.[160]

The first reviews of *Here Is Your War* had come in as well. "I never saw so many wonderful reviews," he gushed to Jerry. And none of them mentioned Ernie's greatest fear—that the book itself wouldn't live up to the hype and the three-dollar price tag.[161] "The status of the book is this now," he continued to Jerry. "They actually made a first printing of 150,000 instead of 125,000, and are already hunting for paper to begin a second printing." In fact, the publisher planned to appeal directly to the War Department for more paper "on the ground that the book is good for national morale." If Holt sold that many copies, some back-of-the-envelope calculations told Ernie, "the goddam royalties will be around $65,000!"[162] Moreover, he reported to Jerry, after meeting with his accountant, "If nothing happens, next year's income should go over $100,000!"

"Aren't those figures ridiculous," he asked. "Why don't we just give up?"[163]

"I told Lee last night," he confided in Jerry, "that although I might have to be gone a year or more on this trip" to cover the Italian campaign, "when I do come back I think it will be for the last time." Ernie knew that was as much as he'd be able to stand. Lee told Ernie that was fine by him and was sure it would be with the rest of those concerned as well.[164] In a November 11 letter, Ernie made his feelings even clearer. To Jerry he promised that if she could "hang on to hope," when he came home from the war again, "it will be to stay.[165]

"I think everybody, including my own conscience," he continued, "will feel that I've done enough by the time I get back again." One of his biggest fears was that even though he'd be surrounded by people from that point forward, he'd really be alone. "But I'll get through it somehow," he promised, "and try not to change too much; and then maybe, when it's all over, we can have the kind of life that I feel we both deserve, and have both earned."[166]

"Whatever this fame business is," he wrote in another letter to Jerry the following week, "you're as much responsible as I am; for you have given me more in character than anyone else in the world. If I could only have your depth of honesty and sincerity, I might think I was really great. But great or not, we've both got so much to live for; we've got everything if we could just have ourselves, and I'm convinced that when I come back again we will have that."[167]

Ernie's commitment to the war, in his mind, wasn't separate from his commitment to Jerry. Good work, Ernie believed, was like a good marriage in that it needed to be dedicated to something larger than his own everyday needs. In this way, what the war needed from Ernie and what Ernie needed from the war began to resemble a marriage in its own right.

11

Before he was finally sent overseas, toward the end of November 1943,[168] Ernie met up with one of Jerry's best friends, a woman named Lucy

"Moran" Livingstone, who had recently moved with her husband from Albuquerque to Washington, DC. According to Pyle's biographer James Tobin, Ernie's relationship with Moran closely resembled his earlier connection with Mabel.[169] Ironically, the go-between who set up Ernie's quiet get-togethers with Moran was his friend and personal secretary Roz Goodman, who had been another of Jerry's best friends back when they all lived in Washington.

Ernie had first met Moran back in the fall of 1941. Her husband was the Albuquerque bureau chief for the Associated Press. According to Tobin, a "warm attraction" grew between her and Pyle because she could, in essence, provide the sympathetic ear he had come to rely on Mabel for, only she wasn't hundreds of miles away in Indiana. Moran, evidently, was not interested at that time in taking their relationship any further.

That all changed two years later, soon before Ernie returned to Italy. The main difference between his relationship with Mabel and his connection to Moran was that Moran's voice in his ear had unlocked something inside him that he wasn't sure still existed. Perhaps Ernie's impotence was more selective than he realized, or perhaps those painful treatments in San Diego were beginning to show results.[170] Regardless, Moran's touch was enough.

"I can't seem to get the wonderful times of Washington out of my head; not that I want to," Ernie wrote to Moran in one letter. In another, he wrote that he couldn't believe it had been only a month since they were together last. "It seems to me ages ago, almost years ago. We had so much fun; I daydream and night-dream about it, and wonder if I'll ever see you again, and if so when, and how I'll feel and how you'll feel and whether I'll have the spirit even to look up after another year and a half of war."

"I can't help but be sad at the end of good times," Ernie confessed. "Actually I'd like to turn around and come home right this minute. Goodbye for a little while darling."[171]

CHAPTER 5

A LONG WINTER OF MISERY

It is one of our popular heroic myths that anybody who comes back from the combat zone begins to itch after a few weeks, and finally get so homesick for the front he can hardly stand it. I've never hated to do anything as badly in my life as I hate to go back to the front. I dread it and I'm afraid of it. But what can a guy do? I know millions of others who are reluctant too, and they can't even go home. So here we go. The decision, it's true, is my own. Nobody is forcing me to go back. Probably that's the reason I feel so glum about it. Going back is all my own fault. I could kick myself.

ERNIE PYLE, "ERNIE PYLE WRITES AGAIN," NOVEMBER 1943[1]

1

The valley floor at the foot of Mount Sammucro in mid-December 1943 was pocked with fresh shell holes and littered with abandoned rifles, empty cartridge belts, blood-crusted bandages, and dead GIs.[2] The graves-registration men, with their stiff, death-tainted leather gloves, hadn't yet arrived to lift the hundreds of lifeless young men into white burial sacks.[3] The smell of mud, sweat, burning metal, and blood saturated the air.

Along the southern slope of Mount Sammucro, where the valley ended and its elevation began, was a small Italian village nestled in a series of terraces: San Pietro Infine. After more than a week of intense attacks and counterattacks, the Americans commanded the heights of Mount Sammucro, where even with the naked eye it was plain to see that the vicious fighting had choked the maze of narrow alleys in the ancient city below with chunks of plaster and splintered beams, broken tiles, and stone. Soldiers on the ground mopping up the last bit of German resistance found a choir loft inside the ghost-quiet Church of St. Michael barely hanging above an altar piled high with rubble.[4] Right above the altar, through a thin curtain of blue battle smoke, they spied a headless Christ still hanging from His cross.[5]

Ernie summited Mount Sammucro sometime on December 16, 1943. "More than half the trail was out in the open," he told his readers, "across bare rocks all under German artillery fire. The top part of the trail was so steep they anchored weights alongside the path for the men to pull themselves upward with." Ernie's guide that day was a rifleman named Fred Ford, a private first class from East St. Louis in Illinois. "He was a tall, rug-

Mount Sammucro, above San Pietro Infine, Italy, December 2019

ged fellow, and he had two weeks of whiskers and grime on his face," Ernie wrote. "He looked sort of ferocious but turned out to be pleasant and friendly."

With heels rubbed raw and taped blisters all over, Ford was supposed to be back behind the lines resting. Instead, he was hiking on his toes to save his heels from rubbing, carrying water to his comrades up at the top. "Sometimes going up the mountain you get to the point where you know you can't make it," he told Ernie, "but somehow you always do."

On their way back down the mountain, German shells landed close to where they'd been, higher up. "If I get to going too fast for you, just yell," Ford said. "When they start shelling we practically fly down the mountain. We don't stop for nothing."

"But I didn't have any pressing business engagements along the way to detain us," Ernie reported in his column, "so Ford and I flew down the mountainside together, going so fast the rocks we kicked loose couldn't even keep up with us."[6]

The most impressive hiker in the outfit Ernie embedded with was a West Virginian named Lester Scarborough.[7] Standing five feet, seven and a half inches and weighing only 135 pounds, Scarborough was a "miniature Paul Bunyan," Pyle wrote, who "could take a full can of water to the top and be clear back down again in two and a half hours, where others took three hours and longer just to get up." Perhaps most impressively, Ernie noted, Scarborough had once climbed to the top of the four-thousand-foot mountain and back four times in a single day—the fourth time to help beat back a German counterattack.[8]

Shortly before noon, seventy-seven years later, I prayed for Scarborough's mule-like strength and endurance as my wife, Ashley, and I drove our black rental van through the Liri Valley south from Cassino, Italy, to modern-day San Pietro. At six foot four and about 250 pounds, I've never been described as a miniature anything, though after several hiking trips in the Wind River Range of the Rocky Mountains in Wyoming during my late teens and early twenties, I concluded that if I did in fact have a spirit animal, it was the unsung pack mule. I'm not a fast hiker, but I can shoulder more than my share, and I can hike all day if I must.

Founded in the Middle Ages, San Pietro Infine had survived several earthquakes and had stood strong against various invaders and brigands in the past.[9] But after the Americans pushed north from their Pyrrhic victory there to the next dead bolt in the German's line of defense, the survivors chose not to rebuild. Of the fourteen hundred or so former residents, most had fled before the fighting began. The several hundred who stayed—mostly women, children, and the elderly—had bunkered in a series of fetid caves near the village, which an army intelligence analyst later described as "the nearest thing to a journey in Dante's *Inferno* that I was to know in the war." Around 140 of them were killed during the fighting. One of them, a baby, was discovered in the mud by an American medic after its lifeless body had been repeatedly run over by a convoy of American military vehicles.[10]

A new San Pietro was later built from nothing a short distance up the valley. To "cancel out in some way the signs of war and revitalize the zone," making it "suitable even for picnics," government officials in this new San Pietro financed a project in the 1970s to plant trees around the ruins they had once called home. By the early 1990s, as the fiftieth anniversary of the battle approached, the deserted village had sunk back into the wilderness and was choked with greenery. To breathe life back into what had become a ghostly grass-and-tree-covered outline, government officials again financed a project, only this time the money wasn't used to cover up the past. Instead, it was used to hire young Italians to clear rubble and brush from the center of the village to attract history buffs and battlefield tourists like myself from around the world. The ruins of San Pietro Infine have since been declared a world monument to peace.[11]

Once my wife and I arrived at the Vecchio Centro, the old center of San Pietro Infine, my GPS directed me to follow a narrow mountain road out of the village into a series of switchbacks that cut through terraced olive groves, buttressed by seemingly endless low stone walls. During the winter of 1943, the Germans dug an organized series of covered terraces in that exact area, east of San Pietro and across the valley west to Mount Lungo. These emplacements were essentially deep pits covered by three layers of logs—and further protected by earth and rocks—that were nearly impervious to Allied artillery fire.[12]

I parked our rental van in a small roundabout overlooking an olive orchard along one of those low stone walls. Normally when we hike, my wife and I have a few children in tow, but because my mother-in-law had agreed to come along with us, we were freed up to hike as fast or as slow as we wanted. I slung a small pack with a few supplies around my shoulders and followed Ashley down a narrow gravel road we found at the end of the roundabout, gaining elevation quickly. After we rounded the first switchback, Ashley spotted the opening to a dirt trail that led up into a shady olive orchard. The trail paralleled a rusty barbed-wire fence, tight and straight. Hiking a few steps behind Ashley, I kept my eyes trained on the ground, trying to read what the earth might be holding.

The trail dead-ended in the corner of the orchard. "Wanna go over or through?" I asked Ashley. With my left foot I stepped down on the lowest rung of wire with my thick-soled hiking boot, and with my bare hands I pulled up hard on the top rung. The rust crumbled off, staining my palms. Ducking as low as she could, Ashley escaped to the other side without a scratch into a tuft of waist-high grass. After tying her long brown hair into a ponytail, she held the fence open for me, and like that we were halfway to the line where the grade became too steep even for a pack mule.

2

To Lieutenant General Mark Clark, the rock-spined mountain that towered above San Pietro was the first of three fortified lines of defense designed to stop him and his Fifth Army from marching victoriously to Rome. Rather than concede central Italy to the Allies, Hitler ordered his commanders to set up a defensive line that stretched from the Tyrrhenian

Sea east across the Liri Valley to the Adriatic, along the Garigliano and Rapido Rivers on the west side of the peninsula and the Sangro River on the east. The Germans would call it the Gustav Line; the Allies the Winter Line.[13] With topography and history on the Germans' side, Hitler had been persuaded by German field marshal Albert Kesselring's argument that instead of strategically retreating north past Rome all the way to the Po Valley,[14] the Germans should make their stand in the mountain ranges south of Rome. It wasn't possible, Pyle later wrote, for the Fifth Army to storm straight up the wide and flat Liri Valley without tremendous losses "because the Germans look down upon you and would let you have it."[15]

Despite General Clark's assessment that the area surrounding San Pietro appeared to be clear of German troops,[16] his infantrymen would soon enough find former wheat and corn fields[17] pregnant with S-mines, razor wire, and interlocking pillboxes.[18] Every mountain ridge would need to be assaulted. Every gun would need to be silenced. When the battle smoke finally cleared on December 17, and after the last infantryman was laid low in the cold Italian ground, the Thirty-sixth Division reported that the Battle of San Pietro cost twelve hundred American battle casualties and another two thousand non-battle losses.[19] The 143rd Regiment alone would require eleven hundred replacements.[20] The "soft underbelly of Europe," as Winston Churchill had called it, was proving itself to be anything but.[21]

3

While the battle for San Pietro raged on, Ernie camped out in a dilapidated cowshed[22] near a battalion aid station at the foot of Mount Sammucro, to the east of San Pietro. He propped his portable typewriter atop a packing case. During the daylight hours, he meandered around in his ragged field jacket and knit cap, chain-smoking and gathering sights and sounds in his mind's eye.[23] It was outside the aid station that Ernie met a young, battle-hardened private with a horrendous case of trench foot. His

name was Riley Tidwell, and he had a story for Ernie about a beloved captain named Henry T. Waskow.

"How 'bout your captain," Ernie said after sidling up to Tidwell while
he had his feet taped up. "Tell me something about him."[24] Tidwell likely
told Ernie the one about how Waskow, before he was killed, had "requisi-
tioned" Thanksgiving Day turkey for his cold and tired men from an inso-
lent army cook who swore there wasn't any more to go around. Waskow
and his men had been patrolling for most of November in the Italian wind
and rain, up and down mountains north of Salerno, without any hot food.
When the cook told Waskow his men would have to go without, Waskow's
dirt-crusted hand slid up the side of his body to his waist, to the holstered
pistol dangling from his webbed belt. His eyes locked with the cook's. Neither man seemed to be breathing. A few seconds felt like an eternity. The
cook blinked first. "We'll give you turkey, Cap'n," he said deferentially, his
eyes lowered to the floor.[25]

Considering the hundreds of young American men who were killed
fighting for San Pietro—hundreds in a list of tens of thousands already
lost—the death of one ordinary man on a lonely mountainside was, for Ernie,
an example of war on a miniature, intimate scale. But for those who were
there when Waskow was killed, it hadn't felt small at all, because Waskow
wasn't like most company commanders. "He had been an original G.I. himself, for one thing," W. B. "Buck" Slaughter said of Waskow after the war.
"He understood the problems of the G.I. insofar as the difference between
just a G.I. and an officer," Slaughter continued. "But Waskow—he was a quiet
man, quite sincere, but he gave the regular G.I.s a break."[26]

By the time Waskow and his men arrived in Italy, he had worked his
way up from the lowest of enlisted ranks, earning his officer's commission
on March 14, 1941, less than four months after his National Guard division
was brought under federal control and mobilized.[27] As a platoon leader,
Waskow showed he knew commanding men in battle was more complicated than barking orders and whipping them into shape. "He'd talk with
you and visit with you about folks, about home," one soldier remembered.

"And the men could talk to him. Wife troubles, or something like that. He never did raise his voice much, never did get mad. When he said something, he meant it to be done. And that's one reason [his men] respected him so much. He didn't chew their ass out or things like that. And he led, instead of driving. If his company was going into attack, he was going to be out there with them. He wasn't going to be behind the lines. He'd be where the action was."[28]

Waskow was promoted to captain in mid-January 1943. Two months later, his new company, along with the rest of the Thirty-sixth Infantry Division, learned they would soon be headed to North Africa, where they would spend the summer training for war in Italy. The first time he and his men heard a shot fired in anger was on the beaches near the ruin of the ancient Greek Temple of Ceres at Paestum, twenty-five miles south of Salerno.[29]

On September 20, eleven days after Waskow and his men landed in Italy, his company was ordered to climb a barren mountain named San Angelo to help repel a German attack. In the report he wrote detailing the action that day, Waskow chalked up the company's success to the strength and courage of his men. "We had never scaled that mountain before in less than three hours," he wrote, "but not a man fell out on this climb. I was more proud of my company that day than at any other time."[30]

4

Before I booked plane tickets for our trip to Italy, I had searched online for as much as I could about how to climb Mount Sammucro. There wasn't much to find. Peakery.com had an entry for Mount Sammucro, but under "Summit," the entry read "no summits yet."[31] If it had been climbed since the end of the war, it hadn't been climbed by anyone who likes to brag on the internet about bagging summits. On top of that, the topographic map of the mountain I found using Google Images didn't show any official hiking trails that led to the summit. If we were going to make it to the top, Ashley and I were going to have to bushwhack our way there. That much I knew. What I didn't know was that we'd have to traverse several fences, hike past grazing cattle, and scramble on all fours up through slippery scree. It didn't occur to me until we were more than halfway up that it was a real possibility that we'd hike back down to find the police waiting alongside our van to arrest us for trespassing. Or perhaps the fences were there to keep grazing cattle from stumbling onto some unexploded ordnance lurking beneath the surface, waiting to claim its victim.

As we emerged from the tree line, Ashley and I found the early after-noon sky sharp and blue, with a stiff and cool wind. The smell of damp rocks and soil being dried by the dappled winter sun filled my nose, and the dull clank of a cow's bell sounded in the hills to our left. During a quick water break, I turned to see the veined valley below, which the GIs had christened "Purple Heart Valley."[32] It was partially hidden beneath a trans-lucent film of clouds. In the far distance, snow-topped mountains seemed to float upon nothing.

Two thirds of the way up to the summit, trees and tall shrubs had all but disappeared. I slipped and slid in the loose and craggy rocks. In a few sections of the climb, it was like trying to summit an A-frame cabin roofed with loose shingles. The first bits of evidence of the battle we found were improvised fighting positions made of stacked-stone walls. With nowhere to dig in, soldiers had to build up defenses with whatever was at hand. For some, those rocks became weapons as well in hand-to-hand combat with the enemy. We also spied along the face of the mountain small clearings large enough for a piece of artillery, marked by low stone walls. The make-shift fighting positions we were passing might even have been forward ob-servation posts, from which a soldier or two could call in artillery strikes. During my examination of one such position, I stumbled upon a heavy, rusty screw cap of some kind, about the size of my palm, with two sets of threads. I took a picture of it and sent it to a good friend of mine who had been an explosive ordnance disposal officer in the air force and is now an expert on arms and military operations for Amnesty International, asking him if it was old munition. I didn't hear back from him until two days after

Ashley and I summitted Mount Sammucro. He messaged me back: "Yeah, the double threads are kinda weird, but probably the top of an old mortar. Glad you didn't blow your hand off picking that up."

5

After nearly a week of fighting on the steep and rocky slopes of Mount Sammucro, the First Battalion of the 143rd Infantry Regiment, which had been made up of over a thousand men when it captured the summit in the fog and darkness of the early morning on December 8,[33] was down to about 150. Waskow's company had been reduced to no more than a platoon.[34] A dozen desperate enemy counterattacks to retake the summit had left the slopes of Mount Sammucro blanketed with hundreds of dead and wounded Germans,[35] making life for those American soldiers still alive at the top more and more unspeakably awful by the day.

At nightfall on December 14, the quiet and unassuming captain and the rest of the First Battalion crept toward a knoll directly behind San Pietro, designated as "Hill 730" on their maps. To reach the hill, the battalion, with Waskow's company in the lead, had to cross a deep saddle[36] and follow a trail across a slippery scree slope that skirted the edge of a ravine. "Wouldn't this be an awful spot to get killed and freeze on the mountain?" Waskow asked his company runner, Riley Tidwell. For some reason, the captain had a sudden craving for toast. He turned to Tidwell once more and added, "When we get back to the States, I'm going to get me one of those smart-aleck toasters where you put the bread in and it pops up."[37]

The men were jolted by the sound of German shells screaming through the air.[38] Captain Waskow pushed Tidwell to the ground. The rocks around the men jumped and twitched. Bullets hissed. Mortars crumped. The bare slopes of the saddles offered nothing for the men to hide behind.[39] In the moonlight, Tidwell flattened himself out like a rat squirming under a door. Through the flashing light of explosions all around him, Tidwell saw Waskow out of the corner of his eye. He was hit. Then he hit the ground, flat on his back. It all happened so quickly. The captain was alive. And then he was not. An indiscriminate fragment of shell, red hot and sharp as a scalpel, had sliced a hole in his chest, killing him instantly.[40] For Tidwell, losing Waskow was "like I'd lost the greatest friend I ever had in my life," he said decades after the war. "Even a father. 'Cause he was that close to me."[41]

6

Soon after the sun set on December 15, Tidwell and Ernie retired to the cowshed to kill time until that night's mule train returned. The mules would be piled high with ammunition and water, Tidwell explained to Pyle, and taken as high up the mountain as they could go—about a third of the way up. From there, the precious cargo had to be unloaded and strapped to the backs of tired soldiers who would then have to hike, and sometimes pull themselves up with guide ropes, the rest of the way to the summit. Once the supplies[42] were unloaded, the mules could then be draped with the bodies of the dead and taken back down the mountain. When the train of mules led by their Italian handlers returned, Tidwell checked each body that had been brought down, with Ernie at his side. They didn't see Captain Waskow's. "Apparently they didn't find him," Tidwell said.[43]

The next morning, Ernie woke from a fitful night's sleep, his back curled like a comma. He decided to wait another day for the captain's body to be recovered. It wasn't.[44] Fed up with the delay, Tidwell stole a mule the night of December 17 and went after Waskow's body on his own. "As soon as it got dark," Tidwell recalled decades later, "I went right where the captain was and stood him up, and picked him up." He was stiff, and very cold. Tidwell strapped the captain's legs to one side of the saddle and his hands to the other so that Waskow's body was trussed facedown across the mule's back. His legs stuck out awkwardly, and his body bobbed up and down as the mule clopped down the steep mountain trail.[45] As the cowshed at the foot of the mountain came into view, Tidwell heard someone yell out: "Here comes Riley with Captain Waskow."[46]

Outside the cowshed, two soldiers unlashed Waskow's body from the mule and gently lifted him down. They laid his body "in the shadow beside the low stone wall," Pyle later wrote in his most famous column, "The Death of Captain Waskow."

"You don't cover up dead men in the combat zone," Ernie reported. "They just lie there in the shadows until somebody else comes after them."

In the stillness of death, there was still plenty of activity. The men who had gathered to receive Captain Waskow's body in the full moonlight seemed reluctant to leave, Ernie noticed. "They stood around," he wrote, "and gradually one by one I could sense them moving close to Capt. Waskow's body. Not so much to look, I think, as to say something in finality to him, and to themselves."

Standing near the back of a mess truck, not far from the body,[47] Ernie studied what happened next like it was an equation waiting to be solved.

One soldier looked down at the captain and said, "God damn it."

Another came and said, "God damn it to hell anyway."

A third man, a fellow officer, came next. His face was bearded and grimy. He seemed to be deeply distressed yet under control and spoke to the captain as if Waskow were still alive. "I'm sorry, old man," was all he could muster.

Then another man came, and in a tender voice said, "I sure am sorry, sir."

Tidwell then squatted down next to Waskow's body, "and he reached down and took the dead hand," Pyle continued, "and he sat there for a full five minutes, holding the dead hand in his own and looking intently into the dead face, and he never uttered a sound all the time he sat there. And finally he put the hand down, and then reached up and gently straightened the points of the captain's shirt collar, and then he sort of rearranged the tattered edges of his uniform around the wound. And then he got up and walked away down the road in the moonlight, all alone."[48]

7

It's not clear how long it took Ernie to write "The Death of Captain Was-kow." In the letters he wrote home from the front lines that are archived at Indiana University in Bloomington, Ernie never shared the intimate details of his writing process. While he frequently complains about not being able to write or falling behind on his cushion of columns or being over-edited by Lee, he never details his strategies for building suspense or even what goals he had for the column.[49] We don't know whether he started with an outline or how much revising he did before he had the story censored and transmitted back to the States.

Lee thought Ernie had written the piece about Waskow in a single day while his mind was still swimming in alcohol from a late night of drinking with Sherman Montrose, a photographer who shared a bottle of eau-de-vie with Ernie back at the Royal Palace at Caserta, south of San Pietro, which the Allies had converted into the headquarters for Mark Clark's Fifth Army.[50] In a letter to Lee, Ernie said that the day he wrote the piece about the captain he felt like death, "but am sort of glad I did it, for I was really low and had the jerks yesterday, and something had to happen."[51] After the war, Ernie's fellow correspondent and friend Don Whitehead told Lee Miller that the war was much harder on Ernie than it had been on him and the other correspondents because Pyle was more sensitive to "the shock of seeing men killed and wounded."[52] Most nights at Caserta, Whitehead re-ported, he and Ernie would get together in Ernie's room and drink and talk. "He suffered some terrible fits of depression in Italy," he told Lee. "The whole campaign was going badly, far more slowly than had been antici-pated, and the strain began to wear on everyone. One night I came in and found Ernie at work. He had been up front to get a series of stories on the mule-pack trains. 'I've lost the touch,' he said. 'This stuff stinks. I just can't seem to get going again.'"[53] The dynamic Ernie confronted, when he felt good work was impossible, was the very dynamic he put into that work—a dynamic that had the power to make the story distinctive and entirely his own.

Ernie trusted Don, so he asked him to look over the column. "The simplicity and beauty of that description brought tears to my eyes," Whitehead told Lee. "This was the kind of writing all of us were striving for, the picture we were trying to paint in words for the people at home."

"If this is a sample from a guy who has lost his touch," Don told Ernie that night, "then the rest of us had better go home."[54]

8

On January 10, 1944, "The Death of Captain Waskow" covered the entire front page of Ernie's flagship paper, *The Washington Daily News*. Only thirty-nine copies of that day's edition were returned from all of downtown Washington. The two hundred other newspapers that ran Pyle's columns at that time also gave it prominent display. One of the most influential news commentators of his era, Raymond Gram Swing, read the column in its entirety on the radio, as did Arthur Godfrey.[55] *Time* magazine reprinted it in full,[56] and the Ruthrauff and Ryan advertising agency asked Lee Miller for permission to use the column to stir emotions in a war bond drive: CAPTAIN WASKOW GAVE HIS LIFE * THE LEAST YOU CAN DO IS BUY WAR BONDS![57] The editor of the *Toledo Blade* predicted that when the war ended "it will be found that Ernie Pyle wrote the most beautiful lines that came out of the whole dark and bitter conflict. His story of the dead men coming down the hill is the most beautifully written newspaper story I have ever read."[58] "I'm going to hang it up and look at it every once in a while," the president of the United Press wrote of the column, "to make me glad that . . . there are still men in [the business] like Pyle who can write stuff like that."[59]

All the mail addressed to "the Family of Captain Henry T. Waskow, Belton, Texas" overwhelmed the Waskow family. The letters came from dozens of states and were filled with words of comfort and expressions of sympathy and condolence. One note of sympathy the Waskows received was written on a tearstained handkerchief.[60]

By writing a true war story about a beloved captain's men paying their last respects, Pyle accomplished something none of the other correspondents who covered the Italian campaign had. Up until the publication of "The Death of Captain Waskow," most news coverage of the war had given American readers only an abstract treatment of death. For many readers, "The Death of Captain Waskow" gently wiped that film from their eyes. Ernie had nudged them to feel that the war their sons and husbands were dying in was not only a world war, to be observed from a safe distance. The war was an emotional war, too. It was an individual war, a personal war. By concentrating on Waskow's individual devotion, suffering, and sacrifice, Pyle used the fallen captain to endow the cause in Italy to which Waskow had given his life with deeper meaning. In a way, Waskow serves as an extension of America, and in a way, America was an extension of Waskow, at least ideally. America was great, Pyle seemed to be saying, because it produced heroic sons like him, and soldiers like Waskow and his men deserved a nation that was worthy of their sacrifice.

9

The Sicily-Rome American Cemetery was closed to the public on Christmas Eve 2019. It wasn't supposed to be closed that day, but the cemetery's superintendent was concerned about the high winds that had been blowing in Nettuno since the night before, which weren't supposed to die down for another day or two. When I pulled up to the cemetery's twenty-foot metal gates, I could see that several limbs from the towering Roman pines that line the perimeter of the cemetery had blown down in the far-left corner of the cemetery. They didn't want anyone to visit until after the debris could be removed, but because I had traveled so far, and Christmas Eve was the only day I could visit, they made an exception.

Luca Tamberiani met me in the parking lot outside the visitors' center.

He was relieved I was by myself. "When I saw your bus pull in," he said, "I thought there was a whole team of people with you!"

Luca was about a decade older than me, and his short black hair was sprinkled with specks of white and gray around his temples. He was Italian, originally from Anzio. His mother was from Naples. He started working at the cemetery as an interpretive guide in 2018 after working for many years as a freelance tour guide at major memorial sites of the Second World War across Italy. "I'm very proud to be a storyteller at this facility," he said as he handed me a stack of literature about the cemetery, including a printout of factoids. "There are thirty sets of brothers and three sets of twins buried here," he said. "That always surprises people."

After I finished watching a short introductory video about the cemetery and made my way through an impressive exhibit of displays that tell the story of the American experience fighting the Germans in Sicily and Italy, Luca said it was time to visit Captain Waskow.

He locked the door to the visitors' center behind me and zipped his dark green coat to his chin. "We have to take the golf cart," he said, "because of safety." I unzipped the plastic door on the cart and slid into the passenger's seat with my pen and notebook in hand. The wind rattled the plastic as Luca pushed the gas and sped us past a large pool with an island in the middle of it.

"What is that thing on the island there?" I asked.

"It's called a cenotaph. It comes from the Greeks," Luca told me. "It's a monument to all those who were killed who are not buried here."

Captain Henry T. Waskow is buried in Plot G, Row 6, Grave 33. Luca didn't need to look up the directions. While Captain Waskow is only one of the more than seven thousand Americans buried at the Sicily-Rome cemetery, he is by far one of the best known, and his headstone is visited frequently by the thousands of Americans who come to the cemetery each year.

"You can tell by the wear and tear on the headstone," Luca explained to me. "The sand we use to highlight their names is quite abrasive—that's why we have to wash it off right away. And over the years, you can see when

The Sicily-Rome American Cemetery and Memorial, Nettuno, Italy, December 2019

a headstone has had sand applied to it and when it hasn't. Most of these boys have never had a visitor."

Luca pulled the cart up close to a row of bushes, in the shade of a line of towering Roman pines that had been trimmed to look like skinny mushrooms. "Otherwise, they act like sails and blow over," Luca told me.

"Why are the rows arranged in such gentle arcs?" I asked as Luca and I hopped out of the cart. "Why not put the headstones in straight lines?"

"It reflects the geometry of the pool near the entrance," Luca explained. "I wondered that, too, when I first started working here."

While I readied myself to take notes and a few pictures, a strong wind blew past us. I turned my back to it and squinted my eyes. Luca gazed up to the tree canopies with a concerned look. As the wind died down, Luca grabbed a red tote with a black handle from the back of the golf cart and led me to the captain's final resting place. Kneeling before the grave, Luca placed his tote down and took out a plywood jig about a foot wide with a handle and two notches cut into it that would show Luca where to plant two small flags—one American and one Italian. Luca placed the jig at the base of the headstone, flat against the ground, then he reached into a small white bucket and pulled out a handful of fine sand. After working it into the shallow carvings of the stone, like a tile-layer spreading grout, Luca reached back once more into his tote of supplies to grab a bottle of water and a small yellow sponge to wipe away the excess sand, leaving only enough to fill each character. The contrast between the ocher sand and the porous white marble was stark, and beautiful:

Captain Henry T. Waskow's grave, Sicily-Rome American Cemetery and Memorial, Nettuno, Italy, December 2019

CHAPTER 6

THE GHASTLY
BROTHERHOOD OF WAR

Buck Eversole has no hatred for Germans. He kills because he's trying to keep alive himself. The years roll over him and the war becomes his only world, and battle his only profession. He armors himself with a philosophy of acceptance of what may happen.

ERNIE PYLE, "BUCK EVERSOLE: ONE OF THE GREAT
MEN OF THE WAR," FEBRUARY 21, 1944[1]

1

Soon after he sent "The Death of Captain Waskow" back to his editor in America, Ernie camped out in the bar in the royal palace at Caserta and tied on a weeklong bender with his roommate, a fellow correspondent named Clark Lee of the Associated Press.[2] Gin and cognac were the only medicines within reach to help stave off the obsessive thoughts that raced through his mind on a never-ending loop. It wasn't the weather or the discomfort or even the danger of the war that depressed him.[3] It was the misery of the "mud-rain-frost-and-wind boys" whom he had grown to love, juxtaposed with his life inside a literal palace built to shame the one in Versailles, that got the best of Pyle if he brooded on it for too long.[4] After the war ended, Clark Lee told Ernie's editor that during that infamous Christmas bender of 1943, "Ernie was in one of his periods of being frightened." That is what Clark remembered most about Ernie. "He would tell you, and convince you, that he was absolutely washed up—he simply couldn't stand the sound of another shell or bullet, or the sight of another bleeding guy."[5]

Once his bender ran out of steam, Ernie came down with another of his "celebrated colds," as Lee Miller described them.[6] Ernie blamed it on the booze. "I think it was really that Christmas spree that weakened me so that I caught this damn cold," he told Lee. Like everyone else in Italy, Pyle opined, he had perhaps "gone a little nuts."[7] A change of scenery seemed to be needed.

After spending four or five days in bed nursing his cold,[8] Ernie left for Naples, even though he hated staying in cities and would much rather bunk in the countryside.[9] The most obvious alternative to the misery and trauma of frontline combat, he decided, was the Air Corps. It wasn't long, however, before he found himself uninterested in their relatively cushy lives.[10] The Air Corps was "colorless and anticlimactic," Ernie confided in a letter to Lee, though he never wrote that explicitly in his column.[11] Instead, he compared and contrasted, leaving it up to the readers to reach that same conclusion on their own.

The airmen Ernie wrote about served in a dive-bomber squadron in the Twelfth Air Force Command. They enjoyed woodstoves and slept in sleeping bags on top of folding cots. They stored their belongings on shelves and ate their meals at tables; electric lights illuminated their rooms, and stools kept them from having to sit on the ground. Unlike their brothers-in-arms serving in the infantry, who had to spend day and night for months on end at the front and who "live and die so miserably" with "such determined acceptance," the Air Forces "die well-fed and clean-shaven, if that's any comfort," Ernie wrote. While infantrymen had to "become half beast in order to survive,"[12] airmen had "an Italian barber, and their clothes are clean and pressed. They enjoy a small recreation room with soldier-drawn murals on the walls. They can go to a nearby town for an evening and see American movies, in theaters taken over by the Army. They can have dates with nurses."[13]

But war wasn't always fun for the Air Forces, Ernie assured his readers.

"The toilets don't work, so you have to flush them with a tin hat full of water dipped out of an always filled bathtub," he wrote. "The lights go out frequently and you have to use candles." Plus, he added a touch sarcastically, as someone who had spent plenty of nights sleeping with his head in the mud, "It's tough getting up two hours before daylight for a dawn mission. The floors are cold, hard tile. There are no rugs. Some of the windows are still blown out."[14] What Ernie failed to mention was that, statistically speaking, the mortality rate among American bomber crews was appallingly high. About 42 percent of all Americans who flew combat missions during the war were killed in action—52,173 in all.[15]

2

The asphalt road that leads from the city of Cassino to the gleaming white Benedictine abbey of Monte Cassino hairpins sharply seven times, cutting deeper and deeper into the steep mountainside. For centuries, pilgrims from around the world have hiked those serpentine switchbacks on foot to pray and to visit the site of the first house of the Benedictine Order, built by Saint Benedict of Nursi in the sixth century.[16] I could have easily driven the five and a half miles to the abbey from the bed-and-breakfast where I was staying, right at the base of Monte Cassino, but that felt like cheating somehow.

It was Christmas Day, and the proprietors of Il Maniero B and B, Julie and Giuseppe, were celebrating with their families. Julie's father, who spoke only a few short phrases of English, had built the B and B out of a bombed-out farmhouse back in 2011. For all those years after the war ended, that farmhouse had stood as a devastating reminder of the war and all that had been lost.

Giuseppe's family's roots run deep in central Italy. "After the war," he told me at breakfast that morning, "The men in my family would walk from here down to Naples or up to Rome, looking for work. They would tell stories about how there was nothing here. It was all destroyed."

"They would walk?" I asked. I had driven in from Rome a couple of days before. Walking that distance must have taken weeks.

"Yes, they would walk. Incredible, I know. Sometimes if they could get bicycles, they would do that. But mostly they had to walk." He paused to refill my espresso. "They had to get money to feed the family. The hardships after the war for the Italian people were . . . well, they were unimaginable."

Giuseppe was about my age, maybe a little older. Every time I saw him, he was wearing a baggy sweatshirt and flip-flops, which clashed with his closely cropped hair and thin mustache. When he and I first met, he struck me as ex-military. I asked him if he had ever served. He thought my question was funny. Not the life for him, he said. He liked to party too much when he was younger. Each morning, either he or Julie would make breakfast for me. I learned that Giuseppe was born in Ohio but moved to Italy when he was ten so that his parents could be closer to their extended families. He and Julie met and fell in love when they were young and moved to the United States. When Julie's mom was diagnosed with an aggressive form of brain cancer, they moved to Cassino to take care of her and help run the B and B. They've been running it ever since.

"This is a very Catholic place of the world," Giuseppe told me when I asked what there might be for me to do during the holidays. "If you think you'd be up for it, you should hike the mountain. Weather is good. The view from the top is incredible. Plus, it beats Netflix, no?"

I had no need for a hat or jacket—the weather was a far cry from the frigid slog Pyle and the infantry experienced in the winter of 1944. As I rounded the first hairpin turn, I tried to imagine Saint Benedict, in 529, hiking that same path to what was at that time a temple to Apollo. According to the only record we have of Benedict's life, "round about it likewise on all sides there were woods for the service of devils, in which even till that very time, the mad multitude of infidels did offer most wicked sacrifice."[17] Soon enough, however, Saint Benedict converted the infidels to Christianity, settled into Apollo's temple, and wrote the Rule of Benedict, which continues to govern much of Western monastic life to this day.[18]

Celebratory firecrackers shook me out of my reverie and brought me back to the road. With each step, the gradient increased until it seemed as if I had to lean forward into the hill to stop myself from rolling back to where I started. Each turn in the road offered successively more beautiful panoramas of the serpentine Rapido River that threaded through the alluvial flats to the south end of the Liri Valley, which ran northwest toward Rome. Before too long, I was walking above a low ceiling of thin clouds that reminded me of ribbed beach sand after a tide has run out.

At the top of the ridge, after five and a half miles of hiking and fifteen hundred feet of elevation gain, the first thing I noticed about the great four-story Abbey of Monte Cassino was its rows and rows of windows, gleaming in the early afternoon sun. Its pearly white limestone was equally harsh on the eyes, making me wish I had brought my sunglasses.

Unlike the rest of Cassino, the abbey was open on Christmas Day. Past a wooden gate with the word PAX carved in stone above it was a cobblestone path that led up a steep incline to the visitors' entrance. Standing behind a glass cabinet in a small room lined with all manner of tourist maps, books, and trinkets, a monk greeted me with a warm hello. I was in luck, I found out, because a tour was about to begin. Two Americans had scheduled it, and if I'd like, the monk told me, he could ask them if it was all right if I joined. He figured they would say yes considering that a tour of the abbey, with admission to the museum, cost thirty euros, and it would be cheaper for all of us if we pooled our money. "And besides," he said with a wry smile, "what American doesn't like to save a little dough?"

3

To appease the head abbot, Gregorio Diamare, Field Marshal Kesselring promised not to use the "immediate vicinity" of the Abbey of Monte Cassino, instituting a neutral zone radiating three hundred meters in all directions from the monastery.[19] The ridge on which the abbey was perched, however, was by far the best defensive position south of Rome,[20] and in mid-December, Kesselring made it clear to his commanders that in addition to the foot of the mountain, everything around the abbey was also fair game. According to a pair of Benedictine monks who kept a record of daily events at the abbey that winter,[21] the Germans honored the neutral zone Kesselring originally promised for a mere three weeks, until January 5. "The saddest of sad days," one of the monks wrote in his diary. "The interpreter for the new Division arrived about 8:30. He asked to speak to the abbot, and he informed him of very painful orders. He declared that by decision of the Supreme Command of the South, the 300-meter zone no longer existed; that all civilians without any exception must be evacuated."[22] Even before then, on the day after Christmas, General Fridolin von Senger granted his men permission to "make defenses right up to the abbey wall if necessary."[23] Two weeks before that, Kesselring had clarified to Senger that it was "the building itself" that "must be spared."[24]

Gregorio Diamare would hear none of it. On January 6, according to the monks' diary, "he protested what had been done and stated his surprise at the German military authorities' reversal of their position towards the abbey." One day, the abbot vowed, the whole world was going to learn the truth about what happened at Monte Cassino. He and the monks, moreover, would not be moved "except by force."[25]

The Germans shrugged, essentially. Heavily fortified observation posts and bunkers drilled into the rock by press-ganged Italian laborers sprung up around the abbey like mushrooms on a rotting log.[26] Adding to the defensive advantages the mountain provided naturally, the Germans made good use of its many limestone caves, which they had dug out to fit an entire platoon to shield them from whatever artillery the Allies fired their way. Antitank guns and thousands of feet of razor wire capped off the Germans' defense measures.

4

In a small entrance cloister outside the visitors' center where I met the monk, I found a bronze statue of Saint Benedict and two men wearing heavy flowing robes. Benedict was looking to the heavens with both arms raised. The two other men were at his sides, wrapping their arms around him in support.

"The design is based on Saint Gregory the Great's description of Saint Benedict's last moments on earth." It was the monk from before. "He passed in 547 AD, forty days after his twin sister, Saint Scholastica, passed. He entered paradise, in Saint Gregory's words, 'on a bright street strewn with carpets.'"

I jotted down what he told me into my small green notebook.

"Are you writing a book?" he asked. "Let me guess," he continued, before I could answer. "It is a book about the Americans and the war and their destruction of this beautiful place."

"Pretty close, actually," I said. "I'm writing a book about a man named Ernie Pyle. He was a journalist who wrote about the war. He lived on the front line with the troops, followed them from England to North Africa, Sicily to Italy. Then he went to France, of course. He was later killed in the Pacific. I'm trying to follow in his footsteps to see the same places he saw."

"He was here, at the monastery?" the monk asked excitedly.

"No," I said, afraid to disappoint him. "He attached himself to a company of soldiers close to here, but he never set foot on Monte Cassino."

"This man was a smart man," he said. "Anyway, I spoke to the two Americans who scheduled the tour," he continued. "They are going to be late. If you like, you can tour our museum on your own before they arrive. Your guide is also running late. Her name is Silena."

I had the abbey's large subterranean museum almost completely to myself. Room after room was packed with display cases full of medieval Catholic splendor and ancient religious artifacts. There were illuminated scrolls and intricately carved cases to hold them. There were also beautiful woven tapestries and paintings by Italian masters of the late Renaissance framed in golden grandeur. When the Germans boxed up and evacuated the art and archives of Monte Cassino to Rome in the beginning of November 1943, they required more than a hundred truckloads to transport everything that was now on display.[27]

After nearly an hour of wandering from room to room, I heard an ominous-sounding bell tolling as if on a loop from a small side room off one of the main display areas. Inside the room were several wooden chairs arranged in front of a big-screen television. Black-and-white photos of the destruction wrought by American bombs advanced across the screen. The bell continued to toll. An Italian voice told a story in somber tones. First a man's voice. Then a woman's. There were no subtitles. The man's voice returned. The bell never stopped. The destruction was always present. The video had no happy ending.

In addition to the television slideshow, the room contained a glass display case of artifacts that must have been uncovered during the reconstruction of the abbey. Rusted bolt-action rifles. Canteens. Brimless German helmets. A long belt of machine-gun ammo. To the left of the television was a room divider accordioned in the corner, with eighteen black-and-white photos pinned to it showing the fighting around the abbey and the resulting devastation.

5

A few days after Company E of the Thirty-fourth Division, 168th Infantry, had taken Cervero, a small town southeast of Cassino, Ernie was introduced to the company's commander, John Sheehy. "He looked so small, unassuming that if I had saw him around on the outside I would have called him 'sad sack, G.I. Joe,'" Sheehy told Lee Miller soon after the war ended.[28] In late January 1944, Ernie's column was being printed in hundreds of papers across the country, and *Here Is Your War* was high on all the bestseller lists.[29] He could have embedded with any frontline rifle company he wanted. He chose Sheehy's Company E because, of the two hundred men who had shipped overseas with the company two years before, only eight remained.[30] Of those eight men, there was one Pyle would come to know well. "He is to me," Pyle later wrote, "and to all those with whom he serves, one of the great men of the war."[31]

This soldier's name was Frank "Buck" Eversole, a shy and courteous sergeant from Iowa with a broad nose who had ridden bucking broncos for $7.50 a ride out West before the war began. At twenty-eight years old, Eversole was considered an "old-timer" among the replacements he led into combat. With a Purple Heart and two Silver Stars for bravery pinned to his chest,[32] he was "more soldier than civilian," a veteran of Tunisia, Salerno,[33] and the more recent fighting on the limestone flanks of Mount Trocchio.[34] Eversole's "commanders depended more on him than on any other man," not only because Eversole had killed so many Germans, Pyle speculated, but also because, like a good cowboy, "he can improvise, patch things, fix things"[35] and because Eversole had become "hard and immensely wise in animal-like ways of self-preservation."[36] If there was a better soldier in the U.S. Army, Pyle hadn't met him yet.

"I'm mighty sick of it all," Eversole told Pyle in a quiet voice while they chatted one afternoon on the edge of Buck's foxhole, "but there ain't no use to complain. I just figured it this way, that I've been given a job to do and I've got to do it. And if I don't live through it, there's nothing I can do about it."[37] Eversole's eyes were the piercing kind, Pyle noticed, and his hands were strong and rough.

Despite his armor of resignation, Eversole was torn by the tremendous losses at the Italian front.[38] By the middle of February, the casualty rate among the rifle companies in the Thirty-fourth Division—including Company E—would total 65 percent.[39] "I've got so I feel like it's me killin' 'em instead of a German," he confessed to Pyle. "I've got so I feel like a murderer. I hate to look at them when the new ones come in."[40]

While Ernie had once noted that it was impossible for America's fighting men to make the change from normal civilians into dispassionate killers and remain the same people, he also stressed that whenever he found time to sit around a foxhole with a man like Buck Eversole, they seemed like "ordinary human beings back home."[41] In Pyle's eyes, that was what set Americans apart from the enemy soldiers they were forced to kill. Even though America's "boys" were drowning in terror, brutality, destruction, and death, there would inevitably come a time when the awfulness of war would end, and they would be able to recover quickly from the temporary madness that overtook them. "The human spirit is just like a cork," Pyle wrote in his second book about the war, *Brave Men*. "A unit may be pretty well exhausted, but if they are lucky enough to be blessed with some sunshine and warmth they'll begin to be normal after two days out of the line."[42]

One man who was in desperate need of a little sunshine and warmth was Sergeant Eversole. He knew Company E would soon be called to attack across the Rapido River toward Monte Cassino, and when he was offered the opportunity to rest up at Caserta for five days, he turned it down so that he could lead his squad during the attack. His platoon leader appreciated his commitment to his men but knew that Buck's feet had swollen so badly inside his boots that he could barely walk and would likely be more of a liability than an asset on the attack. He ordered Buck to rest his trench feet so that he could come back to the company fully healed. Ernie later heard that Buck was "still a little lame" with trench foot, even after a lengthy hospital stay. The army, in its wisdom, decided to send Buck to a camp for replacement soldiers waiting to be assigned to a new unit rather than back to his old one. Not only would he likely never see his men again—at least not in uniform—he had also lost his chance to rotate back to the States. "And unless very lucky," Ernie explained to Lee, "will also lose his sergeant's stripes, all through no fault of his own.

"That's what happens to heroes," he wrote, "so beware."[43]

After Buck left for Caserta, Ernie lay in the darkness, unable to sleep. He thought about Buck's "great and simple devotion" to his men and how Buck had told him he had felt "like a deserter" after he was ordered to the rest camp. In that moment, Pyle felt an overwhelming sense of regret. He regretted that it wasn't possible for all those people back home to see with their own eyes such a powerful example of the "ghastly brotherhood of war."[44]

6

Ernie left Company E the next day, on the morning of January 28—the day they crossed the Rapido River where it ran shallow enough to ford. The night before, the company had received an alert order that they were going to assault the slopes of Monte Cassino toward the southern end, where the monastery stood.[45] Ernie asked Sheehy if he could tag along with the company during their night march to the front and jump off before the shooting started. Some of the soldiers in Company E told Ernie that if they could choose whether to go up to the front or not, they wouldn't. "It's all right for you to be here with us now," they said, according to one of the soldiers, years after the war, "but when we go into the next one, several are not coming back, and if you went with us, you might be one of those."[46] It would be better, they said, if Ernie went back to where he belonged. But Ernie had the final say, and he chose to go. Sheehy said they'd be delighted to have him.[47]

That evening, as the last smudges of violet light faded in the west, the men of Company E waited anxiously for the night to cover their movements past bullet-scarred olive trees, mortar-pocked stone walls,[48] and landslides of Italian rubble. That night was the darkest any of them could remember; they had to tap out every step like blindfolded men. Overhead, shells whistled in and out, fraying nerves and echoing against low-hanging clouds. The crashes and their reverberations blotted out the men's chatter; the only words Ernie heard were cusses[49] when someone slipped and ended up half submerged in the results of Kesselring's "flooding program." In the defensive buildup of Cassio, Kesselring had ordered the destruction of dikes and canals on the Rapido, which created shallow pools of mud and stagnant water in the flats between Mount Trocchio and Cassino.[50]

"He kind of gave the air of 'I've accomplished all of this, now I've got to accomplish what I haven't accomplished yet,'" remembered one of the soldiers Ernie marched with that night, like "'I want to see what combat is really like.'" Ernie had done everything else a fighting man could do, the soldier continued. "He'd been exposed to all the mortar fire and the artillery fire and all of that—the dangers of it—as anyone that was not in a frontline squad, rifle-squad infantryman—he had experienced as much of that as any other person had that was in the service, but he had never experienced that part of being up there."[51]

Before the men reached the front lines, Ernie turned back to the rear. What came next for Company E was nothing short of hell on earth. For three days they ran headfirst into the most formidable German defenses in all of Italy. Ground near the foot of Monte Cassino was won and then lost, won and then lost again. "Every day Cassino is reported taken, every night the rumor is disproved," a Thirty-fourth Division ordnance officer recorded in his diary.[52] Whatever cracks existed in the German lines could not be found, let alone exploited. The Thirty-fourth Division never broke through.[53] The closest Company E ever came to the abbey was four hundred yards away.[54] "I never had more headaches than in that period," General Clark later recalled.[55] On February 14, two weeks after Pyle had left the front lines, the Fourth Indian Division was called forward to relieve the Thirty-fourth. Snow dusted the bodies of dead GIs, so numerous they had to be stacked on top of one another like rolls of coins. "Thank God their mothers couldn't see the sadness and indignity of it all," a British officer wrote.[56]

"It's a damn shame," Ernie believed, "we have to sit here and can't do anything because of that abbey up there." The best course of action, Ernie had convinced himself, was to blow the damn thing off the face of the earth.[57]

7

On February 9, American counterintelligence officers interrogated an Italian who had been inside the abbey several times over the previous month. He said that about eighty German officers and soldiers along with thirty machine guns were "in the buildings," though it wasn't clear whether that meant in the abbey, in the buildings outside the walls of the abbey, or both. Four days later, an artillery unit reported seeing a "great deal of enemy activity in the vicinity of the famous monastery," and the Thirty-fourth Division's monthly intelligence report for January 1944 included the claim, "Orders preventing our firing on this historical monument increased enormously the value of this point to the enemy."[58]

Colonel Edwin Howard, the intelligence officer for the Fifth Army, maintained the view that the abbey must not be bombed. In an interview after the war, he recalled a conversation he had with General Clark about the possible consequences of bombing the abbey. "I had sufficient information to indicate that the abbey was not being used by the Germans for defensive purposes," he said. "There was no reason whatsoever to bomb it. I also said once you bomb it to make it rubble, it will be a better defensive position for the Germans."[59]

On February 14, an American general flew over Monte Cassino to see for himself whether the Germans were using it as a defensive position.[60] He reported seeing "no signs of activity." Bombing the monastery would be "an unnecessary outrage," he wrote in his diary, especially because as many as two thousand Italian refugees were sheltering inside it.[61]

That same day two other American generals took an L-5 Courier plane to have a look of their own. At an altitude of between twelve hundred and fifteen hundred feet on a clear and sunny day, the generals said they could see a radio mast, which they figured was being used to report Allied troop movements to German gun batteries. They also said they saw German uniforms hanging from a clothesline in the abbey's courtyard and machine-gun nests fifty yards from the abbey's outer walls,[62] which one of the generals claimed he could have dropped his binoculars into.[63] An American intelligence report prepared that same day included the key finding that the monastery itself had "accounted for the lives of upwards of 2,000 boys" and that it "*must* be destroyed and everyone in it, as there is no one in it but Germans."[64]

Later that night, a battery of American 105 mm howitzers fired twenty-five rounds of leaflet-stuffed shells[65] that burst three hundred feet above the great monastery, showering it with pleas for the inhabitants to leave before the full weight of American air power rained down upon Monte Cassino:

BEWARE!

We have until now been especially careful to avoid shelling the Monte Cassino monastery. The Germans have known how to benefit from this. But now the fighting has swept closer and closer to its sacred precincts. The time has come when we must train our guns on the monastery itself.

We give you warning so that you may save yourselves. We warn you urgently. Leave the monastery. Leave it at once. Respect this warning. It is for your benefit.

THE FIFTH ARMY

A university student from Cassino and two of his friends volunteered to search out a safe passageway that civilians could take to escape the fighting. They went out the back of the monastery and hiked down the ridge to the hamlet of San Onofrio. They didn't get far. Even though they were carrying a white flag, the three young men were stopped by German soldiers, who trained their machine guns on them and forced them to return to the abbey.[66] The only thing left to do was to burrow as deeply as one could into the bowels of the abbey and pray.

At 5:45 a.m. the next morning, the crews from 144 B-17 Flying Fortress heavy bombers from the Second Bomb Group, out of Foggia, in southern Italy, were briefed on a short mission they'd be flying later that morning. "The target is a huge ancient monastery which the Germans have chosen as a key defense point and have loaded with heavy guns," an intelligence officer told them.[67] Less than an hour later, the planes started taking off, the lead bombers circling above the airfield until all 144 were in the air, divided into four groups.[68] Flying in formation straight up Route 6, the bombers passed over San Pietro at twenty-one thousand feet and into the heart of the Liri Valley.[69] At 9:28 a.m. the first bomber released its payload.[70] The first twelve five-hundred-pound bombs[71] released that sunny February morning[72] thumped into the abbey like hammers in a drop forge. A ravenous pillar of smoke and flame erupted straight into the air,[73] reminding one of the pilots peering down from his cockpit of an exploding volcano. An officer in the Thirty-fourth Division said the dust that exploded out of the abbey's many windows when the roof was pierced looked like "smoke coming out of a man's ears."[74]

During a lull in the bombing, at around 11:15 a.m., the abbot and his monks clawed through the wreckage into the open, where they found scores of dead refugees and many more who had been wounded or who were "crazy with terror."[75] No one knew how many had been buried under the rubble.[76] While Gregorio Diamare was deciding what to do next to protect his monks and the refugees in the now ruined abbey, a first wave of B-26 Marauder medium bombers was on its way to Monte Cassino. After dropping his plane's one-thousand-pound bombs at 1:32 p.m., a staff sergeant in the lead B-26 described the results this way: "Target cabbaged real good."[77]

By two o'clock that afternoon, the great abbey had been disemboweled with high explosives and cremated with incendiaries, reduced to jagged walls, piles of crushed stone, and smoldering embers.[78] No one knows how many refugees perished in the bombing of the abbey on February 15, 1944. Estimates range from one hundred to more than four hundred.[79] After conducting a careful estimate, a local historian put the number at 230. In a macabre method of calculating the collateral damage, 148 skulls were found in the debris after the war;[80] there's no telling how many may have been crushed into dust.[81]

8

Silena was in her early thirties, with long brown hair and tight, thin lips. She was bundled up tightly in a puffy black coat and clutched a heavy set of keys in her fist. We were lucky, she said. Normally the abbey is too full of tourists, but because there were so few people visiting there that day, she could take the three of us to see Saint Benedict's room.

The two Americans on the tour with me were a husband and wife, probably in their late sixties or early seventies. The husband was thick-chested and wore a black sport coat with a gray scarf wrapped around his neck. He walked with a slight limp, and as we descended a dark set of stone steps behind Silena, he pushed his sunglasses up onto his bald head. His wife looked much like Silena. Long dark hair. Black coat. She said her parents were from Italy. Her husband's father had fought in the Polish army, which helped liberate Cassino during the war. This was his first trip to Cassino.

Before we entered Saint Benedict's room, I asked him whether his father had ever talked about his experiences during the war. He chuckled. "He would tell us funny stories sometimes," he said. "It's been so long since he was with us. I don't really remember any of them." He paused for a moment. "He never talked about Cassino, though—it was so traumatic."

From Saint Benedict's room under the basilica, we climbed another set of stairs past ancient fragments from the abbey found in the rubble after the bombing—now displayed on both walls—and into the cloisters, with colonnades and statues of Benedict and Scholastica.

"The Abbey of Monte Cassino," Silena explained, "has been destroyed four times over the centuries. The first time was by the Lombards. That was sometime between 577 and 589 AD, not long after Saint Benedict and his twin sister died. The second time was in 883 by the Saracens. And the third time was in 1389 because of an earthquake. And then, as you know, the fourth time was on February 15, 1944, when the Americans bombed the abbey. They believed, wrongly as it turned out, that the Germans were here using the abbey for their military purposes.

"Monte Cassino is a place of miracles," Silena continued. "The first was when a raven stole a piece of poisoned bread from Saint Benedict while he was standing in this very cloister. Some say that same raven—his name is Niko—can still be seen from time to time perching on the statue of Saint Benedict." Silena pointed over her shoulder to a statue to the left of the grand staircase that leads from the cloister to the basilica above. It shows Saint Benedict holding a scepter with his left hand and a large book under his right arm.

"The second miracle," Silena continued, "is that the statue of Saint Benedict, which was completed in 1736 by a sculptor named P. Campi, was not damaged at all by the American bombing. Everything else around us was destroyed. The colonnades were smashed. The stairs to the basilica were nothing but a big pile of rubble. It was as if God himself placed a protective shield around Saint Benedict.

"There is one more miracle," she said, "and I will tell you about it inside the basilica."

The basilica inside the Abbey of Monte Cassino was breathtaking. Baroque in style, it was dominated by gold leaf decoration and eighty different types of marble. After we passed through the thousand-year-old front door, Silena asked us to turn around and face the back of the basilica. "This is *The Glory of Saint Benedict*," she said. "When I heard you were all Americans, I looked up the conversion. It is 430 square feet big. Impressive, no?"

The Glory of Saint Benedict is a fresco painted in 1983 by an Italian named Pietro Annigoni, who made his mark as an artist by rejecting most

Statue of Saint Benedict, Monte Cassino, Italy, December 2019

modern developments and instead carrying on the tradition of the Old Masters.

"That is Saint Benedict in the middle, of course," Silena explained to us. The basilica was empty and cold. Her voice echoed down the nave to the grand altar. "He is surrounded by monks, nuns, abbots, and bishops. There are also three popes bowing at his feet." As we followed Silena to the altar, I noticed that the ceiling above the nave was a taupe color, rough in texture. It was totally unlike any of the other ornate surfaces in the basilica. I whispered a question about the ceiling to Silena, and she paused our tour.

"You'll notice," she said, "that the frescoes above us have not yet been completed. That is because Pietro Annigoni passed away in 1988, before he was able to finish his work. He completed the dome of the monastery, which we'll see, but since he passed, we've been unable to find someone who can take on such a monumental project."

Below the grand altar, Saint Benedict and his twin sister were entombed in a crypt decorated by mosaics in the Byzantine style that were created by German monks in 1544. "This is the site of the third miracle," Silena told us. "During the American bombing, one of the bombs dropped straight through the dome of the monastery, piercing the altar, and landed right above this crypt. But it didn't explode. In fact, this entire room was left relatively undamaged. The monks who survived the bombing said it was because this is where they had come to pray each day. God would never allow the destruction of such a place."

9

As Colonel Howard had predicted, German paratroopers burrowed deep into the abbey's smoldering rubble and awaited the Allies' assault. Machine gunners poked their barrels out from bits of crumbled masonry. Artillery observers climbed the broken steps to the top of what remained of the abbey's battered ramparts.[82] Because the monasteries' subterranean cellars and vaults were left relatively unscathed, the Germans used them as barracks and to store supplies.[83] What was once Saint Benedict's room was converted into a field kitchen.[84] For three more months, the Germans were able to defend themselves against wave after wave of Allied assaults.[85]

Believing that it simply wasn't possible that even a single German had survived the thunderous Allied bombardment the previous day, a single company of Indian troops was ordered to seize a short slope known as Hill 593, a couple of thousand yards behind the abbey,[86] the day after the bombardment. German paratroopers concealed in the abbey's rubble killed or wounded half the Indian troops before they were able to cover even fifty yards from their line of departure.[87] Known as Monte Calvario, Hill 593 is now home to the Monte Cassino Polish War Cemetery. Over a thousand Polish soldiers who died trying to liberate the abbey from the Germans in May 1944 are buried there. FOR OUR FREEDOM AND YOURS the memorial above the headstones reads, WE SOLDIERS OF POLAND GAVE / OUR SOUL TO GOD / OUR LIFE TO THE SOIL OF ITALY / OUR HEARTS TO POLAND.

For all the worthiness of the cause for which the Allies fought, it cannot be denied that an unacceptable number of innocents were killed that fateful day for no reason at all. While the method was impersonal and the outcome unintended, the result was no less merciless.

Bombing the abbey also resulted in many more casualties for General Clark's Fifth Army. Had he not ordered the bombing of the abbey, he might have been able to find a way around Cassino. But after the Allies needlessly pulverized one of the most venerated Catholic shrines in the world, Clark had to commit his forces to wiping out all German resistance there. "A direct attack on the Monte Cassino features meant that we were committed to success," explained the commander of the Fourth Indian Infantry Division, General Francis Tuker. "We could not stop short and call it a day without acknowledging complete failure."[88]

The Germans slipped out from their positions in and around the abbey in the dark of night three months after the bombing, on May 18, without firing a shot. "There were the dead that had stormed and taken this fortress only yesterday," Peter Stursberg of the Canadian Broadcasting Corporation said of what he found in the Germans' wake. "And there were the dead that had tried to take it months ago. I almost stumbled over a head that had almost mummified. It was not the sight of the dead . . . that turned our stomachs but the stench."[89] Homer Bigart, who was one of the first correspondents to enter Cassino on May 19, wrote about the bleakness and the smoking ruin the city had become after months of bombings and waves of attacks and counterattacks. "With a little sulfur added," he wrote, Cassino "would be more grim than a Calvinist conception of hell."[90]

After three months of being dug in like ticks, the Germans' position in the abbey become untenable not because they suddenly feared being overrun by an Allied frontal assault, but because North African troops had summited the bleak Aurunci Mountains, on the far side of the Liri Valley, unhinging the entire Gustav Line. With their positions in the valley now exposed to the North African troops holding the high ground, the Germans had no choice but to abandon their lines and retreat farther up the valley.[91]

The Abbey of Monte Cassino, in its entirety, has since been rebuilt. The bulk of the construction took nearly twenty years to complete. In 1964, Pope Paul VI consecrated the rebuilt basilica, which looks today exactly as it did before it was bombed, because the abbey's original blueprints were among the archival materials saved by the Germans. One of the few discernible differences between the abbey today and the abbey in the pictures taken before the bombing is that the abbey's new travertine doesn't yet have the aged yellow and gray color it once had. "But it will," Silena said at the end of our tour. "It just takes time."

10

The day after Buck Eversole arrived at the rest camp at Caserta,[92] Ernie made up a ruse about needing Buck to help him with some research and took Buck with him to Naples.[93] They stayed together at an apartment with a beautiful marble entrance[94] that overlooked the harbor.[95] While Buck, the Air Corps major who was in charge of the apartment, and two nurses visited the ruins of Pompeii one day, Pyle finally returned his attention to his columns.[96] In a letter to Jerry, he confessed that he had been "dragging around since the first of the year," and that he had gotten "so low and lackadaisical" that he "had to drop the columns for a whole week." He had neither the physical energy nor the spiritual will to keep on writing.[97] Pyle explained to Lee in another letter that the change of scenery in Naples didn't seem to be enough to pick him back up. "Everybody is low," he wrote, "and the spirit is catching. Not about the outcome of the war or even the Italian campaign, but because we're all bored and there's too much misery and things have been static for so long. I'm in an apartment looking down over what is certainly one of the most beautiful sights in the world, and I don't get even the tiniest thrill out of it."[98]

At least one other good thing, besides lifting Buck's spirits, came out of

Ernie's stay with the Air Corps in Naples. A flight surgeon he made friends with brought an army doctor to the apartment one day when Ernie was feeling particularly unwell. It didn't take long for the doctor to figure out what was really causing Ernie's low mood and energy, at least physiologically. After analyzing a blood sample that showed Ernie's hemoglobin was extremely low, the doctor told him he was suffering from anemia,[99] meaning that his blood didn't have nearly enough healthy red cells to carry the oxygen his body needed to function properly. Maybe that's why he had been feeling dead to the world, he told Jerry.[100]

"So now they've started on a big program of liver injections, polyvitamin capsules, hydrochloric capsules, hydrochloric acid and what not," Pyle explained in a letter to Jerry. The doctors said that within a few weeks he'd be feeling better than he had in years, as long as he limited himself to no more than two drinks a day, which was enough to drive a man to drink, he told Paige.[101] "The Army doctors are grand to me," he told Jerry, "and want to get me built up before I leave for England in about a month. Also the soldiers who run our apartment and mess are grand, and have gone scrounging and actually dug up some eggs (at 25 cents apiece) so that I now have the luxury of eggs and bacon for breakfast." It was a good thing the doctors caught his condition when they did, he told Jerry; "I'll apparently be a Hercules within a month."[102]

CHAPTER 7

THE BITCHHEAD AT ANZIO

When you get to Anzio you waste no time getting off the boat, for you have been feeling pretty much like a clay pigeon in a shooting gallery. But after a few hours in Anzio you wish you were back on the boat, for you could hardly describe being ashore as any haven of peacefulness.

ERNIE PYLE, "NO AREA IS IMMUNE," MARCH 28, 1944[1]

1

The dead men's gear and clothing, mud-caked and bloody, was brought by the truckload, five or six per day, to a salvage dump near the beachhead that was managed by the army's Quartermaster Corps. Black soldiers were tasked with the grisly job of sorting, classifying, and cleaning the litter. "They poke through the great heap," Ernie wrote, "picking out shoes of the same size to put together, picking out knives and forks and leggings and underwear and cans of C-ration and goggles and canteens and sorting them into different piles." Everything that could be used again would be sent back to Naples for restoration and repair. As Ernie looked on, he felt tight-lipped and dejected. The inanimate objects shouted to him from the great pile. There was the helmet with a bullet hole. And an overshoe ripped to hell by shrapnel. Then there was an irreparably smashed portable typewriter. And a pair of muddy pants. One leg was gone.[2]

"This is a new kind of warfare for us," Pyle told his readers of Anzio's suffering.[3] "Here distances are short, and space is confined. The whole beachhead is the front line."[4] Soldiers closest to the German defensive positions flattened themselves into shallow foxholes, which afforded neither comfort nor safety, necessitated by the high water table.[5] Soldiers closer to the coastline had it much better. The sandstone around Nettuno made it possible for enterprising soldiers to mine deep into the substrata.[6] "Men have dug underground and built themselves homes," Ernie reported, complete with pilfered furniture and random bits of detritus that gave the warm and dry lairs a more homey, secure feel.[7]

Ernie's fingers hurt from the cold. They were so stiff he could barely peck at his typewriter keys. It was the middle of March, and spring had not yet sprung along the Tyrrhenian Sea forty miles south of Rome. "We'll have one or two perfectly awful days, cold and dark and pouring rain," Ernie wrote to Jerry, "then about three days of beautiful sunshine and clear skies, warmish in midday but cold at night."[8] As seemed to be the case with Buck and the other frontline soldiers in Italy, Ernie believed a change of scenery, and maybe a letter from home, could pluck him from deep depression that had swallowed him whole. "I've been pretty low for a month and a half," he wrote to Paige on February 16. "Have felt so damn lousy, and no word from Jerry, and the fuckin' war getting under my skin so bad."[9]

Ernie landed at the Anzio beachhead at the end of February,[10] over a month after forty-seven thousand Allied troops stalked across the soft sand, almost completely unopposed, on January 22, 1944.[11] All told, the Allies suffered 110 casualties that first day, with only thirteen men killed in action.[12] The day after the invasion, Pyle's friend and fellow correspondent Don Whitehead reported, "For several hours we have been going around with our mouths open in amazement over the ease with which the Army and Navy managed to land troops behind enemy lines."[13]

The conceptual framework behind Operation Shingle came straight from the top. In December 1943, Winston Churchill, the architect of the disastrous amphibious landing on the Gallipoli peninsula in 1915,[14] proposed landing two divisions of troops at Anzio to outflank the Germans clogging up the Liri Valley.[15] Either German forces on the Gustav Line would stay put—and Rome would fall—or they would be drawn into the fighting for the Italian capital, and Clark's Fifth Army could finally break through at Cassino.[16] On the off chance that the Germans had adequate reinforcements to defend Rome and hold the Gustav Line, the Allies would nevertheless be engaging a sizable number of German divisions that would no longer be available to fight in France once the Allies invaded Normandy. It was a win-win-win, Churchill believed.

General John P. Lucas, who had little confidence in the planning behind the invasion,[17] decided to halt his troops' advance a few miles from the coastline. Wanting to avoid what happened when the Allies landed at Salerno the previous fall—when the Germans nearly pushed the thinly spread Allies back into the sea—Lucas refused to break out of the tiny beachhead and sprint toward Rome until his position on the beachhead was consolidated and he had adequate numbers of men and enough supplies to push back against whatever the Germans threw his way.[18]

In the early days after the invasion, it had appeared, to Whitehead, at least, that "the planners of this operation conceived a brilliant one, for it has gone better than anyone could have dreamed."[19] The way in which the Allies had "gouged a hole in a short time and consolidated their position leaves no alternative but to be optimistic," he told his readers. "Men, guns, armor and supplies have poured across the beach in an unbroken flow and in such proportions that no one I have met has any fears that the Germans will ever be able to threaten a breakthrough such as endangered the Salerno beachhead."[20]

As was often the case during the Italian campaign, however, appearances were deceiving. By the time Pyle arrived at what the soldiers dug in there were calling the "Anzio bitchhead,"[21] the exhausted Allies were mired in a bloody stalemate.[22] And there was no end in sight. By waiting to consolidate his forces at the beachhead, Lucas "achieved the worst of both worlds," wrote the noted military historian John Keegan, "exposing his forces to risk without imposing any on the enemy."[23] Churchill was more poetic, and emphatic: "I had hoped we were hurling a wildcat into the shore," Churchill cabled Field Marshal Alexander, "and what do I find? A whale wallowing on the beaches!"[24]

2

Pyle had decided against embedding with the invasion forces at Anzio. "You will understand by the time you get this letter," he wrote to Lee from the correspondents' apartment in Naples. "If I'm going to get killed I'd rather wait and do it on a bigger show, such as France."[25] In a letter to Jerry, he was less dramatic in his reasons for skipping the landing. "I didn't go on the amphibious landing below Rome which you've now read about in the papers, partly because everybody's stuff had to be pooled and you can't very well pool a column, partly because I still had too much cold, and partly because I didn't want to." After checking out the front lines near Cassino, Ernie planned to fly to London and prepare for the eventual invasion of western Europe. "I read in Stars & Stripes today that there are now 160 correspondents in England to cover the invasion," he wrote to Jerry. "I suppose there'll be 200 by the time it happens." Jerry needn't worry, Ernie assured her: "If and when it does come off . . . I don't intend to go over very early in the game."[26]

Ernie's initial reluctance to land with the first waves in France may have had something to do with the death of his dear friend and fellow Scripps-Howard columnist Ray Clapper. On February 1, 1944, the carrier plane Clapper was riding in collided with another plane over the island of Enewetak, in the North Pacific. Clapper had been in the Marshall Islands to cover the Allied invasion there. "Both planes crashed into a lagoon," a news report said; no one aboard either plane survived.[27] "I'm so upset by it I can hardly think," Ernie wrote to Roz Goodman.[28] "It gives me the creeps, and makes more dominant that perpetual feeling we all have of 'When will my turn come?'"[29] To his editor, Ernie was even more forthcoming about how overwhelmed he was beginning to feel: "The whole thing is getting pretty badly under my skin," Ernie wrote. "I've got so I brood about it, about the whole thing, I mean, and I have a personal reluctance to die that is always in my mind, like a weight. Instead of growing stronger and hard as good veterans do, I've become weaker and more frightened. I'm all right when I'm actually at the front, but it's when I pull back and start thinking and visualizing that it almost overwhelms me. I've even got so I don't sleep well, and have half-awake hideous dreams about the war."[30]

The only thing stopping him from coming home for good was the thought that he wouldn't be able to live with himself if he did. "If I can just see the European war out," he confessed to Lee, "I think I might feel justified in quitting the war."[31]

3

German field marshal Kesselring was surprised by the Allied landings at Anzio. But he was not unprepared. In anticipation that the Allies would eventually try to outflank his forces along the Gustav Line, Kesselring had developed seven plans to counter seven possible Allied advances. Before the sun came up on January 22, Kesselring initiated Operation Richard, which he had developed to counter an invasion that threatened Rome.[32] He dispatched the Kampfgruppe of the Fourth Parachute Division and the Hermann Göring Panzer Division to defend the roads leading from the beachhead to the Alban Hills. At the same time, the equivalent of more than three Wehrmacht divisions were released from France, Yugoslavia, and Germany to join three more divisions already in Italy.[33] "Appreciating the importance of stopping the invading forces before they could advance inland," wrote the military historian Flint Whitlock, "Kesselring was moving whole regiments and divisions around like chess pieces, preparing for the moment when he could unleash a heavy counteroffensive that would block this new threat and turn this impertinent invasion into an unmitigated Allied disaster."[34]

Ernie Pyle eating C-rations, Anzio beachhead
area, March 18, 1944

By January 25, the Germans had surrounded the high ground around
the Allied beachhead.[35] Every square inch of the beachhead was visible
to the German defensive positions, and every square inch was vulnerable to German artillery.[36] By the time Ernie arrived at Anzio, the waterfront villas had been chewed up,[37] and the beaches were scarred with
craters.[38] In the first month alone, more than forty thousand soldiers from
both sides of the line were wounded or killed—a casualty rate of about
20 percent.[39] "Anzio was a fishbowl," one soldier wrote in his diary. "We
were the fish."[40]

After two weeks in Anzio, Ernie wrote to Jerry about his affection for
life on the beachhead. "When I came up," he told her, "I only intended to
stay five days, but found it much more interesting and in a way more satis-
fying than being on the Cassino front or in Naples, so I just stayed on. It's
pretty dangerous here, as the entire beachhead is under shellfire, but there's
a spirit about it that I like better than the other fronts, and my own spirits
are better up here."[41]

4

The censors at Anzio were capricious in their efforts to hide bad news from the folks at home. Under the front-page headline ALLIES GIVE GROUND on February 6, 1944, *The New York Times*' Milton Bracker wrote without hope, "The overall picture of the 156-day-old battle of Italy is not overly encouraging and it is time to say so."[42] After stories like Bracker's had been published, Field Marshal Alexander, acting under orders from Churchill, shut down the radio transmitter that the signal corps had been using to send dispatches back to editors in the States.[43] Churchill was furious that so many alarmist reports were claiming there was little chance that the invasion forces would ever break out of the beachhead. In the House of Commons back in London, Churchill preached, "Such words as 'desperate' ought not to be used about the position in a battle of this kind when they are false. Still less should they be used if they were true." In Washington, DC, the secretary of war, Henry L. Stimson, struck a more conciliatory tone that nonetheless backed Churchill. The correspondents

Ernie Pyle, Anzio beachhead area, March 18, 1944

had been too pessimistic, he said. In the future, they should remember the adage: "Keep your shirt on."[44]

On February 15, Alexander met with a group of correspondents and tried to set them straight on the reality as he perceived it. "There is absolutely no Dunkirk here," he said. "There's no basis for pessimistic rubbish," he continued. "I assure you the Germans opposite us here are a very unhappy party. The Germans realize they've lost the battle, though events have not gone as swiftly as we ourselves hoped."[45] Only after the momentum of the battle seemed to have shifted in the Allies' favor was the radio transmitter reopened.[46]

Casualty lists and the shock of bad news can do one of two things: either they make a nation angry and determined, or they make a nation weary and depressed. Churchill and Stimson feared the latter; the British and American public, in their eyes, still were not prepared psychologically to accept the cruel facts of war. Years after he returned home from Europe, CBS's Eric Sevareid thought back to the decision to shut down the radio transmitter at Anzio and empathized. Had the correspondents accurately described the truth of what the Allies were being forced to endure at Anzio, there would have been a public outcry, Sevareid believed, to stop the "senseless slaughter."[47]

5

The death that plagued Ernie's dreams nearly became reality at Via Gramsci 35 in Nettuno on St. Patrick's Day 1944.[48] At about seven o'clock that morning, Ernie woke and rubbed the sleep from his eyes. The rest of the four-story seaside villa slept. Lying in his bed[49] on the top floor, Ernie was weak. With too little energy to do anything but think, that is precisely what he did. It was a welcome relief from a constant state of weariness to be warm in bed with nothing but the sound of pulsating waves and the smell of the sea. A few minutes after he had woken, booms from an Allied antiaircraft battery nearby barked into the sky, disturbing his peace-

Ernie Pyle at his bed in Nettuno, which he had just
left before the roof fell on it, March 16, 1944

ful morning.[50] The rambling villa he shared with about a dozen other correspondents[51] trembled. With his steel helmet cocked to the side, Ernie
stood at his window, smoking the day's first cigarette, watching the ack-ack
with resigned cautiousness.[52]

At that same moment, a German bomber released two five-hundred-
pound bombs that slammed into the muddy ground only thirty feet from
Ernie's villa.[53] The terrible power of the blast blew apart two of his bedroom
walls and crushed Ernie's still-warm bed with a thousand pounds of rubble.[54] Broken glass sprayed the room,[55] and a thick cloud of dust covered everything, including Ernie's portable typewriter, which he had perched atop
a skinny desk in the far corner of the room.[56] Trembling with a weakness
in his joints,[57] unsure if he was even still alive,[58] Ernie rose to his feet and
patted his stomach and chest, searching for blood. Nothing. His breathing
was short and jerky; there was an empty feeling in his chest.[59] He reached

next for the top of his head as the adrenaline flooded through his veins. His helmet had been blown off. All his fingers felt was dust, shards of glass, and wisps of greasy hair.[60] Then he found the blood.[61] A tiny cut on his right cheek.[62]

"No, I didn't get the Purple Heart, and don't want one, you fuckin hero-worshiper," he later wrote to Paige. "You have to go to the first-aid station and cry, and then you get one. I didn't go cry; a sergeant just came along and spit on his dirty handkerchief and wiped the blood off my face and put some iodine on it."[63]

"When our bombing was over," Ernie later told his readers, "my room was in shambles. It was the sort of thing you see only in the movies. More than half the room was knee-deep with broken brick and tiles and mortar. The other half was a disarray all covered with plaster dust and broken glass." When the other correspondents saw he was all right, they laughed and called Ernie "Old Indestructible"[64]—the luckiest man they knew.

"By mid-afternoon I felt very old and 'beat up,'" he later reported, "and the passage of the afternoon shells over our house really gave me the willies."[65] Like so many of the infantry dug in on the beaches below his villa, Ernie had come down with a case of "Nettuno neurosis,"[66] also known as "Anzio anxiety." Some cases were so severe that the sufferer had to leave the beachhead for a rest. The easiest way to detect such neurosis or anxiety in others was by what Ernie called "that stare." In one of his more poetic columns, Ernie repeats the phrase "It's a look" at the beginning of three sequential sentences to describe that stare. "It's a look of dullness," he wrote, "eyes that look without seeing, eyes that see without transferring any response to the mind. It's a look that is the display room for the thoughts that lie behind it—exhaustion, lack of sleep, tension for too long, weariness that is too great, fear beyond fear, misery to the point of numbness, a look of surpassing indifference to anything anybody can do to you. It's a look I dread to see in men."[67]

Most soldiers with that stare would, according to army doctors, be all right after a few days away from the big guns. "It's one of the perpetual astonishments of war life to me that humans recover as quickly as they do,"

Ernie assured his readers. "You can take a unit that is pretty well exhausted, and if they are lucky enough to be blessed with some sunshine and warmth, they'll begin to be normal after two days out of the line."[68] Only a small minority of soldiers Ernie described as "extreme shock cases" had to be locked away on hospital ships in padded cells with a steel door.[69]

6

Before the war came to Italy, Anzio and Nettuno were comprised of serene waterfront cafés and restaurants, garish bathhouses, and a stunning ancient harbor. "Anzio is where Nero is supposed to have fiddled while Rome burned," Ernie wrote soon after he arrived, "but in more recent years he would doubtless have been sprawling in a deck chair on the patio of his seaside villa, drinking cognac."[70]

I arrived on the crowded narrow streets of Nettuno in the early afternoon. It was Christmas Eve, and there wasn't a seat to be had in any of the seaside eateries, nor was there a parking spot big enough for me to parallel-park the giant bus of a van I was driving. I must have circled Nettuno's clogged downtown, with mopeds buzzing all around me, for at least a half hour before I finally found a spot I could slide into nearly a mile farther down the coast.

There were no reminders, as far as I could see, of the widespread death and destruction that occurred in Anzio and Nettuno during the late winter and early spring of 1944. The pastel-painted shops and cafés facing the water were alive with the fishy, herbal smell of zuppa di pesce and the sound of Mariah Carey's "All I Want for Christmas Is You" mixed with voices and laughter. Nettuno's quiet harbor, beneath a ceiling of wispy clouds, was filled with hundreds of winterized sailboats, their masts bobbing gently. A few hundred yards in from the water's edge, a solid flank of fine stone and stucco buildings stood four or five stories high. Via Gramsci, the main road along the coast, was bracketed by sidewalks laid with cobblestones. Their pattern was curved to match the look of surf falling forward.

The villa where Ernie almost met his end was still there, clad in peach-colored stucco and trimmed with cream-colored stone. Two ornate balconies overlooked the street, which was choked with parked cars and a steady stream of slow-moving traffic. The sound of the sea was faint on the winter wind as I buzzed the button for the apartment on the top floor of the villa, which had, at some point after the war, been converted into a four-flat. No answer. No buzz and click of a lock mechanism disengaging. I buzzed the third floor. No answer. Then the second, and finally, the first. Nothing.

Through a lattice fence of thin metal to the left of the building, I saw a woman dressed in dark jeans and a red turtleneck. She was scrubbing the rust at the bottom of a metal spiral staircase with a wire brush. Behind her the Tyrrhenian Sea was tame and white. The gentle waves broke far out with a slow, majestic sound.

"Scusi," I said timidly through the fence.

"Mi scusi," I said a bit louder, with more confidence.

"Signora!" I shouted above the noise from the street. "Mi scusi, signora!" The woman, in her late thirties or early forties, lifted and turned her head toward the sound of my voice. A streak of blond hair swooped across her face, covering her thin wire glasses. After plucking off her gloves finger by finger, she swept the streak behind her ear, climbed to the bottom of the stairs, and took a few steps in my direction. A small spaniel at her feet yelped in excitement. The woman's impatient eyes squinted in the sun.

"Parla inglese?" I asked with a hopeful upward inflection.

"Um . . . little," she said, taking a few steps closer.

"I am writing a book," I said slowly, using my hands to mimic scribbling in my notebook, "about a man who lived here during the war."

She nodded.

"How long have you lived here?" I asked.

She held up three fingers. "Tre anni."

"Do you know the history of this place? Do you know anything about what happened during the war?"

"No, sorry."

I thought for a moment about what to ask next. "Could I come inside?" I finally asked. "To see what it looks like now?"

"No, sorry."

"Of course, of course," I replied, backing away from the fence. A wave of embarrassment crashed over me. "Grazie. Buona giornata."

The sand below the villa was flat, gray, and hard as concrete. Aside from a pair of short-board surfers with full-body wet suits, the beach was deserted. The air bit a little. Not too sharply. The soothing sound of gentle surf massaging the sand was a comfort at first. Then, walking along the sea's dying edge in the melancholy winter light, I thought about life on the beaches during that miserable winter of 1944, about young lives snuffed out capriciously. After I had walked nearly half a mile, it struck me that life at Anzio was not separate from death; they were knit as tightly as the threads in a carpet. "It must be an awful thing," Ernie wrote of the Battle of Anzio, "to go up to the brink of possible death in the nighttime in a faraway land, puzzled and afraid, knowing no one and facing the worst moment of your life totally alone."[71]

By empathizing with the American infantrymen, by helping make sense of their defeats and their deaths, Ernie helped to maintain morale and stir up the American public to do all that they could to help finish the fighting so that their boys could finally come home. The war was messy and confusing, but it was also necessary. There was no place for judgment. Not yet, anyway. "History is lived forward but it is written in retrospect," the English historian C. V. Wedgwood once wrote. "We know the end before we consider the beginning and we can never wholly recapture what it was to know the beginning only."[72]

7

Ernie stayed at the beachhead for another week after the bombing that destroyed his room. In a letter to Paige, he explained the rationale behind his decision. It wasn't about bravery or courage or needing to show up any of the other correspondents, most of whom had left for England soon after the bombing. Ernie simply needed a little time to get his nerve back, he said—and his self-respect. When he boarded a hospital ship bound for Naples, along with five hundred wounded men, Ernie was feeling "on top of the world," though it was true that for two days after the bombing he had felt "pretty jumpy." After that wore off, he told Paige, "I seemed to be able to take it even better than before. Had several mighty close ones from shells, as well as the bombs. Piss on it."[73]

Ernie had two other things going for him that probably contributed to his renewed sense of courage: temperance and liver shots.[74] For the month he was in Anzio, Ernie hadn't swallowed a drop of alcohol.[75] "My hemoglobin is now so high," he joked to Paige, "they have to drain me a couple times a week to keep me from exploding."[76] Another thing that probably should have buoyed him during that difficult time was the fact that *Here Is Your War* had sold over 225,000 copies—and was soon going to be coming out in the People's Book Club and Overseas Pocketbooks.[77] On top of that, Ernie's column was now being published in 270 papers,[78] second only to Drew Pearson's Washington Merry-Go-Round and Walter Winchell.[79]

Back home in Albuquerque, Jerry had been giving ground in the battle with her demons. In early February, Lee had cabled Ernie to tell him that Jerry had been sick since the first of the year[80] and that her sister Poe[81] had brought her to Denver.[82] "I suppose it's the same old business," Ernie relayed to Paige.[83] A month later, Ernie learned Jerry's "sickness" wasn't the flu or common cold. She had suffered a complete nervous collapse soon after New Year's.[84] Her doctor had prescribed Jerry an antacid formulated to relieve pain and stress even though it contained two toxic substances—sodium bromide and acetanilide.[85] Soon after beginning the treatment, Jerry became weak and delirious—two common symptoms of bromide poisoning. "I can't see anything for it but one swing of the pendulum after another until it's all over," Ernie confided in Paige. "I feel so goddam sorry for her I could weep." But what was he supposed to do about it from Italy? "It's been proved that me being there doesn't help any," he continued, "so there's no use for me to quit and come home and go nuts too."[86]

On March 30, Ernie finally worked up the courage to write to Jerry about the distress he felt after learning how much she was suffering at home without him. "I do love you as I always have," he told her. "Your being well again is the only thing that really means anything in my life." In the same letter, however, Ernie couldn't resist heaping his own distress onto Jerry. "I've given up all hope of ever hearing from you," he wrote, "but will keep on writing to you, and hope you want me to. I have days when I feel so close to you and long so to be with you that I can hardly keep from crying to myself, and yet at other times when I try to write you like now, I feel that we've so lost contact that I hardly know what to say to you. I can't and don't want to heckle you about not writing me, but how I do wish you could, just once in a while."[87]

On April 5, Ernie boarded an army cargo plane in Naples, final destination London.[88] "There's such a thing," he wrote, "as pressing your luck too far in one spot."[89] The fighting he left behind him at Anzio would last for another two months.[90] Jerry had not yet told him whether or not she wanted him to come home.[91]

8

It's funny to hear them talk," Ernie wrote of the infantrymen he embedded with near Cassino in a column published on January 8, 1944. "One night in our cowshed I heard one of them say how he was going to keep his son out of the next war. 'As soon as I get home I'm going to put ten-pound weights in his hands and make him jump off the garage roof, to break down his arches,' he said. 'I'm going to feed him a little ground glass to give him a bad stomach, and I'm going to make him read by candlelight all the time to ruin his eyes.'"[92]

Had slashing a bloody valley in the underbelly of Europe been worth the suffering? The commanders and politicians responsible for the campaign believed it was. "Our war of attrition is doing its work," President Roosevelt said of the Mediterranean strategy.[93] The value of that work, Field

Marshal Alexander later wrote, "must be expressed not in terms of the ground gained, but in terms of its effect on the war as a whole."[94] By the time Rome fell on June 5, 1944, six of Kesselring's divisions had been badly bloodied, and a total of fifty-five German divisions that might otherwise have been used to reinforce the French coastline in Normandy were instead deployed along the Mediterranean fronts to thwart any further encroachment on Hitler's Reich.[95] Nearly a decade after it ended, Churchill wrote of the Italian campaign: "The principal task of our armies had been to draw off and contain the greatest possible number of Germans. This had been admirably fulfilled." The Allies had devoured the German army, Churchill stated unequivocally. "There have been few campaigns with a finer culmination."[96]

Historians of the Second World War have been much less laudatory in their analysis of a campaign that was so poorly planned and incompetently commanded. B. H. Liddell Hart was a British veteran of World War I who later became an influential historian and military theorist. He concluded that rather than devouring the German army, as Churchill had claimed, the Italian campaign had subtracted heavily from Allied war resources.[97] The British historian John Ellis wrote that the Mediterranean campaign has been "consistently over-emphasized in most English studies of the war," and that "it might well be thought that the whole campaign barely merits an extended footnote."[98] In the words of another British historian, Correlli Barnett, the entire Mediterranean war was a preposterous cul-de-sac that gave the Allies something to do but didn't take them anywhere. The fighting in Italy was nothing more than "mere byplay in the conclusion of a war," he continued, "that had been won in mass battles on the Eastern and Western fronts."[99]

The American historian Robert W. Love went further in his history of the U.S. Navy, arguing that it was Churchill's imperial ambitions and Roosevelt's "vacillation" that were to blame for a "wasteful peripheral strategy in the Mediterranean" that gave the Germans two extra years to finish construction of its formidable Atlantic Wall.[100] Even more bitingly, the American historian David M. Kennedy called the campaign "a needlessly costly sideshow" and a "grinding war of attrition whose costs were justified by no defensible military or political purpose."[101]

Historical debates aside, for those soldiers who survived the misery, destruction, and frustration that defined the Allied campaign in Italy, it took time, introspection, faith, and a little imagination to justify or give meaning to what they were forced to endure. Ernie was no exception. "There has been some exhilaration here and some fun, along with the misery and the sadness," he wrote of the Italian campaign in a column published on May 4, 1944, "but on the whole it has been bitter. Few of us can even conjure up any truly fond memories."[102]

While there seemed to be no way to rationalize what had happened during the campaign, to make sense of why things were the way they were, Ernie took his best shot. "I look at it this way," he told his readers. "If by having only a small army in Italy we have been able to build up more powerful forces in England, and if by sacrificing a few thousand lives here this winter we can save half a million lives in Europe this summer—if these things are true, then it was best as it was."[103]

In fact, the Italian campaign cost many times more than a few thousand lives. All told, the Americans alone suffered upward of 120,000 battle casualties to liberate Italy, including 23,501 killed in action.[104] But for Ernie, who never reported on the dubious decision-making that resulted in so much needless death, the horrible sacrifices he witnessed *had* to be worth it. The mayhem and violence *had* to have meaning. The bloody calculus of combat *had* to add up to something. "I'm only saying," he told his readers, "that you've got to look at it that way. Or else you can't bear to think of it at all."[105]

9

Stuffed at the bottom of Ernie's leather-handled barracks bag, below two bottles of whiskey and a sherry he planned to gift to the young woman who had nursed him through the worst days of his anemia, rested a lumpy reversible parka—olive green on one side and snow white for winter fighting on the other.[106] A day or so before he joined Company E back near Cassino, the men had been issued the newly designed parkas, which came with a heavy fleece inner lining. "Ernie had mentioned that he liked them very much," John Sheehy remembered after the war, "so we decided to give him one as a remembrance from the company."[107] After the war ended, the parka found its way to the archives of the Indiana State Museum in Indianapolis.

"To Ernie Pyle," one of the company's sergeants wrote under the collar on the white inner lining. Below the inscription, the bubbled letters INF serve as the background for a two-dimensional eagle with its wings spread wide. Crossed rifles and a circle of fourteen five-pointed stars round out the design of the division's crudely drawn insignia. Underneath, the names of every man in the company are handwritten in four neat columns. One hundred sixty-three names in all. Eight of those names are now etched into white marble at the Sicily-Rome American Cemetery in Nettuno, not far from where Pyle nearly lost his life were it not for his nicotine addiction.

From a distance, their names are as indecipherable as Henry T. Waskow's was before Luca massaged in a handful of fine sand. To read the names, you'd have to kneel before them and squint your eyes. There was PFC Thomas B. Doolin. He was from Massachusetts and died on January 30, 1944, two days after Ernie parted ways with Company E. Six men later died fighting for control of Monte Cassino: PFC Francis J. Stelzer from Ohio and Private Joe J. Najpauer from Connecticut were killed on February 8, and three days later Sergeant John J. Morton from Illinois and Private Arbeth L. Taylor from Tennessee, along with PFC Minton B. Mattice and Private Charles J. Gubbins—both from New York—lost their lives. Then there was PFC Edward Krzyzak, also from Illinois. He survived the fighting at Cassino only to lose his life at the end of May, after the company had been redeployed to the Anzio beachhead.

"It was quite a touching gift," Pyle wrote once he was back in London, seven short weeks before the planned invasion of Normandy.[108] "I thought I'd write about it," he told Lee, "but it seemed so damned immodest I gave it up."[109]

What should have taken Ernie two days—flying from Naples to the English capital by way of North Africa—ended up taking nearly a week because of four days of bad weather in Casablanca.[110] He found the flights themselves quite peaceful.[111] During the first, from Naples to Algiers, he draped his frail and haggard body atop a pile of canvas sacks full of GI mail and slept half the trip away. On the next flight, he found a blanket and stretched his skinny limbs out on the floor, as the plane's throbbing motors hummed him to sleep. When he awoke with a start a short time later, the sun was beginning to set.

"I've written many times that war isn't romantic to the people in it," he later wrote about that flight. But then, all of a sudden, the romance became impossible to ignore. "A heavy darkness had come inside the cabin," he continued. "Passengers were indistinct shapes, kneeling at the windows to absorb the spell of the hour. The remnants of the sun streaked the cloud-banked horizon ahead, making it vividly red and savagely beautiful."[112]

Through the cabin window, Pyle spied the green peaks of the Atlas Mountains under the softening shroud of dusk. Their loveliness reminded him of the Sandias outside Albuquerque.[113] "And there high in the sky above and yet part of it all were plain Americans incongruously away from home," he wrote. "For a moment it seemed terribly dramatic that we should be there at all amid that darkening beauty so far away and so foreign and so old. It was one of those moments impossible to transmit to another mind. A moment of overpowering beauty, of the surge of a marching world, of the relentlessness of our own fate. It made you want to cry."[114]

He was torn. Part of Ernie wanted to stay in Italy, to see the campaign through to the end. "In a way," he wrote to Jerry, "I hate to leave this theater—I've been with it so long and feel so much a part of it that I almost feel like a deserter at leaving."[115] The other part of him—the more vocal part—knew it was time to leave. There were other beaches to storm, new villages to liberate, more young men to bury. "Don't worry about me," Ernie wrote in the final line of a letter to his father on April 14, "for I'll be in no danger now for awhile."[116]

CHAPTER 8

WALKING THE LONG THIN
LINE OF PERSONAL ANGUISH

••• ••• ▬▬▬▬▬ ••• •••

Now that it is over it seems to me a pure miracle that we ever took the beach at all. For some of our units it was easy, but this special sector where I am now our troops faced such odds that our getting ashore was like my whipping Joe Louis down to a pulp.

ERNIE PYLE, "A PURE MIRACLE," JUNE 12, 1944[1]

1

Most of the men in the first wave never stood a chance. In the predawn darkness of June 6, 1944, thousands of American soldiers crawled down swaying cargo nets and thudded into wooden-hulled landing craft bound for the Norman coast. Once their shoebox of a boat chugged away from its mother ship, the young men's senses were choked with the smells of wet canvas gear, bitter seawater mixed with chunky vomit,[2] and acrid clouds of powder from hundreds of huge naval guns erupting close over their heads.[3]

As the first wave of landing craft drew close to shore, the deafening roar stopped, quickly replaced by German artillery rounds crashing into the pewter-colored water all around them. The flesh under the men's sea-soaked uniforms prickled. That many of them would die was a matter of necessity. Which of them would die, exactly, was a matter of circumstance—and they knew it. So, they waited, barely daring to breathe.

Ten to fifteen stories in height, the bluffs ran the length of the beach and ended with massive cliffs on the Americans' right flank. The Germans could not have asked for a more favorable topography on which to mount their defenses. Behind a blanket of smoke and dust, nearly two thousand German defenders hid from the men's view atop the heavily fortified bluffs above the beach. From eight massive concrete bunkers and thirty-five smaller pillboxes, the Germans would concentrate their fire on the five draws (or "exits") that rose steeply from the beaches to three Norman villages strung along the bluffs. German infantrymen manned trenches at the lower end of the bluffs, halfway up, and at the top. Also scattered along the slopes of these draws were hundreds of what the Germans called "tobruks," which were concrete-lined holes large enough for a mortar pit (there were six of those), a machine-gun team, or even the turret of a tank.[4] In addition, four open field positions for German artillery, eighteen antitank-gun pits, forty rocket-launching sites, and at least eighty-five machine-gun nests[5] had been constructed by French slave labor.

If the Germans were going to toss the Allies back into the sea, they needed to transform the five miles of pancake-flat beach at Omaha into a corpse-clogged shooting gallery.[6] Hunched behind a machine gun in a nest guarding the beach exit below the village of Colleville, a twenty-one-year-old German corporal named Hein Severloh repeated in his head the strict order passed down that morning: "Hold your fire until the enemy is coming up the waterline."[7]

"They must be crazy," a German sergeant named Krone said to no one in particular. "Are they going to swim ashore? Right under our muzzles?"[8]

As soon as the steel landing ramps of the first wave of boats slapped down into the surf all along the beach, a catastrophic hail of gunfire erupted from German guns hidden in the bluffs. The ensuing slaughter, as Rommel had foretold, was merciless. "We hit the sandbar," one soldier recalled after the war, "dropped the ramp, and then all hell poured loose on us. The soldiers in the boat received a hail of machine-gun bullets." In another lead boat, every one of the three dozen soldiers aboard were killed before their ramp lowered even an inch. "It just vaporized," the veteran continued. "No one ever learned whether it was the result of hitting a mine" or if German artillery had struck a direct hit.[9]

Another German soldier manning a machine gun, a teenager named Franz Gockel, remembered a temporary lull between the first and second waves of soldiers. "Again we opened fire," he said after the war. "The beach became strewn with dead, wounded and shelter-seeking soldiers. They reached the low stone wall, but the safety offered there was temporary. Our mortar crews had waited for this moment and began to lay deadly fire on present coordinates along the sea wall. Mortar rounds with impact fuses exploded on target. The shell splinters, wall fragments, and stones inflicted severe casualties. The waves of attackers broke against our defenses."[10]

But the Americans kept landing, wave after wave, and by midday, some five thousand soldiers[11] had crossed the sandy killing ground, moving single file across the stretch of mine-laden marsh below the bluffs[12] and up through thick smoke cover to drive the Germans from their defensive entrenchments below the beach exits near Saint-Laurent-sur-Mer and to the east of Colleville-sur-Mer.[13] By the end of D-Day, the most intense fighting had moved at least a mile inland.[14] For their heroism on Omaha Beach, 153 men would receive the Distinguished Service Cross, the American military's second-highest honor.[15] In the biggest and most complicated amphibious operation in military history, it wasn't the bombs, artillery, or tanks that overwhelmed the Germans; it was men—many of them boys, really— slogging up the beaches and crawling over the corpses of their friends that won the Allies a toehold at the western edge of Europe.[16]

2

Four days after he left Italy,[17] Ernie arrived safely in London dressed like some freedom fighter who had outfitted himself with castoffs from the battlefield. His jacket was British and his olive-drab wool trousers

American. He had no pinks to strut around town in, and his dark leather boots matched those of the infantrymen. For twenty-five bucks, Ernie bought himself an American army officer's uniform so he could avoid getting picked up by the military police for not looking the part.[18]

Ernie waited for nearly two months in England for the invasion of Europe to finally begin. During that time, his feelings vacillated from bad to worse. At times he felt overwhelmed with invitations and requests. The UK's Foreign Office wanted to interview him about his "views" on the Mediterranean campaign. Two men from what Ernie called the "Special Services" paid him a visit one day asking if he could write a "certain piece" for the army newspaper *Stars and Stripes.* To Lee he reported that the two gentlemen had "put it in a way I just couldn't turn down."[19] Before long, Ernie made himself a blanket policy—which he relayed to Lee back in Washington—to turn down all requests, except those made by the army. It was all too much for him.

Ernie had been so close to the high tension and mass suffering of war for so long that he no longer felt he could adjust to normal people, in normal places. He was "very allergic to raids," he told Lee, and "can hardly get my breath when the guns start." At other times, Ernie felt a numb sense of disappointment, like when he heard from Moran about her drunk driving accident. "I'm afraid Moran, like all the rest of us," Ernie wrote to Lee, "is a little psychopathic." Or when he dug through a pile of mail waiting for him in London and found a "rather pathetic note" from Jerry that Jerry's sister Poe had enclosed in a letter of her own. The note said nothing, he told Lee, "outside of pretending that she would soon be allright and back on the job. She apparently was in some dreadful shape. I'm afraid there's little hope."[20]

During those tense and busy days in the late spring of 1944, Ernie left the city whenever he could to spend time with the troops out in the field. When back in the city, he'd hole up in his room and peck out columns and letters home to build his cushion back up and assure his loved ones he was fine, all things considered.[21] All that writing was made a bit easier by a farewell bottle of bourbon a general in Italy had given him and the two dozen duck eggs a friend brought him from Ireland, which Ernie cooked up right in his room.[22]

When he wasn't writing or scrambling eggs for breakfast, Ernie dined in high-end restaurants with the likes of Edward R. Murrow, the American broadcast journalist whom Ernie always "liked very much";[23] endured the stabs of required inoculations—followed by, unsurprisingly, at least a day or two of recovery in a "little postage-stamp" room at the Dorchester;[24] and chain-smoked through military briefings on the Allied invasion plans.[25]

Even though he wasn't sure when he'd get home next,[26] there was no need to fret about his safety, Ernie wrote to Jerry several times in the lead-up to the invasion. "I'll not be going over till things are well established," he wrote, "and I'll be in no danger so you mustn't worry about me."[27] At the end of April, despite a growing sense of dread,[28] he wrote again, urging Jerry not to lose heart. "Darling," he wrote, "it's true that everybody has a normal chance of something happening to him, but actually with me it's very slight, and I am as careful as I can be."[29]

3

Late one afternoon, Ernie and friends were tying one on in the crowded bar of Ernie's hotel. One of those friends, a well-known theater critic by the name of John Mason Brown, would later remember Ernie "looked made over" that day. The color had returned to his face—"red meat and rest," Ernie explained. As happened so often wherever American men in uniform congregated, two young pilots spotted Ernie and leaned over from their nearby perches. "Isn't that Ernie Pyle?" one of them whispered to John. When John nodded, the pilot nudged his friend to grab his attention. "The two of them were as excited as if they had just completed a successful mission over Berchtesgaden," Ernie's friend wrote.[30]

The two pilots introduced themselves as Lindsey Greene of San Francisco and Jack Arnold of East St. Louis, Illinois. Arnold's friends called him "Red Dog," mostly because of his ginger locks,[31] but also because, according to his crew, Arnold wasn't afraid of anything.[32] The two tables got to talking, and after a couple of rounds of drinks, they all decided to leave together, not quite ready to call it a night. Outside the pub, the damp night air was steeped in heavy smells—cheap coal and old woodsmoke.[33] "We adjourned from one place to another," Ernie wrote, "as Damon Runyon would say, and kept on adjourning throughout the evening, and a good time was had by all."[34] Above their heads, beams of light shining up from searchlights raked the sky, searching for German bombers. Even though the fantastic raids by hundreds of bombers had come to an end, most nights a few planes, here and there, still flew over to "keep alive the threat of death," as one army historian put it.[35] Below their feet, hundreds of Londoners with terror left over from 1940 on their pinched faces sheltered from the threat of German bombs in the confines of the fetid Tube.[36]

At some point in the night, Arnold asked Ernie whether he wouldn't want to come visit him and his crew, maybe even come up on a bombing mission with them. Being nothing if not accommodating, Ernie agreed to pay their airdrome a visit, though he had no intention of tagging along on a bombing mission—"I told them I was allergic to missions," he told Jerry.[37] Still, he was curious to learn more about what it was like to be a member of a B-26 crew, flying near-daily missions over enemy-held territory. That, and he had had all he could take of city life, with all its official duties, friendly obligations, and noisome intrusions. Dozens of letters arrived each day. Ernie couldn't answer even half of them and figured at least a third demanded "some kind of attention."

All the nervous tension that came with being so easily reachable in the city and having to please so many masters was taking its toll. In addition to "crossed and blurry" eyes, Ernie's stomach seemed to have "started to go to hell in a mild way," he told Lee. "For several days I've had queer pains in it and now and then feel nauseated." After all those years of drinking, Ernie figured maybe he was developing an ulcer, as Jerry had when Ernie was reporting from Canada before the war.[38] Ernie was still optimistic, though, that once the invasion began, he could get out with the troops, and the deadly simplicity of life at the front would render moot all the pressure

Ernie's type of fame brought with it. He also had no illusions that the war and all the obligations and expectations that came with it were going to end anytime soon. His plan regardless, he told Lee, was to travel to India and China over the winter and return to London for the spring of 1945—if the fighting hadn't ended by then.[39]

On May 2, Ernie left London and made his way northeast to Earls Colne, west of Colchester, to the airdrome where Arnold and his crew were stationed.[40] What seemed like miles of green-painted steel huts and low concrete barracks blended almost seamlessly into the bucolic English landscape. The countless structures were spread throughout an old grove of giant elms and chestnut trees. When Ernie walked from one barracks to another, under the shade of such big-trunked and wide-branched behemoths, searching for Arnold, it gave him a feeling of peace and contentment. He hadn't felt that way in he didn't know how long, and as he finally spotted that red mop of hair atop Arnold's pale head, he knew he might never feel that way again.[41]

"Red Dog" Arnold was twenty-two years old, though he seemed older to Ernie. He was friendly yet serious. When he joined the army right out of high school, he had started off as an infantryman, but after a year and a half, his higher-ups decided he'd be of better use as an officer in the Army Air Corps. When Ernie met him in April 1944, Arnold had been in the service for four years and was making a living as a bombardier on a B-26 Marauder tactical bomber in the Ninth Air Force.[42] Their mission, Arnold explained to Ernie, was threefold. First, they needed to rid upper France and the Low Countries of German fighter planes to clear the path for heavy bombers on their way to Germany.[43] They accomplished this by laying waste to German factories, especially those tasked with producing plane engines and propellers. *Can't fly without those!* Second, to prepare the way for an eventual land invasion of France, the bombers targeted railroad marshaling yards and disrupted Germany's ability to resupply their western front by leveling rail yards, repair shops, bridges, signal systems, switches, and rolling stock.[44] In May 1944 alone, Allied planes taking off from Britain dropped seventy-six thousand tons of high explosives on railway targets—over four times more than they had dropped in May 1943.[45] According to historian Stephen E. Ambrose, "Some 1,700 locomotives and 25,000 wagons had been destroyed or put out of action, which sounded impressive, but which constituted only 13 percent and 8 percent respectively of the pre-raid figures." In many cases, Ambrose continued, the Germans were able to clear damaged equipment and reopen the destroyed rail lines within a day or so.[46] Still, according to German generals after the war, there was a "strong belief" that "various air attacks were ruinous to their counter-offensive plans" after the invasion began.[47]

Such destruction also came at a heavy human cost.[48] Despite the Allies' dropping warning leaflets from planes before each bombing raid, many French civilians had no idea how much danger they were in during the lead-up to the invasion.[49] Around fifteen thousand would die before an American soldier ever set foot on the beaches of Normandy.[50] Many thousands more lost their homes and nearly everything else they owned, too. Such "collateral damage" was caused mostly by inaccuracy on the part of the bombers. Even in ideal conditions, only about half of all the bombs they dropped landed within a quarter mile of their intended targets.[51]

Third, and most important to Ernie and the thousands of soldiers who would someday soon land somewhere on the western coast of France, the B-26s had been entrusted with crippling, if not destroying, the infamous Atlantic Wall Hitler had built to repel an Allied invasion. Given the enormous strategic importance of this endeavor, Hitler dispatched arguably his most brilliant field commander, the "Desert Fox" himself, Erwin Rommel, to oversee the construction of fortifications from Spain to the Arctic. An Allied invasion would most likely take place, Hitler came to believe, at the Pas-de-Calais, where the English Channel was at its narrowest. It was also a much straighter line from the port city of Calais to the industrial heartland of Germany, and ultimately, to Berlin. By the spring of 1944, Calais became, according to Ambrose, "by far the strongest fortified portion" of the Channel coast. "It was there that the Atlantic Wall came closest to what German propaganda claimed it was, an impregnable fortress."[52] Hitler believed that if the Germans were able to repel an Allied invasion at Calais, that would knock the British and the Americans out of the war—at least for as long as it took them to lick their wounds and mount another offensive somewhere else. With the western front no longer at great risk, Hitler could concentrate his armies in the east against the Soviets.[53]

Upon first visiting the Normandy coast in January 1944, Rommel parroted his Führer's convictions: "The war will be won or lost on the beaches. We'll have only one chance to stop the enemy and that's while he's in the water, struggling to get ashore." He knew the first twenty-four hours of the invasion would decide the fate of Germany. "For the Allies, as well as Germany," he continued, "it will be the longest day."[54]

Arnold and his squadron tried to assure Ernie they were getting the job done, regardless of whatever the Germans did to steel themselves against the impending invasion. "I told them if they hadn't," Ernie wrote, "I was going to be plenty sore at them some fine day, because I might be in the vicinity and if there was anything that made me sick at the stomach it was an enemy military installation in good working order."[55]

None of the fliers in Arnold's crew could put into words what they were fighting for, exactly, but they knew it had to be done, Ernie told his readers. "The boys didn't especially hate the Germans," he continued, "and they certainly didn't like the war, yet they understood that the only way out of the war was to fight our way out."[56] They did it willingly, Ernie concluded, and "with spirit." Arnold was the best example of this. "He figured that as a bombardier," Ernie wrote in his column, "he had killed thousands of Germans, and he thought it was an excellent profession." His "finest bombing experience," Arnold confided in Ernie, had been the time he missed his intended target and accidentally dropped his plane's payload on a barracks building full of German soldiers. Hundreds of them were killed.[57] It was the happiest accident of Arnold's young and deadly serious life.

After only a few days at the airdrome, where "nobody harassed you all the time," the vague pains in Ernie's stomach[58] disappeared and he felt fine once again. His eyes went back to normal, too. But still, Ernie was lonely. "It's the loneliness of being surrounded by people," he explained in a letter to Jerry, "when I'd really like them to be different people in a different place."[59]

4

It's not clear how Ernie ended up getting assigned to cover the invasion. At one point he explained it to Jerry this way: "I truly did plan to go slow on this one—not to come over for two or three weeks, after things were well established. But what happened was this—a certain very important general let it be known informally that I and one other correspondent were very acceptable to go with him." Turning down this invitation from General Omar Bradley would be akin to turning down an invitation for dinner at the White House from FDR himself. He simply couldn't refuse.[60] But in a cryptically worded May 1 letter, Lee wrote to Ernie, "Your friend, who shall be nameless, phoned from New York day before yesterday about your plans." Lee wasn't happy about Ernie's decision to turn down the general and ride with the infantry instead, regardless of how it was reached. But he knew it was hopeless to try to talk Ernie out of it. "I don't know what in the hell I can do about it," he confessed, "except to hope for the best."[61] Ernie wasn't happy, either. The thought of waiting offshore with General Bradley as the troops landed on the beaches was one he didn't relish. "It was really, to me, worse than the thought of going ashore on D-Day," he told Jerry. Once it was decided that Ernie would tag along with the invasion forces, he continued, "there was no way for me to let you know."[62]

On one occasion before the invasion, the war correspondents who would be participating in the initial landings gathered in the theater of a military club in central London.[63] "Of the 28 correspondents in the Assault Group about two-thirds had already seen action in various war theaters," Ernie reported, "people such as Bill Stoneman, Don Whitehead, Jack Thompson, Clark Lee, Tex O'Reilly and myself."[64] Never knowing how to say no to the army, Ernie resigned himself to a fate he was sure awaited him. "I stayed up for a couple of nights with a hammer and saw," he wrote of finding out he'd be covering the invasion from the surf and sand. Ernie was "preparing a large box for myself," he joked, "with horseshoes tacked all over it."[65] Without their own lucky box, some other correspondents who had been

picked to cover the invasion got cold feet and "backed out of their assign-
ments at the last minute," Ernie reported back to Lee. "I guess all of us feel
that way, but there's nothing to do for it but to go on and go. I'll sure be glad
when the first month is over."[66]

A hush settled over the men as General Eisenhower strolled to a po-
dium at the front of the theater. "I've been informed by the newspapers that
an operation is pending," he began. The newspapermen chuckled respect-
fully, the way staff officers do. "Our countries fight best when our people
are best informed," the Supreme Allied Commander continued. "You will
be allowed to report everything possible, consistent, of course, with military security. I will never tell you anything false." To prove his sincerity,
Eisenhower leveled with the men. He had no illusions as to the magnitude
of the task that lay before them. "It will be no basket of roses," he said.[67]

Reports from the French underground and Allied reconnaissance
photos showed how formidable the German defenses along the Normandy
coast had become, the general continued.[68] Based on an elaborate formula
known as Love's Tables, Eisenhower told Ernie and the other correspondents that he expected D-Day to cost the Allies about 12 percent casualties—
or almost nineteen thousand men. Ernie's favorite division—the First
Infantry—had been picked to land first on a flat, sandy beach, code-named
Omaha, because of their ferocious fighting spirit, which Ernie had told
America all about during the North African campaign. Under "maximum
conditions" on the invasion beaches, as Eisenhower described the worst-
case scenario, the First Infantry Division would likely lose a quarter of its
men on the first day alone.[69]

5

The sand-strewn parking lot near the metal wings of the memorial
sculpture Les Braves, on Omaha Beach, was empty when my friend
Jennifer and I arrived in my rental car a little before eleven o'clock in the
morning. The first week in December, as it turns out, is a fantastic time to

visit Normandy if, like Ernie, you're not such a fan of crowds. Many of the D-Day-related museums and attractions, especially the smaller, more niche ones, are closed during the winter months, though plenty more remain open and are not too crowded.

I first came into contact with Jennifer Orth-Veillon, my Franco-American friend, who teaches at the university in Lyon, back in 2016, when I was teaching a writing seminar for student veterans, many fresh from tours in Afghanistan, at the University of Wisconsin–Stevens Point. That year, unbeknown to each other, Jennifer and I each began projects related to the First World War. She was hired to curate the United States World War I Centennial Commission's WWrite Blog, which explored the war's lasting impact. As for me, my university's archives partnered with the surrounding county's historical society to draw the community's attention to a trove of letters written home by local soldiers on the western front in France that the university had archived. Over the course of a semester, my students read every one of the hundreds of letters, noting any information they found particularly interesting or noteworthy—especially if anything they read reminded them of their own experiences in Iraq and Afghanistan or elsewhere. The letters did not disappoint.

The first time Jennifer and I met in person was at a war writers' conference hosted at the U.S. Air Force Academy, north of Colorado Springs, in the fall of 2018. We bonded that weekend over our shared academic training in the history of the Holocaust and in the fact that both of us were researching and writing about what our respective grandfathers had experienced during the war and how they had lived when they came home. Jennifer's grandfather, a physician who served across western Europe and helped liberate concentration camps, turned to alcohol after the war to help deal with what he had experienced, as my grandfather had. Neither of our grandfathers was talkative when it came to their wars, though Jennifer's at least kept correspondence and other primary sources of information that she'd used to round out the picture of him in her mind.

A pall of smoky gray clouds hung above the bluffs and beach to our west and north on that late December morning in 2021. The strong, swirling tides of Omaha Beach were high that time of day, shifting the contours of the tabletop-flat coastline as they rolled in and out. The sounds I can re-member from the D-Day scene at the beginning of *Saving Private Ryan*—the rips and thuds of whizzing German bullets, chest-thumping explosions, heavy splashes, shouts for a medic, hushed prayers, and screams of agony—had been replaced by the steady lapping of waves, stiff winds, the squish and rub of sand beneath our soles, an occasional gull, and our own hushed voices.

6

On April 9, Liz Shaffer sent a letter to Lee Miller. She was terribly con-cerned about Jerry, she wrote—Sister Margaret Jane was, too. Not long after Jerry had been checked into one of the cottages on the grounds outside of St. Joseph's Hospital[70] in Albuquerque, Liz went to visit and was "both shocked and puzzled." Jerry's spirits had completely collapsed, the result, Sister thought, of her "driving herself beyond her capacity" at work. "She was terribly weak, physically," Liz reported to Lee, "and I have never seen such apathy in anyone."[71] To Liz it seemed as if Jerry wasn't so much depressed as she was apathetically resigned to the fact that Ernie probably wouldn't make it back home from the war. There was no point in hoping for the best; it was time to rehearse for the worst.

Jerry returned home for most of the month of February. She would later tell Ernie she had no memory of the month of January. Somehow, Sis-ter Margaret Jane managed to take care of an emaciated and mentally un-healthy Jerry at her and Ernie's home while also managing to run a hospital during a time in which there was a shortage of doctors because of the war. For about a month, Sister kept it all together, hoping she could eventually convince Jerry to return to the hospital's cottages. Sister always was given to optimism.[72] Sister finally got through to her, but then Jerry's sister Poe drove down from Denver and brought Jerry home with her so that she could be treated by Dr. Richards instead. When Jerry returned to Albuquerque in

mid-March, Liz thought she seemed "wonderfully better, really like herself again."

One Friday toward the end of March, Jerry was granted permission to
return to her house so that she could supervise a cleaning woman. The plan
was for Jerry to return to the hospital grounds once the cleaning woman
had finished her work, but in the late afternoon, Jerry called Liz to tell her
that while she would definitely return to the cottages, it wouldn't be that
day. "I realized from her voice that she had been drinking quite a lot," Liz
wrote to Lee. Jerry "did a lot of drinking that weekend, not going back to
the hospital until Tuesday morning."

"I can't stress too strongly," Liz wrote, "that I think, and Sister thinks,
that there is a lot more involved than just drinking will account for." What
exactly? Liz couldn't be sure, though she told Lee that she and Sister believed Jerry was going to "crack up completely or else gradually drift to a
point where she is beyond the reach of anyone."[73]

The main reason for Liz's letter, it seems—besides updating Lee on
Jerry's condition—was to let him know they were going to need more money
for Jerry's treatment. At the beginning of April, Dr. McLin, another doctor
from the Lovelace Clinic in Albuquerque, proposed a new, monthslong
course of treatment. "I think the idea," wrote Liz, "is to try to build her up
to the point where she will be able to stand some shock treatments." None
of that was cheap. "Although the sanitarium is somewhat more expensive than the cottage," Liz wrote, the largest expense would be for the
three round-the-clock nurses Jerry needed, the "various shots" the doctor
wanted to give her to help rebuild her lost strength, and the eventual shock
therapy.

Liz asked Lee not to tell Ernie what bad shape Jerry was in that spring.
She and Sister didn't want to worry Ernie and distract him from his work,
and besides, Liz continued, "there is nothing to indicate, from the effect
that the interlude last fall had, that his coming home would do anything
good." Liz also feared what Jerry might think if she knew Liz had gone behind her back to Ernie. "From the attitude she took when we notified him
of her first illness," Liz reminded Lee, "she would completely resent his

being told and be only more upset."[74] Three days after Liz mailed her letter, on April 12, Lee wrote to Ernie with news that Jerry's doctor was planning to administer a "series of special hospital treatments" and that Jerry was "showing an encouraging determination to do something about herself."[75]

At the end of April, Ernie wrote a long letter to Jerry in which he confided in her that he was sick of the war, wanted desperately to come home, but also knew that he couldn't—not yet, anyway. "I've been a part of the misery and tragedy of it for so long that I've come to feel a responsibility to it or something. I don't quite know how to put it into words, but I feel if I left it, it would be like a soldier deserting."[76]At the same time, Ernie was heartened by the assurances Dr. McLin expressed to Liz regarding Jerry's treatments. "Somehow," he wrote to Lee, "I have to hope that some good will come out of it."[77]

But still he dreamt of home and a future in which he and Jerry could finally be together. Ernie wanted to build another house, this time far off in some untouched land that wasn't Albuquerque. He wanted lots of "wild and unplanned land around us," he told Jerry, where he could sit and relax, which was all he seemed to want to do after the war. Albuquerque wasn't going to cut it. Aside from being built at the wrong altitude, which Ernie blamed for the tension he felt to stay busy whenever he was home, their little white house on Girard Boulevard would never, Ernie knew, be secluded enough to grant him the peace he so desperately desired. "Especially with this fame or whatever you call it that has grown up," Ernie wrote to Jerry, "it would be utterly impossible for us ever to live on a street or be accessible." Jerry agreed. Perhaps Southern California, nearer to Paige and his wife, would be best, Ernie thought. "We could have the mountains and the desert and isolation, and still be close to things." There was no rush to decide, Ernie concluded, because "there can be no building until after the war anyhow, so we've got lots of time to think about it."[78]

Jerry returned home from the sanitarium on May 8. One nurse stayed with her from seven o'clock in the morning until three o'clock in the afternoon, and another stayed with her from then until eleven at night.[79] From around 8:00 a.m. until lunchtime, Jerry and the first-shift nurse liked to go on walks together[80] and work in the yard and around the house. Jerry planted lots of flowers that spring, proof that "her outlook is improving," Sister Margaret Jane reported to Lee.[81] In the afternoon, Jerry was supposed to "officially relax" for a few hours.[82] And while Sister maintained that Jerry was not yet well, she was making progress. "She is absolutely off liquor and aside from one bad spree she has had very little to drink since the first of February."[83]

7

A couple of weeks after Ernie arrived in London, he set out for an army hospital up in the Midlands of England, where the architect who designed his and Jerry's house in Albuquerque—"Little Arthur" McCollum—was stationed. Little Arthur had written to Ernie with a plea for a visit. He had been saving a bottle of bourbon for eight months, and a visit from Ernie would certainly be considered a special enough occasion to finally imbibe.[84] Several months before Ernie arrived back in London, Little Arthur's son, Ross, had been listed as missing in action when the bomber he was flying over Germany was shot down. Months had passed without a word. Nothing from the Red Cross reporting that he'd been imprisoned by the Germans. Nothing. At first, Little Arthur crumbled. "He said he was lower than anybody would ever know for a couple of months," Ernie reported back to Jerry. But then, somehow, Little Arthur found some way to compartmentalize his agony and despair, in the face of all the evidence that Ross had been killed. "He looked and acted perfectly normal and fine," Ernie said of Little Arthur. "He is quite hopeful for Ross, but after hearing the details it doesn't look very good to me."[85]

Ernie and Little Arthur made short work of the bourbon. It was a Saturday, the twenty-second of April, and Ernie felt a wave of relief as his experience of London receded. The snowed-under and confused feelings he'd been carrying around his neck melted as the simplicity of life in the field came into view.[86] "We both got pissy-assed," he confided to Paige. After they finished the bourbon, they scrounged a bottle of gin. While they were in the deepest depths of their drunkenness, Ernie and Little Arthur opened up to each other. Both men were grieving: Little Arthur a son; Ernie a wife. And once they'd finished pouring themselves out, they changed the subject to less vulnerable, more "electrifying" topics, such as how nice it would be to sleep with some women they knew back in Albuquerque. "We succeeded in embarrassing the commandant and losing Mac's overcoat," Ernie continued to Paige, "and it took me two days to get normal, so the party was a success."[87]

A few days after he returned from his visit with Little Arthur, Don Whitehead rang Ernie in his hotel room at the Dorchester. It was about ten o'clock in the morning. "You've won the Pulitzer!" he blurted out. Ernie thought Don was kidding him. The Pulitzer was for *serious* newspapermen— not human-interest columnists like him. The year before, Hanson Weightman Baldwin had been awarded the Pulitzer for correspondence. He was the longtime military editor for *The New York Times* and earned his prize for his coverage of the early days of World War II from Guadalcanal and the western Pacific. Because he didn't think it was for folks like him, Ernie didn't think he would care so much about the prize, but in fact he was really quite touched. "I feel mighty good about it," he confided in Lee, "for I truly didn't expect it. I've got fairly dulled to accolades, but when Don told me I damn near started to cry."[88]

By the end of May 1944, Ernie was more famous than any other war correspondent in American history. Over the span of a few days, he was awarded the Pulitzer, a memorial award named for Ray Clapper, and the Outstanding Hoosier Award. "So many clippings and awards and plaudits and things are rolling in," he wrote to Jerry, "that I feel almost ashamed."[89] Ernie's edited collection of columns from North Africa, *Here Is Your War*, was still in the top five of bestselling books a year after it was published, according to both *The New York Times* and the *New York Herald Tribune*.[90] The book had made $80,000 for Ernie by December 1943, he bragged to

Paige, and that was after only half the sales returns had been tabulated.[91] (That's about $1.3 million in 2022 dollars.) His publisher was also considering putting together another collection, this one to include his best work from Sicily, Italy, and France, and a third book for whatever was after that.[92]

Everybody, it seemed, wanted Pyle. His column ran in all but two of the biggest one hundred cities in America (only Omaha and Spokane hadn't yet jumped on the Pyle bandwagon). A few weeks before D-Day, Lee wrote to Ernie: "Orders for the column continue to drift in; three new ones yesterday—Mobile Press Register, Minot (N.D.) Daily News and Okmulgee Times." He wasn't sure the exact number, but Lee figured Ernie's column was running six days per week in close to five hundred newspapers around the country—including the weeklies that were covered in a deal Scripps-Howard struck with the Western Newspaper Union.[93] After much back-and-forth during which many noteworthy names were bandied about, actor turned soldier Burgess Meredith was granted leave from the army long enough to play the title role in *Ernie Pyle's Story of G.I. Joe*. A young Robert Mitchum was cast as "Captain Bill Walker," a beloved officer who is killed on a mountainside in Italy.[94] Mitchum's portrayal of a character who was essentially Captain Waskow would earn him an Academy Award nomination for Best Supporting Actor.

Ernie didn't find that it got to his head. What was the point of being the greatest at something that was probably going to kill you? What matter did it make how much money he made if he'd never be around to enjoy its fruits? "I've been fighting the deadline so close," he explained to Paige, "and holding tense against all the intrusions and petty details so much that I'm all tied up in knots in the back of my neck." Add to that the desperate hopelessness he felt for Jerry in the back of his mind. "Jerry has left the hospital," he continued. "I'm not working up too much hope for the long run," he confessed. In the meantime, he told Paige, "All I do is drink and work and wait." He was sorry he couldn't write a funny letter with the invasion coming up, but "I don't feel very funny right now," he confessed. "I just feel tired and sleepy." Throughout their friendship, Ernie would often close out his letters to Paige with some ironic or silly or off-color signature. For his

May 26, 1944, letter to Paige—the last he would write before the invasion—Ernie took a decidedly more confessional tact, signing off as Ernest Taylor Pyle, "The Unhappy Warrior."[95]

8

On Monday, May 22,[96] Ernie dined with Don Whitehead, Duke Shoop of *The Kansas City Star*, and Gordon Gammack, a staff writer for the *Des Moines Tribune*. It's not clear who came up with the ruse, but somehow the restaurant manager, his wife, and all his staff were conned into believing Ernie was Dr. Ernest T. Pyle, an allegedly famous American professor of psychology. Ernie's friends came up with decoy stories to complement Ernie's. Even though they weren't that much younger than the graying Pyle, Ernie's pals pretended they were three of his prized pupils. This last dinner, they explained to their hosts, was a reunion of sorts. That part, at least, was true.

To help the old friends celebrate such a joyous occasion, the restaurant manager made sure the men had the best of everything—no "austerity bread," made with a soft breath of sawdust, or "victory coffee," brewed from acorns.[97] At one point in the festivities, Ernie turned serious, expressing a deep fear that he wouldn't live long enough to see a world without war. "I have an awful feeling that I won't live through this one," he confessed that night. "It's a terrible feeling. I can't sleep, and it is like a constant weight, night and day."[98]

Ernie, Don, Duke, and Gordon were supposed to meet up again the next morning so Ernie could take them on a tour of Kensington Gardens. Instead, the following day Ernie, Don, and the other twenty-six correspondents[99] received the call they had been waiting for.[100]

The army said it was going to give the correspondents at least a day's notice before they were to leave London, but when Ernie's hotel phone rang at nine o'clock that fateful morning, he was told he had ninety minutes to meet at a "certain place" with all his field gear packed and ready to go. "As we arrived one by one at the appointed place," Ernie wrote, "we looked both knowingly and sheepishly at each other."[101] While his room at the Dorchester continued running up a bill, Ernie set out to witness and report on the largest amphibious landing in the history of warfare.[102]

"Tell me, Mr. Pyle," Bill Stoneman asked Ernie as the two waited at that "certain place" for a departure into the unknown, "How does it feel to be an assault correspondent?"

Bill was holding a pencil and a notebook, fully committed to act out the entire scene with him.

"It feels awful," Ernie replied.[103] Bill was being sardonic; Ernie was as serious as he'd ever been about anything.

The Allied armada poised for the invasion of France numbered nearly seven thousand destroyers, cruisers, battleships, and minesweepers—all dark-turreted and gray hulled.[104] They filled every berth in every English port from Felixstowe on the North Sea to Milford Haven in Wales, with others moored in the Humber, the Clyde, and Belfast Lough.[105] "As far as you could see in every direction," Ernie wrote, "the ocean was infested with ships."[106]

Ernie was supposed to have boarded the USS *Augusta*, General Bradley's headquarters ship.[107] But when he reached Falmouth Harbor,[108] south of London, he discovered there had been some kind of mix-up in arrangements and he had been assigned to bunk with an army colonel aboard an LST,[109] a flat-bottomed ship designed to transport tanks.[110] By the time Ernie reached the ship, it was already nearly loaded with trucks, armored cars, and soldiers, with its ramp down in the water, several yards from the shore. "Being an old campaigner," Ernie waded aboard with a heart heavy with dread,[111] soaking his feet, as the officer in line behind him yelled up at the deck, "Hey, tell the captain to move the ship up closer."[112] While the men waited for the ship's ramp to lower onto dry ground, Ernie felt the weight of his field kit bag hanging at the end of his arm. Inside he had neatly packed eleven bottles of liquor he had squirreled away, an assortment of good-luck charms, his trusty Remington portable, spare bits of clothing, the sleeping bag Jerry had sent him, a few letters, and a notice of the Pulitzer Prize he'd been awarded.[113]

Ernie could feel the deep gnaw of the LST's screws churning the choppy Channel water as he steeled himself to the reality of going back to war. "Now you were committed," Ernie wrote of that moment. "It was too late to back out now, even if your heart failed you."[114]

9

Dressed for winter and prepared for rain, Jennifer strolled ahead of me along the "Easy Red" section of Omaha Beach, which the troops later renamed "Bloody Red." I followed perfect imprints made by her rain boots in the moist sand for a spell, my eyes trained downward, trying to come to terms with the scale of the fighting and the dying that took place on that shore all those decades ago.

"Dave! Hey, Dave!" Jennifer shouted over the wind. "Come check this out!"

She was kneeling down when I caught up to her. She swiped a curly brown strand of hair out of her face and tucked it behind her ear, and with the other, still gloved, she poked a Baltic blue and translucent blob nestled in the packed sand. It was a blue jellyfish.

"Ernie wrote about seeing jellyfish washed up on the shore the day after the invasion," I said. "He wrote there were millions of them.

"Did you know that Juno Beach was almost code-named 'Jelly Beach'?" I asked. Jennifer looked at me with a skeptical side-eye. "It's true," I protested. "The American beaches were named after places—Omaha and Utah—and the other beaches were going to be named after fish—Gold Beach came from goldfish, Sword Beach from swordfish, but then instead of calling it Jelly Beach, which Churchill thought was undignified, they renamed it Juno, after the wife of a Canadian officer."

We also spied evidence of modern life common to any coastal region, washed up above the high-water line, at the bottom of an angled wall of huge black boulders that separated the beach from a coastal road to Vierville. Tumbleweeds of blue and orange and green nylon fishing line and rope, a lonely blue rubber glove—the sort a fisherman on a commercial boat might use—discarded hospital masks, a soggy bandanna, and black plastic pots with slits carved in the sides and a hole drilled in the bottom. They looked like flowerpots to me, but then Jennifer pointed to markers out in the surf. The Normandy coastline was rich with oysters, mussels, and scallops, she explained. These were traps, washed up after breaking loose from some setup nearby.

At the end of the beach, we reached the concrete remnants of a mostly intact bunker that once guarded the Vierville beach exit the Americans needed to use to push off Omaha and into the hedgerow country beyond. Over eighty years of coastal weather seemed to have done more damage to the bunker than American firepower had. A marker nearby told the story in French and English of how the Allies eventually prevailed. On D-Day, it read: "The 88mm-anti-tank gun in front of you faced around thirty tanks that had landed on the beach. Despite suffering losses, the American tanks finally managed to destroy the gun that morning." With the big gun disabled, hundreds of infantrymen scaled the steep earthen banks beyond, where they could flank German gun emplacements along the top of the bluffs.

"You up for a little hike?" I asked with a grin. Jennifer pushed up the knit cap that had slid down her forehead, overshadowing her eyes. She looked up at me standing next to another, smaller bunker farther up the bluff from the Vierville exit. With one eye squinting into the partly cloudy sky, she gave me the look a mother gives when their child asks for ice cream on a hot summer day. It wasn't a no, but it wasn't a yes, either. "Come on," I urged. "It'll be fun."

10

On D-Day itself, Ernie was trapped offshore, still aboard ship. "Funny little things happen in a convoy," he explained to his readers. In the early-morning hours of D-Day, Ernie's ship veered off course because of engine trouble and was adrift in a section of the English Channel that hadn't been swept clear by Allied minesweepers.[115] Ernie was in bed when he heard the news from his bunkmate, an army colonel commanding the troops aboard the ship. The day before, the colonel had revealed the entire invasion plan to Ernie—"the secret the whole world had waited years to hear." The fighting onshore would be tough, the colonel admitted, and "our own part would be precarious."[116] The hope, of course, was to sustain as few casualties as possible—but there *would* be casualties, he said to Ernie.

"One engine has broken clear down," the colonel told Ernie after returning from the bridge, "and the other can only run at third speed." Instead of cruising with the ships in their convoy,[117] where they were supposed to be, their ship was steering straight, drifting west with the wind and tide.[118] "From a vague anticipatory dread," Ernie later wrote, "the invasion now turned into a horrible reality to me. In a matter of hours the holocaust of our own planning would swirl over us. No man could guarantee his own fate. It was almost too much for me. A feeling of utter desperation obsessed me throughout the night."[119]

Exhausted by all the uncertainty, Ernie dosed himself with seasickness pills[120] and drifted off to sleep around four o'clock that morning—and even then, "it was a sleep harassed and torn by an awful knowledge."[121] If they couldn't get the engines repaired in time, Ernie knew, they'd continue drifting until they ran aground on a hostile beach. If Ernie and the rest of the troops aboard were lucky, they'd spend the rest of the war in a German prison camp—if they didn't brush up against a mine or two first.

By dawn, when Ernie woke for good, the ship's engines had been repaired and were firing on all cylinders. The ship had steered back into mineless waters, though they had lost their spot in the column. As committed as he had been to cover the invasion from the beaches, Ernie wouldn't be going ashore until the morning after.[122]

"My devastating sense of fear and depression disappeared when we approached the beachhead," he confessed to his readers about that longest of days. "There was the old familiar crack and roar of big guns all around us, and the shore was a great brown haze of smoke and dust, and we knew that bombers would be over us that night. Yet all the haunting premonition, the soul-consuming dread, was gone."[123]

With a front-row seat to a "great military epic," Ernie stood at his ship's rail, balls of cotton stuffed in his long ears, and watched as salvo after salvo arched over his head and exploded on the beaches and bluffs. Hot air blasted against his face with each big gun's report. Before long, whatever view Ernie had of the German's defensive positions was enveloped by debris and clouds of smoking marsh grass.[124] Still unobscured from view were the hundreds of wooden shoeboxes full of first-wave assault troops leapfrogging past thirty-ton "swimming" Sherman tanks floundering in the gray waves.[125] All but two of twenty-nine tanks in one battalion sank to the bottom of the Channel; all but three in another sank as well.[126] Some of those tanks still rest beneath the waves to this day. With his tired eyes, Ernie traced red-hot .50-caliber bullets fired from the back of the landing craft as they stabbed through the smoke. "Occasionally a dead man floated face downward past us," Ernie reported without much emotion.[127] That was the closest he would come to death that day on Omaha Beach.

11

The weather was still too cold for Ernie on June 7, even though the winds had dropped, the skies had cleared, and the English Channel had calmed since the day before. Bundled up against the icy ocean spray, Ernie caught a ride to shore on a large pontoon barge with outboard engines the army called a Rhino. The first thing Ernie did after splashing onto the beach was search for his friends. "I went ashore in a jeep with Private William Bates Wescott," he wrote.[128] Wescott was a handsome, intelligent man—a salesman for a dairy farm in California before the war started.[129] It didn't take them long to find a small gaggle of correspondents, milling around a cluster of hastily dug foxholes.[130] They all looked exhausted in body and spirit. Their faces were unshaven, their eyes bloodshot. They moved, in Ernie's estimation, like elderly men with achy joints.[131] Ernie first picked out Jack Thompson's conspicuous beard from among all the two-day stubble. Jack sat on the edge of his foxhole, lacing up his paratrooper boots. In a hole kitty-corner to Jack's, Ernie found his dear friend Don Whitehead wrapped in an army-issue blanket, barefoot and seemingly asleep.[132]

"Get up, you lazy so-and-so," Ernie said with a smile.

With his eyes still closed, Don returned the smile. He would have known that gentle voice anywhere. But his eyes stayed shut. Overnight, under a blanket of red tracers and antiaircraft fire, Don couldn't find sleep, even though he had totally exhausted himself the day before, so he'd taken a sleeping tablet that forced his body to find rest.[133]

"I don't know why I'm alive at all," Don confessed after coming to later that morning. "For hours there on the beach the shells were so close they were throwing mud and rocks all over you." All the violence and death and dying all around him was so terrible, he confided in Ernie, that "after a while you didn't care whether you got hit or not."[134]

As he spoke, Don gathered whatever strength he could, and by the time he was finished, he was up and out of his foxhole, bent over a cardboard ration box, fishing for a cigarette. He pulled out an envelope of anti-seasickness tablets and threw them into a nearby bush with a flick of his wrist. "They ain't worth a damn," he said when he noticed Ernie watching him. Don stood, trying to pinch a cigarette from its pack. "I was sicker than hell while we were circling around in our landing craft waiting to come ashore." He lit the cigarette and took a long draw of its smoke. "Everybody was sick," Don said with a wince before exhaling. "Soldiers were lying on the floor of the LCVP, sick as dogs."[135]

"I think I have gone on one too many of these things," he continued between exhales. D-Day had been his sixth amphibious landing—four of which were "murderously tough," Ernie told his readers. "Not because of what might happen to me personally," Don explained, "but I've lost my perspective. It's like dreaming the same nightmare over and over again, and when you try to write you feel that you have written it all before. You can't think of any new or different words to say it with." Ernie knew only too well what Don was feeling in that moment.[136]

Most of the other correspondents had also pulled through all right, Ernie learned. "One had been killed," he wrote, "and one was supposed to have been lost on a sunken ship, but we didn't know who. One or two had been wounded. Three of our best friends had not been heard from at all, and it looked bad. They subsequently turned up safe." Safety was a relative term. "They had carried ashore only their typewriters and some K rations," he wrote. "They had gone two days without sleep, and then had slept on the ground without blankets, in wet clothes. But none of that mattered too much after what they had been through. They were in a sort of daze from the exhaustion and mental turmoil of battle. When anyone asked a question it would take them a few seconds to focus their thoughts and give an answer."[137]

Jack Thompson told Ernie, "You've never seen a beach like this before. Dead and wounded men were lying so thick you could hardly take a step. One officer was killed only two feet away from me."[138]

"War is so romantic," Ernie told his readers. But only if you're "far away from it."[139]

12

By the time the correspondents had finished catching up and fortifying themselves for another day of combat reporting, the clouds that had made it so difficult the day before for Allied bombers to take out the Germans' coastal defenses were beginning to burn away. The soldiers on the ground, fighting in the hedgerows around Omaha Beach, would go from freezing to baking in their gas-impregnated "skunk suits" beneath the early-summer sun.[140] Two of the three villages along the bluffs above Omaha Beach—Colleville-sur-Mer and Saint-Laurent-sur-Mer—had been cleared of

Germans[141] and reduced to mounds of smoldering wood beams and honey-combed stone. More than two thousand French civilians were killed on D-Day, mostly by the Allies' pre-invasion bombardment. "In the skeletons of churches, and collapsed cottages and beachside villas," writes historian Alex Kershaw, "villagers formed shocked groups and mourned their dead neighbors, not sure whether their liberators were about to be kicked back into the sea."[142]

For a couple of hours that first day on the beach, Ernie walked alone along the ragged line where the ocean meets the sand, his tired eyes trained downward. He was dressed in army coveralls a few sizes too large for him, like a "short scarecrow with too much feet," in the words of a combat historian who met Ernie on the beach that day.[143] Half-submerged tanks, disabled jeeps, and beached landing craft dotted the pitiful areas around the heavily defended beach exits.[144] When the tide was low, demolition men moved carefully and deliberately, blowing up thousands of wood pilings and iron barriers Rommel had decorated with mines and dug into the tidal flat.[145] Soldiers on armored bulldozers cleared patches of the beach near the seawall[146] while others paved open routes up and through the beach exits. Engineers erected signs to guide incoming landing craft, blew gaps in the Germans' nine-foot-tall antitank wall,[147] and organized supply dumps.[148] "Phase Number One," as Ernie termed it, "was the highly vital task of getting ashore at all," he explained a couple of weeks after D-Day. "We either had to break a hole in the beach defenses and have our men flowing through that hole within a few hours, or the jig was up."[149]

Above the high-water line, doctors in makeshift casualty clearing centers treated wounded men the best they could before they were loaded on empty landing crafts and sent to a hospital ship in the Channel for further treatment. Many wounded men died from shock and exposure during the night after the invasion began.[150] Those who weren't going to live were jabbed with morphine to numb the pain and given plasma to help keep them as warm as possible. Because there were so many casualties to treat, many grievously wounded men were "left alone to whatever fate would befall them," as British military historian Antony Beevor put it.[151] Outside the clearing centers, gloved grave-registration men laid waterlogged and bullet-ridden bodies in neat rows beneath wool blankets. "We all seemed in a trance," one man remembered, "removing dog tags and other morbid duties." German soldiers who had surrendered received double rations if they volunteered to dig graves for fallen Americans.[152] Many more uncollected bodies remained. They sprawled grotesquely, half hidden in the sand or by the high grass beyond the beach.[153]

Later that evening, right before sunset, Ernie and his driver left the bivouac area near the beachhead and set out for the front lines. It was dark by the time they found a grape and apple orchard on a hillside several miles from Omaha Beach. All along the route, bodies clogged the ditches between the narrow, sunken lanes and the thick hedgerows of tangled roots and raspberry bushes that lined the thousands of tiny farm fields. There were American and German bodies, Ernie noted, but they were "mostly German." Ernie later figured that by the end of June he'd seen upward of five hundred dead men in Normandy. Those villagers still alive near the beachhead smiled and waved as Ernie and Wescott passed by in their jeep. "Others kept their heads down and wouldn't look up," Ernie reported.[154]

Wescott pulled the jeep under a tree in the orchard. After other soldiers in the area were posted as sentries, Wescott pulled some crackers and sardines from a big ration box in the back of the jeep. As they washed it all down with some grapefruit juice, German planes appeared overhead in the dusky sky. One bomber released its payload not far from Ernie—"near enough to give us our first touch of the nerves," he later wrote. "There were antiaircraft guns all around and they made an awful racket," he continued. "The night began to take on an ominous and spooky aspect."[155]

In the early hours that night, Ernie and Wescott were finally ready to turn in. They covered the jeep with a camouflage net and cursed the fact that they didn't have bedrolls. To stay warm, Ernie curled up under the jeep's fender, with his head resting right behind the front wheel. "It was a good place," he later recounted, "but the headroom was so scant that every time I turned over I got a mouthful of mud from the fender."[156]

When they awoke with the sunrise, the orchard they had made their home for the night revealed itself to be full of dead Germans, killed the day before. A colonel who came across Ernie and Wescott while on a reconnaissance tour informed them that they'd need to help bury the fifty or so bodies, including American bodies, to stop them from rotting in the open.[157]

That morning, Ernie helped carry a young German's body to a central spot in a nearby pasture, where it would be buried by another group of soldiers. The German couldn't have been older than fifteen, Ernie figured. "His face had already turned black," he wrote, "but you could sense his youth through the death-distorted features."[158] After spreading out an army blanket on the damp ground beside the dead boy, Ernie gripped one of his lifeless ankles while another soldier grabbed the other; another pair of soldiers picked him up by the arms and hoisted him onto the blanket.

"One of the two soldiers was hesitant about touching the corpse," Ernie continued. "Go on, take hold of him, dammit," the other soldier growled. "You might as well get used to it now, for you'll be carrying plenty of dead ones from now on. Hell, you may even be carrying me one of these days."[159]

The four Americans carried the dead German across two fields, each holding a corner of the blanket. "The boys made wisecracks along the way to cover up their distaste of the job," Ernie wrote. When they reached the designated burial site, the men didn't know exactly where the officer in charge wanted the cemetery started, so Ernie and the others set the dead boy on the ground so they could rest before receiving further orders. As they turned from the blackened corpse, one of the soldiers who had helped carry the body whipped around and shook his finger the way a mother might scold a child. "Now don't you run away while we're gone," he said.[160] Ernie chuckled. "This war is constantly producing funny things as well as tragic things," he wrote.[161] There was no way to hide from all the death—or from the psychic numbing that comes with too much of it.[162]

13

For days after the landing, no one back home in America had any real sense of how the invasion was progressing or how many Americans were being killed.[163] There were no photographs flashed instantly to the news media, no hot takes on whether Eisenhower was a hero or a failure. The few correspondents who landed on the beaches with the troops that day were hampered by the danger and chaos of battle, and then by strategic censorship and long delays in wire transmission back to London.[164] The first to announce the invasion was the Trans-Ocean News Service, Germany's news agency, a mere forty-three minutes after the opening salvos of the Allies' pre-invasion bombardment.[165] Not knowing whether the story was a feint to draw out the French Resistance prematurely, *The New York Times* published a headline only, without a story. At half past nine o'clock in the morning in London, General Eisenhower issued a brief announcement, confirming German reports that "Allied naval forces, supported by strong air forces, began landing Allied armies this morning on the northern coast of France."[166] That was all he revealed. The first newspaper articles Americans read were based almost entirely on such military press releases. After several days without a new Pyle column to read, many newspapers began printing daily notices explaining that no copy had yet been received from the most beloved war correspondent in America.[167]

Pyle spent a few days after D-Day holed up in General Bradley's headquarters ship, pecking away on his typewriter. Once he had written several columns,[168] he handed them off to a courier who ferried them back to England to be censored and pooled with other copy being sent in from the other correspondents. When copy was pooled, that meant newspapers back home could choose from a wide variety of pieces to construct articles and columns for their respective readers.

To return to Normandy, Ernie climbed down the USS *Augusta*'s net into a small boat that took him, an intel photographer weighted down with a large movie camera, and a young naval officer carrying an equally heavy still camera that would be used to make intelligence reports. "When we waded ashore, Ernie was next to me," the officer recalled after the war. Halfway through the surf, Ernie tapped the officer. "Come on," he said. "Give it to me now. It's my turn." The officer hesitated. Ernie looked so frail, and the camera was no picnic to haul. "His carrying it was a point of pride," the officer said. "Not to have given him the camera would have been to hurt his feelings." The officer handed Ernie the camera, and even though he struggled at first, sagging under the weight, Ernie quicky found his grip. "When he took it," the officer continued, "there was a moment when I thought that both he and the camera were lost for good." This insistence upon sharing the burden was typical Pyle, and it made that young officer, John Mason Brown, understand why, as they plodded down "dusty and traffic-jammed" roads toward the front, one bone-tired young soldier after another would notice Pyle. "Hi-ya, Ernie," they'd shout. "Glad to see ya!"[169]

14

Ernie's first column about the D-Day landings, published on June 12, 1944, gave his readers an honest accounting of how daunting the invasion had been—and what a miracle it was that the Allies had taken the beaches at all. "The advantages were all theirs," he said of the German defenders: concrete gun emplacements and hidden machine-gun nests "with crossfire taking in every inch of the beach," immense V-shaped ditches, buried mines, barbed wire, "whole fields of evil devices under the water to catch our boats" and "four men on shore for every three men we had approaching the shore. . . . And yet," Ernie wrote, "we got on.

"Before long," he continued, "it will be permitted to name the units that did it. Then you will know to whom this glory should go. They suffered casualties. And yet if you take the entire beachhead assault, including other units that had a much easier time, our total casualties in driving this wedge into the continent of Europe were remarkably low—only a fraction, in fact, of what our commanders had been prepared to accept."[170] His intent with this first column seems to have been simple: to elicit pride and appreciation for such a monumental achievement and solemn gratitude for "those both dead and alive" who had clawed their way up the beaches and overpowered Hitler's Atlantic Wall.

Ernie's second column from the Normandy beaches, published ten days after D-Day, was markedly different from anything he had previously filed. "It was a lovely day for strolling along the seashore," he wrote, reeling the reader in with a cheerful opening. "Men were sleeping on the sand, some of them sleeping forever. Men were floating in the water, but they didn't know they were in the water, for they were dead."

Ernie then cataloged the vast wreckage of military matériel, what he termed the "shoreline museum of carnage": the "scores of tanks and trucks and boats" resting at the bottom of the Channel, jeeps "burned to a dull gray," and half-tracks blasted "into a shambles by a single shell hit." To soften the unvarnished facts, Ernie followed them with reassurances that the losses were an acceptable price for the victory. Ernie had seen a small group of German prisoners of war atop the bluffs, overlooking the sea. "They didn't say a word to each other," Ernie told his readers. "They didn't need to. The expression on their faces was something forever unforgettable. It was the final horrified acceptance of their doom." He balanced these optimistic notes with descriptions of the "awful waste and destruction of war."[171] He was building up to something he hadn't exactly done before.

The next day, June 17, newspapers across the country published Ernie's third column describing the D-Day beachhead. By allowing the objects he saw in the sand to tell an eloquent story of loss, he showed his readers the true cost of the fighting, without explicitly describing the blood and man-gled bodies. "It extends in a thin little line, just like a high-water mark, for miles along the beach," Ernie wrote about the detritus of the battle. "Here in a jumbled row for mile on mile are soldiers' packs. Here are socks and shoe polish, sewing kits, diaries, Bibles and hand grenades. Here are the lat-est letters from home. . . . Here are toothbrushes and razors, and snapshots of families back home staring up at you from the sand. Here are pocket-books, metal mirrors, extra trousers and bloody, abandoned shoes."[172]

Ernie often included himself in his stories, addressing his readers directly and letting them see him in the scene, a reassuring presence who was keeping his eye on things for them, reducing sprawling events to their digestible essentials. But here Ernie depicted himself as stunned and confused—a dazed witness to gambles and losses on a scale that *nobody* could comprehend. "I picked up a pocket Bible with a soldier's name in it, and put it in my jacket," he wrote. "I carried it half a mile or so and then put it back down on the beach. I don't know why I picked it up, or why I put it back down."[173]

By the end of the column, Ernie's readers were confronted with outright horror: "As I plowed out over the wet sand of the beach," he wrote, "I walked around what seemed to be a couple of pieces of driftwood sticking out of the sand. But they weren't driftwood. They were a soldier's two feet. He was completely covered by the shifting sands except for his feet. The toes of his G.I. shoes pointed toward the land he had come so far to see, and which he saw so briefly."[174] This was a different Ernie Pyle than the one millions of Americans knew from the newspapers that kept them company at the breakfast table or on the train home in the evening. If Ernie's reporting before D-Day was aimed at comforting the disturbed readers back home with optimism, tales of the soldiers' endurance, and poetic lines more palatable than the gritty truth, his reporting from the beaches of Normandy was aimed at disturbing the comfortable.

To his own surprise, his dispatches about D-Day's vast losses were not met with censorship or rejection. In fact, the effect they had was quite the opposite. In addition to the five hundred or so daily and weekly newspapers that subscribed to Ernie's column,[175] and the untold number of outlets that had access to his copy through the pool, *Life* magazine requested permission to run an excerpt, and radio programs quoted Ernie's words in plugs to implore listeners to buy war bonds. The big New York newspapers ran editorials about the columns, and *The Washington Post* featured Ernie's reporting on page 1. In the chambers of the nation's capital, meanwhile, two of Ernie's D-Day columns were reprinted in the official Congressional Record.[176] "It's getting so you can't pick up any damned publication at all without seeing you mentioned," Lee Miller wrote to the reporter a few days after the last column in the series ran.[177] At *The Washington Daily News*, Lee said they gave the same play to the last piece as they did to the Waskow column. The headline that ran beneath the masthead and over the bumped-up type of the column itself read: THIS IS THE WAY IT WAS . . . BY ERNIE PYLE.[178] "There was much debating," he told Ernie, "as to which was the better piece."[179] The publisher of Ernie's first book, *Here Is Your War*, loved Ernie's invasion columns so much they decided then and there to rush the publication of a follow-on book. "They expect a first print of 100,000," Lee told Ernie in early July. "Their salesman reported orders of 15,000 in their first four days on the road, which apparently is very hot. The goddamned book may turn out to be as big a seller as the other."[180]

"America must be very emotional about the invasion," Ernie wrote to Lee on the first day of July, "to compare that beachhead litter piece with the Waskow piece. It was very inadequate in expressing what you really saw.

"But of course," he added, "I'm glad people liked it."[181]

15

Ten days after the landings, the awful tension of life at the violent end of enemy bombs and exploding antiaircraft shells had eaten away at Ernie's already fragile mental state. Even though his nights were terrifying, noisy, and sleepless, he told Jerry he'd had "no bad times at all," that he was "as comfortable as anybody could be in the field," and that the nervous tension he had felt before the invasion kicked off was "disappearing under the simple life here in the field."[182]

With Lee, he was more forthright. "I didn't have a bad time at all on the crossing or the landing," Ernie wrote to him, "but the nights have not been pleasant since then." His stomach was what bothered him most, he explained. It had to be from the constant stress and lack of sleep, he figured.[183] It was impossible for Ernie to steal any rest unless he went to bed good and drunk. So that's what he tried to do as often as he could.[184] Soon enough, he knew—a couple of months at the most—the hell of it all was going to catch up with him. He told Jerry as much when he opened up to her about having felt as if he'd "run my race and served my purpose" and that he knew he couldn't keep up this pace forever. "But we will see," he wrote.[185]

"My spirit of depression comes and goes," he explained to Lee in a letter at the end of June. "Although I don't often stick my neck out," he continued, "just the normal presence in the zone is precarious enough that anything might happen and I still get moody about it." One night, an unexploded German antiaircraft shell buried itself less than a stone's throw from Ernie's tent.[186]

And then there were the aggravations that came along with Ernie's rising celebrity status. While he was embedded with an antiaircraft unit set up near the beachhead for a couple of nights, Ernie lost an entire day being "trundled against my will" from battalion to battalion to help raise the troops' morale.[187] General Bradley said on more than one occasion that his men always fought harder when they knew Ernie was around. "Your average doughfoot will go through his normal hell a lot more willingly," Ernie wrote once, "if he knows that he is getting some credit for it and that the home folks know about it."[188]

The biggest unanswered question Ernie faced with regards to his own morale was whether, when the time came, he'd have enough courage to quit before the war broke him beyond repair. He also had to make sure that before that time came, he was financially secure enough to walk away and still be able to afford the care Jerry needed. It was odd, then, that around the time Ernie's D-Day series hit newsstands, he turned down an offer from the Westinghouse Electric and Manufacturing Company that would have paid him $12,000 per month to read his already written columns onto a recording disc three times per week. All he'd have to do, they said, was read exactly what he wrote, for later rebroadcast across the country. They promised Ernie no extra work at all, except for the time it took to record the columns. If we account for eight decades of inflation, that means Ernie passed up an offer that would have paid him about $49,000 per week, or more than $2.5 million per year. Even after paying all the commissions and taxes,

Ernie figured he'd be able to bring home $30,000 per year (or about $490,000 in 2022 dollars).[189]

Lee thought the offer was too good to turn down. But W. W. Hawkins, the chairman of Scripps-Howard's board, hoped Ernie wouldn't accept it. Roy W. Howard, the president of the E. W. Scripps Company, which operated nineteen newspapers, was apparently dead set against the deal mostly because he hated anything having to do with radio. Plus, Ernie had been turning down offers to do radio left and right for months.[190] What was different about this offer? Was it simply a matter of money?

Part of Ernie felt miffed that his bosses thought it was their business to tell him what money he could make and how. Especially Roy, who Ernie thought "a little free with his objections" to offers that would likely never be made again. Another, more grace-giving part of himself tried to reframe the situation. Between the movie royalties and the returns he'd likely see from future collections of his columns, well, he rationalized to Lee, "I guess that ought to bring in all any human should want."[191] In a letter to Jerry, he figured that with another book and a movie that did all right, "we should have enough clear to give us a grand total of something like $75,000 in the bank by the end of next year. Which is a pittance to what it might be if we went after everything, but which ain't chicken feed at that."[192] Plus, Ernie didn't want to be cross with his bosses; they'd already done so much to support his career for so long. More than anything, Ernie worried that whenever he *did* stop writing the column, everything he had built would dry up and he wouldn't have enough to fall back on.

It only took an hour of mulling before Ernie sent a cable to Lee letting him know he should kindly refuse the offer. "Maybe I'm making a mistake," he confessed to Jerry. "Thirty thousand a year clear is a lot of money. But I'm a little afraid of anything extra-curricular." On top of that, he continued, "I've been out in this other world so long I guess I've sort of lost my perspective about what money means. Somehow it just seemed to make me like a good joke to turn down $150,000 a year for doing nothing. People are getting killed for 50 bucks a month, so what the hell. I suppose I'll regret it in my old age."[193]

Two weeks later, Ernie tried to convince Lee he was glad the Westing-house offer had fallen through. Turning down that kind of money had emboldened him to some extent. He figured that by deferring to his bosses on such weighty professional matters he had retained the freedom to quit the column "any damn moment I want to." And that moment, he warned Lee, was fast approaching. "I'm beginning to feel," he confessed, "that I've run my road in this war, and can't keep going much longer."[194]

CHAPTER 9

WINNING THEIR BATTLES

A stack of muddy, rusted rifles is a touching sight. As gun after gun came off the stack I looked to see what was the matter with it—rifle butt split by fragments; barrel dented by bullet; trigger knocked off; whole barrel splattered with shrapnel marks; guns gray from the slime of weeks in swamp mud; faint dark splotches of blood still showing. I wondered what had become of each owner. I pretty well know.

ERNIE PYLE, *BRAVE MEN*, 1944[1]

1

Nearly three weeks after the Allies invaded France, Ernie woke from a drunken half-sleep to the smell of steak sizzling in a pan outside his six-man tent. It was a Monday, the twenty-sixth of June. For a week and a half, Ernie had been hanging out with troops from the Ninth Division, along with Robert Capa and fellow correspondent Charles Wertenbaker. The division raced west to the seaside town of Barneville to sever the Normandy peninsula before wheeling north along the coast to Cherbourg, a deep-port city the Allies needed to take if they wanted to be able to quickly resupply the million or so Allied troops that had crossed the English Channel by the end of June.[2] Nearly every day with the Ninth, Ernie, Capa, and Wertenbaker found themselves in the thick of action.

The Allies had planned to capture Cherbourg within a week of the

D-Day landings,[3] but for a variety of reasons, progress had been much slower than anticipated. Unless Cherbourg fell soon, General Bradley feared, Normandy could turn into another Anzio. The troops themselves could not be blamed; they had fought ferociously. The Ninth Division, in particular, had impressed the hell out of Ernie. From what he saw of them in France, they had lost none of the fighting spirit he had seen in them back in North Africa, despite the obstacles they had to overcome before they could capture Cherbourg. "The Ninth is good," Ernie wrote in his column. "It performed like a beautiful machine in the Cherbourg campaign." He praised the way the division "kept tenaciously on the enemy's neck. When the Germans would withdraw a little the Ninth was right on top of them. It never gave them a chance to reassemble or get their balance."[4]

The biggest obstacle, other than the horrendously stormy summer weather, was the particular characteristic of the Norman landscape known as the bocage[5]—an ancient patchwork of small farm fields separated by thick banks of earth, matted with roots. "Irregular in length and height," writes historian Timothy M. Gay, "the hedgerows had been designed two millennia before, during Julius Caesar's conquest of Gaul, to mark property boundaries and keep Norman cattle from wandering."[6] Out of these woven embankments grew thick tapestries of weeds, bushes, and trees up to twenty feet high. "I couldn't imagine the bocage until I saw it," General Bradley would say after the war.[7]

The Allies called them hedgerows, and the Germans turned them into an attacking army's worst nightmare in what they called their *schmutziger Buschkrieg*, or "dirty bush war."[8] Snipers strapped themselves up in the trees. Machine gunners and riflemen prepared hidden firing holes through the dense brush. Mortars and other heavy weapons were hidden, protected by timber-covered trenches dug on the far side of each hedge. Horizontal curtains of German fire cut men down like piles of muddy laundry or knocked them backward as if they'd been jerked with a rope. Each one of the hedgerows was a "wall of fire," one soldier later put it, "and the open fields between were plains of fire."[9]

"We had to dig them out," Ernie explained. After several platoons learned the hard way how well defended the far side of each hedgerow's opening was,[10] the Americans took to splitting up into smaller groups, a handful of men at the most. With a few yards between each soldier, they stalked down either side of the hedgerow, grenades at the ready. Step. Squat. Wait. Then rise slowly. Step. Squat. Wait. Once they were close enough to strike, the rest of the platoon on the far side of the field would open up with everything they had, hosing the hedgerow with thousands of red-hot rounds. "That pinned the Germans to their holes while we sneaked up on them," Ernie continued. "The attacking squads sneaked up the sides of the hedgerows while the rest of the platoon stayed back in their own hedgerow and kept the forward hedge saturated with bullets."[11]

The fighting Ernie witnessed during that phase of the campaign ended in one of three ways. The Germans came out of their holes with their hands up. Or maybe some would try to make a run for the next hedgerow. They'd be mowed down from behind before they made it even halfway. And for those too stubborn or too scared to surrender or retreat, Ernie said, "a hand grenade, thrown into their hole, finished them off."[12] That's how the fighting was. "This hedgerow business," he wrote, "was a series of little skirmishes like that clear across the front, thousands and thousands of little skirmishes. No single one of them was very big. Added up over the days and weeks, however, they made a man-sized war—with thousands on both sides getting killed."[13]

2

Developed in 1938 by researchers at the Quartermaster Subsistence Research and Development Laboratory in Chicago, the U.S. Army-issue C-rations at first consisted chiefly of canned corned beef or bacon and hardtack biscuits. By 1944, the selection had expanded to include spaghetti and tomato sauce, eggs and potatoes, meat and noodles, and chicken and vegetables.[14] Halfway through the American campaign to capture Cherbourg, Ernie couldn't stomach another bite, no matter how hard he tried. Because

Ernie's friend and reporting partner Robert Capa never could enjoy a C-ration, either, one night the two men hatched a plan.

"We got a friendly mess sergeant to drum us up some cans of Vienna sausages, some sugar, canned peas, and what not, and we put them in a pasteboard box," Ernie wrote. "Then we walked around a couple of hedgerows to our motor pool and dug out Pvt. Lawrence Wedley Cogan from the comfortable lair he had prepared for himself in an oat field." Cogan drove jeeps for the military intelligence officers of the Ninth Infantry. When Ernie caught Cogan between tasks for an officer, he could talk him into driving him somewhere. Cogan was good people. Only nineteen years old, he'd been in the army for two years already. He was born and raised outside Washington, DC, in Alexandria, Virginia. "He is one of the nicest human beings you ever met," Ernie told his readers. "We piled in and directed Chauffeur Cogan to set out for the nearby village of Les Pieux," Ernie continued. "When we got there, Capa, who speaks eight languages—and as his friends say, 'none of them well'—went into a restaurant to make his investigations. Pretty soon he came to the door and motioned. So Cogan parked the car behind a building, we took our box of canned stuff, and in we went."

Nearly eight decades later, all efforts to locate this anonymous establishment turned up empty. Ernie, unfortunately, didn't offer many helpful clues. He never gave the name of the restaurant, and in his column, all he wrote to describe it was that it was made up of four or five separate dining areas and had low ceilings, and the floors sagged. "It was crammed with French people," Ernie continued, "for we had only just taken Les Pieux and not many Americans had found the place yet."[15]

The three men, dirty with grease and dust, were seated at a long table with several people from the old and worn-looking village who were eager to make their acquaintance. "Pretty soon," Ernie wrote, "we were in the thick of conversation. That is, Capa and the French were in conversation, and occasionally he would relay the gist of it to Cogan and me, the hicks."[16]

Capa reached an agreement with the woman who ran the restaurant. The three Americans would trade their army rations for the restaurant's regular dinner. He didn't want to take anything away from a people who had already had so much stripped from them. "We had expected to pay the full price anyhow," Ernie wrote later, "but when the bill came they charged us only for the cooking, and wouldn't take a bit more."[17]

Some of the restaurant's patrons told Capa all about the Nazi occupation, and according to Ernie, they hadn't said much bad about the Germans. "To be honest about it," Ernie later wrote, "we can't sense that Normandy suffered too much under the German occupation. That is no doubt less because of German beneficence than because of the nature of the country. For in any throttled country the farm people always come out best."[18]

During Jennifer's search for this anonymous restaurant before my arrival in France, she met a pub owner named Casimir who invited us to share a drink with him during our visit to Les Pieux. Even though he couldn't claim to own the same restaurant Pyle, Capa, and Cogen had visited, Casimir knew more than most about Les Pieux's history during the war and had collected dozens of old photographs from aging neighbors who had survived the Normandy campaign.

The light inside Casimir's pub was the color of honey. Casimir greeted us from behind his dark wood bar. He was an older man, graying in the beard, with short dark hair and a thick chest. He loved America, he told me in broken English as he tugged down on the bottom of his T-shirt so that I could make out the image of the Texas Hill Country. He'd bought the shirt in Bandera, Texas, he explained to Jennifer in French too fast for me to follow word for word. He and his wife, Ingrid, had visited America back before the pandemic began. They'd rented an RV and driven with another family of friends north through Yellowstone National Park and east to the Black Hills of South Dakota to visit the final resting place of Old West heroes Wild Bill Hickok and Calamity Jane.

Both Casimir and Ingrid wore face masks, pulled down around their chins. Casimir and Jennifer chatted briefly about how difficult the pandemic lockdowns in France had been on his business while Ingrid showed me to a booth with red velvet seat cushions at the front of the pub. She was wearing a denim dress with buttons. Her sleeves were rolled up halfway to her elbows, and her dirty-blond hair kissed the tops of her shoulders. Her spoken English was as rusty as my French, so we sat quietly for a moment with polite smiles as Jennifer sat down with her thick winter coat still on.

After I explained a bit more to Ingrid, through Jennifer's translations, what I was hoping to find in Les Pieux, Casimir motioned for me to come look at something behind the bar. He was standing at a laptop computer, and old black-and-white photos of the destruction in Cherbourg slid across the screen. With his reading glasses perched halfway down his nose, Casimir looked down through the lenses until he found what he was looking for—the image of what appeared to be a bombed-out school. "This is the school that my father attended in Carentan," he explained. Another image showed a destroyed bridge near Cherbourg, and another was of the victory parade the local residents threw when the Normandy campaign ended.

I asked about the damage done to Les Pieux during the fighting, and he corrected me. There wasn't much fighting, if any, that took place in Les Pieux. "We're not important enough to fight over," he said. What he meant was that there wasn't anything particularly important or strategic about Les Pieux. It wasn't located at an important crossroads or transportation junction. There was no decent high ground or natural defensive positions.

After we returned to the booth, Casimir plunked four short snifters on the table and poured shots of calvados, an apple brandy that can only be produced in Normandy. Strong and harsh, the liquor offers notes of baking spices and flowers, though apple is by far the dominant flavor.

"Ernie made a joke about calvados," I said as the alcohol went straight to the front of my brain. "He said it was so bad that any soldier who drank it should receive the Purple Heart." I chuckled. Jennifer translated. Casimir smiled. "That's why the people back then made '44," he said.

From a closet behind the bar, Casimir retrieved a liter-sized glass jar with a wide mouth containing a sickly-brown liquid. He popped the seal when he cranked the top off the jar. An astringent aroma of orange and coffee jolted my senses. As he told me the story behind this concoction, Casimir dipped a small metal ladle into the drink and poured me three fingers' worth.

Through Jennifer's translation, I learned that after the fighting had pushed past their village, some enterprising residents took what they had readily available and designed a premixed calvados cocktail they called '44, which the Americans preferred to straight apple brandy.

"Is it named for the year—1944?" Jennifer asked.

"Yes," he replied as he gently filled the other snifters on the table.

"But also because of how it is made," Casimir continued. "First, you take a peeled orange, and then you have to stab it forty-four times with an American paratrooper knife," he began. Then you must jam a coffee bean into each of the fresh stabs and drop the bean-stuffed-fruit into an empty jar. After adding forty-four spoonfuls of sugar and filling the jar to the brim with calvados, the mixture is supposed to rest for at least forty-four days.

"This batch has been resting for several years now," Casimir said with a smile, "so it should be quite smooth."

The liquor spread out in my belly like a warm blanket, opening up the veins in my head. For the first time in I couldn't remember when, I was totally relaxed, widening to the possibilities of whatever came next.

Casimir said something to Ingrid under his breath. Ingrid turned to me, sheepishly. When she spoke, she kept her eyes on me, only glancing at Jennifer periodically to make sure she comprehended before translating.

"After the Germans left this place," she said, "my grandmother was dragged by a mob of her neighbors to the city square. There they shaved her head. She had fallen in love with and married a German who was stationed here."

There was a long pause. Casimir reached for his wife and caressed the space between her shoulder blades with the fingers on his right hand. She took a deep breath. Jennifer asked something in French, and Ingrid explained that her grandmother had four children total, two with her first husband, whom she divorced, and two more with a German man who had fled Hitler's Germany for France but was drafted into the German army once the war began. According to Ingrid, her grandfather never supported what happened and was a most reluctant soldier. None of that mattered.

Guilty of "horizontal collaboration" with the enemy, many French women had their heads shaved, swastikas scrawled between their breasts or on their foreheads, then were paraded half-naked through the streets while their neighbors jeered. This *tonte ritual*, as it was called, was replicated throughout France and received plenty of press coverage, though never from Ernie. "Historians have seen the ritual as an attempt on the part of French men," writes Mary Louise Roberts, "to restore domination over women's bodies, thus recuperating their masculinity and 'the virility of the nation itself.'"[19]

Ingrid's family's shame didn't end there. During her childhood, her father, the son of a German, was routinely ostracized by his French neighbors. Sometimes the revulsion turned violent, as when her father was a young man going door to door to sell stamps for a school fundraiser. A neighbor who knew who Ingrid's father was and where he had come from wanted nothing at all to do with him and even threw heavy rocks at him until he fled. With no friends and no support from her community whatsoever, Ingrid's grandmother remained in Les Pieux, where she died resentful of how self-serving her punishers had been.

"There were some members of the French Resistance here," Casimir added, "but many people decided they needed to hurt their neighbors to prove they themselves were not collaborators."

3

Once past the bloody hedgerows, on the way toward Cherbourg, the Americans found fewer fields, more forests, and higher hills. "The Norman country is truly lovely in many places," Ernie told his readers of the Allied advance. "Here in the western part of the peninsula the ground becomes hilly and rolling. Everything is a vivid green, there are trees everywhere, and the view across the fields from a rise looks exactly like the rich, gentle land of eastern Pennsylvania." Like many parts of Tunisia, Sicily, and central Italy, Normandy seemed too beautiful to be a theater of war. "Someday," Ernie joked, "I would like to cover a war in a country that is as ugly as war itself."[20]

After breakfast on June 26, Ernie, Capa, and Wertenbaker took a jeep to a church at the end of a narrow lane in a western suburb of Cherbourg, close to the front lines. An American infantry regiment had converted the church into a makeshift command post.[21] It was early afternoon when Ernie and his friends arrived. Intending only to take a quick look around, maybe have a chat or two, Ernie stuck close to the company commander, a Bostonian who was about to deliver his mission briefing. "Below us there were big fires and piles of black smoke," Ernie wrote of his view from the church. American shells flew overhead, exploding with a crash in the near distance, creating even more fire and smoke. In response, German shells stabbed through the smoky air, hitting somewhere in the distance behind the command post. The ground below Ernie's boots quaked with each detonation.[22] Offshore, big American naval guns hammered at enemy strong points, including a mountaintop fortress overlooking the harbor.[23]

Ernie and his friends listened in on a briefing that concerned a French hospital up ahead. Since the invasion began, more than a hundred wounded Americans had been imprisoned there, and the front lines had finally receded far enough that it was possible to mount a rescue operation. As the briefing was ending, a young lieutenant by the name of Orion Shockley approached Capa, unfolded a map, and pointed to a street intersection about a half mile down the street from the church.[24] "Our company is starting in a few minutes to go up this road and clean out a strong point," Shockley said. "There are probably snipers in some of the houses along the way." Then he lifted his gaze toward the sounds of fighting over Ernie's shoulder. "Do you want to go along with us?" Ernie did not, but he joined Capa and Wertenbaker in saying yes. "Going into battle with an infantry company is not the way to live to a ripe old age," he later kidded in his column. "But when you are invited, what can you do?"[25]

"This is how we'll do it," Shockley continued. "A rifle platoon goes first. Right behind them will go part of a heavy-weapons platoon, with machine guns to cover the first platoon. Then comes another rifle platoon." Bringing up the rear, he added, would be another rifle platoon and the rest of the heavy weapons "to protect us from behind." Then he turned to Ernie. "We don't know what we'll run into," he said, "and I don't want to stick you right out in front, so why don't you come along with me? We'll go in the middle of the company."[26]

Shockley and the other grunts in the company looked haggard and sunken eyed. They'd been fighting for nearly three weeks without much rest, and it showed. Besides their tired eyes, the men's chins and cheeks were studded with two-week-old growth, their uniforms were slick with grease and sweat, and they stank like sour milk. As soon as the company of men set out on their patrol, the skies opened up, and the pouring rain quickly soaked through the men's clothes, right down to the skin.[27]

Then suddenly: WHAP! WHAP! WHAP! Shockley knew the sound instantly. "It's those damn 20-millimeters again," he told Ernie. "Better hold it up a minute." The antiaircraft rounds, fired from a cannon on wheels, "whanged" through the air into a grassy hillside beyond the American position. Crouched low behind a high wall, Ernie felt little fright in that moment—he seldom did, he told his readers, once whatever was going to happen happened. The anticipation of combat always worried him more than combat itself.

Once the firing stopped, Shockley ordered his men to cross a culvert and turn down the road leading to the hospital. "The men went forward one at a time," Ernie later wrote. Some fixed grenades at the ends of their rifles. Others carried Browning automatic rifles. Everyone crouched when they ran, including the soldier with the bazooka. With "confused excitement and a grim anxiety in their faces," they trotted softly and silently across the open ground. Unlike the German boots, which clacked on the cobble-stones, the rubber-soled American combat boots whispered across the pavement. The quiet jingle of buckles and buttons, punctuated by the sound of breath, was the only noise a running soldier made.[28] Safely on the far side of the culvert, the infantrymen "filtered to either side of the road, stopping and squatting down every now and then to wait a few moments."

"They weren't heroic figures as they moved forward one at a time, a few seconds apart," Ernie reported to his readers. "You think of attackers as being savage and bold. These men were hesitant and cautious. They were really the hunters, but they looked like the hunted."

"They seemed terribly pathetic to me," he continued. "They weren't warriors. They were American boys who by mere chance of fate had wound up with guns in their hands sneaking up a death-laden street in a strange and shattered city in a faraway country in a driving rain. They were afraid, but it was beyond their power to quit. They had no choice."[29]

Practically all the "combat replacements" Ernie met in the weeks after D-Day had received little if any small-unit or field training. Men who had been trained as "mail orderlies, cooks, officers' orderlies, truck drivers etc., for periods ranging from six months to a year, who had been sent over, assigned to a combat unit, and thrust into combat within 24 hours," one report on combat effectiveness in Normandy read. "These men were definitely inadequately prepared, both psychologically and militarily, for combat duty."[30]

Even if they weren't born killers, Ernie wrote, "they win their battles. That's the point."[31]

When it was Ernie's turn to take that lonely dash, he was busy chatting up some of the soldiers in line behind him. Before he could get their names and addresses penciled into his handheld notebook, a sergeant motioned for him. With shoulders hunched and knees bent, Ernie moved forward in a short burst to a little bush halfway to the other side—"as though that would have stopped anything," he later joked. The man in front of him had pulled up short, and to avoid bunching up into a more enticing target for an enemy gunner, Ernie froze in a tightly wound ball of energy until the rest of the opening was clear to burst across.

It was another hour before he was able to catch back up with those soldiers he'd befriended. With the rain still pouring down, soaking everyone's khaki jackets, pants, and gaiters, they each took a turn holding Ernie's helmet above his bent knee so he could use it to write without soaking his notebook. There was Joseph Palajsa from Pittsburgh, and Arthur Greene, who was from Auburn, Massachusetts, and spoke with a heavy New England accent. There was Dick Medici out of Detroit and a "soldier-looking" lieu-tenant named James Giles, from Athens, Tennessee. Arthur Slageter told Ernie he'd been a fan of his column from way back. They loved Ernie in Cincinnati, Ohio, he told him. Ernie spent a bit more time chatting with Robert Eddie, a private from New Philadelphia, Pennsylvania. He was the oldest of the bunch, at thirty, and had worked in a brewery before the war. Normally he carried a bazooka, but his was broken, so they shoved a rifle in his hand. Then there was Ben Rienzi of New York City and Robert Hamilton of Philadelphia proper, who'd been wounded in North Africa. Lastly, there was a sergeant named Joe Netscavge, from Shenandoah, Pennsylvania, who sported a dent in his helmet where a German sniper's bullet had grazed him.[32]

"The city around us was still full of sound and fury," Ernie wrote. The soldiers stayed close to the walls of the buildings on either side of the street. Most stayed crouching most of the time. It was impossible to tell where any of the firing or explosions were coming from, Ernie said, because the streets and buildings had been abandoned, and "shots, incidentally, always sound louder and distorted in the vacuum-like emptiness of a nearly deserted city." The only other sounds that could be heard, besides the pelting rain, were the clapping and banging of abandoned doors and unfastened shutters.[33]

Up ahead of Ernie's position in the formation, the narrow street wound around a bend. The ghostly sounds of the abandoned neighborhood suddenly ended with the sharp crack of an American rifle, followed by the rat-tat-tat of an American machine gun. Then there was a much quicker report, the unmistakable blurp-blurp sound of a German MG 42 machine gun. "For a long time we didn't move at all," Ernie wrote. It was hard to know exactly what was going on up ahead. "One side will bang away for a while, then the other side," Ernie explained. "Between these sallies there are long lulls, with only stray and isolated shots." Before too long, word made it back to Lieutenant Shockley that the street had been cleared all the way to the hospital, less than a quarter mile ahead. "There were lots of our own wounded in that hospital," Ernie continued, "and they were now being liberated."[34]

Still keeping close to the building facades along the sidewalk, Ernie rushed from doorway to doorway, along with Shockley, Wertenbaker, and Capa. "I lost the others before I had gone far," he wrote. "As I would pass doorways soldiers would call out to me and I would duck in and talk for a moment and put down a name or two."[35]

One soldier in particular had a bone to pick with Ernie. "Why don't you tell the folks back home what this is like?" he demanded, with a belligerent edge. "All they hear about is victories and a lot of glory stuff. They don't know that for every hundred yards we advance somebody gets killed. Why don't you tell them how tough this life is?" By the war's end, the Ninth Division had spent 264 days in combat. They suffered nearly thirty-four thousand casualties—more than any other American infantry division in Europe—and their turnover rate was an undeniably hellish 240 percent.[36] If Americans at home didn't know before, Ernie was going to make sure they learned.[37]

"That's what I try to do all the time," Ernie told the young soldier. And just in case this exchange might unnecessarily worry any of his readers, Ernie made sure to add that the man was probably exhausted, that people say odd things when they feel that tired. "A few days' rest usually has him smiling again," Ernie assured them.[38]

It took nearly half an hour for Ernie to make his way to the hospital—"and then," he concluded his column that day, "the excitement began."[39] Another block past the hospital, Ernie spotted two American tanks camped out in the middle of the street, spaced about fifty yards apart. As he approached the closest tank, its 75 mm cannon coughed out a terrific concussive blast that shattered nearby windows and shook the narrow street. Fearing whatever the tank shot at would return fire, Ernie ducked into a nearby doorway. Inside he found a dirt-floored cellar that had served as a wine shop before the war. After tipping over several empty bottles, Ernie moved back to the doorway.

The tank lumbered backward like a frightened elephant. From the safety of a tall brick door casing, Ernie watched as a German Panzerfaust whooshed at knee level down a side street and exploded into the heavy steel brace the tank's tread ran on. Then a second round, with the same whoosh, ripped into the pavement with a dull thud along the tank's vulnerable track. Smoke poured from the wounded armor as its crew popped themselves up and out of the turret, one after another. "Grim as it was," Ernie wrote, "I almost had to laugh as they ran toward us. I have never seen men run so violently. They ran all over, with arms and heads going up and down and with marathon-race grimaces."[40]

For the next hour or so, Ernie sat on overturned boxes in an empty hallway with the adrenaline-fueled crew. "The escaped tankers naturally were excited," Ernie wrote, "but they were as jubilant as June-bugs" until one of them realized they'd left their tank, which they had named "Be Back Soon," with the engine running. "We could hear it chugging away," Ernie continued. It wasn't good for the engine to let it idle like that, but none of the tankers was especially excited about running back out into harm's way. The first three weeks of the invasion were the only three weeks they'd ever been in combat, and this was the third time their tank had been shot out from under them. This time, Ernie learned during his chat with the five-man crew, when they fired their cannon at a reinforced concrete bunker in the niche in the wall of a building about a block farther up the street,[41] the round backfired and filled the inside of the tank with blinding smoke. When Ernie had watched the tank backing up, that was the driver trying to get his bearings back. "Unfortunately," Ernie wrote, "he stopped exactly at the foot of a side street. More unfortunately there was another German pillbox up the side street. All the Germans had to do was take easy aim and let go at the sitting duck."

"The first shot hit a tread, so the tank couldn't move," he continued. "That was when the boys got out. I don't know why the Germans didn't fire at them as they poured out."[42]

While Ernie was collecting material for his column, Robert Capa found his way into the liberated hospital, where he found more than two hundred wounded paratroopers from the Eighty-second Airborne Division. He overheard someone say the hospital's basement was stuffed to the ceiling with the best wine and brandy in Normandy. Capa stole down the stairs to the basement. "Every soldier of the 47th Infantry already had his arms, jacket, and pockets bulging with precious bottles," he wrote after the war. When he asked if he could bum a bottle from a young soldier, he was met with a laugh. "Only if you're Ernie Pyle," he responded. Capa stopped another soldier. "Say, could I get one of those, there? Just one." Then a pause. "It's for Ernie Pyle. THE Ernie Pyle, that's right." This time, there was no hesitation. The young soldier shoved a bottle into Capa's hand with a smile that said, *Tell 'im this one's on us.*[43]

Once the fighting had died down a bit, Ernie and the tank's commander, a Chicagoan named Martin Kennelly, snuck up the street until they were nearly even with the thirty-three-ton roadblock.

"Say! It went right through our lower ammunition-storage box!" Kennelly told Ernie in amazement. "I don't know what kept the ammunition from going off. We'd have been a mess if it had. Boy, it sure would have got hot in there in a hurry!"

Farther down from the disabled tank, about two blocks away, Ernie saw a bombed-out German truck beached in the middle of the street like a charred whale. Its tires had burned off, and there wasn't another human being in sight.

That lull in the fighting lasted about an hour. The one operable tank left had pulled back from the line of fire from a third pillbox and waited. "Now and then blasts from a 20-mm. gun would splatter the buildings around us," Ernie wrote. "Then our second tank would blast back in that general direction, over the low roofs, with its machine gun. There was a lot of dangerous-sounding noise, but I don't think anybody on either side got hit."[44]

Several minutes later, a bedraggled band of Germans ready to surrender appeared up ahead, beyond the burned-out truck. An unarmed officer with his metal helmet strapped tightly under his chin led the small procession. Above his head, he carried a large white flag. The defeated men marched slowly along the far side of the street, a few feet from a tall wall of brick shaded under even taller leafy trees. Eight other Germans behind him shuffled along, carrying two wounded comrades on canvas litters.

More Germans walked behind the wounded with their hands up. Ernie assumed they'd been the crew manning the pillbox up ahead that had taken out the tank.

Robert Capa wheeled down the street, pulling up shy of a T-intersection covered by two American soldiers with carbines. He lifted his Leica to his eye and snapped an iconic image.[45] The first American, closest to the intersection, had turned to peer in Capa's direction as the shutter clicked. A lit cigarette hangs from his left hand. The butt of his carbine digs into his right hip, the muzzle pointing up and away. A second soldier, closer to Capa, kept a tight grip on his weapon. His gaze is locked on the German officer leading the pack.

"Folge mir! Folge mir! Diesen weg!" Capa shouted at the officer. No doubt relieved to hear his native tongue, the German followed Capa, leading his men over to the American side of the "invisible fence of battle," as Ernie described it, to the hospital where their wounded could be looked over.

"I didn't stay to see how the remaining pillbox was knocked out," Ernie concluded his column. "But I suppose our second tank eventually pulled up to the corner, turned, and let the pillbox have it. After that the area would be clear of everything but snipers."[46]

Later that day, the German general in command of Cherbourg, Karl-Wilhelm von Schlieben, along with eight hundred of his men, surrendered to General Manton S. Eddy, the commander of the Ninth Infantry Division. Ernie was there to see it for himself. These Germans from Cherbourg were no supermen. As one army officer put it, "There is a missing generation in Germany now. It's under the sod. Instead we have kids and middle-aged burghers."[47]

After a long debriefing, General Eddy gave American photographers permission to take pictures of the captured enemy general. "They stood in a group in an orchard while the photographers snapped away," Ernie wrote. Von Schlieben's sullen demeanor turned to self-righteous despondency. General Eddy had an interpreter explain to his German counterpart that this minor inconvenience was the price of being a general. Von Schlieben snorted in response.

"Tell the general that our country is a democracy," General Eddy continued, "and therefore I don't have authority to forbid these photographers to take pictures."

Von Schlieben snorted once more. Ernie chuckled behind his weeks-old stubble. It was the "slickest example of working democracy we had ever seen. And General Eddy had the appearance of the traditional cat that swallowed something wonderful."[48] The next day, four hundred more Germans surrendered moments before the Forty-seventh Infantry was set to assault the last fortified holdout on the western side of the city. Cherbourg had fallen.[49]

4

On June 29, Ernie left Cherbourg and moved into a six-man tent pitched in an apple orchard on the grounds of a stone castle in the rich farm country of Bessin, where the tiny village of Vouilly lies.[50] A couple of miles southeast of Isigny-sur-Mer and some fifteen miles north of Saint-Lô, the Château de Vouilly, managed by the matriarch of a family named Hamel, served for five weeks that summer of 1944 as the headquarters for Allied combat correspondents in France.[51] Waiting for Ernie there inside his tent was the first batch of letters he'd received since D-Day, including two from Jerry. "They sounded very fine," he reported to Lee. "I really am beginning to have hopes for her again."[52] Jerry was no longer taking medication and was laying off alcohol and getting more sleep.

Ernie's outlook on the war had turned equally hopeful. "You can't tell for sure yet, but I've at last let myself get optimistic about the war," he wrote to Paige, who at the time was acting as Ernie's consiglieri on set in California during the lead-up to filming *The Story of G.I. Joe*. From inside Ernie's tent in Vouilly, surrounded by the tranquility of farming country, undisturbed

by enemy fire, it appeared as if the war might even end later that fall.[53]
"Several months of course and lots of hard fighting yet," he wrote to Jerry.
"Admitting that to ourselves is like seeing the first faint light at the far end
of a dark tunnel."[54]

Once he finished catching up on news from home, Ernie and one of
his tentmates, a photographer named Bert Brandt, of United Press International, worked together in the loveliest weather they'd seen all summer
to turn their army-issued canvas enclosure into a proper home office. They
laid a long rug on the bare ground between their two cots and "requisi-
tioned" a few essential items from captured German headquarters units,
including a skillet and spatula, drinking glasses, a wide assortment of
canned rations, and even a few radios.[55]

"I got him started on being neat in his tent and providing yourself with
a few little common comforts, such as ash trays from ration cans, a box beside your cot to put things on, and such stuff," Ernie wrote to Jerry in a five-
page letter dated July 1, 1944. "Bert fell in with the idea like a child, and
since he's a natural-born scrounger, he comes back every evening with all
the junk he can carry." The only comfort they lacked was electric lighting.[56]

One day, another of their tentmates, Don Whitehead, returned from a
foraging trip with a couple of dozen eggs, jam, and "other junk."[57] For the
next several mornings, Ernie acted as his tent's very own short-order cook.[58]
After waking with the apricot glow of morning, Ernie fried bacon and
cooked eggs over Bert's Coleman stove—enough to feed Bert, Don, and Ernie's other three tentmates: Hank Gorrell of the United Press, Jack Lee of
the International News Service, and A. J. Liebling of *The New Yorker*.[59] "He
would fry the eggs with bacon," Liebling remembered fondly after the war,
"over a Coleman stove in the mornings, creating a smoke smudge behind
which you could have deployed a battalion of tanks."[60]

"He knew how big a figure he had become in the United States," Liebling, the consummate New Yorker, continued. "But the discovery had
not affected his unassuming kindliness. I thought then that he clung to his
homespun manner the way a baseball player hangs on to a lucky bat, but
that was probably unkind. I think now that he just didn't have any other

manner—that if he hadn't been born into his honest Hoosier character (and for all I know he had), he had at least grown into it so solidly that he couldn't change."[61]

During their stay at the château, the correspondents converted a large room at the end of a long hallway on the château's main floor into their press copy room. It was outside that same room that James Hamel, whose family has called the château home since before the war, explained to me and Jennifer that the hallway outside the room, tiled in a black-and-white checker pattern, had not been altered at all since the war and that the pull in the middle of the door to the press copy room was also the original. James waved to me to come closer.

"This is the same pull Mr. Pyle touched with his own hands," he said. "Please, you should pull it, too."

The air on the other side of the door was cold and dry. During warm months, James rents out the rooms on the château's second floor and serves breakfast in the old press copy room, but because it's way too expensive to heat an entire old castle in the winter, James and his family live on one end of the château and close off the other rooms until spring. James was making an exception for us, and after I stepped into the room, I could understand why. The dark-wood walls were covered with portraits of uniform-clad men, old battle maps, and pictures of all the famous men who called this place home that fateful summer. On the far wall, between two giant curtained windows, was an image I had seen many times before, of Ernie bent over a typewriter in a makeshift newsroom stuffed with other correspondents plucking away at their own workstations.

"Where you are standing now," James said to me, "this is where Ernie was seated. This spot. And nothing has changed here except these curtains."

Giddy with excitement, I asked if we might be able to re-create the scene for a photo. "Is there a small desk like this we could use?"

James's brown eyes twinkled as a sly smile spread across his face. He had figured I'd ask and had prepared a small folding table like the one Ernie was seated at in the photo, along with a typewriter of that era and a leather bomber jacket with the words U.S. WAR CORRESPONDENT and an American flag printed on the back. Being too burly for the jacket, I settled for a staged photo of myself seated in the same sort of setup as Ernie, in the same spot as Ernie, with my back curved and neck cranked like Ernie sweating over a column.

In the next room over, through a set of tall double doors, the army's censors set up a space of their own. It was there, through a haze of cigarette smoke, that General Bradley's public relations officers conducted their daily morning briefings. After downing one last cup of coffee, the correspondents, fully briefed, would head out in pairs or groups of three with a jeep and a driver, searching for a story. At the end of their day, they'd head back to Vouilly and set up in the press copy room, oftentimes with censors clutching blue grease pencils lined against the walls, glaring over the correspondents' shoulders as they typed.[62] The correspondents' commute to the war, A. J. Liebling later quipped, became as routine as taking a taxi from uptown to downtown Manhattan.[63]

Ernie preferred to do his writing at a folding table in the quiet of his tent. "I'm several days ahead and the columns couldn't keep at all close to the news anymore," he explained in a long letter to Jerry, "so I'm now dropping back to my old routine of just sawing wood." There would be no danger for him to avoid, he assured her, while he pecked out a series or two about the ordnance units he'd spent time with in the first week or so after D-Day. The supply and maintenance battalions were "doing such marvelous work here," he told her, but they got so little credit.[64] In a letter to Lee, he added that their work was most dramatic right now because without their tireless effort, the Allies would never get enough men and matériel in France to break out of Normandy.[65]

5

One evening, late in July, Ernie and the other correspondents camped outside the Château de Vouilly were summoned to General Bradley's briefing room. "We correspondents could sense that a big drive was coming," Ernie wrote. "There are many little ways you can tell without actually being told, if you are experienced in war."[66]

"It will start on the first day we have three hours good flying weather in the forenoon," General Bradley told them of his plan to finally break out of the hedgerows west of Saint-Lô.[67]

"Once a hole was broken," Ernie wrote of the operation's objective, "the armored divisions would slam through miles beyond, then turn right toward the sea behind the Germans in that sector in the hope of cutting them off and trapping them." That hole Ernie spoke of would be broken by what Ernie described as a "gigantic two-hour air bombardment by 1800 planes—the biggest, I'm sure, ever attempted by air in direct support of ground troops." The plan, in Bradley's mind, was simple. Bomb the absolute hell out of a four-mile stretch of the Germans' front line and unleash the tanks and infantry to pour through the softened defenses. Next stop: Berlin. "It was a thrilling plan to listen to," Ernie continued. "There isn't a correspondent over here, or soldier, or officer I ever heard of who hasn't complete and utter faith in General Bradley." Another officer added that this operation—known as Cobra—was "no limited objective drive." The beginning of the end was finally upon them.[68]

On July 21, 1944, Ernie joined the Fourth Infantry Division on their march south and west to their final assembly area, about five miles west of Saint-Lô, a transportation hub the Allies needed to capture before they could liberate the rest of France. During his first night with the division, Ernie slept in a tent at the division's command post, and on the second, he curled up on the floor of a stone farmhouse a little closer to the front. After a third night sleeping at the bottom of a foxhole along the edge of an orchard, Ernie found himself a spot about eight hundred yards north of the Périers–Saint-Lô road,[69] in a barnyard behind an abandoned stone farmhouse.[70] Ernie chose the Fourth Infantry Division because it had been picked to spearhead the initial attack. Nervous that the infantry wouldn't get its due credit in what he called one of the "great historic pinnacles of this war," Ernie didn't want to miss the "mighty surge out of our confined Normandy spaces."[71] When he stayed away from the front for too long, a shame would wash over Ernie until he steeled himself enough to return. "Any correspondent who wasn't in it," he later told Jerry of Operation Cobra, "violated his right to be over here at all."[72]

General Bradley wanted his men as close to the bomb line as possible to ensure they could quickly sweep aside any remaining German resistance before the enemy had a chance to recover and regroup. The bomber men under Bradley's command wanted the troops dug in at least three thousand yards back from the bomb line—nearly two miles. They knew all too well that even in perfect flying conditions with no enemy gunners trying to shoot them down, heavy bombers didn't always hit their targets. Anything closer than three thousand yards, one air commander once quipped, is like "bombing between the Army's legs."[73] General Bradley countered with twelve hundred yards. The soldiers under his command, Bradley later wrote, were "nothing more than tools to be used in the accomplishment of the mission." He believed then and after the war that he simply could not do his job and concern himself with the "dignity of man." As he once told Ernie, "I've spent thirty years preparing a frame of mind for accepting such a thing."[74]

The bomber men also knew more than Bradley about ballistic coefficients and dropping angles, which led them to conclude that his plan to funnel hundreds of bombers into a one-mile corridor in a single hour would be impossible. The full bombing run would take closer to three.[75]

From his spot in a barnyard near a stone farmhouse about half a mile from the bomb line,[76] Ernie watched through cupped hands in the early morning sun as the first American fighter-bombers barreled straight out of the sky at forty minutes past nine in the morning, right on time. For the next twenty minutes or so, they pummeled the far side of the road with pinpoint accuracy. Even though the men had been under the "strictest orders" to stay down in their foxholes during the raid, many were sitting or standing on top of their vehicles, cheering on the annihilation of the army across the way.[77] "The air was full of sharp and distinct sounds of cracking bombs and the heavy rip of the planes' machine guns and the splitting screams of diving wings. It was all fast and furious, but yet distinct, as in a musical show in which you could distinguish throaty tunes and words."[78]

At around ten o'clock, more than a thousand B-17 Flying Fortresses and B-24 Liberators flying in waves of seventy or so droned over the heads of the cheering Americans, perpendicular to the bomb line.[79] All that could be heard in the level countryside was a sound "deep and all-encompassing with no notes in it," Ernie wrote, "a gigantic far-away surge of doomlike sound. It was the heavies. They came from directly behind us. At first they were the merest dots in the sky. You could see clots of them against the far heavens, too tiny to count individually." With a certain "ghastly relentlessness," as Ernie put it, the procession of planes seemed without end. "What the Germans must have thought," he added, "is beyond comprehension."[80]

Then the bombs began to fall. They tumbled through the blue sky in large clusters and smacked the earth with a sound that "instantly swelled into a monstrous fury of noise that seemed surely to destroy all the world ahead of us," Ernie continued. "A wall of smoke and dust erected by them grew high in the sky. It filtered along the ground back through our own orchards. It sifted around us and into our noses. The bright day grew slowly dark from it."[81]

The first wave or two struck their intended targets, but soon the bomb line was obscured by smoke and dust. "We were horrified by the suspicion that those machines, high in the sky and completely detached from us," Ernie later reported, "were aiming their bombs at the smokeline on the ground—and a gentle breeze was drifting the smokeline back over us!"[82]

After realizing how much danger they were in, some soldiers dug in at the very tip of the spear threw orange smoke grenades in a last-ditch effort to warn the bombardiers up above. It was no use. With no radio link between the bombers in the air and the troops on the ground, there was no way for the bombers to know they were killing their own men.

An indescribable panic washed over Ernie. His muscles were both tense and frozen, trapping his body in a momentary feeling of suspended animation. Then he dove. The closest shelter was a wagon shed at the end of the stone house. He remembered hitting the ground flat and spreading out thin, "like the cartoons of people flattened by steam rollers," and squirming for his life to get under a heavy wagon he found parked in the middle of the shed.[83]

"An officer whom I didn't know was wriggling beside me," Ernie wrote. They stopped flailing for cover at the same time, knowing deep down how hopeless it was to waste another second of energy. American bombs crashed all around them as Ernie and his new friend lay on their stomachs, with their heads up and facing each other, "like two snakes." With his eyes, Ernie tried to ask him what they should do, and with his, the officer answered. There was nothing either one of them *could* do. They were being bombed by their own side. Either a bomb would land near enough to kill them, or it wouldn't. If it did, there was nothing they could do about it. If it didn't, well, they'd have to stay put, with their chins in the dirt, "gaping at each other in a futile appeal," Ernie continued, "our faces about a foot apart, until it was over."[84]

During the short time Ernie had spent with the ordnance units in the rear near the beachhead after the fall of Cherbourg, he had felt an outsize sense of guilt for not being up with the "real troops." Now all he wished was for the flutters of air drumming and ringing against his chest and eyes to stop, for the terrifying rattle of death in his ears to end, and for the darkness to lift. "I can't record what any of us actually felt or thought during those horrible climaxes," Ernie confided. "I believe a person's feelings at such times are kaleidoscopic and uncatalogable. You just wait, that's all."[85]

6

A gentle rain picked at my down coat. Jennifer's boots clicked on the pavement at a faster cadence than my long strides. A gentle breeze occasionally patted the microphone in my iPhone, which Jennifer was using to film my totally unscientific method of measuring out eight hundred meters from the "Rue de Resistance" north, where Ernie said he had survived the botched Cobra bombing.

"How many more do you have left, Dave?" she asked. Along the road a wire-and-post fence separated the ditch from the thick overgrowth of leafless trees and bushes.

"That's, um . . ." I had to stop. "That's five hundred and . . . seventy-nine." I then briefly chuckled at the absurdity of my search. What did I think I was going to find? *Seven hundred and ninety-nine . . . and . . . eight hundred! Here we are! Here's where Ernie almost died all those years ago. Check that one off the list!*

"OK, we'll see you on the other side," Jennifer responded before turning off the camera.

If it weren't for a pair of Mustang fighters, "flying like a pair of doves," that day, the death toll on the American side of the bombing line might have been far worse. The two pilots, Ernie wrote, had somehow figured out that most of the bombs were dropping short, so they patrolled the skies, back and forth, out in front of each oncoming wave of bombers. When it was safe to release their bombs, one of the Mustangs released a flare from the belly of the plane. "The flare shot forward," Ernie wrote, "leaving smoke behind it in a vivid line, and then began a graceful, downward curve that was one of the most beautiful things I've ever seen. It was like an invisible crayon drawing a rapid line across the canvas of the sky, saying in a gesture for all to see: 'Here! Here is where to drop. Follow me.'" Before long the bombs were falling where they were intended, on the German side of the line. "There was still a dread in our hearts," Ernie admitted, "but it gradually eased as the tumult and destruction moved slowly forward."[86]

For the German soldiers on the south side of the bombing line, the horror of it all was beyond comprehension. "The whole place looked like a moon landscape," wrote a German commander after the war. "Everything was burned and blasted. It was impossible to bring up vehicles to recover the ones that were damaged. The survivors were like madmen and could not be used for anything."[87] Many of the German prisoners of war taken that day were literally babbling, an American doctor noted in his diary. They had been "knocked silly" by the bombardment.[88] Deranged, they ran in tight circles or wandered through the smoldering wreckage until they were cut down by advancing American infantrymen.[89] Before the sun set that day, over a thousand Germans had been slaughtered. In a frantic message to his higher-ups back in Germany, the commander, General Fritz

Bayerlein, put it this way: "My grenadiers and the pioneers, my anti-tank gunners, they're holding. None of them have left their positions, none. They're lying in their holes, still and mute, because they are dead. Dead. Do you understand?"[90] At least 70 percent of his troops were dead, wounded, numb, or out of their minds.[91] The German commander later concluded that he didn't believe "hell could be as bad as what we experienced."[92]

7

On the American side of the bomb line during Operation Cobra, some infantrymen from the Thirtieth Division searched desperately for General Lesley J. McNair, who had flown in from England to observe Operation Cobra. When they finally found his remains, sixty feet from his foxhole, they knew it was him only because of the three blackened metal stars pinned to a collar.[93] A 1904 graduate of West Point, McNair had been one of the most respected men in the U.S. Army; the chief of staff, General George C. Marshall, once referred to McNair as "the brains of the Army" in tribute to the tremendous role he played in developing doctrine and training methods.[94] Up until that point in the war, McNair was the highest-ranking officer in the American military to die in combat.[95] Another 110 Americans were also killed that day, and 490 more were wounded.[96] According to historian Rick Atkinson, "The star-crossed 30th Division took more casualties from the Army Air Forces (AAF) on this Tuesday forenoon than from the enemy on any day in the war."[97]

And yet, of the three divisions tasked with attacking after the bombing ended, only two units were unable to attack within an hour, and not a single unit was knocked out of the fight entirely.[98]

Once the bombing ended and the noise subsided, after Ernie slithered out from underneath the heavy wooden cart that saved his life, he found a colonel friend of his walking up and down behind the farmhouse, snapping his fingers. "Goddammit, goddammit!" he said over and over again to himself. When he noticed Ernie noticing him, he stopped and stared. "God-dammit!"

"There can't be any attack now, can there?" Ernie asked, standing there spiritless and abandoned.

"No," the colonel replied. Then he turned and walked away, snapping his fingers and muttering to himself once again.

"The leading company of our battalion was to spearhead the attack forty minutes after our heavy bombing ceased," Ernie told his readers. "The company had been hit directly by our bombs. Their casualties, including casualties in shock, were heavy. Men went to pieces and had to be sent back. The company was shattered and shaken."[99]

The Fourth Infantry Division later reported that "all men and officers who were under the bombing testify to the terrific shock effect. A great number of the men were in a daze for a while, just staring blankly and unable to understand when spoken to." In the Thirtieth Division, 164 men were evacuated after succumbing to combat exhaustion.[100] All told, around thirty thousand cases of combat exhaustion had been reported in France since D-Day—about one in four casualties were "neuropsychiatric" in nature.[101]

And yet they advanced. "Within an hour they sent word back that they had advanced 800 yards through German territory and were still going," Ernie continued. "Around our farmyard men with stars on their shoulders almost wept when the word came over the portable radio.

"The American soldier," Ernie concluded, "can be majestic when he needs to be."[102]

Jennifer's and my shadows were growing long and dark on the still-wet pavement as we continued to look for Ernie's farmyard. The wind picked up significantly. I was beginning to lose hope when Jennifer pointed at an old farmhouse suddenly in view, poking through a thick and tangled mass of leafless trees.

As we approached the house, I turned back toward the road, back to where we had started from. Behind me were thirty-foot-tall evergreen bushes, trimmed flush with a rickety chipped-white, split-rail fence.

We walked closer to the farmhouse, a two-story stone structure with steep ceilings and two dormer windows in the attic. A fat pine tree, wider than the house, it seemed, marked the far edge of the lot.

"This looks abandoned," I said after noticing the broken windows on the side of the house closest to us.

Behind a low concrete fence topped with two rows of rusted metal pipes for added height, the gray, pink, and tan brick house with sand-colored grout was not only abandoned but also totally open to the elements. The first-floor windows on both sides of the tall white front door were smashed and open and creaked as they swung in the stiff breeze. On the right, it looked as if someone had thrown a long metal tube like a javelin that broke the pane and got stuck hanging halfway out the window. I shouldered my way in through the front door.

Inside we found nothing but peeling wallpaper and plenty of evidence that someone came to hang out there from time to time. In one of the rooms, with pale orange wallpaper, we found a half-finished beer in a clear glass bottle, with half a dozen bees floating dead inside it. In front of a small fireplace were an assortment of magazines and a few comic books. In the back corner, someone had fashioned a bench out of two overturned ceramic flowerpots and a wood door pried off one of the kitchen cabinets. Jennifer had no interest in exploring the unfinished attic, so I took the phone from her and marched up. Beneath a large hole in the thatched roof, a soiled mattress collected drips of rainwater from the shower that had passed through.

Out back behind the house, Jennifer found it—a brick barn similar in appearance to the one Ernie described seeking shelter in. Half-dead ivy crawled up its face, digging into the spaces between the stones, slowly eating away at the sand-colored mortar.

"This has to be our best bet of where Ernie survived the bombing," I said to Jennifer as I stood in the center of this old, abandoned barn behind an old, abandoned stone farmhouse five miles west of Saint-Lô. "Assuming that the place where Ernie survived is still standing, that is."

Jennifer agreed.

There was nothing special about the inside of the barn. It very much resembled the ground floor of the barn my grandfather owned in central Wisconsin. Farm-animal dirt and grime, whitewashed stone, and simple post-and-beam construction. Probably used to house pigs, I figured, judging by the way the pens were set up and how caked with filth the bottom of the walls were.

Looking back on that disastrous bombardment, the worst case of American mass-casualty friendly fire of the war, Ernie struck a sympathetic note for his readers, writing that he was sure that fateful night, back in their huts on some airdrome in England, the crews wept for what had happened, in what he described as "the awful knowledge that they had killed our own American troops."

"But I say this to them," Ernie continued, addressing his friends in the Air Corps directly. "Anybody makes mistakes.... And in this case the percentage of error was really very small compared with the colossal storm of bombs that fell upon the enemy."[103]

With Lee Miller, Ernie was a little less magnanimous. "That bombing," he wrote at the end of a letter, "was the most sustained horrible thing I've ever gone through. I really don't believe I could go through the whole thing again and keep any sanity."[104]

Physically, he claimed, he felt fine after the bombing—once he returned to his tent at Vouilly. But then the next morning he woke with body aches, a fever, and a bout of the "famous Army diarrhea" that laid him low for almost a week, even after a heavy dosage of paregoric and bismuth tablets.[105] "Think it was just kind of a 'collapse' reaction from being so long under such strain and tension, during the big attack." It took another four or five days after he started feeling better before he regained enough strength to write up what he had lived through. "Went through a hell of a period of depression," he confided to Lee. "Just barely managed to drag out one column a day."[106]

It was time to come home, he told Jerry. Ernie's war, the war of "little things," as he put it, was ending. "The war seems to be rushing toward a climax," he wrote to her, and what readers seemed to want now was stories about "miles gained and signs of complete enemy collapse."[107] That wasn't the war Ernie had the inclination to cover. Gone were his plans to fly to India and China for the winter. "I find I can't take as much as I could a year or two ago," he told Lee. "Out in the field I wear out awfully easily, and when I come back have to rest before writing."[108] Perhaps after a few months of rest, when he didn't feel harassed by the pressure of writing a daily column, he'd regain some perspective? Perhaps the war in the Pacific would appreciate a little of the "Pyle treatment"?[109] "At least it'll be something different," he concluded. With the realization that he'd have around a hundred thousand dollars stowed away—"even after taxes"—by the end of 1944, he could finally stop worrying about maintaining his column to earn enough to cover Jerry's medical expenses. He could finally stop pushing, at least for a little while. And for the first time in almost a year, he could sit with Jerry under the warm New Mexico sun, a cold drink melting in his hand.[110]

"I don't have much feeling one way or the other about our present fame," he wrote to Jerry. "It's nice in a way, but I'm afraid it's going to make life almost unlivable when I get home." If his time in France was any indication, all that peace and quiet Ernie was hoping for might not materialize. "Everywhere I go I have to autograph hundreds of franc-notes for soldiers (although I enjoy that); but now it's got so soldiers come to the camp just to see me, and they don't know when to leave and it slows me up. One boy rode a bicycle five miles the other day to come here."[111]

8

Soon after Ernie's stomach was settled enough for him to get down to writing, Little Arthur McCollum, as he lived and breathed, strolled into Ernie's tent at the camp outside the Château de Vouilly. Arthur's hospital had come over from England and set up shop in Cherbourg at the beginning of August. As soon as he was able to get away, Arthur set out on a search for his old friend from Albuquerque. Since the last time they'd tied one on together, before the invasion, Arthur had learned that his son had been killed in action when the plane he was piloting was shot down by German antiaircraft guns. He couldn't stand all the sympathy he was getting at the hospital. "Actually," Ernie told Jerry, "he is taking Ross's death perfectly fine."[112]

Ernie asked a couple of other correspondents to take Arthur along with them for the day while Ernie dedicated himself to column writing. When they returned later that evening, Arthur broke out a bottle of Scotch he'd been saving.[113] A day or two later, after Ernie had caught up on his cushion a little, he and Arthur went for a jeep tour close behind the front lines, which at that point in August were fluid.[114]

"In wandering around our far-flung front lines," Ernie later wrote in his column, "we could always tell how recently the battles had swept on ahead of us." Turning to his tried-and-true writing tool, anaphora, Ernie listed both the big and little things, repeating the phrase "From the . . ." no fewer than eight times:

From the scattered green leaves and the fresh branches of trees still lying in the middle of the road.

From the wisps and coils of telephone wire, hanging brokenly from high poles and entwining across the roads.

From the gray, burned-powder rims of the shell craters in the gravel roads, their edges not yet smoothed by the pounding of military traffic.

From the little pools of blood on the roadside, blood that had only begun to congeal and turn black, and the punctured steel helmets lying nearby.

From the square blocks of building stone still scattered in the village streets, and from the sharp-edged rocks in the roads, still uncrushed by traffic.

From the burned-out tanks and broken carts still unremoved from the road.

From the cows in the fields, lying grotesquely with their feet to the sky, so newly dead they had not begun to bloat or smell.

From the scattered heaps of personal gear around a gun.[115]

From all such things, Ernie continued, he and Arthur could tell when they reached Le Mesnil-Tôve, about fifty miles straight south of Vouilly, that the sweet old stone village had been the scene of recent and intense fighting. It was the "men so newly dead that they seemed to be merely asleep" that gave it away. What stood out most of all was the "inhuman quiet" of the vacuum left behind fast-moving combat. "The Germans would stand and fight it out until they saw there was no hope," Ernie wrote. "Then some gave up, and the rest pulled out and ran for miles." All that remained was the "lifeless debris, the sunshine and the flowers, and utter silence."

"Everything was dead," Ernie wrote, "the men, the machines, the animals."[116]

9

The ditches were clogged with dead men. Their battered helmets and broken rifles rested askew all around their bloating pink and blue bodies. Ernie and Arthur drove along slowly in their jeep. A headless, legless, and armless torso stole their words. All they could do was stare. "There was so much uncertainty in all the silence," Ernie later reported. "There was no live human being, no sign of movement anywhere."[117] He'd asked the driver to take him and Arthur about a quarter mile or so outside of Le Mesnil-Tôve, a village of not more than fifty buildings, most of which had recently been reduced to blackish-gray ruins. "It was necessary for us to wreck almost every farmhouse and little village in our path," he explained in one of his columns from France. "The Germans used them for strong points or put artillery observers in them, and they just had to be blasted out. Most of the French farmers evacuated ahead of the fighting and filtered back after it had passed."[118]

Ernie asked the driver to stop. The young man jammed the stick into neutral and turned off the engine. On the far side of the field, a stranger stood, silhouetted with the sun at his back. Ernie waved from the back seat of the jeep. The man on the far side of the field waved back. Satisfied that the stranger was friendly, Ernie and Arthur hopped out onto the gravel road, stepped over a low hedge, and walked toward the middle of the matted farm field. To their left they noticed two smashed planes in an adjoining field. Both were British, Ernie figured. One lay right side up, and the other rested on its back. Nothing else about them stood out.

After Ernie introduced himself and Arthur, the stranger, a young second lieutenant dressed in coveralls named Ed Sasson, shook their hands before asking what brought them this way. After explaining the reason for their joyride, Ernie learned Sasson was a graves-registration man attached to an armored division that had fought through there. It was Sasson's job to follow behind the front, scour the fields, and locate any American remains so that they could be identified and properly buried. He told Ernie and Arthur he was happy to have the company, for "it is a lonely job catering to the dead," he said.[119]

Another soldier ran up to the trio, interrupting their conversation. In between gasps of breath, he squeezed out the message: "Hey!" A breath. "There's a man alive." Another breath. "In one of those planes across the road!" A swallow and one long, deep breath. "He's been trapped there for days."

Ernie ran along with Sasson, Arthur and the other soldier following close behind. "That one! There! The upside-down one!" Ernie dropped to his hands and knees to peek through a hole in the side of the downed plane. He saw a man lying on his back, strapped in so that he hung upside down in the cramped cockpit. "His feet disappeared somewhere in the jumble of dials and pedals above him," Ernie later reported. "His shirt was open and his chest was bare to the waist. He was smoking a cigarette."[120]

"Oh, hello," the man said in his "typical British manner of offhand friendliness."

"Are you all right?" Ernie asked. He didn't know what else to say.

"Yes, quite," the pilot replied. "Now that you chaps are here." His name was Robert Gordon Follis Lee.

"How long have you been like this?"

The pilot couldn't say. Time had lost all meaning. He did know the date he was shot down, though.

"Good God!" Ernie replied. "This man's been trapped, lying there for eight days!"

Right at that moment, several more Americans emerged through a nearby hedge. They tore at the sides of the plane, some with pliers or wire clippers, others with their bare hands or a crowbar. "It seemed as if it would take hours to make a hole big enough to get the pilot out," Ernie wrote. "The ripping and pounding against the metal sides of the hollow plane made a thunderous noise."

Ernie peered back inside. "Does the noise bother you?" he asked.

"No, I can stand it," the pilot replied matter-of-factly. "But tell them to be careful when they break through on the other side—my leg is broken, you know."[121]

"His left leg was broken and punctured by an ack-ack burst," Ernie wrote. "His back was terribly burned by raw gasoline that had spilled. The foot of his injured leg was pinned rigidly under the rudder bar. The space was so small he couldn't squirm around to relieve his own weight from his paining back. He couldn't straighten out his legs, which were bent above him. He couldn't see out of his little prison. He had not had a bite to eat or a drop of water." For eight days, no less.[122] "Yet when we found him," Ernie added, "his physical condition was good, and his mind was calm and rational."[123]

"God," one of the soldiers exclaimed, "these Limeys have got guts!"[124]

10

On my last day in Normandy, I checked out of my airborne-themed B and B in Carentan and drove about an hour and a half south to Le Mesnil-Tôve in search of the field where Ernie and Arthur had found the downed pilot. Jennifer was back in Lyon with her husband and daughter. There were university courses to teach and final exams to grade. I wasn't sure there would be anything to find on my own, except the village itself. A battlefield tour guide Jennifer had befriended a few months back had never heard of Ernie's series of columns on the trapped pilot, and he knew Normandy and its battlefield history better than most.

A hazy white sun glowed through thinning clouds above, drying the wet pavement on the road leading into town. The stone buildings were either square or rectangular, with barnlike features and rooflines. They were built close to the two-lane road that cut the village down the middle. After hanging the first right I could make, I circled around the church of Saint-Jean-Baptiste, a small, gray-stoned Catholic church with deep-red front doors and a black roof, surrounded by a small cemetery and a low stone wall. Past the church, I pulled over into a small gravel parking lot across the narrow lane from an open-air dairy barn ripe with black-and-white milking cows. It wasn't yet lunchtime, and I had yet to see another living soul out and about on this Thursday in early December.

Outside my car window I noticed a historical marker with the title BIEN-VENUE AU MESNIL-TÔVE. I couldn't translate every word, but I gathered the gist. "The terrible events of 1944," the narrative began, "which are told to you in the panels making up this circuit . . ." I looked down below the text to find a map of a wonky square with rounded edges, laid out in green, that I could follow if I wanted to see where two Royal Air Force pilots had crash-landed on August 7, 1944, "in the heart of the front between Americans and Germans." The last stop on the circuit, the map showed, was city hall. I was clearly not the only one who had come around, knocking on doors and asking questions, hoping to retrace the steps of America's most beloved war correspondent.

Back behind the wheel, I drove slowly past the church and hung a right onto La Boutinais, the village's main road. Instead of proceeding straight onto La Piloisière, I was, according to the map, supposed to merge right onto an S-shaped stretch of road that cut through a small cluster of homes before slicing through fenced-in pastures of milking cows. Outside my windows I saw gentle shadowy hills rolling back into the village beyond. The church's steeple, black and slick like a blade, cut into the sky where the horizon met the clouds. I slowed my pace to a crawl, scanning from the ditches to the distant horizon. No sign of commemoration or memorialization—not even a simple recognition of the spot where Ernie and Arthur had witnessed the miracle rescue.

Another right. The road narrowed. Up ahead, the hazard lights on the back of a tractor with giant farm tires blinked methodically. From behind the driver's cockpit, an orange mechanical arm with a high-powered mower at its business end trimmed the top of a deep-green and brown hedgerow alongside the road. I tried to imagine, with the grinding of wood and foliage as my soundtrack, how much the people of Le Mesnil-Tôve were affected, long after the battles that raged in their backyards and outside their church had ended. All I'd been able to find during my research was that Le Mesnil-Tôve's steep-sided valleys and patchwork of small hedgerowed fields made the village relatively easy for even a small contingent of Germans to frustrate the American advance with a few antitank weapons, some artillery support, and a couple of heavy machine guns. "Losses on both sides were heavy," I'd read before my trip, "and the civilian population took an equal measure of suffering." The worst of it took place at a farm owned by the Chevalerie family, where thirteen French civilians were caught in the crossfire between the Third Battalion of the American 119th Infantry Regiment and part of the German army's right flank, made up of soldiers from the Second SS Panzer Division, the same group of hard-liners that on June 10, 1944, murdered 642 French civilians, including women and children, from the village of Oradour-sur-Glane. While the "Battle of the Hedgerows around Mesnil-Tôve and Mesnil-Adelée," as it is known today, lasted only about a day and a half, it took nearly a week for the Americans to finish mopping up enemy resistance.

Then my mind turned to Ernie's recounting of the rescue operation. I couldn't remember if he'd mentioned a second pilot. Perhaps the other pilot was killed in the crash—and Ernie didn't think that detail merited mention? Or maybe that other pilot was able to escape and return safely to Allied lines? The road came to a dead end at the driveway of a farm. A quick Y-turn took me back the way I came.

Feeling stymied, I returned to Ernie's description of the rescue. As soon as the hole the soldiers were cutting into the cockpit was large enough, Ernie stuck his slim shoulders and head through far enough that he could hand a canteen of water to the desperately thirsty man. After the pilot had emptied it, he placed the canteen down on his bare chest and held it close with both hands. "By God," he said, "I could drink a river dry."[125]

Ernie wetted a dirty handkerchief and rubbed the sweat and smudge from the pilot's forehead. "His hair was nut brown in color and very long," Ernie later recounted. "His whiskers were reddish and scraggly and he had a little mustache. His face seemed long and thin, and yet you could tell by his tremendous chest that he was a big man and powerful. His eyes were not glassy, but I was fascinated by his eyeballs. They didn't protrude; it was just that they were so big. When he turned them toward you, it was as though he was slowly turning two big brown tennis balls."[126]

"Is there someone else in the plane?" Ernie asked. The stench inside the pulverized metal was almost unbearable. Surely a copilot must be festering underneath all that wreckage.

"No," the pilot answered. "This is a single-seater, old boy." That meant only one thing: gangrene must have set in to one of his wounds.[127]

The first German machine-gun round that hit his night fighter knocked out the motor, the pilot explained to Ernie. "It was too low to jump," he added, "so I turned on my lights to try a crash landing." That's when the enemy "really poured it on him." A second bullet clipped the fingers on his right hand to the bone, and a third landed in his leg.[128]

"I can move my right leg," the pilot said. "It's all right. In fact I've had it out from here several times, and moved it around for exercise. But the left one I can't move."

He had left his wheels up, and when the plane's belly hit the earth, it dug a groove about fifty yards long. "Then the plane flopped, tail over nose, onto its back," Ernie told his readers. "The pilot was absolutely sealed into the upside-down cockpit."

"That's all I remember for a while," the pilot told Ernie. "When I came to, they were shelling all around me."

"For days afterwards," Ernie wrote, "the field in which he lay passed back and forth between German hands and ours. The pasture was pocked with hundreds of shell craters. Many of them were only yards away. One was right at the end of his wing. The metal sides of the plane were speckled with hundreds of shrapnel holes. He lay there, trapped in the midst of that inferno of explosions. The fields around him gradually became littered with dead."[129]

"Where did you get the cigarette you were smoking when we got here?"

"Your chap gave it to me," the pilot responded. "The one who came first. He lighted it for me and stuck it in through the hole, and went searching for the rest of you."

"Probably not so wise to light up in a wrecked plane," Ernie chided him.

"I'll tell you about that," the pilot said. "Do you see that woods a little way north of us?" There were several small woods all around, but Ernie said sure, he saw.

"Well," the pilot said, "that first night they set fire to that woods. I could tell it by the glow in the cockpit. And here the plane was soaked with hundred-octane gasoline. I thought the fire would spread right across the field. But it didn't." Ernie knew that wasn't what happened—the fire he saw was the neighboring town, which had been shelled. "I didn't bother to tell him," Ernie later wrote, "for he was alive, and after all what could the technicalities matter?"[130]

"The days passed," Ernie added in his column. "He thirsted terribly. He slept some; part of the time he was unconscious; part of the time he undoubtedly was delirious. But he never gave up hope."[131]

The nearest aid station to the downed pilot's plane was nearly six miles away. It took an hour for a medical captain and three medics to arrive. After assessing the scene, the captain asked for morphine. The pilot held out his right arm. The captain stuck the needle into the bend in the pilot's elbow.

"You're in good condition," the captain assured the pilot. "This is just to make it easier for you when we start to pull you out."

They waited a few minutes, long enough for the morphine to kick in. "I am delaying you from your work," the pilot said to the aid men. "I'm frightfully sorry about it."

"Good God, Lieutenant," one of the aid men blurted. "You aren't delaying us. This is what we're here for. We're just sorry we've been so long getting out."

The pilot closed his eyes. Then he placed his hand on his forehead. He took a breath. "Well, I don't know what I should do without you."

With web belts looped around the pilot's armpits, and with a couple of medics holding on to the pilot's trapped foot, ready to wiggle it free, the men prepared to pull. "It's my back that's weak," the pilot said. "All the strength seems to be gone from the small of my back. You'll have to help me there."

"They pulled," Ernie recounted. "The pilot, although without food for eight days, was tremendously strong, and he reached above his head to the plane's framework and helped lift himself. The belts slipped, and the soldiers took them off. They knelt and lifted his shoulders with their hands."

"We'll be as easy as we can," the medical captain said. "Tell us when to quit."

"Go ahead," the pilot said. "I'll stand it as long as I can."

After sliding the pilot a few inches through the cut opening in the side of the cockpit, the pilot suddenly yelled out for the men to stop. "My back! It's stuck to the ground. We'll have to break it loose slowly." They stopped pulling. "I can't raise my behind at all," he added.[132]

When I reached the main road once again, I turned right and pulled even with a steep-roofed provincial building with tall second-story windows and a French flag flying high from a white pole out front. The empty parking lot told me I had arrived at city hall, apparently too late to catch anyone before they headed home for lunch. After parking close to the locked entrance, I walked to the edge of the road to take a picture or two. That's when I noticed it—another historical marker, this one with a grainy picture of four pilots standing shoulder to shoulder, all suited up before takeoff. Ernie's misspelled name jumped out at me immediately, right there in the first paragraph of the two-column narrative: "Le journaliste Ernie Pyles a raconté cette histoire de survie au Coeur des combats, huit jours enfermé dans son avion retourné, dans le journal 'Stars and Stripes' de l'époque le 23 août 1944." There followed a long excerpt from one of Ernie's columns that describes the rescue operation.

Farther down the sidewalk, in the shadow of a tall hedgerow, another marker told the story of the second pilot—a stern-looking Royal Air Force lieutenant by the name of William "Killy" Kilpatrick. In my rough translation from the French, the story went something like this:

On August 7, 1944, his squadron was sent from the B3 aerodrome of Sainte Croix sur Mer to attack enemy transports near Condé sur Noireau. The pilots found no targets. So they headed south to Saint Jean des Bois where Killy's group of Typhoons launched an attack. While flying at low altitude, the engine of his Typhoon was damaged by the flak.

Knowing there were about two minutes left before the engine stopped, he headed southwest where the Allied line was. He remembers having flown over a forest, probably the forest of Mortain. Immediately after, the engine stopped. Killy saw a field beyond the trees and he turned to make a hard landing. As he approached the field at high speed, he saw another Typhoon roll back into the field. It was Bob Lee's Typhoon of 245 Squadron which had just crashed after attacking German tanks at the Battle of Mortain.

The field was on the border of the American and German armies.

As Killy's plane was under attack, he got out of the plane and ran toward some pits. There was a German tank on the other side of the
hedge. The village of Le Mesnil-Tôve was being stormed, so he hid
under the tank hoping to escape later. That evening he was arrested
by a German officer and taken east to the Falaise Pocket where he
spent several days under attack from the RAF and U.S. Air Force.

Killy met an American prisoner who was also a pilot. So the two
men persuaded their guards to surrender and guide them to the Allied lines. They had to pass through an SS headquarters where the
plan was nearly uncovered. Eventually twenty-four German soldiers joined the group and were persuaded to surrender to the two
pilots. Soon contact was made with the Free French Forces and the
German prisoners were placed in a camp, while the two pilots went
first to Le Mans and then to their bases.

King George VI later presented Lieutenant Kilpatrick with the Distinguished Service Order, one of the highest distinctions a British service
member can receive. Killy also returned to the scene of events, the narrative read, in the fall of 1944. A black-and-white picture shows a battered Typhoon with its belly buried in rich topsoil. The front props are twisted and
looking filed down, like mini-golf pencils too short to hold comfortably.
Two men in civilian dress stand on the downed plane, one in the cockpit
and the other on the wing. The man on the wing has his knuckles dug into
his hips with his elbows jutting out, like Superman. Whoever took the picture was too far away to capture the details of their faces. One of the men
must be Killy, I thought. But is the other this "Bob Lee," the man Ernie met
and chatted with, who survived eight days of excruciating pain without
food or water?

Not likely, I learned. Military censors back at Vouilly wouldn't allow
Ernie to reveal the name of the Royal Air Force pilot he had helped rescue
until several days later—after the pilot's family and proper military authorities had been notified. Ernie also didn't know whether the dispassionate
and brave-beyond-belief Robert "Bob" Lee was going to live or not. He did

in fact live. Nine months after the crash, the pilot's father, Frank Lee, re-ported to the press that after months of painful rehabilitation, "Robert has recovered from his wounds apart from the injury to his left leg." It would still take some time, though, "before it is well and of use to him."[133]

11

Not long after his conversation with the medic in the bar of Hôtel Scribe, Ernie was granted permission to return to the United States. Before flying to London to catch the *Queen Elizabeth*, whose decks would be crowded with wounded GIs,[134] Ernie returned for a few days' rest to the Château de Vouilly, where General Bradley had set up his headquarters.[135] Arriving on September 2, "worn out, thin, and badly in need of a shave," as one of Bradley's staff officers later reported, Ernie said his goodbyes.[136] Bradley told him he ought to not only go home but stay home.[137] Forget that nonsense about covering the Pacific. Ernie had done more than enough, Bradley tried to convince him.

It's not clear if Ernie finished the last chapter of *Brave Men* while camp-ing at Vouilly or if it was in another "French orchard," but when I told James Hamel that Ernie had described finishing his book "under an apple tree in a lovely green orchard in the interior of France" in the "latter part of August 1944," his eyes lit up.[138] There used to be an apple orchard on the back corner of the property, near where many of the army's tents had once been erected. The trees were no longer there, he said, but if Jennifer and I liked, he could walk us out to the spot to see for ourselves.

He led us out a glass-paned side door at the back of the château, where the vines and growth crawling up the stucco exterior were a dead-looking grayish brown, devoid of all springtime green. We crossed a gravel-packed stone bridge across the château's shallow moat, which stretched thirty feet from the exterior walls to the stone wall that surrounded the main house, and headed to a back corner of the property. We passed under a giant, sprawling walnut tree and followed a trail mowed through matted-down grass to a small pond. In leafless trees on the far side, small bundles of mistletoe dotted the space between branches. The murky pond was calm and clear as we skirted its marshy shoreline and stepped into a large unplanted field of grass ringed by short hedgerows and sixty-foot maples. The ground was squishy beneath my shoes.

James stood next to me with his hands buried in the front pockets of his black windbreaker. His thinning white hair waved in the breeze. He pointed to where I was standing. Mostly through Jennifer's translations, he explained to me that where I stood was where that famous portrait of Pyle typing under an apple tree was taken. He's seated at a folding table big enough for a single person, with legs that fold in like a card table, a leather strap to hold down the legs, and a handle to carry it around. His left leg is crossed over his right, under the table, and his correspondent's case is open on his lap, pressed between his torso and the edge of the table. He's shuffling papers, it seems, like he's recently finished a column and is about to straighten the loose pages and slide them back into his case. It doesn't appear he knows he's being photographed; his eyes are trained on the task at hand, and his face is lost looking and tired, as if he's rushing to meet a deadline and isn't sure if there will be enough time to do the subject justice.

I can't be totally sure that photo was taken on James's property, though I am inclined to take his word for it. According to the photographer who snapped it, he came across the scene of Ernie writing on July 12, 1944, which checks out,[139] as far as when Ernie stayed at the press camp. But there isn't much in the way of background that lines up with what we see today. Still, it's very much possible.

Standing there in the silence, I found it easy to imagine Ernie pitched in the shade, a metal cup of booze within reach, out past the château's ancient moat. I could see him pecking at the keys on his typewriter with the broken carriage return. "It could well be that the European war will be over and done by the time you read this book," Ernie wrote in his conclusion to *Brave Men*. "Or it might not. But the end is inevitable, and it cannot be put off for long. The German is beaten and he knows it."[140]

But how did it come about? How were the Allies able to rally together to defeat the Nazis? How were average folks from humble beginnings able to endure so much for so long? First off, there was the fact, he knew, that the Axis powers had been weakened from those earlier battles Ernie had seen for himself. He started there. Then there were America's brave men, of course, but there was also "Russia, and England, and the passage of time, and the gift of nature's materials." The Allies did not prevail, Ernie wrote, "because destiny created us better than all other peoples." It was, in fact, Ernie's sincerest hope that the hundreds of thousands of words he wrote during the war would lead Americans to show more gratitude than pride, for "the dead men would not want us to gloat." Instead, he concluded, "All we can do is fumble and try once more—try out of the memory of our anguish—and be as tolerant of each other as we can."[141]

CHAPTER 10

NOTHING LEFT TO DO

■■ ■■ ■ ■■■■■■■■■ ■■■■

The methods of war, the attitude toward it, the homesickness, the distances, the climate—everything is different from what we have known in the European war.

Here in the beginning, I can't seem to get my mind around it, or my fingers on it. I suspect it will take months to get adjusted and get the "feel" of this war.

ERNIE PYLE, "EUROPE THIS IS NOT," FEBRUARY 16, 1945[1]

1

The month of October was a hectic one for Ernie. First there was a visit from Paige. Then Lester Cowan arrived in Albuquerque and stayed for three days. The movie producer and the man he had chosen to direct *The Story of G.I. Joe*, William Wellman, both updated Ernie on their progress and made a final pitch for Burgess Meredith to play Ernie. As an enlisted soldier, Meredith needed the army's permission to take enough time off to shoot the film. Ernie had to call in a favor from General Alexander Surles to make it happen.[2] When Cowan and Wellman returned to California, Wellman "went back and killed 90 percent of the dialogue" in the script, "which I'm sure is just as well," Ernie told Lee.[3]

Ernie figured that after they all left, he had half a week's worth of letters that needed to be written—plus there were all those piles that arrived every afternoon from all corners of the country and from battlefields across Europe, letters Ernie desperately wanted to read and reply to, but he knew that without a secretary they'd likely rot where they were laid in batches.[4] "When that's finished," he told Lee at the beginning of October, "I can relax."[5] If only it were that simple.

The phone rang at least a half a dozen times per day with offers to speak or write or to be presented with some kind of honor or award.[6] "People call from all over the country wanting me to make speeches," Ernie complained to Lee, "but it's easy to say no. I turned down Bob Hope, Eddie Cantor and the Treasury Dept all in one day."[7] Ernie also told Lee to decline an offer made by the Madison Avenue marketing firm Young & Rubicam. In early October, they had sent a man to meet with Lee about a five-thousand-dollar retainer for Ernie *if and when* he decided to do some radio work, as long as he agreed to do it through them. Lee thought the offer sounded fishy.[8] Ernie agreed. He told Lee to tell Young & Rubicam "nuts on that if and when contract business." Besides, Ernie added, "I don't need the money now and I've definitely decided a flat no on all radio nibbles, now and forever."[9]

Perhaps the most flattering request for Ernie's time came one morning when he found the president and two deans from the University of New Mexico camped in his front yard.[10] They wanted to know if Ernie would accept an honorary doctorate of letters. "I didn't see why not," he told Lee.[11] On the day of the big ceremony, Ernie was still drunk from the night before but somehow managed to get through it "without keeling over or disgracing myself." Fortunately, he continued, "I was in such a daze I didn't know where I was so didn't even mind the crowd. The worst part was when it was over I had to sign autographs for an hour."[12] Upon receiving his first honorary degree, Ernie could only squeak out a nervous "Thank you" to the adoring crowd. Later, grinning, he admitted when pressed that he was in fact pleased. A month later, he endured a repeat performance while being awarded a doctorate of humane letters from Indiana University in Bloomington, the first such degree the school ever bestowed. "They sent my old friend Dean Edmondson," Ernie explained to Lee, "with special papers telling me about it." Could they award him the degree in absentia? Absolutely not, the dean told him. What if they arranged a special convocation? "My natural impulse is to tell them to stick it up their ass," he wrote to Lee, which may or may not have been entirely true. "A good bucket of shit is of more importance to me than one of these damn things, yet in this case you just can't turn it down. So I've got to go."[13]

Perhaps the greatest work-related barrier to Ernie's finding balance between his profession and his family was erected by the U.S. Navy,[14] which had stepped up its pressure campaign on Lee Miller after Ernie mentioned the Pacific in his farewell to Europe. It seems clear, judging from Lee's correspondence with Ernie,[15] that the navy wanted Lee to put his thumb on the scale in Ernie's mind about whether to stay home with Jerry or go warhorsing across the Pacific.

Was Ernie concerned about censorship? No problem. They were working something out. "This Captain Waldo Something-or-other who has been lousing up press and censorship at Pearl Harbor has been jerked," Lee assured Ernie. Waldo had been replaced, he continued, with someone "who will make things smoother for the correspondents."[16]

What about the field conditions over there—the heat, the bugs, the malaria, and the dysentery? The navy assured Lee that Ernie could have "anything the Navy's got," and that no matter where he wanted to go, the navy would get him there, from "carrier to battleship to buoy."[17]

On top of all that, the navy had recently commissioned author and fellow Scripps-Howard journalist Max Miller, who would be assigned to accompany Ernie to the Pacific as his official liaison—"assuming that you don't change your mind," Lee stipulated to Ernie. "Captain Campbell of Navy public relations assured me that once you had a cushion of a week's columns you would have no worries at all about keeping up daily continuity," he continued. "They're putting in a big transmitter at Guam, and they catapult planes to deliver copy from warships, and so on."[18]

Then there were Ernie's publisher's expectations, which added to the pressure being exerted by the navy. By the beginning of October, Henry Holt and Company had already sold over 100,000 copies of Brave Men in advance of its publication at the end of the year. At first, they had only

enough paper to print 170,000 copies,[19] but then they were able to comman-
deer more paper from the publisher's textbook department so they could
print nearly 200,000 copies for the New Year's Eve 1944 release.[20] Ultimately, Holt wanted to publish a three-in-one book someday, a book that
wove together *Here Is Your War*, *Brave Men*, and a "theoretical book on the
Pacific." Ernie was a cash cow, plain and simple. In 1944, Holt sold nearly
46,000 copies of *Here Is Your War*, a whole year after it was published, earning Ernie a little over twelve thousand dollars (about two hundred thousand dollars in 2022 money).[21] Add to that the extra money Lee negotiated
out of Lester Cowan. "This would lift the ceiling on your 10% of profits," he
explained to Ernie in a letter, "and it might mean several hundred thousand, to which you certainly are entitled in view of the fact that he is in effect buying two books instead of one."[22]

"I hate and dread to go so terribly that when I let myself think about it
I get clear down in the dumps," Ernie confided in Lee. "I wish I could somehow feel free to stay here just as long as I wanted to, until I really got itchy
to get going again."[23] Ernie wasn't the only one who wanted him to stay. Sister Margaret Jane pleaded with Ernie not to leave again. She told him Jerry
wouldn't survive him going overseas. "But what can I do? I don't want to
go either," he explained to Lee, "but if I stay at home I suppose I'd get so I
couldn't live with myself, for not going . . . And if I go and she should die,
it would haunt me the rest of my life. I'm really in the dumps about it."[24]

2

Midway through October, Ernie traveled to California for a few days
of work on the movie. Paige had insisted he come so that Ernie could
"talk privately to the people who will really make the picture—the associate producer, the art director, the writers, and so on," Ernie recounted in a
letter to Lee. Apparently, the folks who were making the movie were all
feeling a bit hobbled by Cowan and his seemingly endless flow of "ideas."
Paige believed that if Ernie could "talk to everybody and as an outsider see

the whole thing sort of clearly," and then convey to Cowan and Wellman what he thought, "it would solidify and clarify things for them," he explained to Ernie, "and get them started into action, instead of just forever having new ideas."[25]

"I had a medium good time in Hollywood," Ernie later reported to Lee, "and think some good was done." He and Paige set up shop in Paige's shady backyard. "We just sat there in state in the garden and had all the underlings—such as producers, directors, cameramen, ward-robe men, writers, art directors and what not come to us one at a time for 'conferences.' Think it worked out pretty well."[26] Even though he didn't care much for the movie's proposed title, Ernie was starting to come around to the conclusion that the film might be a hit.[27]

What Ernie had wanted since the end of the North African campaign, more than money—and a hell of a lot more than fame—was a calm, peaceful life with an intelligent, healthy, and sober woman who could devote herself to him, even when all they had to do on any given day was sit out on their little terrace,[28] sip iced gin drinks, and read from their mountain of books in the New Mexican sunshine on a warm afternoon.[29] For a week or so, Ernie thought maybe he had finally found what he was yearning for. "When I came home," he confided in a letter to Lee, "she was mentally herself for the first time in many years," meaning that she hadn't been drinking or abusing drugs, mainly. Since he was last home, Jerry had aged considerably—"15 years since I saw her last,"[30] Ernie figured—"and obviously was far from recovered either physically or mentally, but she had made wonderful progress and God how she had tried this time."[31] But then after Ernie returned from working on the set in California, "she started into one of these things that psychologists call manic depressions. The doctor says it was probably caused by nothing specific at all. That it was just the swing of the cycle."

"As I say," Ernie continued to Lee, "I've had no rest, and it hasn't all been due to family troubles." After several weeks of the mail piling up, Ernie hired Shirley Mount to provide some relief. She could fire off a couple dozen letters a day, but most of what needed to be done had to be done by Ernie himself. Letters had to be returned: From soldiers Ernie befriended. From the War Department. From old friends checking up on him. "The requests, demands, pleas and what not for me to write something or do something are just unbelievable in number," he lamented. "And so many of them are the kind that it's almost impossible to turn down."

"There is by no means a constant stream of visitors at the door," he continued, "yet there are just enough that you never feel for one hour that you're alone in your own home."[32]

3

After Ernie left for an appointment with the dentist downtown, Jerry's nurse, Mrs. Ella Streger, asked Jerry to join her outside in the garden. Jerry refused, choosing instead to retire to her room at the front of the house. Even though it wasn't part of Ms. Streger's official job description, there was housework to be done, so she left Jerry sitting alone on her bed. After pulling up and tucking in Ernie's bedsheets in the next room over, between Jerry's room and the bathroom, Mrs. Streger parked herself on a footstool to sew a missing button back onto one of Ernie's shirts.[33]

From a skinny drawer in her little writing desk, Jerry pulled out a pair of long narrow scissors. They had been gifted to Ernie by the Ringling Bros. and Barnum & Bailey Circus years before. Was this the first time she ever held them while contemplating her own destruction? Did it give her an odd sense of security to know they were there, in that skinny drawer, when she was ready for them, once she was ready to erase the stillness that hung between her and Ernie, the silent sadness that filled the house like a noxious gas?

Jerry would have lifted the scissors shoulder height, with the tips together and pointed down at a violent angle. Did her hand tremble? Did she need both hands to steady herself? How many times had she raised that same pair of scissors, only to drop her arms and toss the shitty souvenir to the back of the skinny desk drawer?

Before she could find a reason not to, Jerry plunged the scissors into the middle of her throat, below her Adam's apple. To drive them deeper, she pounded on them with her hand as if she were slapping the ketchup out of a glass bottle. With her windpipe sliced, she moved the scissors to the right side of her neck, below the jawline and in front of her ear.[34]

Cheetah, the family border collie, dashed into Ernie's room and jumped up onto Mrs. Streger's lap, jumped back down, and then back up.[35] When that didn't garner enough attention, Cheetah ran in a tight circle and darted out of the room, back to the coppery smell of blood. Mrs. Streger followed. "And there was Jerry," Ernie recounted to Lee, "standing before her little writing desk, absolutely covered with blood, and pounding the scissors into her neck."[36]

Jerry stared at Mrs. Streger hatefully, as if daring her to intervene. The pounding continued as the nurse lunged for her. Dodging her would-be tackler, Jerry retreated behind a big chair, still pounding on the scissors. "When Mrs. Streger got too close," Ernie continued, "she pulled the scissors out and started at Mrs. Streger with them." A tussle ensued until Mrs. Streger pried the bloody shears from Jerry's hand. "In her excitement," Ernie wrote, Mrs. Streger "laid them on the book shelf, and in a moment Jerry had them back again and started jabbing her wrists." Once more, Ella was able to wrestle the scissors away; this time she held them tight against her chest while with the other hand she phoned Jerry's doctor.[37] While the telephone line rang in Mrs. Streger's ear, Jerry stumbled out of her room and into the bathroom, locking the door behind her. She rifled through the medicine cabinet until she found what she needed—Ernie's razor. As she went back to work, this time on her left wrist and breast, Ernie pulled back into the driveway with a numb jaw and eight new fillings.[38]

Later that night, after Ernie and Mrs. Streger left Jerry in her room at the sanitarium, around eleven o'clock, Jerry's doctor came back to the house to talk. The neighbor girl, Shirley Mount, was there, too. Mrs. Streger had been through such a horror that she couldn't bear the thought of being home alone that night; Shirley was there to "make it moral." The four of them sat and drank until the early hours of the next morning, mostly out of relief that the day's ordeals had finally ended. Dr. Lovelace told them that he had talked with Jerry earlier that evening, and he was convinced that Jerry recalled nothing whatsoever. "She told him the first thing she remembered," Ernie told Lee, "was when the surgeon was sewing up her neck, and she wondered how it happened." Dr. Lovelace told Ernie what likely happened was that she had become "intoxicated almost to the point of mental blankness by this desperate depression."[39]

Still, the doctor assured Ernie, there was nothing he or anyone else could have done, especially because, according to Ernie, no one had sensed any "suicidal instincts" in the weeks leading up to her assault on herself. "Of course I lived for ten years in a horror that she would commit suicide," Ernie wrote to Lee, but in recent years, Ernie and Jerry's various doctors had decided she didn't have what it took to end her own life—"that her indirect threats were all part of her act." Jerry's previous attempts to kill herself were botched so badly "they were almost laughable," Ernie wrote, "and convinced us she was acting. In the last couple of years I had ceased to worry that she would ever do it. There has been nothing at all lately to indicate she was thinking along that line, even as an act. But brother this one was no act."[40]

Ernie and Jerry's doctors may not have seen her suicide attempt coming, though they did know *something* was bound to happen. In a letter dated October 8—over three weeks before Jerry's suicide attempt—Ernie wrote to Lee Miller that Jerry cried half the day in pain that he described as a "muscular ache that's like a tooth-ache all over."[41] Nine days later, Ernie wrote to Lee again. "She has good days and bad days," he wrote, "but she is so physically weak, and she still gets all knotted inside and gets panicky, and she can't sleep at night without sedatives—and really she must be under daily care of doctor and nurse." Even though Jerry's doctor visited her at home twice per day, and even though Jerry required nursing care night and day, and even though her doctors refused to give her anything for the pain—all things he reported to Lee—Ernie seemed to have forgotten it all by the end of that same month. "Even though she's so much better," he continued to Lee, "I see not much more recovery, and I get terribly depressed about it."[42]

"I've long given up hope for Jerry," he confessed, "yet there's nothing to do but hope."[43]

The day before Jerry tried to take her own life, Ernie wrote to Paige that she had fallen into a "horrible new depression" and that it was "part of the pattern," according to the doctor. "Starting Thursday evening it became drastic fast," he continued. "Since then she has only sat on the edge of her bed and stared, saying nothing, only occasionally answering you, most of the time just staring right through, other people as well as me."[44] Expecting her to get worse and worse for about five days until she "reached a climax," Dr. Lovelace implored Ernie and Mrs. Streger to ready themselves as if preparing for a storm.[45]

The night before that fateful day, Jerry had asked if she could cook Ernie dinner. Certainly, he said. They ate together and talked. "Although she wasn't wholly normal," he later wrote, "she seemed practically so compared to the previous several days." According to Ernie, Jerry went to bed "seemingly happy." Several times during the night, Jerry woke and came to Ernie's room to talk a little more. "I became convinced she was pulling out of it," he told Lee.[46]

Now Dr. Lovelace recommended that Jerry be committed for a least a month without any outside visitors, including Ernie.[47] "Starting in a couple of days," Ernie explained to Paige, "they're going to begin electrical shock treatments. One a day for about 30 days. They say it's terrific, but the doctor says it's the only hope."[48]

"It's the same as electrocution," Ernie told Lee, "only they stop in time. It induces a convulsion, and unconsciousness for about two hours. The doctor says it is the same as dying each time."

"The theory of this thing, the best I can make of it," Ernie continued, "is that it breaks up all the maze of 'thought patterns' that are attached to each other. As the doctor says, Jerry is in a condition similar to ringing a doorbell, but instead of a bell ringing at the other end of the wire, 20 sticks of dynamite go off. These treatments are to disconnect the wire from the dynamite, as he puts it, although the dynamite will still be there."[49]

Jerry's doctor, whom Ernie found to be "the best yet,"[50] had supreme confidence in electroconvulsive therapy. Ernie did not.[51] "It's too goddamned deep for me and I have little faith in it, but there's no harm in trying."[52]

4

Jerry seemed to be responding well to the shock therapy. At times she even became "somewhat cheerful," the doctors told Ernie, "and rational too." For about a week, she looped through a cycle of depression and "normalcy," he added, "and was batty as hell." Ernie even found some of it funny, like how Jerry was apparently convinced that either the Democrats or the Republicans—Ernie couldn't remember which—had conjured up an "evil plot" they were carrying out against her.

"There's no telling how Jerry will come out of this," Ernie continued in a letter to Lee. "If there's any indication that this recent tendency still exists, she'll just have to be institutionalized." Ernie wrote that he dreaded the thought of such a fate, but at the same time, he added, "we can't go on living in constant fear day and night that she'll do it again."[53]

Back at the house on Girard Boulevard, Mrs. Streger diligently showed up for work each morning, to fix Ernie's meals and serve as a "general all-round house companion." Despite all that had happened, she was committed to remaining Jerry's caretaker.

On November 12, 1944, Ernie wrote a letter to Paige laying out the next steps he had planned for Jerry. After she consented to being transferred to a private hospital, Dr. Lovelace suggested Ernie travel with her to Pasadena, to Las Encinas, a "beautiful and high-class" hospital that offered mental health services, both inpatient and out, with a focus on psychiatric stabilization and chemical-dependency issues. "We talked it over," Ernie wrote, "when Jerry was in one of her lucid periods, and she finally consented to go voluntarily, provided we would not tie her up so she couldn't leave. We agreed."[54]

After only a few more weeks in the hospital in Albuquerque, Jerry was back home with Ernie, who had nurses ready to care for Jerry around the clock. "Six hours after she got home," Ernie confided in Lee, "she was back in the hospital—under restraint. Yet next day she was home again, and as normal as she's been in a long time. She had two good days, but has been low and stayed in bed the last two days."

"It's an awful problem," Ernie added, "and I'm almost whipped. There's only one thing to do, and I can't do it. I just don't know what to do."[55] A week later, even though Jerry had been "haywire through it all," Ernie still had not decided what was to be done. "She can't be left at home even with nurses," he told Lee, "because it would take two per shift, and you can't get that many. Whatever we do has got to be for a long period of time, for if she's left fluctuating she'll be back home in a few weeks and the problem will start all over again, and with nobody here to handle it."[56]

Ernie and Jerry flew to Los Angeles to celebrate Christmas at Cicero's, on Sunset Boulevard in West Hollywood, with Paige and his wife.[57] The next day, Mrs. Streger took Jerry back to Albuquerque. The hospital Dr. Lovelace had recommended in Pasadena had no room for Jerry to stay while Ernie made his way across the Pacific. After several days hanging out with Burgess Meredith and the rest of the crew on set, supervising the filming of *The Story of G.I. Joe*, Ernie and his personal naval liaison, Max Miller, left Los Angeles on a train headed north to Camp Roberts in central California, the largest army basic training installation in the country,[58] for "two nights and days of 'inspecting' and travel with no sleep." From there they trekked farther north to San Francisco, a major port of embarkation for troops heading to the Pacific theater.[59]

At half past eight in the morning on January 8, an army driver picked up Ernie and Max from their hotel and took them for a tour of the port. "First we went to see the General in command, who was very nice, and then went on his private yacht over to Angel Island," home of Fort McDowell.

Waiting for Ernie and the general at the pier were a few colonels and a fifty-piece army band to serenade the special guests while the yacht was docked. For about an hour after that, Ernie was jeeped around the island, "stopping at various places and being shown around," he complained to Jerry. "It was all fairly boring, but something we had to do."[60]

The last stop on the tour was the base's cavernous drill hall, where over a thousand soldiers were assembled, waiting to greet Ernie before shipping out to uncertain futures.

One of the colonels put Ernie on the spot. "Would you mind saying a few words to the boys?"

"Oh my God no," Ernie replied. "I can't speak. Never do."

"But it was too late," he wrote to Jerry. "They had me trapped."

The band was back and playing with full and powerful lungs as Ernie, Max, and the officers entered the hall, traipsed down the center aisle, and mounted the stage at the front of the mass of grateful men. One of the colonels made a "little flattering speech" about Ernie. "And then I had to step up and face it," he wrote later.

He said half a dozen sentences, tops. Something to the effect of, "I can't make you a speech, because I was born tongue tied. This is the first one I've ever made, and I hope the last one.

"I've been two and a half years on the other side of the war," he continued, still trembling, "and now I'm headed for your side. A lot of you are too. So wish me luck." His voice cracked. "And I'll wish you luck." He paused. "And thanks a lot."[61]

The next night, Ernie and Max were comped tickets to *The Shaking Vanities*, a "big musical extravaganza" on roller skates instead of ice. It was "really terrific," Ernie reported to Jerry. He also had to grant interviews to reporters from local papers who "insisted on the most stupid and un-understanding" inquiries.[62] "You say a word or two about hating to go back to war and not getting much rest at home," he complained to Jerry, "and they seize on it and dramatize it out of all proportion."[63]

Jerry wanted Ernie to come home, to be with her. Ernie dismissed her pleas, despite his own reservations. It was simply too late to turn back now, he explained in a long letter. "You know that I don't want to go any more than you want me to, but the way I look at it it's something almost beyond my control. If I stayed I'm afraid that would defeat both of us, for I'd probably gradually work up a guilty feeling that would haunt me. I hate it, but there's just nothing else I can do."[64]

Having followed his chosen path for so long, through so much trauma, Ernie had reached a kind of threshold where his freedom to choose had been replaced by an understanding that he was made for the world in a particular way and that this way of being was nonnegotiable. Like the mountains or the sea, it simply *was*. It was as if, in other words, he had chosen and chosen until there was actually no choice at all.

Jerry blamed herself. If only she was better, more worthy of Ernie, she convinced herself, then he would want to stay. Ernie couldn't disagree more. "I've noticed both before and after your last relapse," he wrote, "that you were damning yourself unmercifully for the things you had done and hadn't done, and looking upon yourself as bad, which you are not.

"I know how you love me," he assured her, "and I am grateful for that. But I don't want you to let your feelings crucify you. Just try to achieve above all an inner calmness, and since we do still love each other in spite of all the world and personal turmoils we've been through, I know we can still have a fine and wonderful life together.

"If you do feel a debt to anyone," Ernie added, "you can best repay it by abandoning your present feelings of remorse and shame and self-condemnation, and being cheerful and accepting and becoming vitally interested in something."[65]

Above all else, Ernie tried to convince Jerry, he wanted for her to get well, to be her old self. "I want your mind to be calm and clear," he told her, "and for you to enjoy being alive, and be interested in things. I know how hard you are trying and how I admire you for it."[66] Ernie needed her to get well, for when he finally returned home, when the war was finally over, when he could finally put an end to all that wandering, he wanted to make the most of the time he had left with Jerry. He wanted to live simply and love deeply.

"I couldn't go on forever leading this frenzied goldfish life of the past few months," he confided in her. "We'll just have to drift out of the limelight and let it die its natural death, that's all."[67]

5

Around breakfast time on Thursday, January 11, 1945, John Steinbeck learned Ernie was staying at the hotel right across the street from where he and his wife, Gwyn, were sharing a room with their son, Thom, and his nurse for a three-day trip away from home back in Monterey.[68] Gwyn was sour with John after he had abandoned her bedside at Christmas to be with his sister while Gwyn was still recovering from the flu.

Ernie and Max stopped over about an hour before lunchtime to chat for a minute before heading over to the navy yard. They found photographers everywhere they went. At lunchtime, they stopped for a bite at the Palace Hotel, where "hotel photographers" interrupted the meal. Afterward, he spent an hour signing copies of *Brave Men* and "seeing everybody and listening to the same talk and answering the same questions."[69]

At four thirty, Ernie had the Steinbecks over to his hotel room for a drink, which quickly turned into four. "In San Francisco before he went to the Pacific," Steinbeck recounted years later, "he seemed a little numb. The rest hadn't rested him. His eyes were deep and tired and restless."[70]

Ernie strangled a glass of whiskey, his jaw muscles tight. To Steinbeck, he looked sick. "I don't know why I have to go back but I do," Ernie said. "It's my business." Then he pinched at his new uniform and cap. "These are a waste of money," he said. "I won't need them."

"I don't know whether I can write anymore," he added.

With their bellies warmed with brown liquor, John and Gwyn asked Ernie and Max to join them for dinner, but Ernie was too "washed up," he said. Instead, Ernie ate dinner alone and called it an early night.[71]

6

Fortune had come to Ernest Taylor Pyle—close to half a million dollars in the last two years of his life and millions more surely on the way—and he was being read daily in four hundred newspapers and weekly in three hundred more by an estimated fourteen million readers. His version of the war had become America's version. For some men, that might have been enough. But not Ernie. That's not how he saw it. The war was like a marriage to Ernie. It couldn't be something you suffered through for an acceptable amount of time before abandoning. He'd learned that lesson from Jerry. His marriage to her resembled his companionship with the misery, desolation, and exhilaration of war and the men who waged it, and the war, unlike Jerry, was not a spouse that would entertain the idea of divorce. His connection to the war had become part of who Ernie Pyle was, and he behaved as if he had no power to obliterate that version of himself.[72] The enemy would have to. Or the war would end. Those were the only two endings Ernie could see for himself. "I'm going simply because I've got to go," he told his readers, "and I hate it."[73]

Ernie and Max Miller left San Francisco on a Sunday afternoon. Ernie telegraphed Jerry that he was off and that he thought it was best that way—better than a phone call, at least. "I hope you feel the same way," he wrote to her. "There's nothing we need to say—for we know."[74]

Ernie and Max arrived in Honolulu, still hungover from a night of drunken adventure in Marin County followed by milk spiked with gin for breakfast.[75] The American Pacific-island-hopping campaigns were mostly complete by then; only the Philippines, Iwo Jima, and Okinawa remained before the Allies could mount an invasion on the Japanese mainland itself. During his short stay in Hawaii, the navy managed to carve out for Ernie a couple of quiet days for him to pound out eight columns. Then he met with reporters from the local papers, both of which published big write-ups. "Then the deluge began," Ernie recounted to Jerry. He and Miller had lunch or dinner with three admirals and two generals, and a prominent local businessman named Earl Thacker threw Ernie a little cocktail and dinner party, complete with Hawaiian singers.[76]

On January 21, Ernie landed on the island of Guam, now the headquarters of the American Pacific Fleet. There he struck up a friendship with Robert Sherrod, the intrepid correspondent for *Time* magazine and author of *Tarawa: The Story of a Battle*. Convinced that the two well-respected correspondents could help raise the navy's profile, Ernie and Sherrod were given "the purple treatment," including privileged accommodations and exclusive interviews with high-ranking officers. "The Navy has been won-

Ernie Pyle visited leathernecks of the Third Marine Division, where, along with talking to the veterans of the fight on Bougainville and Guam, he observed the famous Marine Corps war dogs for the first time. Shown here on January 24, 1945, talking to Jeep, a scout and security patrol Doberman pinscher, Ernie was impressed with the high standards set by the dogs and their outstanding battle records to date in the Pacific. Jeep was eighteen months old and had been overseas only a short time.

derful to me," Ernie wrote to Jerry, "and give me the best of everything and try to make things smooth for me."[77]

The grim view of the war that overtook Ernie on the beaches of Normandy—the sense that perhaps the losses were simply beyond bearing—seemed to follow him to the Pacific, like a shadow, until he found some semblance of peace on the island of Saipan, in the Mariana Islands. From the porch of a B-29 squadron commander's beachfront house, Ernie threw off the "awful inner horror of coming back" that had obsessed him. He wasn't sure what exactly caused such a dramatic change in attitude, but it had something to do with the quality time he was spending with his radio-operating nephew Jack Bales and his bomber buddies. Not being constantly pestered by soldier fans helped, too. Over the course of three days, Ernie had enough uninterrupted work time to write a batch of seventeen columns, matching his all-time record for a single stretch of writing. "There is no quality in the columns," he confessed to Jerry, "but quantity is what I'm after now."[78]

As far as his column was concerned, Ernie's biggest worry was that the navy would so censor his pieces that they'd lack whatever it was that made him such a mainstay for so many readers back in America. "Censorship is much different, due to a different type of security necessity," he explained to Jerry, "and I'm afraid I may be frustrated quite a bit in trying to give the average guy's picture of the war." By early March, after a column Ernie wrote had all the sailor's names cut out, he told the censors that "if the ruling weren't modified so I could use people's names, I'd simply have to go on to the Philippines or go home. So they've temporarily relaxed the rule, but it isn't official yet, and I don't feel yet permanently settled."[79]

Plus, there was the fact that Lee wouldn't be back in DC waiting patiently at the office to "translate" Ernie's sometimes garbled transmissions. Like Ernie, he was on assignment in the Pacific, covering the fighting in the Philippines. "But maybe it will work out better than I think," he added with uncharacteristic optimism. "There hasn't been anything in them yet worth losing, but maybe they can improve as I get back into the swing. It will probably take me another month to get clear back into the one-tracked mental world of war."

"The islands where I am are very pretty, and the climate really is nice," he added. Other than the warm and wet weather causing Ernie to break out with "little water blisters," he felt better than when he left California. "We live wonderfully here," Ernie wrote.[80]

Far from the appalling hardships incurred during amphibious assaults and frontline fighting in places like Iwo Jima, Ernie chose to focus his reporting on what he saw as the major differences between the doughfoot's war winding down in Germany and the "endless sameness" he found in the vast expanses of the Pacific. In a column titled "Europe This Is Not," Ernie laid out his conclusions: "The methods of war, the attitude toward it, the homesickness, the distances, the climate—everything is different from what we have known in the European War.[81]

"Another adjustment I'll have to make is the attitude toward the enemy," Ernie continued. "In Europe we felt our enemies, horrible and deadly as they were, were still people." Not true in the Pacific, where Ernie gathered the feeling that "the Japanese are looked upon as something inhuman and squirmy—like some people feel about cockroaches or mice." The only Japanese people he'd yet come across were prisoners of war fenced behind wire. "They were wrestling and laughing and talking just as humanly as anybody," Ernie reported. "And yet they gave me a creepy feeling and I felt in need of a mental bath after looking at them."[82]

After talking with marines who had squared off against the Japanese, Ernie began to "get over that creepy feeling that fighting Japs is like fighting snakes or ghosts." The truth was that they while they were, "indeed, queer," they were not "slippery or rat-like." It was much simpler than that. The Japanese were modern soldiers with weapons and training that made them "good, tough soldiers." Plus, Ernie told his readers, most of whom were well used to the racist framing used to discuss Japanese people, "the Japs are human enough to be afraid of us."[83]

Even though Ernie acknowledged that it "looks like soul-trying days for us in the years ahead," the Pacific war he described to his readers back in America was a softer, easier sort of war. "Health conditions among our men are excellent," he reported. "They work in shorts or without shirts and are deeply tanned. The mosquito and fly problem has been licked. There is almost no venereal disease. Food is good. The weather is always warm but not cruelly hot. Almost always a breeze is blowing. Anywhere you look, you have a pretty view."[84]

In early February, Ernie flew to the tiny island of Ulithi, where he boarded the USS *Cabot*, a light-aircraft carrier Ernie described as both "noble" and lacking all "poise"[85] for a "three-week tussle with that ol devil sea."[86] Top-heavy and lopsided, the profile of the *Cabot* reminded Ernie of a "well-fed cow,"[87] and its mission, as he understood it, was to carry planes that would bomb the Japanese mainland and heavy artillery that would support the landings on Iwo Jima.[88] "It doesn't cut through the water like a cruiser, knifing romantically along," Ernie explained to his readers. "It doesn't dance and cavort like a destroyer. It just plows." Since leaving home in November 1943, Ernie reported, the *Cabot* had sunk twenty-nine big Japanese ships and blasted five enemy planes out of the sky. Her aircraft,

Marine staff sergeant Elwood P. Smith, right, and another marine officer converse with Ernie Pyle on Ulithi, March 24, 1945

meanwhile, had been credited with 238 enemy planes destroyed during air battles, and "her bombs and aerial torpedoes have smashed into everything from the greatest Jap battleships to the tiniest coastal schooners."[89] The *Cabot* and her crew had also weathered five typhoons, which explained her nickname: "The Iron Woman."

"She has known disaster" as well, Ernie added. Twice the *Cabot* was struck by Japanese bombs. Both times the crew held mass burials, "with her dry-eyed crew sewing 40-mm shells to the corpses of their friends, as weights to take them to the bottom of the sea."[90]

For all their hardships, however, Ernie believed the sailors he met lived much better that even the best-treated GIs in Europe. "Their food is the best I've run onto in this war," he reported. "They take baths daily, and the laundry washes their clothes." Sure, their quarters were crowded, and the monotony of the Pacific could be difficult to deal with, but "each man has a bunk with a mattress and sheets, and a private locker to keep his stuff in." The work was hard, Ernie had no doubt, "but their hours are regular."[91]

Ernie Pyle being transferred by breeches buoy from the USS *Cabot* to the USS *Moale*, February 23, 1945

The worst offense, in Ernie's mind, was that some of the sailors he met didn't seem to appreciate how good they had it. They feel they're "being persecuted by being kept out of America a year," is how Pyle framed it. "I've heard some boys say," he added, "'I'd trade this for a foxhole any day.' You just have to keep your mouth shut to a remark like that."[92]

Not everyone appreciated Ernie's characterizations of sailor life in the Pacific. A scathing personal rebuke printed in *Brief,* the Army Air Corps magazine, concluded with a rhetorical question about Ernie's honesty as a reporter: "You're making liars out of a lot of soldiers here, Ernie. Or is it the other way around?"[93]

7

Back home in New Mexico, Jerry managed to talk Dr. Lovelace into letting her return to the house on Girard Boulevard.[94] Mrs. Streger stayed with her at night,[95] and Dr. McLin visited nearly every day.[96] In letters to Ernie, Mrs. Streger stressed that she was still quite worried about Jerry, though she could report that Jerry was getting through her days without any Benzedrine and sleeping through most of the night without a single Seconal.[97] "She is still admittedly very confused and unsure of herself," Ernie confided in Paige, "and vacillates back and forth half a dozen times over small decisions and then worries about it." Still, it was a vast improvement compared to before. Her memory was also improving, and she managed to spend her waking hours "puttering around doing things to the house," in Ernie's words, "and pondering over having it painted and setting out shrubs."[98]

Jerry's letters to Ernie seemed so full of eagerness, he thought. She told Ernie she was glad to be alive, which was the first time Ernie could remember ever hearing her say that. Her biggest challenge in living a full life, other than Ernie being gone, was a "terrible" and "pathetic" confusion that washed over her whenever her shock-treated brain couldn't help her decide what project around the house to tackle next. "I think it might be wise if you could follow a plan of having just one thing done at a time, and seeing it through," Ernie advised her. "One of the things you've had to cope with, you know, is over-enthusiasm at first, and then a sudden disinterest and complete dropping of something before it was finished."[99]

"I know you will get better," Ernie assured Jerry, "and I have utter faith in you. I want you to get well as I've never wanted it before, and I know you do too and that helps me."[100]

CHAPTER 11

AN END TO ALL THAT WANDERING

And so it is over. The catastrophe on one side of the world has run its course. The day that it had so long seemed would never come has come at last.

ERNIE PYLE, IN A DRAFT COLUMN DISCOVERED
THE DAY HE WAS KILLED, APRIL 18, 1945[1]

1

Even though Ernie told Jerry he had no interest in seeing any more war up close, and even though he worried constantly that he'd "crack wide open and become a real case of war neurosis" if he was ever in real combat again, and even though he wouldn't give "two cents for the likelihood of me being alive a year from now,"[2] he nonetheless chose to board an assault transport with units of the First Marine Division bound for Okinawa.[3] "Some of them are going into combat for the first time," Ernie told his readers. "Others are veterans from as far back as Guadalcanal. They are a rough, unshaven, competent bunch of Americans. I am landing with them. I feel I am in good hands."[4]

"I hate it that this letter is so short, so inadequate," he wrote to Jerry on March 26, less than a week before invasion day. "It is the last one I can write for some little time.

"I love you," he added, "and you are the only thing I live for."[5]

Ernie Pyle watching a marine play casino aboard USS *Charles Carroll* while en route to Okinawa, March 29, 1945

After a ham-and-egg breakfast at half past four in the morning on Easter Sunday 1945, Pyle boarded a landing craft stuffed full of marines bound for shore. Dreading the sight of another beach littered with mangled American bodies, Ernie "felt miserable" with "that awful weight" still tugging at his heart, he wrote of his long and lonely climb down the cargo net. "There's nothing romantic whatever in knowing that an hour from now you may be dead."[6]

When he and the marines of the Fifth Regiment realized the landings were "absolutely unopposed," Ernie saw it as a sign. That was it for him, the final invasion. There was no way any future invasion could possibly go so well. "You can't know the relief I felt," Ernie wrote to Jerry a week later, "for as you know I had dreaded this one terribly."

"I will never make another landing," he promised. "In the future I'll make some more trips with the Navy, but they will be on big ships where there's almost no danger at all."[7]

The architect of Japan's defenses on the island, Colonel Hiromichi Yahara, had learned from recent battle losses to the Americans that it was mostly pointless to try to throw the invading force back into the sea. Instead, he concentrated most of his forces in the southern third of the island, below several heavily fortified lines north of Shuri Castle, where the Japanese army dug its underground headquarters. More than sixty miles of underground tunnels, fortifications, hospitals, and command posts protected the Japanese defenders from basically any number of enemy bombs and artillery fire. Or, as Yahara put it, "Against steel, the product of American industry, we would pit our earthen fortifications, the product of the sweat of our troops and the Okinawan people."[8]

Over the course of many toiling months, "several jagged lines of ridges and rocky escarpments" were turned into a "formidable nest of interlocking pillboxes and firing positions," according to historian Saul David. All were "connected by a network of caves and passageways inside the hills that allowed the defenders to move safely to the point of attack."[9] American troops would need to root out their heavily entrenched enemies cave by cave, one at a time.

From the uncontested landing beaches, Ernie followed a marine headquarters platoon for about a mile and a half inland, stopping every now and then to slough off his pack and rest while others forged ahead. "A lifetime of sin and crime finally does catch up with you," he quipped to passersby.[10]

The land was mainly cultivated, Ernie wrote of Okinawa, and "rose gradually from the sea in small fields." It was not unlike his native Indiana in late summer, he thought, "when things have started to turn dry and brown, except that these fields were much smaller."[11] Edged by ditches and small two-foot-wide dikes, they were filled with sugarcane, sweet potatoes, and wheat. Farther inland the fields gave way to rougher, hilly country with less cultivation and more trees.

Not so attractive were the farmhouses destroyed by the American bombardment, some reeking of the "sickening odor of death." There were, Ernie knew from experience, "always people who won't leave, no matter what." Those Okinawans who had survived were either "very old or very

Ernie Pyle, fourth from left, on the trail with a group of marines, Okinawa, April 8, 1945

young" and all "very, very poor." The women were dressed in traditional Okinawan kimonos, the old men "in skintight pants." All were filthy and seemed "shocked from the bombardment."[12]

That night, Pyle dug his foxhole alongside the marines at the foot of a small embankment and inflated three life preservers to use as an improvised mattress, a trick he had picked up in France. At dusk the next morning, three planes flew overhead, prompting what felt like the entire American fleet and all the anti-aircraft batteries already ashore to pepper the sky with bursts of fire.

Lying in his foxhole, Ernie could clearly make out the low voices of nearby officers directing their troops by field telephone and radio. Every now and then the stillness was broken by the boom of a naval gun, a violent burst of machine-gun fire, or a few lonely rifle reports. These sounds were eerily familiar to Pyle, "unchanged by distance or time from war on the other side of the world." It was a pattern, he told his readers, "so embedded in my soul that, coming back to it again, it seemed to me as I lay there that I'd never known anything else."[13]

When Ernie joined another company of marines dug in on a hill beyond Yontan airfield the following night, he was given the choice of bedding down in the company's command post—"a big, round Japanese gun emplacement made of sandbags," as historian Saul David described it—or in a "little gypsylike hideout" a couple of soldiers had built for themselves halfway down the hill. One of the soldiers, a corporal by the name of Martin Clayton from Dallas, whom everyone called "Bird Dog," was "tall, thin, and dark, almost Latin-looking," and sported a "puny mustache he'd been trying to grow for weeks." The other soldier, William Gross of Lansing, Michigan, noted Pyle, was "very quiet, and thoughtful of little things, and both of them looked after me for several days."[14]

After more than a week of patrolling with marines on the northern third of the sixty-seven-mile-long island and avoiding any "special excitement," other than the platoon he was embedded with capturing two Japanese prisoners one morning,[15] Ernie boarded the Seventy-seventh Infantry Division's command ship, USS *Panamint*, where he shared a comfortable cabin with Robert Sherrod and two naval officers. His uniform was dirty,

Ernie Pyle rests on the roadside with a marine patrol, April 8, 1945

and his body was exhausted. "I guess I can't take the field life as well as I used to," he admitted to Jerry.[16]

With at least four days' worth of writing to peck out, Ernie shaved, showered, and slept, and in the morning, he changed into clean socks, but because he didn't have anything else clean to change into, he started poking at his typewriter in a pall of cigarette smoke, still dressed in his muddied herringbone fatigues.[17] Before he could get much accomplished, though, Ernie felt the beginnings of another one of his infamous colds.

Soon after checking into the ship's hospital quarters, Ernie learned that the Seventy-seventh Infantry Division was preparing to land on Ie Shima,[18] an island barely three miles off the western tip of Okinawa's Motobu Peninsula. Rectangular in shape, Ie was an unsinkable aircraft carrier with multiple landing strips that could be used to support the main assault on Okinawa and firebombing missions over the Japanese home islands. Intelligence reported Ie was defended by a garrison of barely two thousand men, many of whom were not seasoned combat troops.[19]

Jerry had heard from Max Miller that Ernie had made his final landing and was no worse for wear. In a letter Ernie would never receive, Jerry thanked her husband. "If it means no more such landings as you have described in your columns," she wrote, "I am thankful for that, Ernie—I am thankful for whatever it is that has made me feel through the years that as long as you were somewhere, nothing could be completely wrong—or hopeless."[20]

2

Ernie landed on a hostile beach for the last time on April 17, 1945. Keeping with the spirit, if not the letter, of his promise not to tag along for another invasion, he waited until the day after the Seventy-seventh began landing on Ie Shima, after they captured the island's main airfield and nearly two thirds of the ten-square-mile island. It's not clear what ultimately changed Ernie's mind. One account of the lead-up to Ernie's death suggests that he went ashore at Ie because he'd been disappointed in how little action he'd seen with the marines.[21] Another suggests that somehow Ernie knew getting back into the mud with the soldiers would cure whatever was ailing him. Robert Sherrod, who shared a cabin with Ernie for over a week before the Ie Shima invasion, came up with what may be the best explanation. "I never learned which doughboy of the Seventy-Seventh Division persuaded Ernie to change his mind and go on the Ie Shima invasion," Sherrod wrote after the war. "But Ernie rarely refused a request from a doughboy, or any other friend."[22]

The weather on Ie the day Ernie landed was his kind of weather—balmy but not suffocating, and bright sunshine.[23] He landed on a sector of the beach code-named Red Beach No. 2 and climbed up and out of the Higgins boat dressed in khakis, looking the part of a general coming ashore to inspect the rearguard troops. Some of the officers waiting for Ernie on the beach were concerned his choice of outfit would attract snipers, so they persuaded him to don a jungle-green coat before they guided him to the command post for the 305th Regiment, on the outskirts of Ie's main town, Tegusugu.[24] At some point along the way, one of the soldiers Ernie was marching with stepped on a mine right in front of Ernie. Shaken, all he could muster when asked if he was all right was, "I wish I was back in Albuquerque."[25]

3

The jeep full of military men[26] was on its way to a new command post, closer to the front, when the zipping and pounding of a Nambu machine gun erupted from a terraced coral ridge to the left of their position, about a third of a mile away.[27] The country there was open, with no cover aside from shallow ditches on either side of the narrow road. A split second later, the brakes locked, and the engine whined down as the jeep's tires skidded to a stop. Ernie, the regimental commander, Lieutenant Colonel Joseph B.

Coolidge,[28] and an enlisted man named Dale W. Bassett raced into the ditch that ran along the right side of the road, close to a crossroads.

"We all jumped out of the jeep and dived into a roadside ditch," Coolidge told Grant MacDonald, a photographer for the Associated Press who reported on Ernie's death because he was the first on the scene. "A little later Pyle and I raised up to look around. Another burst hit the road over our heads and I fell back into the ditch." Visibly shaken, the distinguished commander's grief-stricken eyes pooled with tears.[29] The next picture of Pyle he had in his mind's eye was of the frail-looking newspaperman lying motionless in the dirt, faceup to the brilliant sky. "At the time no blood showed," he added, "so for a second I could not tell what was wrong."

Ernie had been killed instantly and was never in any pain, that much Coolidge was sure of—"the bullet entering his left temple just under his helmet."[30] Coolidge later told a reporter from *The New York Times* that Ernie had raised his head to check on one of the other men from the jeep. "Are you all right?" were, in Coolidge's telling, Ernie's final words.[31] A few soldiers who had overheard their anguished commander came up to MacDonald and showed him autographs Ernie had signed for them less than an hour before he set off with Coolidge.

Ernie's death that morning transformed Grant MacDonald into a reporter with a story no one else could tell.[32] After gleaning the details from Coolidge, he determined Ernie had been killed around 10:15 a.m. local time; forty-five minutes later, MacDonald was hunched over his typewriter, pounding out the story. The navy's censors didn't clear everything he had written—Pyle had been killed by a burst of three machine-gun bullets, all in a single instant, not one—and they wouldn't transmit MacDonald's account until after Ernie's family had been notified.[33]

While MacDonald pecked at his typewriter, the battle for Ernie's body was raging. The commander of the Seventy-seventh Division, General Andrew D. Bruce, ordered tanks to retrieve the body, but enemy machine-gun fire made it impossible for the tankers to leave the relative safety of their thirty-three tons of steel.[34] About four hours after Ernie was killed, a squad of litter bearers led by an army chaplain named Nathaniel B. Saucier volunteered to crawl if they had to along the road's ditch, litter in tow.[35] Corporal Alexander Roberts of New York City tagged along and was the first to reach Ernie's body. From a worm's-eye view, Roberts snapped the photograph that was until 2008 thought to be lost to history.

With Ernie's dead body on the litter, the men inched back down the ditch to the division's command post, still under sniper fire. Ernest Taylor Pyle, the roving correspondent from Indiana, was forty-four years old.

It's this version of events that spread across the world, repeated again and again for decades. The problem with this version is that it is a little too neat, a little too convenient.[36] A clue from Roberts's photograph of Ernie's dead body may help explain what really happened the morning Ernie was killed. At the rim of the ditch he sought shelter in, the soft dirt had clearly been eaten away into a half-moon shape, about thirty-six inches long and eighteen inches deep. If the dirt had in fact been eaten away by the Nambu machine gun's .31-caliber bullets, that could help explain how the three fire-hot machine-gun rounds that killed him lacked the velocity they'd normally have to explode. Had he been struck by three rounds above the left temple straight on, there would have undoubtedly been a much bloodier mess, if there was anything left of his skull at all. But that's not what Roberts found, and that's not what his photograph shows.

What it does show is a man dressed in the khaki uniform of a war correspondent,[37] lying on his back, slumped down a sandy berm, with his head resting in a steel helmet against the dirt. His upper body is slightly twisted to the right. A pair of sunglasses with a missing left lens have slid down his straight nose and cover his lifeless eyes. Folded across his midsection, small hands touch with dead fingers a jungle-green billed cap.[38] Aside from a dried tear of blood that trickles down from the corner of his mouth, it appears as if he's napping in the warmth of the tropical sun.

In the Pacific theater, war correspondents generally had no trouble jumping in a jeep and driving right up to the front line in broad daylight without drawing a storm of artillery or getting knocked out by mines, as in Europe. And that is precisely why more American correspondents were killed in the Pacific, according to Ernie's friend and fellow newspaperman

Homer Bigart. "The newcomer gets a false sense of security," he told his readers of the Pacific theater. "Hearing none of the usual din of battle, he comes jeeping along, admiring the scenery, when—ping—a sniper's bullet shatters his daydreams."[39]

"It was so peaceful a death," Corporal Roberts said sixty-three years after capturing the picture on his Speed Graphic camera, "that I felt its reproduction would not be in bad taste."[40] Taken after an "unbelievably slow, laborious, dirt-eating crawl" to where Ernie's body fell dead, the photograph was so rare that even the top photo archivist at the National Archives, the largest repository of military records in the United States, claimed never to have seen it.[41]

4

Once Ernie's body was finally recovered, a corporal named Landon Seidler of Richmond, Virginia, hammered together a coffin for him out of flimsy pine boards.[42] Another soldier, Sergeant Irvin Steifel of Camden, New Jersey, fashioned a white cross and a sheaf made of flowers and grain.[43] Seidler also constructed a crude wooden sign, painted white with black lettering,[44] to mark the ground where Ernie was killed. It read:

AT THIS SPOT

The 77th Infantry Division
LOST A BUDDY
ERNIE PYLE
18 April 1945

On April 20, General Bruce and a few dozen of his men, helmeted and solemn looking, paid their respects during a hasty burial service led by the same chaplain who had helped recover his body, Nathaniel B. Saucier. The chaplain finished his funeral prayer with the extra request that "God will bless him doubly—our comrade, Ernie Pyle."[45]

"With the exception of an occasional blast of distant guns and the murmuring of the waves 100 yards away," Saucier later recalled, "all was quiet" during the ten-minute service.[46] Grant MacDonald was there, again, to capture the scene. "The surroundings seemed fitting for Ernie, who had seen action on so many battlefronts," MacDonald wrote. "Even the funeral party, on the way to the cemetery, had to duck mortar shells."[47] When the service was concluded, General Bruce drove off in his jeep to a command post, and the other soldiers in attendance slogged back up toward the front.

Ernie was buried that day in his uniform with his helmet on, in a long row of graves, with full military honors.[48] An infantry private rested on one side of him, a combat engineer on the other. Around his wrist was the watch he'd received thirteen years earlier from his friend Amelia Earhart, who'd gifted it to him at a small ceremony put on by the early aviation community at Washington-Hoover Airport to thank Ernie for his coverage of their exploits.[49]

5

Jerry's doctor, W. R. Lovelace, and Liz Shaffer broke the news of Ernie's death to her once it had been confirmed.[50] "'That Girl' in Ernie Pyle's stories," The New York Times reported on April 19, "was grief-stricken today at her husband's death." When a reporter called the house on Girard Boulevard in Albuquerque, Jerry answered "in a calm but very low voice." She had not yet received any details of his death, she said.[51] Dr. Lovelace later reported that "Mrs. Pyle was prostrated with grief and under his care."[52]

The news of Ernie's death hit the press wires around 10:25 a.m. in New York City. Even seasoned newspapermen were momentarily stunned. In Knoxville, a columnist named Bert Vincent remembered after the war that in the News-Sentinel newsroom, the "usual clatter and noise in the room stopped suddenly. You could have heard a pin drop. Then shocked men and women here who knew Ernie almost as if he worked right here with us, yelled: 'What! Surely not!'" The newspaper's switchboard operator, Jane Sterchi, said the phone lines that day were overwhelmed by readers calling to ask if the news they had heard was true. "I've never seen the board more jammed in my eight years," she said. "There was scarcely a household in the whole country, certainly none that had sons overseas, where his name was unknown," the *Washington Post* editorial board wrote.[53]

The loss hit even harder among those who had known him well, or worked alongside him, chronicling the war. Kenneth L. Dixon of the Associated Press reported on the stunned disbelief felt by everyone at the Ninth Army press camp in Germany. Once it settled in, he wrote, "All that the boys could talk about was Ernie." Robert Vermillion of United Press said of Ernie, "He was the soldier's idea of what a war correspondent should be. He will be mourned by thousands of men and they'll say as they've said of so many comrades, 'it's always the good ones who get it.'" Ronald Stead, who wrote for *The Christian Science Monitor*, said that whenever he chatted with a soldier, they'd inevitably ask him if knew Ernie. "That was the sincerest tribute to a man we all admired personally and professionally."[54] In Leipzig, Robert Capa heard the news from Hal Boyle: "Ernie got it." Capa sat down and drank himself stupid in silence.[55]

Back in Ernie's hometown, Nellie Hendricks, who lived across a field from the Pyle family farm, first heard the news of Ernie's death on the radio. She sprinted to tell Ernie's father and his aunt Mary Bales.[56] Both were reportedly stunned. Another neighbor, Ella Goforth, told *The New York Times*, "They're not taking the news very well."[57] Neither his aging father nor any other family member spoke to the press the day they learned of Ernie's death; they were too distraught.[58]

General Eisenhower felt the loss of Ernie deeply. "The G.I.s in Europe— and that means all of us—have lost one of our best and most understanding friends."[59] George C. Marshall, the army chief of staff, told reporters that "Ernie Pyle belonged to the millions of soldiers he had made his friends.

His dispatches reached down into the ranks to draw out the stories of individual soldiers. He did not glorify war, but he did glorify the nobility, the simplicity and heroism of the American fighting man. The Army deeply mourns his death." The secretary of war, Henry L. Stimson, was quoted as saying that the day Ernie was killed was the day that soldiers "lost a champion." He added, "The understanding of Americans in battle which ran through all of Ernie Pyle's dispatches was drawn from hours spent with them under fire, sharing dangers they endure." Even Lieutenant General Mark Clark had kind words to say about a man who never disparaged him in the press, even though he would have been justified in doing so. "His reporting was always constructive," Clark said of the roving correspondent who "marched with my troops through Italy, took their part and championed their cause both here and at home." The young soldier-cartoonist Bill Mauldin said, "The only difference between Ernie's death and that of any other good guy is that the other guy is mourned by his company. Ernie is mourned by his army."[60]

From the White House, Harry Truman told the nation he was saddened by the death of Ernie Pyle. Speaking to Ernie's impact as a correspondent, America's new president concluded:

No man in this war has so well told the story of the American fighting man as American fighting men wanted it told. More than any other man he became the spokesman of the ordinary American in arms doing so many extraordinary things. It was his genius that the mass and power of our military and naval forces never obscured the men who made them. He wrote about a people in arms as people still, but a people moving in a determination which did not need pretensions as a part of power. Nobody knows how many individuals in our forces and at home he helped with his writings. But all Americans understand now how wisely, how warmheartedly, how honestly he served his country and his profession. He deserves the gratitude of all his countrymen.[61]

The former First Lady, Eleanor Roosevelt, wrote in her daily column that Ernie's reporting had "brought the best understanding of the human side of our fighting men." She added that she would never forget how much she admired "this frail and modest man who could endure hardships because he loved his job and our men."[62]

Four days after Ernie was killed, Republican senator Raymond E. Willis proposed that Ernie be posthumously awarded the Congressional Medal of Honor, the highest military award a soldier can earn, for Pyle, in Willis's words, was "as much a part of America as Mark Twain, or the corner drugstore, or the church in every town."[63] A few days later, a soldier named Karl Detzer Jr. and fifty other combat veterans signed a letter Detzer mailed to *Stars and Stripes* to lend their support. "Although in the past we have objected strenuously to the presentation of military decorations to civilians, (we) veterans of infantry combat suggest that the Congressional Medal of Honor be posthumously awarded to Ernie Pyle, soldier."[64] Despite receiving President Truman's support for the award a month later, that's as far as it went. He never did receive the Medal of Honor.[65]

One tribute that wasn't made public until five decades after Ernie's death came from John Steinbeck, who found himself inundated by telegrams asking him to write an appreciation of some kind. While Steinbeck worried about how to handle such an assignment, he reached out to Scripps-Howard to see if they'd be interested in publishing an obituary of sorts that Steinbeck had penned a week or so after Ernie's death.[66] This long-unpublished Steinbeck original was written at a time when Steinbeck was overcome with grief by what he saw as the needless death of a dear friend—a truth the powers that be likely weren't ready to hear. "Ernie Pyle didn't want to go back to the war," Steinbeck wrote. "When he left France, he set down his disgust and fear and weariness. He thought he could rest a little, but he couldn't."[67] It's possible, of course, that in the back of Steinbeck's mind there lurked the thought that had he not turned down a request similar to the one Pyle received from the navy to cover the war in the Pacific, he might have met the same fate.

Scripps-Howard replied by wire that Steinbeck's submission had been sent too late for use in their publications. "This was ten days after his death," he lamented to his agent, Elizabeth Otis, "and he was no longer news to Scripps-Howard whom he had been practically supporting."

Who was to blame for Ernie's death? That was simple, Steinbeck concluded. It was Ernie himself. Sure, there were plenty of people pressuring him, subtly and not, to continue covering the war, but "he could have overcome that," Steinbeck continued. What Ernie couldn't overcome was "his own sense of responsibility. He had become identified with every soldier in the army." That stubborn sense of duty, of dedication to the cause—that's what finally caught up with the rail-thin son of an Indiana tenant farmer all those thousands of miles from the "sad, slow wind" that drove him like a coachman cracking a whip to parts unknown.

"Everyone expected him to go back," Steinbeck wrote. "Everyone except Ernie thought Ernie was imperishable."[68]

<h1 style="text-align:center">6</h1>

Once the bloody three-month-long battle for Okinawa was complete, men from the Seventy-seventh Division's combat engineer group terraced a platform near the spot where Ernie was killed and erected a four-foot-tall cement cenotaph that took the three-dimensional form of the "Statue of Liberty" division's insignia. Embedded in its concrete face are a blue enameled plate depicting the Statue of Liberty and a relief plaque made of brass shell casings that is inscribed with the same words as the original memorial marker.

On July 2, 1945, a hot and humid day, the Ernie Pyle Monument was officially dedicated by General Edwin Randle, the Seventy-seventh Division's assistant commander. Rather than being afforded the opportunity to pay their respects, Ernie's beloved enlisted men were corralled behind barbed wire, evidently to keep them out of the line of the many news cameras that were there that day to record the ceremony. After briefly addressing the assembled crowd, General Randle tugged at a release cord and a parachute-silk shroud fell to the ground, revealing a stout obelisk that remains there to this day. It is one of only three American monuments that the Japanese government agreed to maintain once the United States returned Okinawa's sovereignty to it in the spring of 1972.

"Ernie Pyle didn't like to report battles," General Randle began his opening remarks; "he liked to go among the soldiers and talk to them and write about them." Behind the general, flanking him, stood two soldiers with flags dipped in respect to Pyle. Behind them were several more high-ranking officers and a small group of war correspondents. Behind them, a young broadcaster was making an on-the-spot transcription of the ceremony. Standing at attention in orderly rows of sand-colored khaki on three sides of all that pomp was an honor guard, and all around, still and movie cameramen swarmed and jockeyed for the best shot of the proceedings.[69] "It was a very military ceremony," one soldier-reporter by the name of Jack Briggs[70] wrote after the war.[71]

Far removed from all those important people, behind a barbed-wire fence, stood hundreds of "dusty sweating people Ernie Pyle said were his friends," Briggs continued. "They stood silently under the fierce sun, watching the backs of the Generals and their friends. Some GIs wore khaki. Some wore fatigues. Many were bare to the waist, and sweat made little grooves as it trickled in crooked streams down their burned chests."

As the general continued his remarks, one of the soldiers near Briggs made his resentment clear. "Look at that chickenshit sonofabitch," he said, motioning to the general. "Ernie Pyle wouldn't have pissed on him."

"This is a stirring and historic occasion," a radio announcer near Briggs said into his microphone. "A great newspaperman who lies at rest among 354 of his friends in a near-by cemetery is now receiving the homage of the brave men whose lives he reported honestly and well. He sleeps among other soldiers who gave their lives for their country. He sleeps among his humble friends."

"Tell them the humble friends of Ernie Pyle are behind barbed wire today," Briggs called out to the announcer. "Tell them that, Mac." But before Briggs had gotten the word "barbed" out of his mouth, the announcer had flipped the on/off switch on his recording machine, "lest my softly spoken 17 words became part of the prepared lie," Briggs wrote. The announcer flipped his device back on and "looked embarrassed and nettled and resumed his speech," Briggs added, "with a cautious and fearful eye fixed upon us, with his hand upon the switch."

When taps sounded from the end of a brass bugle, all the men in uniform saluted. Behind Briggs one soldier remarked, "Jesus, that's a beautiful monument." Another soldier voiced his agreement. A third man wasn't having any of it. "The hell with it," he snorted. "Why didn't they leave that old board there? That old board was like Ernie Pyle; there wasn't no brass or blue enamel about that guy."

Under his breath, another soldier leaned over to Briggs. "Remember Tom Sawyer?" he asked. "How he came back and walked in on his own funeral?"

"Yeah," Briggs replied softly.

"Suppose Ernie Pyle came back today," the GI continued. "Boy, would he piss up a storm when he seen this!"[72]

7

Efforts to honor Pyle and his legacy back home abounded. The fanciest and most ambitious plan had to have been the 120-acre park many important people wanted to build in Dana, Indiana, to serve as the final resting place for Ernie's remains. Admirals Ernest J. King and William D. Leahy, the heads of the American Federation of Labor and the Congress of Industrial Organizations, numerous veterans' organizations, and "thousands of newspapermen" were all on board, and a New York public relations firm spearheaded the effort to raise millions of dollars for its construction. According to the firm, Jerry signed off on their plans in June 1945, but by the end of August, she had changed her mind. She was, she said, "unalterably opposed" to the project, which she described as "a pretentious park and cemetery that is entirely out of keeping with everything that Ernie ever did, or said, or thought, or was."[73] Leave him buried, she said, "with the

The body of Ernie Pyle was laid to final rest in the new National Memorial Cemetery of the Pacific, Honolulu, July 19, 1949.

men he loved." Jerry would, in fact, "never consent to having his body moved."[74] The editors of the *Omaha World-Herald* agreed with Jerry's veto. "It would verge on the improper to erect a fancy memorial to this fine, simple man. Memorials, if they are to have dignity, must be simple."[75]

Soon after the war ended, in the early fall of 1945, the army exhumed Pyle's remains from Ie Shima and reinterred them at a U.S. military cemetery on Okinawa before permanently relocating them to the National Memorial Cemetery of the Pacific in Honolulu, Hawaii, in 1949. In the spring of 2021, I flew to Honolulu, and on my first full day there, I found Ernie under pleasant tree-cast shade, in plot D 109, beneath an unembellished gray marker. On either side of him are the remains of two unidentified soldiers, "known unto God." For a man who paid the ultimate price to immortalize the ordinary soldiers who took the worst of it and kept on marching, it was somehow a fitting tribute.

8

Edwin Waltz, Ernie's personal secretary at Pacific Fleet Headquarters back in Guam, was tasked with processing Ernie's personal effects,[76] many of which Ernie had wanted either burned or thrown away so as not to upset Jerry. One artifact Waltz didn't throw out was a two-page story, handwritten on cheap pulp paper, that was discovered in one of his pockets before he was buried. The draft column was not so much a dispatch from the Pacific as it was a meditation on the end of all the killing. "Last summer," it began, "I wrote that I hoped the end of the war could be a gigantic relief, but not an elation. In the joyousness of high spirits it is so easy for us to forget the dead." That was a relief Ernie knew was simply unavailable to himself and millions more and a fact that no one should be allowed to forget.

"There are so many of the living who have had burned into their brains forever the unnatural sight of cold dead men scattered over the hillsides and in the ditches," the draft column continued. "Dead men by mass production in one country after another, month after month and year after year. Dead men in winter and dead men in summer. Dead men in such familiar promiscuity that they become monotonous. Dead men in such monstrous infinity that you come almost to hate them.

"Those are the things that you at home need not even try to understand," he continued in his loopy cursive. "To you at home they are columns of figures, or he is a near one who went away and just didn't come back. You didn't see him lying so grotesque and pasty beside the gravel road in France. We saw him, saw him by the multiple thousands. That's the difference."[77]

Pyle's editors at Scripps-Howard chose not to release the draft column to its papers. Perhaps they were indifferent to Ernie's truth, or simply decided his readers weren't ready to hear it. "Perhaps they guessed it would puzzle his readers, even hurt them," one of Pyle's biographers noted. "Certainly it was darker valedictory than they would have expected from him."[78]

Currently, the handwritten pages are on display at the New Mexico History Museum in Santa Fe.

During his career as a frontline war correspondent, Pyle was embraced by enlisted men, officers, and a huge civilian public as a voice who spoke for the common infantryman. With his traumas in Sicily, Italy, and France, he had, in essence, become one of them. After sharing so much of their experience, their pain and their purpose, he understood better than most how gravely war can alter the people who must see it and fight it and live it. He knew that many survivors would come home with damage that is profound, aching, and long-lasting. It was a truth that he found hard or even impossible to communicate to his readers back home—and it's a truth that is still difficult and troubling now, all these decades later.

By the time Ernie landed on Ie Shima, nearly seven thousand miles from home, the insights he gleaned while living with the effects of war had fully solidified for him. Not even the end of the war, not even victory and that last trip home, would be able to bring back all the people killed or counteract the damage done to the war's survivors. By the time unconditional Allied victory was within grasp, Ernie had come to believe that there was simply no way the war could ever simply be a story with a happy ending. And now it was truly over, an end to all that wandering.

ACKNOWLEDGMENTS

This book wouldn't exist were it not for the support and guidance I received from dozens of people. Thank you to my dear friend and mentor, Brian Castner, who listened to my pitch over beers at the Falcon Club for a Tony Horwitz–style book where I would retrace Ernie Pyle's steps through the war and told me, at long last, "That's the one. Write that." From there, my agent, Stuart Krichevsky, suggested I write an article about Ernie to see whether anyone outside the world of war correspondents still remembered Ernie. My editor at *The New York Times*, Lauren Katzenberg, afforded me the opportunity to remind readers about Ernie's reporting from the beaches of Normandy for the seventy-fifth anniversary of D-Day, back in 2019. Special thanks to my fact-checker and editor, David Georgi. I'm a better writer today thanks to him. Not long after the article went live, I was inundated with a tremendous outpouring from readers from across the globe. I received handwritten letters at work from people whose father or grandfather had once met Ernie at an airdrome in Algeria or during the horrendous mountain fighting in Italy. Others told me of the scrapbooks their parents kept of Ernie's clippings and how there would never be another correspondent like Ernest Taylor Pyle.

A few days after the article was published, I received an email from

Scott Moyers, who said that if I wanted to talk about writing a book about Ernie he was more than interested. Even as I type these words, the last words I will type into this manuscript, I cannot believe how incredibly fortunate I am. When I told Scott over the phone one afternoon in June 2019 my plan to tell the story of Ernie's war reporting in the style of Tony Horwitz's *Confederates in the Attic: Dispatches from the Unfinished Civil War*, there was a pregnant pause at the other end of the line. After what seemed like forever, Scott replied, "Well, you know I was Tony's editor for his last book, don't you?" I promise you, dear reader, I had no idea whatsoever. Tony died at the end of May 2019 of a sudden cardiac arrest while he was on tour for *Spying on the South: An Odyssey Across the American Divide*. While there will never be another writer quite like Tony Horwitz, I hope this book will have a similar effect on my readers as Tony's had on me.

Thank you to the entire team at Penguin Press. Special thanks especially to Helen Rouner, Carlynn Chironna, and Aly D'Amato. Greg Villepique copyedited the book and helped me make it even stronger with his insightful comments and keen attention to details. Darren Haggar designed the cover, which still gives me chills every time I look at it. Quite frankly, I doubt there is another image of Ernie out there that better captures his essence.

I'm in debt to Thomas Brennan and the wonderful team he's built at The War Horse, an award-winning nonprofit newsroom and the most trusted source for bulletproof reporting on the human impact of military service. I'd also like to thank the incredible staff at the Logan Nonfiction Program, which graciously extended me a fellowship while I was writing the first half of this book, during the darkest depths of the COVID-19 pandemic. Huge thank you to Zan Strumfeld, Carly Willsie, and Viviane Galloway. Without the support I received from David Logan and the Logan Nonfiction Program's incredible advisory board, this book would not have become what it is today. Special thanks to Josh Friedman and Mark Bowden for reading early chapters and providing excellent feedback to me on how to tell this story the way it needed to be told.

Librarians and archivists are some of the best people I've ever met, and without them we wouldn't know half of what we know about Ernie Pyle. Thank you to Katherine Gould, who introduced me to the archives at the Indiana State Museum and who digitized hundreds of letters between Ernie and his editor, Lee Miller. The entire staff at Indiana University's Lilly Library were incredibly helpful, as were the staff at the Albuquerque Museum of History & Art, the University of New Mexico archives in Albuquerque, and the Texas Christian University in Fort Worth. I'd especially like to thank Doug Hess and the other incredible people who manage the Ernie Pyle World War II Museum in Dana, Indiana, Ernie's hometown. I'd also like to extend my sincerest gratitude to Jerry Maschino and his team at the Ernie Pyle Legacy Foundation. During my travels, I visited three American battlefield cemeteries managed by the American Battle Monuments Commission and the National Memorial Cemetery of the Pacific in Hawaii. It's impossible to visit these places without walking away with an overwhelming sense of awe and gratitude.

There are so many more people I'd like to thank: Jennifer Orth-Veillon, who served as my translator and travel companion in France and who introduced me to Yomna Mansouri. Thank you to Yomna's entire family for all their support and for showing me their family's home, and to Kirk Hendricks, who took me all over Hawaii to see the sights many tourists overlook. Special thanks to my dear friend Annie Erling Gofus, who took all the stress out of my travel planning and made sure I had everything I needed on my various research trips. And thanks to all those many people I met across the world who brought me into their homes, shared their stories with me, and helped me make sense of what Ernie must have experienced during all those many months at war.

NOTES

The following abbreviations are used for some of the more frequently cited persons and institutions in letter citations.

EP   Ernie Pyle

ISMA   Indiana State Museum Archives

JP   Jerry Pyle

LL   Lilly Library, Indiana University

LM   Lee G. Miller

MCBL   Ernie Pyle Manuscript (MS 141), Special Collections, Mary Couts Burnett Library, Texas Christian University

MD   Indiana State Museum and Historic Sites, Miller Donation

PC   Paige Cavanaugh

CHAPTER 1: WARHORSING AROUND

1. "Farewell to Europe," Sept. 5, 1944, in David Nichols, ed., *Ernie's War: The Best of Ernie Pyle's World War II Dispatches* (New York: Random House, 1986), 357–59.
2. Rick Atkinson, *The Guns at Last Light* (New York: Henry Holt, 2013), 171.
3. Antony Beevor, *D-Day: The Battle for Normandy* (New York: Penguin Books, 2019), 496.
4. EP letter to JP, Aug. 24, 1944, LL.
5. Mary Louise Roberts, *D-Day Through French Eyes: Normandy 1944* (Chicago: University of Chicago Press, 2014), 161.
6. Richard Collier, *Fighting Words: The War Correspondents of World War Two* (New York: St. Martin's Press, 1989), 171.
7. Brian Best, *Reporting the Second World War: The Battle for Truth* (South Yorkshire, UK: Pen and Sword Military, 2015), 164.

8. Beevor, *D-Day*, 495. See also Atkinson, *Guns at Last Light*, 173.

9. John Keegan, *Six Armies in Normandy: From D-Day to the Liberation of Paris June 6th–August 25th, 1944* (New York: Viking Press, 1982), 298.

10. Beevor, *D-Day*, 484.

11. Atkinson, *Guns at Last Light*, 173.

12. Ronald Weber, *Dateline—Liberated Paris: The Hotel Scribe and the Invasion of the Press* (New York: Rowman & Littlefield, 2019), 43. See also Atkinson, *Guns at Last Light*, 173.

13. Keegan, *Six Armies in Normandy*, 298–99. See also Andy Rooney, *My War* (New York: PublicAffairs, 1995), 204.

14. Henry T. Gorrell and Richard D. McMillan. See "Liberating the City of Light," Aug. 28, 1944, in Nichols, ed., *Ernie's War*, 351–54. See also Marc Lancaster, "Liberation Day: When Paris Went Mad," ww2ondeadline.com, Aug. 25, 2020.

15. Weber, *Dateline—Liberated Paris*, 28.

16. "Liberating the City of Light," Aug. 28, 1944, in Nichols, ed., *Ernie's War*, 351–54.

17. Atkinson, *Guns at Last Light*, 172.

18. "Liberating the City of Light," in Nichols, ed., *Ernie's War*, 351–54. See also Ernie Pyle, *Brave Men* (Lincoln: University of Nebraska Press, 2001), 484.

19. Pyle, *Brave Men*, 485.

20. "Liberating the City of Light," in Nichols, ed., *Ernie's War*, 351–54.

21. "Liberating the City of Light," in Nichols, ed., *Ernie's War*, 351–54.

22. "Liberating the City of Light," in Nichols, ed., *Ernie's War*, 351–54.

23. "Liberating the City of Light," in Nichols, ed., *Ernie's War*, 351–54.

24. Pyle, *Brave Men*, 488.

25. Rooney, *My War*, 215. Clark Lee of INS was there in the lobby with Pyle that day, and he quoted Ernie as saying, "Anybody who doesn't sleep with a woman tonight is just an exhibitionist." See Phillip Knightley, *The First Casualty: From the Crimea to Vietnam: The War Correspondent as Hero, Propagandist, and Myth Maker* (New York: Harcourt Brace Jovanovich, 1975), 327.

26. Mary Louise Roberts, *What Soldiers Do: Sex and the American GI in World War II France* (Chicago: University of Chicago Press, 2014), 167.

27. Weber, *Dateline—Liberated Paris*, 58.

28. Atkinson, *Guns at Last Light*, 171.

29. Weber, *Dateline—Liberated Paris*, 58. See also Beevor, *D-Day*, 496.

30. Column from Sept. 2, 1944, in Nichols, ed., *Ernie's War*, 356–57 and 359. See also Pyle, *Brave Men*, 490.

31. "Farewell to Europe," Sept. 5, 1944, in Nichols, ed., *Ernie's War*, 357–59.

32. Weber, *Dateline—Liberated Paris*, 56–57.

33. During the war, Lee Miller also became Ernie's agent and power of attorney. Lee G. Miller, *The Story of Ernie Pyle* (New York: Viking Press, 1950), 162. See also Nichols, ed., *Ernie's War*, 5.

34. Nichols, ed., *Ernie's War*, 357.

35. Mack Morriss, "Pyle Goes Home," *Yank*, Oct. 6, 1944; reprinted as "Friend of the GIs," *New York World-Telegram*, Oct. 30, 1944, and in *Publisher's Auxiliary* 79:45, Nov. 4, 1944.

36. Frederick C. Painton, "The Hoosier Letter Writer," *Saturday Evening Post*, Oct. 2, 1943.

37. EP letter to William Pyle, June 1, 1943, LL, LMC 1879, Indiana University.

38. Painton, "The Hoosier Letter Writer."

39. Ernie Pyle, *Here Is Your War* (New York: Henry Holt, 1943), 241.

40. "Farewell to Europe," in Nichols, ed., *Ernie's War*, 357–59.

41. "Farewell to Europe," in Nichols, ed., *Ernie's War*, 357–59. He wrote to a soldier friend later: "When I was there I felt as though I were living in a whorehouse—not physically but spiritually." See Knightley, *The First Casualty*, 327.

42. Ben Shephard, *A War of Nerves: Soldiers and Psychiatrists in the Twentieth Century*

(Cambridge, MA: Harvard University Press, 2001), 245. See also Rebecca Jo Plan, "Preventing the Inevitable: John Appel and the Problem of Psychiatric Casualties in the US Army during World War II," in *Science and Emotions after 1945: A Transatlantic Perspective*, ed. Frank Biess and Daniel M. Gross, published to Chicago Scholarship Online.

43. "Farewell to Europe," in Nichols, ed., *Ernie's War*, 357–59. Later he wrote: "You begin to feel that you can't go on forever without being hit. I feel that I've used up all my chances. And I hate it . . . I don't want to be killed." See Knightley, *The First Casualty*, 327.

44. EP letter to LM, Oct. 31, 1944, MD.

45. EP letter to LM, Oct. 31, 1944, MD.

46. EP letter to PC, Oct. 31, 1944, LL.

47. EP letter to LM, Oct. 31, 1944, MD. See also EP letter to PC, Oct. 31, 1944, LL.

48. Pyle, *Here Is Your War*, 241.

49. EP letter to LM, Oct. 31, 1944, MD.

50. EP letter to LM, Oct. 31, 1944, MD.

51. "In 1913, a young doctor named William Randolph Lovelace moved his frontier practice to [Albuquerque, New Mexico]. Before long he was renowned for his skill as a surgeon and his extraordinary compassion for his patients. Joined by Dr. Edgar T. Lassetter and eventually by other physicians, Dr. Lovelace modeled his pioneering group practice, the Lovelace Clinic, after Minnesota's respected Mayo Clinic." See "History of Lovelace Health System," https://lovelace.com/about/history.

52. EP letter to LM, Oct. 31, 1944, MD.

53. EP letter to PC, Oct. 31, 1944, LL.

54. EP letter to LM, Oct. 31, 1944, MD.

55. EP letter to PC, Oct. 31, 1944, LL.

56. EP letter to LM, Oct. 31, 1944, MD.

57. Clipped from *Albuquerque Journal*, Jan. 23, 1959, 37, www.newspapers.com/clip/12730981/albuquerque-journal.

58. EP letter to LM, Oct. 31, 1944, MD.

59. Miller, *The Story of Ernie Pyle*, v. Reading his columns provided a much-needed relief for Americans, who desired information on the soldiers rather than the strategies and tactics, which were supplied by other correspondents.

60. Miller, *The Story of Ernie Pyle*, 146.

61. Nichols, ed., *Ernie's War*, xiii.

62. Michael S. Sweeney, *The Military and the Press: An Uneasy Truce* (Evanston, IL: Northwestern University Press, 2006), 99.

63. "The Press: Ernie Pyle's War," *Time*, July 17, 1944.

64. Nichols, ed., *Ernie's War*, 137.

65. James Tobin, *Ernie Pyle's War: America's Eyewitness to World War II* (New York: Free Press, 1997), 4. Many authors have written about Pyle, although much of that material has appeared in newspapers or obscure magazines. Lee G. Miller, in addition to his biography of Pyle, put together a picture-narrative, *An Ernie Pyle Album: Indiana to Ie Shima* (New York: William Sloane Associates, 1946). Others have written more focused, lesser-known biographies. See Rudy Faircloth and W. Horace Carter, *"Buddy," Ernie Pyle, World War II's Most Beloved Typewriter Soldier* (Tabor City, NC: Atlantic Publishing Company, 1982), and Richard Melzer, *Ernie Pyle in the American Southwest* (Santa Fe: Sunstone Press, 1995). Several graduate students have written theses about Pyle. David Nichols penned long introductions to two collections of Pyle's writings. Even a few foreign authors and translators have written brief evaluations of Pyle and his reporting.

66. Robert W. Desmond, *Tides of War: World News Reporting 1931–1945* (Ames: Iowa State University Press, 1982), 462. See also Ray Moseley, *Reporting War: How Foreign Correspondents Risked Capture, Torture and Death to Cover World War II* (New Haven: Yale University Press, 2017), 7.

67. "Mencken's Dark Side," *Washington Post*, Dec. 5, 1989, www.washingtonpost.com/archive /lifestyle/1989/12/05/menckens-dark-side.

68. Knightley, *The First Casualty*, 332–33.

69. Jackson J. Benson, *The True Adventures of John Steinbeck, Writer* (New York: Viking Press, 1984), 518–19.

70. Knightley, *The First Casualty*, 276.

71. LM letter to EP, July 27, 1943, MD.

72. LM letter to EP, Oct. 4, 1944, MD.

73. LM letter to EP, Oct. 17, 1944, MD.

74. Yoni Appelbaum, "Publishers Gave Away 122,951,031 Books During World War II," *Atlantic*, Sept. 10, 2014, www.theatlantic.com/business/archive/2014/09/publishers-gave-away -122951031-books-during-world-war-ii/379893.

75. EP letter to LM, Oct. 20, 1943, MD.

76. EP letter to LM, Dec. 11, 1944, MD. "As for 1945, it looks to me like the income will be around $275,000, which would mean a quarterly tax payment of around $60,000." Lester Cowan was also in talks with Ernie about working together to produce "three extremely expensive and high-class shorts per year out of the old columns." Cowan wanted Lee Miller, Paige Cavanaugh, and Ernie to share ownership in the company: "Lester wants to fix it so you and Cavanaugh and me will all share in the thing. His tentative proposal is to give you and Cavanaugh 5 percent of the company or the profits of something, and me ten percent. In addition, Cavanaugh would continue working for him at a good weekly salary, this to be booked against his share of the profits." Five percent of the profits, Lester estimated, would be at least $40,000 per year, which is about $642,000 in 2022 dollars. See EP letter to LM, Dec. 3, 1944, MD.

77. EP letter to LM, Dec. 3, 1944, MD.

78. "Hardly a vacation," Feb. 8, 1945, in Nichols, ed., *Ernie's War*, 365.

79. EP letter to LM, Dec. 3, 1944, MD.

80. Tobin, *Ernie Pyle's War*, 236.

81. Tobin, *Ernie Pyle's War*, 236.

CHAPTER 2: AT LAST THEY ARE IN THE FIGHTING

1. "Tank Battle at Sidi-Bou-Zid," March 1, 1943, in David Nichols, ed., *Ernie's War: The Best of Ernie Pyle's World War II Dispatches* (New York: Random House, 1986).

2. Rick Atkinson, *An Army at Dawn: The War in North Africa, 1942–1943* (New York: Henry Holt, 2002), 350.

3. Martin Blumenson, *Kasserine Pass: Where America Lost Her Military Innocence* (Boston: Houghton Mifflin, 1966), 134.

4. Atkinson, *Army at Dawn*, 349.

5. Atkinson, *Army at Dawn*, 350.

6. "Tank Battle at Sidi-Bou-Zid," in Nichols, ed., *Ernie's War*, 92.

7. Atkinson, *Army at Dawn*, 338.

8. Lee G. Miller, *The Story of Ernie Pyle* (New York: Viking Press, 1950), 14.

9. EP letter to PC, Sept. 11, 1939, LL.

10. Miller, *Story of Ernie Pyle*, 25–26, 27, 36, 37, 39–40, 41, 47. Ernie cut his reporting teeth as a cub reporter in La Porte, Indiana, before moving to Washington, DC, to report for the Scripps-Howard *Washington Daily News*. Around the time Charles Lindbergh was flying the *Spirit of St. Louis* from New York to Paris, Ernie and Jerry were driving across the country in a Ford roadster Ernie had bought for six hundred dollars. They had grown bored with life in the capital and wanted to try out the Bohemian lifestyle for a bit. When they returned to the East Coast, Ernie quickly found a job on the copy desk of the *New York Evening World*

and later at the *New York Post*. After less than a year, Lee enticed Ernie to return to Washington. During the day, Ernie edited telegraphs, and in the evening, he prowled the airports around DC, talking with pilots and watching them work. In the spring of 1928, Ernie asked Lee, who had become managing editor of the paper, whether he could try writing a column on the side. He wanted to tell the story of America's budding aviation sector. The new assignment gave Ernie the chance to immerse himself in something exciting and new and challenged him to explain what he saw to a readership of outsiders that had likely never even seen a plane. See Nichols, ed., *Ernie's War*, 6–7. "The column was marked by a preoccupation with people and with 'little things,'" Lee Miller later wrote. "It made good reading, even for many with no intrinsic interest in aviation." See Miller, *The Story of Ernie Pyle*, 42.

11. Miller, *Story of Ernie Pyle*, 44–49, 53.

12. Nichols, ed., *Ernie's War*, 7.

13. Miller, *Story of Ernie Pyle*, 53.

14. Nichols, ed., *Ernie's War*, 8.

15. Miller, *Story of Ernie Pyle*, 33.

16. For a description of Ernie and Jerry's sparsely decorated apartment, see Miller, *The Story of Ernie Pyle*, 37. In a letter to Paige Cavanaugh on Oct. 29, 1940, Ernie says that he doesn't have "nerve enough to ask the Millers and other for our furniture back" to move it into the new house in Albuquerque, "so will have to get new stuff." See EP letter to PC, Oct. 29, 1940, LL.

17. Miller, *Story of Ernie Pyle*, 34.

18. Miller, *Story of Ernie Pyle*, 53.

19. Nichols, ed., *Ernie's War*, 8.

20. James Tobin, *Ernie Pyle's War: America's Eyewitness to World War II* (New York: The Free Press, 1997), 27.

21. Ernie Pyle, *Home Country* (New York: William Sloane Associates, 1947), 72.

22. Pyle, *Home Country*, 98–100.

23. Steve Hockensmith, "The Home Front," *Chicago Tribune*, Aug. 6, 2000, www.chicagotribune .com/news/ct-xpm-2000-08-06-0008060013-story.html.

24. William Rice, "A Journey through 1930s America with Ernie Pyle," *Chicago Tribune*, Aug. 27, 1989, www.chicagotribune.com/news/ct-xpm-1989-08-27-8901070986-story.html.

25. Miller, *Story of Ernie Pyle*, 57.

26. Miller, *Story of Ernie Pyle*, 60.

27. Miller, *Story of Ernie Pyle*, 72.

28. Rice, "A Journey through 1930s America with Ernie Pyle."

29. Pyle, *Home Country*, 119.

30. David Nichols, ed., *The Best of Ernie Pyle's 1930s Travel Dispatches* (New York: Random House, 1989). See also Rice, "A Journey through 1930s America with Ernie Pyle."

31. Miller, *Story of Ernie Pyle*, 64–65.

32. EP letter to PC, Sept. 11, 1939, LL.

33. In a letter to Paige, Ernie said that Jerry threatened to "jump out a high window" if he enlisted in the military. Ernie seemed undaunted. "If the damn war lasts long enough," he told Paige, "I'll bet I get some kind of a look at it." See Miller, *The Story of Ernie Pyle*, 118.

34. Salutatorian of her high school class, Jerry took a business course upon graduation, got a civil service job in Washington, DC, and left Minnesota for good in 1918 at the age of eighteen. She met Ernie Pyle five years later, shortly after he had arrived in Washington—and started dating him seriously a year after that.

35. Miller, *Story of Ernie Pyle*, 34.

36. Miller, *Story of Ernie Pyle*, 35.

37. Miller, *Story of Ernie Pyle*, 35.

38. Lila Noll Liggett, "That Girl of Ernie Pyle's," *The Woman with Woman's Digest*, July 1945.

39. Esther C. Robb, "Jerry, His Wife: Here Is a Story Never Told Before About 'That Girl'—Ernie

Pyle's Wife," *Golfer & Sportsman* 20, no. 4 (Apr. 1947), 4. Some of this material was reworked for publication by Edwin G. Robb, "JP: Ernie's Afton Connection," *The Afton* (MN) *Paper*, Apr. 1994, 12–13.

40. Miller, *Story of Ernie Pyle*, 38–39.

41. Tobin, *Ernie Pyle's War*, 42. See also Miller, *Story of Ernie Pyle*, 122.

42. We also know that she typed and retyped his drafts and helped him edit and correct them. Jerry also did some writing of her own, which was of a quite different style, but rather than submitting it somewhere for publication, destroyed it so that Ernie would not be offended. She decided that having two writers in one family could be difficult.

43. "Mrs. Ernie Pyle, 45, War Hero's Widow," *New York Times*, Nov. 24, 1945, https://times machine.nytimes.com/timesmachine/1945/11/24/88316545.html?pageNumber=19. During his years as a roving reporter, Ernie frequently referred to Jerry as "that girl who rides beside me." See Miller, *The Story of Ernie Pyle*, 70.

44. While he was in college, Ernie wrote an editorial in his journalism class on what made for the "ideal girl." He said that when a man "begins to think seriously of a wife and home of his own, his mind turns to an entirely different type of girl. The type who is willing to share your troubles, sympathetic with you in your periods of adverses, and makes your interests her interests." See Miller, *The Story of Ernie Pyle*, 18.

45. Liggett, "That Girl of Ernie Pyle's."

46. To Jerry, Ernie once wrote, "Do wish you were going [to New York] with me. I suppose it would be foolish for such a short trip, but I can hardly bear to go East alone, without you to lean on and 'protect' me. I mean it." See Miller, *Story of Ernie Pyle*, 115.

47. Miller, *Story of Ernie Pyle*, 69–70, 122.

48. Miller, *Story of Ernie Pyle*, 146.

49. Miller, *Story of Ernie Pyle*, 70.

50. Miller, *Story of Ernie Pyle*, 146.

51. When Jerry preceded Ernie back from South America at the end of 1938, she buried herself in a hotel room and nearly drank herself to death. See Miller, *Story of Ernie Pyle*, 98, 105.

52. Atkinson, *Army at Dawn*, 230.

53. Ernie Pyle, "Albuquerque at Last," *Albuquerque Tribune*, no date.

54. EP letter to PC, Oct. 29, 1940, LL.

55. Ernie Pyle, "Why Albuquerque?," *New Mexico Magazine*, Jan. 1942.

56. EP letter to PC, Oct. 29, 1940, LL. See also Miller, *Story of Ernie Pyle*, 132.

57. Miller, *Story of Ernie Pyle*, 140.

58. Miller, *Story of Ernie Pyle*, 132, 136.

59. EP letter to PC, Oct. 29, 1940, LL.

60. Miller, *Story of Ernie Pyle*, 137.

61. Miller, *Story of Ernie Pyle*, 137.

62. Miller, *Story of Ernie Pyle*, 137.

63. EP letter to PC, Nov. 15, 1940, LL. See also Miller, *Story of Ernie Pyle*, 138.

64. EP letter to JP, Nov. 26, 1940, LL.

65. EP letter to PC, Oct. 29, 1940, LL.

66. EP letter to PC, May 4, 1940, LL. See also Miller, *Story of Ernie Pyle*, 125–26.

67. EP letter to PC, May 22, 1940, LL. See also Miller, *Story of Ernie Pyle*, 126.

68. EP letter to PC, May 22, 1940, LL. See also Miller, *Story of Ernie Pyle*, 126.

69. EP letter to JP, Jan. 5, 1942, LL.

70. "A Dreadful Masterpiece," Dec. 30, 1940, in Nichols, ed., *Ernie's War*, 42–44.

71. EP letter to JP, Jan. 5, 1942, LL.

72. EP letter to JP, Jan. 12, 1941, LL. See also Miller, *Story of Ernie Pyle*, 149.

73. Miller, *Story of Ernie Pyle*, 147.

74. EP letter to JP, Dec. 15, 1940, LL.

75. EP letter to PC, Apr. 1, 1941, LL.

76. Miller, *Story of Ernie Pyle*, 152.

77. Mike Lunsford, "Celebrate Ernie Pyle for What He Was: A Great Writer," *Tribune-Star* (Terre Haute, IN), July 29, 2018, www.tribstar.com/news/news_columns/mike-lunsford -celebrate-ernie-pyle-for-what-he-was-a-great-writer.

78. Richard Lewis, "Dad Stood There Watching As Ernie Ran for His Plane," *Indianapolis Times*, Mar. 28, 1941.

79. She was the "feisty and liberated daughter of the owner of the hardware store in Nashville, the county seat of Brown County and a traditional gathering place for artists." See Owen V. Johnson, "Darling Jerry, Darling Mabel, Darling Moran: Ernie Pyle and the Women Behind Him," paper prepared for presentation to the History Division, Association for Education in Journalism & Mass Communication, San Francisco (Aug. 2–5, 2006).

80. Pyle's stay in Brown County was recalled by Rex Redifer, "Ernie Pyle Enjoyed Summer in 'Spoiled' Scenic Setting," *Indianapolis Star*, Sept. 29, 1985, Sect. F, 1, 4. The columns that resulted from Pyle's stay were gathered together in Ernie Pyle, *Images of Brown County* (Indianapolis: Museum Shop, 1980).

81. Johnson, "Darling Jerry, Darling Mabel, Darling Moran."

82. Johnson, "Darling Jerry, Darling Mabel, Darling Moran."

83. Johnson, "Darling Jerry, Darling Mabel, Darling Moran."

84. Johnson, "Darling Jerry, Darling Mabel, Darling Moran."

85. See Johnson, "Darling Jerry, Darling Mabel, Darling Moran."

86. Johnson, "Darling Jerry, Darling Mabel, Darling Moran."

87. Ernie Pyle, "Picket Fence," July 8, 1941, LL.

88. EP letter to PC, June 5, 1941, LL.

89. "Close Friend of Ernie Pyle Dies," *Albuquerque Tribune*, Aug. 5, 1974, C12.

90. This project was photographed by Ferenz Fedor, and the photos were used in the article "Why Albuquerque?," published in the Jan. 1942 issue of *New Mexico Magazine*. See Richard Melzer, *Ernie Pyle in the American Southwest* (Sunstone Press, 1996), 128.

91. Ernie Pyle, "Picket Fence."

92. Johnson, "Darling Jerry, Darling Mabel, Darling Moran."

93. Johnson, "Darling Jerry, Darling Mabel, Darling Moran."

94. EP letter to PC, June 25, 1941, LL. See also Miller, *Story of Ernie Pyle*, 164.

95. Miller, *Story of Ernie Pyle*, 164.

96. Miller, *Story of Ernie Pyle*, 167.

97. Miller, *Story of Ernie Pyle*, 166.

98. Miller, *Story of Ernie Pyle*, 167.

99. EP letter to PC, Sept. 4, 1941, LL.

100. EP letter to PC, Sept. 4, 1941, LL.

101. EP letter to LM and Walker Stone, Sept. 24, 1941, MD.

102. Miller, *Story of Ernie Pyle*, 170.

103. EP letter to PC, Sept. 27, 1941, LL. See also Miller, *Story of Ernie Pyle*, 170.

104. EP letter to LM and Walker Stone, Sept. 24, 1941, MD.

105. EP letter to LM and Walker Stone, Sept. 24, 1941, MD.

106. Miller, *Story of Ernie Pyle*, 165.

107. EP letter to LM and Walker Stone, Sept. 24, 1941, MD.

108. EP letter to LM and Walker Stone, Sept. 24, 1941, MD.

109. EP letter to LM and Walker Stone, Sept. 24, 1941, MD. See also EP letters to PC, Sept. 27, 1941, and Oct. 11, 1941, LL; and Miller, *Story of Ernie Pyle*, 170.

110. EP letter to LM and Walker Stone, Sept. 24, 1941, MD.

111. EP letter to LM and Walker Stone, Sept. 24, 1941, MD. See also Miller, *Story of Ernie Pyle*, 169.

112. EP letter to LM, Sept. 30, 1941, MD. See also EP letters to PC, Sept. 27, 1941, and Oct. 11, 1941, LL.
113. Miller, *Story of Ernie Pyle*, 172.
114. Miller, *Story of Ernie Pyle*, 173.
115. EP letter to JP, Jan. 4, 1942, MD.
116. EP letter to LM, Jan. 4, 1942, MD. See also EP letter to LM and Walker Stone, Sept. 24, 1941, MD.
117. Johnson, "Darling Jerry, Darling Mabel, Darling Moran."
118. Pyle, "Why Albuquerque?"
119. Pyle, "Why Albuquerque?"
120. Miller, *Story of Ernie Pyle*, 176.
121. EP letter to PC, Nov. 8, 1941, LL.
122. EP letter to LM, Walker Stone, and George "Deac" Parker, Oct. 28, 1941, MD.
123. Miller, *Story of Ernie Pyle*, 174.
124. EP letter to LM, Aug. 18, 1941, MD.
125. EP letter to LM, Walker Stone, and George "Deac" Parker, Oct. 28, 1941, MD.
126. EP letter to LM, Oct. 28, 1941, MD. See also EP letter to LM, Walker Stone, and George "Deac" Parker, Oct. 28, 1941: "[War with Japan] would be either in Manila, Chungking, Singapore or the East Indies, any of which would be far safer than London was last winter, when we were under raids almost every night. It seems to me the Japanese ships or bombers aren't likely to get very close to any of those places."
127. EP letter to LM, Aug. 18, 1941, MD.
128. EP letter to LM, Oct. 28, 1941, MD. See also EP letter to LM, Walker Stone, and George "Deac" Parker, Oct. 28, 1941.
129. Johnson, "Darling Jerry, Darling Mabel, Darling Moran." Letter was dated Nov. 24, 1941. For Mabel, the departure was traumatic. She wrote her thoughts on the back of an 8 x 11 picture of himself that Pyle gave her.
130. EP letter to PC, Dec. 9, 1941, LL.
131. EP letter to LM, Walker Stone, and George "Deac" Parker, Oct. 28, 1941, MD.
132. EP letter to PC, Dec. 9, 1941, LL.
133. EP letter to PC, Dec. 9, 1941, LL.
134. EP letter to JP, Dec. 17, 1941, LL. See also EP letters to JP, Feb. 20, 1942, and Mar. 1, 1942, LL.
135. EP letter to JP, Jan. 30, 1942, LL.
136. EP letter to JP, Feb. 20, 1942, LL.
137. EP letter to PC, Mar. 19, 1942, LL. See also Miller, *Story of Ernie Pyle*, 188.
138. EP letter to PC, Mar. 19, 1942, LL.
139. EP letter to JP, Mar. 15, 1942, MD.
140. EP letter to JP, Jan. 21, 1942., MD.
141. EP letter to LM, Jan. 14, 1942, MD.
142. EP letter to JP, Jan. 21, 1942, MD. See also EP letter to JP, Mar. 1, 1942.
143. EP letter to LM, Jan. 14, 1942, MD.
144. EP letter to LM, Jan. 14, 1942, MD. In a Jan. 14, 1942, letter from Seattle, Washington, to Jerry, Ernie wrote: "I feel maybe that this is t last turning point you'll have to go thru. I'm hoping t boost from yr transfusion will give you enough strength that you won't need yr Benzedrine any more—and I do feel strongly that you will never be completely well until you have stopped them completely." See also EP letter to JP, March 15, 1942, MD.
145. JP letter to EP, Feb. 5, 1942, MD. To Lee Miller, Ernie wrote, "I can't go on forever traveling alone and keeping a nurse with her just for company. But I suppose I will." Feb. 26, 1942, MD.
146. JP letter to EP, Feb. 5, 1942, MD.
147. EP letter to JP, Mar. 15, 1942, MD.
148. EP letter to JP, Mar. 15, 1942, MD.
149. EP letter to LM, Feb. 28, 1942, MD.

150. EP letter to JP, Mar. 15, 1942, MD.

151. EP letter to JP, Mar. 15, 1942, MD.

152. "Tank Battle at Sidi-Bou-Zid," Mar. 1, 1943, in Nichols, ed., *Ernie's War*, 93.

153. Reporter Philip Jordan wrote that central Tunisia was "that half-world where cultivation does not quite know where to cease or the desert to begin." See Atkinson, *Army at Dawn*, 309.

154. "Tank Battle at Sidi-Bou-Zid," in Nichols, ed., *Ernie's War*, 93.

155. Atkinson, *Army at Dawn*, 350.

156. Column from March 2, 1943, in Nichols, ed., *Ernie's War*, 94.

157. EP letter to JP, Dec. 24, 1942, LL.

158. Gene Eric Salecker, *Rolling Thunder Against the Rising Sun: The Combat History of U.S. Army Tank Battalions in the Pacific in World War II* (Mechanicsburg, PA: Stackpole Books, 2008), 351.

159. Miller, *Story of Ernie Pyle*, 191.

160. EP letter to LM, Apr. 14, 1942, MD. See also EP letter to PC, Apr. 23, 1942, LL.

161. Miller, *Story of Ernie Pyle*, 191.

162. Miller, *Story of Ernie Pyle*, 192.

163. Nichols, ed., *Ernie's War*, 12.

164. Nichols, ed., *Ernie's War*, 12.

165. Miller, *Story of Ernie Pyle*, 187.

166. EP letter to LM and Walker Stone, Apr. 23, 1942, MD. See also EP letter to PC, Apr. 23, 1942, LL; EP letters to JP, Dec. 24, 1942, and Feb. 9, 1942, LL; and Miller, *Story of Ernie Pyle*, 214.

167. EP letter to LM and Walker Stone, Apr. 23, 1942, MD.

168. Miller, *Story of Ernie Pyle*, 193.

169. Nichols, ed., *Ernie's War*, 12.

170. EP letter to LM and Walker Stone, Apr. 23, 1942, MD.

171. EP letter to LM and Walker Stone, Apr. 23, 1942, MD.

172. EP letter to LM, Apr. 27, 1942, MD.

173. EP letter to LM, Apr. 27, 1942, MD.

174. EP letter to JP, May 8, 1942, MD.

175. EP letter to JP, May 8, 1942, MD.

176. EP letter to JP, May 19, 1942, MD.

177. After the United States entered World War II, amendments to the Selective Training and Service Act on Dec. 20, 1941, made all men between the ages of twenty and forty-four liable for military service, and required all men between the ages of eighteen and sixty-four to register.

178. EP letter to JP, May 8, 1942, MD. On May 19, he wrote to Jerry that he had passed his army physical and was officially draft eligible.

179. EP letter to JP, May 8, 1942, MD. The three papers were in Detroit, MI; Akron, OH; and Miami, FL.

180. EP letter to JP, May 8, 1942, MD.

181. EP letter to JP, June 1, 1942, MD.

182. Johnson, "Darling Jerry, Darling Mabel, Darling Moran." This paper refers to additional letters to individuals, copies of which have been made available to the author. Particularly valuable is the correspondence to Mabel Calvin, copies of which the author acquired in March 2006.

183. Johnson, "Darling Jerry, Darling Mabel, Darling Moran." A year later, on July 24, 1943, Mabel married Ralph Burkholder, editor of *The Indianapolis Times*, then serving on leave as executive officer of the Postal Division of the U.S. Office of Censorship. He later was an editorial writer for the *Miami Herald*, and taught journalism at Indiana University and Brown County (IN) High School. He died in 1978, after what family members describe as "a stormy marriage."

184. EP letter to JP, June 1, 1942, MD.

185. EP letter to JP, June 9, 1942, MD.

186. EP letter to JP, June 9, 1942, MD.

187. EP letter to PC, May 27, 1942, LL. See also Miller, *Story of Ernie Pyle*, 158, 199.

188. "Colorado Mental Health Institute at Pueblo," *Colorado Encyclopedia*, https://colorado encyclopedia.org/article/colorado-mental-health-institute-pueblo-cmhip.

189. EP letter to "Papa & Auntie," May 28, 1942, MD. See also EP letter to JP, June 9, 1942, MD.

190. EP letter to JP, June 9, 1942, MD.

191. EP letter to PC, May 27, 1942, LL.

192. EP letter to JP, June 9, 1942, MD.

193. EP letter to JP, June 9, 1942, MD.

194. Miller, *Story of Ernie Pyle*, 200.

195. EP letter to JP, June 9, 1942, MD.

196. EP letter to PC, Aug. 8, 1942, LL.

197. EP letter to JP, July 27, 1942, LL.

198. EP letter to JP, Aug. 17, 1942, LL.

199. EP letter to JP, Sept. 26, 1942, LL.

200. EP letter to JP, Sept. 26, 1942, LL.

201. Miller, *Story of Ernie Pyle*, 211.

202. EP letter to JP, Sept. 26, 1942, LL.

203. EP letter to JP, Sept. 26, 1942, LL.

204. Miller, *Story of Ernie Pyle*, 205.

205. In a letter to Paige, Ernie says, "Lee writes that the draft board has decreed they want me to stay over here instead of come home. But my number was passed in August, so the minute I do return I'm in the Army." See EP letter to PC, Nov. 3, 1942, LL.

206. EP letter to JP, Sept. 26, 30, 1942, LL.

207. EP letter to PC, Aug. 8, 1942, LL.

208. Nichols, ed., *Ernie's War*, 15. See also A. J. Liebling, "Pictures of Ernie: An Intimate Reminiscence on Ernie Pyle, Who Fled Blindly from Personal Fears to Become the Hero and the Victim of War," *Esquire*, May 1, 1947.

209. Atkinson, *Army at Dawn*, 13.

210. Atkinson, *Army at Dawn*, 14.

211. Atkinson, *Army at Dawn*, 31.

212. Atkinson, *Army at Dawn*, 27, 66–67.

213. EP letter to JP, Nov. 26, 1942, LL.

214. Atkinson, *Army at Dawn*, 129. See also Blumenson, *Kasserine Pass*, 3.

215. Blumenson, *Kasserine Pass*, 25.

216. "Scared Stiff," Dec. 9, 1942, in Nichols, ed., *Ernie's War*, 61.

217. Atkinson, *Army at Dawn*, 272–73. See also Blumenson, *Kasserine Pass*, 83, 383–84.

218. Blumenson, *Kasserine Pass*, 83.

219. Atkinson, *Army at Dawn*, 124.

220. Atkinson, *Army at Dawn*, 129.

221. Atkinson, *Army at Dawn*, 27, 66–67.

222. Blumenson, *Kasserine Pass*, 45. See also Atkinson, *Army at Dawn*, 171.

223. Atkinson, *Army at Dawn*, 169–70.

224. EP letter to JP, Nov. 26, 1942, LL.

225. EP letter to JP, Nov. 26, 1942, LL.

226. Column from Dec. 24, 1942, in Nichols, ed., *Ernie's War*, 63–64.

227. Atkinson, *Army at Dawn*, 124.

228. Column from Dec. 24, 1942, in Nichols, ed., *Ernie's War*, 63–64.

229. Atkinson, *Army at Dawn*, 124.

230. Column from Dec. 31, 1942, in Nichols, ed., *Ernie's War*, 64.

231. Atkinson, *Army at Dawn*, 124.

232. Column from Dec. 24, 1942, in Nichols, ed., *Ernie's War*, 63.

233. EP letter to JP, Dec. 24, 1942, LL.

234. EP letter to JP, Dec. 8, 1942, LL. See also EP letter to JP, Dec. 24, 1942, LL.

235. James Tobin interview with Ralph Martin, date not recorded, LL. Each day, according to Martin, an intelligence officer would brief the correspondents to let them know where the action was happening. Most war correspondents interested in the daily news would then hop in a jeep and get out there as quickly as they could. "Two or three guys would have a driver and a jeep," Martin remembered, "and they would go to an agreed area, usually near the front, where the action was."

236. Tobin, *Ernie Pyle's War*, 67. John Sorrell's letter to Walker Stone, Nov. 21, 1942, ISMA.

237. EP letter to JP, Dec. 24, 1942, LL.

238. Liebling, "Pictures of Ernie."

239. Column from Dec. 8, 1942, in Nichols, ed., *Ernie's War*, 60.

240. "Scared Stiff," Dec. 9, 1942, in Nichols, ed., *Ernie's War*, 61.

241. Column from Dec. 15, 1942, in Nichols, ed., *Ernie's War*, 63.

242. "Scared Stiff," Dec. 9, 1942, in Nichols, ed., *Ernie's War*, 62.

243. "Killing Is All That Matters," Dec. 1, 1942, in Nichols, ed., *Ernie's War*, 59.

244. "Killing Is All That Matters," in Nichols, ed., *Ernie's War*, 60.

245. Atkinson, *Army at Dawn*, 59–61.

246. Atkinson, *Army at Dawn*, 59.

247. Atkinson, *Army at Dawn*, 247–48.

248. Atkinson, *Army at Dawn*, 237.

249. Atkinson, *Army at Dawn*, 249.

250. Atkinson, *Army at Dawn*, 60–61.

251. Atkinson, *Army at Dawn*, 260.

252. Blumenson, *Kasserine Pass*, 73–74. See also Atkinson, *Army at Dawn*, 249–50. In a message to Washington and London, Eisenhower wrote: "Due to continual rain there will be no hope of immediate attack on Tunis. May be possible later by methodical infantry advance. Am attempting to organize and maintain a force to operate aggressively on southern flank."

253. Liebling, "Pictures of Ernie."

254. Owen V. Johnson, ed., *At Home with Ernie Pyle* (Bloomington: Indiana University Press, 2016), 194.

255. EP letter to JP, Feb. 21, 1943, LL. See also Miller, *Story of Ernie Pyle*, 230.

256. EP letter to JP, Feb. 21, 1943, LL.

257. In a Jan. 7, 1943, letter to Jerry, Ernie said that there was "nobody at all I feel really close to or intimate with, and I suffer from a deep fundamental loneliness. My chronic depression of spirit hangs on, and I just can't rouse in myself a genuine interest in anything." See EP letter to JP, Jan. 7, 1943, LL.

258. Liebling, "Pictures of Ernie."

259. "Snakes in Our Midst," Jan. 4, 1943, in Nichols, ed., *Ernie's War*, 65.

260. Atkinson, *Army at Dawn*, 159.

261. "Snakes in Our Midst," in Nichols, ed., *Ernie's War*, 65.

262. "Snakes in Our Midst," in Nichols, ed., *Ernie's War*, 65.

263. "Snakes in Our Midst," in Nichols, ed., *Ernie's War*, 65.

264. Atkinson, *Army at Dawn*, 159.

CHAPTER 3: DISAPPOINTING THE FOLKS AT HOME

1. "A Humiliating Predicament," Feb. 23, 1943, in David Nichols, ed., *Ernie's War: The Best of Ernie Pyle's World War II Dispatches* (New York: Random House, 1986), 87.

2. EP letter to JP, Feb. 21, 1943, LL.

3. Column from Feb. 26, 1943, in Nichols, ed., *Ernie's War*, 89.

4. Martin Blumenson, *Kasserine Pass: Where America Lost Her Military Innocence* (Boston: Houghton Mifflin, 1966), 86.

5. Rick Atkinson, *An Army at Dawn: The War in North Africa, 1942–1943* (New York: Henry Holt, 2002), 274–75.

6. EP letter to JP, Feb. 21, 1943, LL.

7. Blumenson, *Kasserine Pass*, 74. See also Atkinson, *Army at Dawn*, 270–71.

8. Atkinson, *Army at Dawn*, 281.

9. Atkinson, *Army at Dawn*, 307.

10. Atkinson, *Army at Dawn*, 303.

11. Lee G. Miller, *The Story of Ernie Pyle* (New York: Viking Press, 1950), 226.

12. Miller, *Story of Ernie Pyle*, 230.

13. "The Velvet Is Gone," Feb. 20, 1943, in Nichols, ed., *Ernie's War*, 83–84.

14. Miller, *Story of Ernie Pyle*, 227.

15. Miller, *Story of Ernie Pyle*, 230.

16. "Night Convoy," Feb. 16, 1943, in Nichols, ed., *Ernie's War*, 80.

17. Miller, *Story of Ernie Pyle*, 230. See also Timothy M. Gay, *Assignment to Hell: The War Against Nazi Germany with Correspondents Walter Cronkite, Andy Rooney, A. J. Liebling, Homer Bigart, and Hal Boyle* (New York: The Penguin Group, 2013), 110, and EP letter to JP, Feb. 21, 1943, LL.

18. Miller, *Story of Ernie Pyle*, 230.

19. EP letter to JP, Feb. 21, 1943, LL.

20. "Life at the Front," Feb. 19, 1943, in Nichols, ed., *Ernie's War*, 81.

21. "The Velvet Is Gone," in Nichols, ed., *Ernie's War*, 83–84.

22. "Night Convoy," in Nichols, ed., *Ernie's War*, 80–81.

23. "Night Convoy," in Nichols, ed., *Ernie's War*, 78.

24. "Night Convoy," in Nichols, ed., *Ernie's War*, 80.

25. "Night Convoy," in Nichols, ed., *Ernie's War*, 80–81.

26. Column from Feb. 26, 1943, in Nichols, ed., *Ernie's War*, 89.

27. Atkinson, *Army at Dawn*, 325.

28. Column from Feb. 26, 1943, in Nichols, ed., *Ernie's War*, 89.

29. Column from Feb. 24, 1943, in Nichols, ed., *Ernie's War*, 88. See also James Tobin, *Ernie Pyle's War: America's Eyewitness to World War II* (New York: The Free Press, 1997), 81.

30. Column from Feb. 24, 1943, in Nichols, ed., *Ernie's War*, 89.

31. Atkinson, *Army at Dawn*, 307–8.

32. Atkinson, *Army at Dawn*, 307–8. See also Blumenson, *Kasserine Pass*, 4.

33. Atkinson, *Army at Dawn*, 310–11.

34. Atkinson, *Army at Dawn*, 275.

35. Atkinson, *Army at Dawn*, 310–11.

36. Atkinson, *Army at Dawn*, 310–11.

37. Atkinson, *Army at Dawn*, 223.

38. On Feb. 2, the 1st Armored Division was ordered to end its attacks and concentrate their forces. See Edwin V. Westrate, *Forward Observer* (Philadelphia: Blakiston, 1944), 109–17. See also Major General I. S. O. Playfair et al., *The Mediterranean and Middle East: The Destruction of the Axis Forces in Africa*, History of the Second World War United Kingdom Military Series (Uckfield, UK: Naval & Military Press, 2004), 204.

39. Atkinson, *Army at Dawn*, 203.

40. Atkinson, *Army at Dawn*, 203, 311.

41. Atkinson, *Army at Dawn*, 311.

42. Atkinson, *Army at Dawn*, 317.

43. Column from Feb. 26, 1943, in Nichols, ed., *Ernie's War*, 90.

44. Column from Feb. 26, 1943, in Nichols, ed., *Ernie's War*, 90.

45. Column from Feb. 26, 1943, in Nichols, ed., *Ernie's War*, 90–91.

46. Column from Feb. 26, 1943, in Nichols, ed., *Ernie's War*, 91.

47. Atkinson, *Army at Dawn*, 327.

48. Atkinson, *Army at Dawn*, 339–40.

49. Blumenson, *Kasserine Pass*, 134. See also Atkinson, *Army at Dawn*, 341–42.

50. Atkinson, *Army at Dawn*, 325.

51. Atkinson, *Army at Dawn*, 325.

52. Atkinson, *Army at Dawn*, 339–40.

53. Atkinson, *Army at Dawn*, 339–40.

54. Atkinson, *Army at Dawn*, 342.

55. Atkinson, *Army at Dawn*, 342.

56. Atkinson, *Army at Dawn*, 343.

57. "Tank Battle at Sidi-Bou-Zid," Mar. 1, 1943, in Nichols, ed., *Ernie's War*, 93–94.

58. Atkinson, *Army at Dawn*, 350.

59. Blumenson, *Kasserine Pass*, 141–42.

60. Atkinson, *Army at Dawn*, 351.

61. Column from Mar. 2, 1943, in Nichols, ed., *Ernie's War*, 94.

62. Atkinson, *Army at Dawn*, 350.

63. Blumenson, *Kasserine Pass*, 122.

64. Column from Mar. 3, 1943, in Nichols, ed., *Ernie's War*, 96–97.

65. Column from Mar. 3, 1943, in Nichols, ed., *Ernie's War*, 96.

66. Atkinson, *Army at Dawn*, 352–53.

67. Atkinson, *Army at Dawn*, 352–53.

68. Atkinson, *Army at Dawn*, 367–68.

69. Blumenson, *Kasserine Pass*, 229.

70. Atkinson, *Army at Dawn*, 364.

71. Bruce Allen Watson, *Exit Rommel: The Tunisian Campaign, 1942–43* (Mechanicsburg, PA: Stackpole Books, 2007), 80.

72. Blumenson, *Kasserine Pass*, 215.

73. Watson, *Exit Rommel*, 80.

74. Watson, *Exit Rommel*, 81.

75. Atkinson, *Army at Dawn*, 369.

76. Atkinson, *Army at Dawn*, 369–70.

77. Blumenson, *Kasserine Pass*, 230.

78. Atkinson, *Army at Dawn*, 369.

79. Atkinson, *Army at Dawn*, 366.

80. Atkinson, *Army at Dawn*, 367–68.

81. Atkinson, *Army at Dawn*, 366–67.

82. Blumenson, *Kasserine Pass*, 221. See also Atkinson, *Army at Dawn*, 369.

83. Blumenson, *Kasserine Pass*, 239.

84. Atkinson, *Army at Dawn*, 371.

85. Blumenson, *Kasserine Pass*, 189.

86. Blumenson, *Kasserine Pass*, 189.

87. Atkinson, *Army at Dawn*, 360–61.

88. Blumenson, *Kasserine Pass*, 190–91.

89. "The night was heavy with low cloud, and always that intolerable wind . . . and all the inevitable turmoil and confusion of night movement," wrote A. D. Divine. "Clouds were red with the burning of the Sbeïtla dumps." See Atkinson, *Army at Dawn*, 366.

90. Atkinson, *Army at Dawn*, 360–61.

91. Atkinson, *Army at Dawn*, 364.

92. A. J. Liebling, "Pictures of Ernie: An Intimate Reminiscence on Ernie Pyle, Who Fled Blindly from Personal Fears to Become the Hero and the Victim of War," *Esquire*, May 1, 1947.

93. Even when a story had nothing even remotely controversial in it, the military censors could take days, sometimes weeks, to approve it and transmit it back to the States. See Gay, *Assignment to Hell*, 65. While stateside journalists had their copy approved by the Office of Censorship, which was hastily cobbled together a mere nine days after the Japanese attacked Pearl Harbor, correspondents like Pyle had their articles censored by military public affairs officers. The higher-ups at the Office of Censorship figured that officers closer to the action would have the greatest understanding of what sorts of information was too risky to publish. See Michael S. Sweeney, *The Military and the Press: An Uneasy Truce* (Evanston, IL: Northwestern University Press, 2006), 71.

94. Gay, *Assignment to Hell*, 65.

95. Fletcher Pratt wrote: "The official censors pretty well succeeded in putting over the legend that the war was won without a single mistake by a command consisting exclusively of geniuses." See Phillip Knightley, *The First Casualty: From the Crimea to Vietnam: The War Correspondent as Hero, Propagandist, and Myth Maker* (New York: Harcourt Brace Jovanovich, 1975), 276.

96. Sweeney, *Military and the Press*, 103–4.

97. Sweeney, *Military and the Press*, 104, 107.

98. Column from Feb. 28, 1943, in Nichols, ed., *Ernie's War*, 91.

99. "A Humiliating Predicament," Feb. 23, 1943, in Nichols, ed., *Ernie's War*, 87.

100. "A Humiliating Predicament," in Nichols, ed., *Ernie's War*, 86. See also Blumenson, *Kasserine Pass*, 4–5.

101. "A Humiliating Predicament," in Nichols, ed., *Ernie's War*, 86.

102. "A Humiliating Predicament," in Nichols, ed., *Ernie's War*, 86.

103. Atkinson, *Army at Dawn*, 366.

104. Atkinson, *Army at Dawn*, 370. See also Blumenson, *Kasserine Pass*, 239.

105. Blumenson, *Kasserine Pass*, 239.

106. Blumenson, *Kasserine Pass*, 243–44.

107. Atkinson, *Army at Dawn*, 378.

108. Atkinson, *Army at Dawn*, 371.

109. Atkinson, *Army at Dawn*, 377.

110. Atkinson, *Army at Dawn*, 372.

111. Atkinson, *Army at Dawn*, 379.

112. Atkinson, *Army at Dawn*, 381.

113. Playfair et al., *Mediterranean and Middle East*, 301.

114. Atkinson, *Army at Dawn*, 387, 398. See also Gay, *Assignment to Hell*, 104.

115. Gay, *Assignment to Hell*, 104. See also Atkinson, *Army at Dawn*, 389.

116. Atkinson, *Army at Dawn*, 390.

117. Atkinson, *Army at Dawn*, 390. Butcher was an American radio broadcaster who served during World War II as the naval aide to General Dwight D. Eisenhower from 1942 to 1945. See Harry C. Butcher, *Three Years with Eisenhower* (New York: Simon & Schuster, 1946), xiii.

118. Atkinson, *Army at Dawn*, 389.

119. EP letter to JP, Feb. 21, 1943, LL.

120. EP letter to PC, Feb. 28, 1943, LL.

121. EP letter to JP, Feb. 21, 1943, LL.

122. EP letter to JP, Feb. 21, 1943, LL.

123. EP letter to JP, Feb. 21, 1943, LL.

124. Knightley, *First Casualty*, 315.

125. Knightley, *First Casualty*, 317.

126. Knightley, *First Casualty*, 308.

127. Miller, *Story of Ernie Pyle*, 226.

128. Column from March 10, 1943, in Nichols, ed., *Ernie's War*, 97.

129. EP letter to JP, Mar. 2, 1943, LL.

130. Miller, *Story of Ernie Pyle*, 241.
131. Gay, *Assignment to Hell*, 95.
132. Miller, *Story of Ernie Pyle*, 230.
133. EP letter to JP, Mar. 13, 1943, LL.
134. EP letter to JP, Feb. 21, 1943, LL.
135. Miller, *Story of Ernie Pyle*, 240.
136. Column from March 3, 1943, in Nichols, ed., *Ernie's War*, 97.
137. David Sedaris, "And While You're Up There, Check on My Prostate," *Calypso* (New York: Back Bay Books, 2018), 242.

CHAPTER 4: DRIFTING WITH THE WAR

1. "One Dull, Dead Pattern," Aug. 25, 1943, in David Nichols, ed., *Ernie's War: The Best of Ernie Pyle's World War II Dispatches* (New York: Random House, 1986), 153.
2. EP letter to JP, May 14, 1943, MD.
3. EP letter to JP, May 19, 1943, MD.
4. EP letter to JP, May 14, 1943, MD. See also EP letter to JP, May 19, 1943.
5. EP letter to JP, May 14, 1943, MD.
6. EP letter to JP, May 19, 1943, MD.
7. Clarence E. Redman, "That Girl," *Bombsight*, Christmas 1943. In a letter from Roz, Ernie learned that Jerry was "doing two people's work." See EP letter to JP, May 19, 1943, MD.
8. EP letter to JP, Nov. 16, 1943, MD.
9. EP letter to JP, May 19, 1943, MD.
10. EP letter to JP, May 19, 1943, MD. See also EP letter to JP, May 26, 1943, MD.
11. EP letter to JP, May 19, 1943, MD. See also EP letter to LM, May 20, 1943, MD.
12. EP letter to JP, May 19, 1943, MD.
13. EP letter to JP, May 26, 1943, MD.
14. EP letter to JP, May 14, 1943, MD.
15. EP letter to JP, May 19, 1943, MD.
16. EP letter to JP, June 14, 1943, MD.
17. EP letter to JP, May 19, 1943, MD.
18. EP letter to JP, May 19, 1943, MD.
19. EP letter to JP, May 19, 1943, MD.
20. EP letter to JP, May 19, 1943, MD.
21. EP letter to JP, May 19, 1943, MD.
22. EP letter to JP, May 19, 1943, MD.
23. EP letter to PC, June 11, 1943, MD. See also EP letter to JP, June 14, 1943, MD.
24. EP letter to William Pyle, June 1, 1943, LL, LMC 1879, Indiana University. See also EP letter to PC, June 11, 1943, MD.
25. EP letter to PC, June 11, 1943, MD. See also EP letter to JP, May 26, 1943, MD.
26. EP letter to JP, June 14, 1943, MD.
27. EP letter to PC, June 11, 1943, MD. See also EP letter to JP, June 14, 1943, MD.
28. EP letter to JP, May 26, 1943, MD.
29. EP letter to PC, June 11, 1943, MD; and EP letter to LM, May 30, 1943, MD.
30. EP letter to PC, June 11, 1943, MD.
31. EP letter to LM, May 30, 1943, MD.
32. EP letter to LM, May 30, 1943, MD.
33. EP letter to PC, June 11, 1943, MD.
34. EP letter to JP, May 19, 1943, MD. See also EP letter to William Pyle, June 8, 1943, LL, LMC 1879, Indiana University.
35. EP letter to JP, May 14, 1943, MD.
36. EP letter to JP, May 26, 1943, MD.

37. LM letter to EP, May 28, 1943, MD.
38. EP letter to JP, May 19, 1943, MD.
39. EP letter to JP, May 26, 1943, MD.
40. EP letter to JP, May 26, 1943, MD.
41. EP letter to JP, June 20, 1943, MD.
42. EP letter to PC, June 11, 1943, MD. See also EP letter to JP, May 26, 1943, MD.
43. EP letter to PC, June 11, 1943, MD.
44. EP letter to PC, June 11, 1943, MD.
45. EP letter to JP, June 15, 1943, MD.
46. LM letter to EP via George Lyon, OWI, June 21, 1943, MD.
47. Eleanor Roosevelt, "My Day," June 21, 1943, www2.gwu.edu/~erpapers/myday/displaydoc
    .cfm?_y=1943&_f=md056527.
48. Eleanor Roosevelt, "My Day," Nov. 5, 1943, www2.gwu.edu/~erpapers/myday/displaydoc
    .cfm?_y=1943&_f=md056638.
49. Eleanor Roosevelt to EP, Oct. 1, 1943, MD.
50. EP letter to PC, June 11, 1943; and EP letter to JP, June 14, 1943, MD.
51. EP letter to JP, June 22, 1943, MD.
52. EP letter to JP, June 22, 1943, MD.
53. EP letter to JP, June 22, 1943, MD.
54. EP letter to JP, July 11, 1943, MD.
55. Ernie Pyle, *Brave Men* (Lincoln: University of Nebraska Press, 2001 [1944]), 4. See also Nichols, ed., *Ernie's War*, 141.
56. Pyle, *Brave Men*, 4.
57. Pyle, *Brave Men*, 4.
58. Column from July 16, 1943, in Nichols, ed., *Ernie's War*, 141. See also Pyle, *Brave Men*, 5.
59. Column from July 16, 1943, in Nichols, ed., *Ernie's War*, 5.
60. Pyle, *Brave Men*, 5.
61. Pyle, *Brave Men*, 6.
62. Column from July 16, 1943, in Nichols, ed., *Ernie's War*, 141.
63. Pyle, *Brave Men*, 27–28, 30. See also Ray Moseley, *Reporting War: How Foreign Correspondents Risked Capture, Torture and Death to Cover World War II* (New Haven: Yale University Press, 2017), 208.
64. Pyle, *Brave Men*, 26.
65. Pyle, *Brave Men*, 25.
66. Pyle, *Brave Men*, 27.
67. Pyle, *Brave Men*, 28.
68. Pyle, *Brave Men*, 32.
69. Pyle, *Brave Men*, 29, 34.
70. Pyle, *Brave Men*, 33.
71. Column from Aug. 6, 1943, in Nichols, ed., *Ernie's War*, 144.
72. "What Is These Barons, Anyway?," Aug. 20, 1943, in Nichols, ed., *Ernie's War*, 152. Later on in the campaign, Ernie's opinion of the Sicilian people evolved. "Whatever else you can say about them, the Sicilians don't seem lazy. One soldier summed it up when he said: 'After living nine months with Arabs, the sight of somebody working voluntarily is almost too much for me.'"
73. "An Easy Landing," July 17, 1943, in Nichols, ed., *Ernie's War*, 143. See also Pyle, *Brave Men*, 34.
74. EP letter to JP, July 11, 1943, MD.
75. "An Easy Landing," in Nichols, ed., *Ernie's War*, 143. See also Pyle, *Brave Men*, 34.
76. "An Easy Landing," in Nichols, ed., *Ernie's War*, 142.
77. EP letter to JP, July 11, 1943, MD.
78. EP letter to JP, July 11, 1943, MD.
79. Pyle, *Brave Men*, 36.

80. Pyle, *Brave Men*, 42.
81. EP letter to JP, July 18, 1943, MD.
82. EP letter to JP, July 18, 1943, MD. See also Pyle, *Brave Men*, 47.
83. Pyle, *Brave Men*, 47.
84. Column from Aug. 6, 1943, in Nichols, ed., *Ernie's War*, 144.
85. "An Easy Landing," in Nichols, ed., *Ernie's War*, 143.
86. Column from Aug. 6, 1943, in Nichols, ed., *Ernie's War*, 144.
87. Pyle, *Brave Men*, 29.
88. Pyle, *Brave Men*, 33.
89. Ralph G. Martin, *The GI War: 1941–1945* (Boston: Little, Brown, 1967), 76.
90. Martin, *The GI War*, 80.
91. EP letter to LM, Aug. 3, 1943, MD.
92. Ernie wrote to Lee Miller, "I've just read over a couple of weeks clippings re the first days of Sicily and the Navy, and your job of translating was uncannily good. Out of the whole batch I found only a couple of slight misinterpretations; plus one omission which apparently was radio garbled, and a couple of small ones which probably were censorship." See EP letter to LM, Aug. 20, 1943, MD.
93. EP letter to LM, Aug. 3, 1943, MD.
94. EP letter to LM, Aug. 3, 1943, MD.
95. EP letter to LM, Aug. 3, 1943, MD.
96. Pyle, *Brave Men*, 85.
97. Pyle, *Brave Men*, 86.
98. Pyle, *Brave Men*, 86.
99. Martin, *The GI War*, 76.
100. Alex Kershaw, *Blood and Champagne: The Life and Times of Robert Capa* (New York: Da Capo Press, 2002), 105. See also Moseley, *Reporting War*, 211.
101. Pyle, *Brave Men*, 63. See also column from Aug. 27, 1945, in Nichols, ed., *Ernie's War*, 154–55.
102. Column from Aug. 27, 1945, in Nichols, ed., *Ernie's War*, 155.
103. "A Spectacular Engineering Job," Sept. 3, 1943, in Nichols, ed., *Ernie's War*, 159–60. See also Pyle, *Brave Men*, 63.
104. "A Spectacular Engineering Job," in Nichols, ed., *Ernie's War*, 159–60. See also Pyle, *Brave Men*, 70.
105. Pyle, *Brave Men*, 72.
106. EP letter to JP, Aug. 15, 1943, MD.
107. "A Spectacular Engineering Job," in Nichols, ed., *Ernie's War*, 159–160. See also Pyle, *Brave Men*, 71.
108. "A Spectacular Engineering Job," in Nichols, ed., *Ernie's War*, 159–160. See also Pyle, *Brave Men*, 71.
109. "A Spectacular Engineering Job," in Nichols, ed., *Ernie's War*, 159–160. See also Pyle, *Brave Men*, 71.
110. "A Spectacular Engineering Job," in Nichols, ed., *Ernie's War*, 159–160. See also Pyle, *Brave Men*, 71.
111. "A Spectacular Engineering Job," in Nichols, ed., *Ernie's War*, 159–160. See also Pyle, *Brave Men*, 74.
112. "A Spectacular Engineering Job," in Nichols, ed., *Ernie's War*, 159–160. See also Pyle, *Brave Men*, 69.
113. "A Spectacular Engineering Job," in Nichols, ed., *Ernie's War*, 159–160. See also Pyle, *Brave Men*, 74.
114. EP letter to JP, Aug. 15, 1943, MD.
115. "A Spectacular Engineering Job," in Nichols, ed., *Ernie's War*, 159–60. See also Pyle, *Brave Men*, 74.

116. "The Kind of Bridge That Wins Wars," Sept. 6, 1943, in Nichols, ed., *Ernie's War*, 164. See also Pyle, *Brave Men*, 74–75.

117. "The Kind of Bridge That Wins Wars," in Nichols, ed., *Ernie's War*, 164. See also Pyle, *Brave Men*, 75.

118. Column from Aug. 9, 1943, in Nichols, ed., *Ernie's War*, 145–46. See also Pyle, *Brave Men*, 50.

119. Column from Aug. 9, 1943, in Nichols, ed., *Ernie's War*, 145–46. See also Pyle, *Brave Men*, 48, and EP letter to JP, Aug. 2, 1943, MD.

120. Column from Aug. 9, 1943, in Nichols, ed., *Ernie's War*, 145–46. See also Pyle, *Brave Men*, 48.

121. Pyle, *Brave Men*, 57.

122. Column from Aug. 9, 1943, in Nichols, ed., *Ernie's War*, 145–46. See also Pyle, *Brave Men*, 48.

123. Column from Aug. 9, 1943, in Nichols, ed., *Ernie's War*, 145–46. See also Pyle, *Brave Men*, 54.

124. EP letter to JP, Aug. 2, 1943, MD.

125. "One Dull, Dead Pattern," in Nichols, ed., *Ernie's War*, 154.

126. EP letter to JP, Aug. 15, 1943, MD.

127. EP letter to JP, Aug. 15, 1943, MD.

128. Pyle, *Brave Men*, 96.

129. EP letter to LM, Aug. 20, 1943, MD.

130. EP letter to LM, Aug. 20, 1943, MD. See also EP letter to JP, Aug. 15, 1943, LL.

131. EP letter to parents and Mary Bales, Mar. 14, 1940, LL.

132. Roy Simmonds, *John Steinbeck: The War Years, 1939–1945* (Lewisburg, PA: Bucknell University Press, 1996), 187.

133. "Fed Up and Bogged Down," Sept. 11, 1943, in Nichols, ed., *Ernie's War*, 166–67.

134. "Fed Up and Bogged Down," in Nichols, ed., *Ernie's War*, 166–67.

135. EP letter to LM, Sept. 30, 1943, MD.

136. EP letter to LM, Oct. 10, 1943, MD.

137. EP letter to LM, Oct. 15, 1943, MD. See also EP letter to LM, Oct. 16, 1943.

138. EP letter to LM, Oct. 24, 1943.

139. EP letter to LM, Oct. 15, 1943, MD.

140. EP letter to PC, Oct. 21, 1943, MD.

141. EP letter to LM, Oct. 10, 1943, MD.

142. EP letter to LM, Oct. 20, 1943, MD.

143. EP letter to LM, Oct. 20, 1943, MD. "As for Cowan's writer (Lester always referred to him as 'my writer' and I never realized he had a name till he got here—it is Arthur Miller, and truthfully I'm very much impressed with him. He is a young New York playwright, and his ideas about a movie are just like yours and mine, if not more so."

144. Arthur Miller, *Situation Normal* (New York: Reynal & Hitchcock, 1944), 163.

145. Miller, *Situation Normal*, 164.

146. Miller, *Situation Normal*, 170.

147. Miller, *Situation Normal*, 167.

148. Miller, *Situation Normal*, 165.

149. Miller, *Situation Normal*, 164.

150. See EP letter to LM, Oct. 20, 1943, MD.

151. EP letter to PC, Oct. 21, 1943, LL.

152. EP letter to PC, Mar. 31, 1944, LL.

153. EP letter to PC, Mar. 31, 1944, LL. See also EP letter to PC, Mar. 24, 1944, LL, and EP letter to LM, Oct. 20, 1943, MD.

154. EP letter to LM, Oct. 20, 1943, MD. See also EP letter to PC, Mar. 31, 1944, LL.

155. EP letter to LM, Oct. 20, 1943, MD.

156. EP letter to LM, Oct. 20, 1943, MD.

157. EP letter to PC, Mar. 31, 1944.

158. EP letter to JP, Oct. 28, 1943. See also EP letter to LM, Oct. 20, 1943, MD.

159. EP letter to LM, Oct. 24, 1943, MD.

160. EP letter to JP, Nov. 1, 1943, MD.

161. EP letter to LM, Oct. 16, 1943, MD.

162. EP letter to JP, Nov. 1, 1943, MD.

163. EP letter to JP, Nov. 6, 1943, LL.

164. EP letter to JP, Nov. 1, 1943, MD.

165. EP letter to JP, Nov. 11, 1943, LL.

166. EP letter to JP, Nov. 11, 1943, LL. See also EP letter to JP, Nov. 16, 1943, MD.

167. EP letter to JP, Nov. 16, 1943, MD.

168. EP letter to JP, Nov. 16, 1943, MD. See also EP letter to LM, Nov. 28, 1943.

169. James Tobin, *Ernie Pyle's War: America's Eyewitness to World War II* (New York: The Free Press, 1997), 127.

170. Tobin hints there was a brief intensive relationship with a woman in California. In fact, Pyle cabled Moran from San Francisco on Feb. 5, 1942: "You've found your man so stop shuddering. Your old friend is still the same lifeless rake as always. Last night he so captivated your sister that the traditional bestial appetite of the shepherds was overcome and we forgot to eat. That's more than you ever did for me." The sister was apparently Moran's sister, Elizabeth (Lisbeth) Krohn. See Tobin, *Ernie Pyle's War*, 63.

171. Owen V. Johnson, "Darling Jerry, Darling Mabel, Darling Moran: Ernie Pyle and the Women Behind Him," paper prepared for presentation to the History Division, Association for Education in Journalism & Mass Communication, San Francisco (Aug. 2–5, 2006).

CHAPTER 5: A LONG WINTER OF MISERY

1. David Nichols, ed., *Ernie's War: The Best of Ernie Pyle's World War II Dispatches* (New York: Random House, 1986), 171.

2. Homer Bigart, "San Pietro a Village of the Dead; Victory Cost Americans Dearly," in *Reporting World War II: American Journalism 1938–1946* (New York: Library of America, 2001), 371–74. The article was originally published in the *New York Herald Tribune* on Dec. 20, 1943.

3. Rick Atkinson, *The Day of Battle: The War in Sicily and Italy, 1943–1944* (New York: Henry Holt, 2007), 292.

4. Bigart, "San Pietro a Village of the Dead," in *Reporting World War II*, 371–74.

5. Atkinson, *Day of Battle*, 291.

6. Ernie Pyle, No. 26 (For Release Friday, Jan. 7), Jan. 3, 1944, MCBL. The source is a manuscript of Pyle's book *Brave Men* with annotations and corrections by an unknown editor. I chose to quote from this manuscript, as opposed to the published version of *Brave Men*, because this particular manuscript is comprised of copies of the dispatches Ernie wrote as they were first received from abroad, before they were synthesized and woven together to form the published manuscript.

7. James Tobin interview with Riley Tidwell, May 25, 1994, LL. Tidwell told Tobin that Pyle hiked the mountain with PFC Lester Scarborough, but in his "Human Supply Trains" article, Pyle says that Scarborough "had left the area when I was there and I never did get to see him. He was somewhere in West Virginia."

8. "Human Supply Trains," Jan. 7, 1944, in Nichols, ed., *Ernie's War*, 192–93.

9. Atkinson, *Day of Battle*, 279.

10. Atkinson, *Day of Battle*, 292.

11. Matthew Evangelista, "Manipulation and Memory in John Huston's *The Battle of San Pietro*," *Film & History: An Interdisciplinary Journal* 46, no. 1 (Summer 2016): 4–20.

12. Lance Bertelsen, "San Pietro and the 'Art' of War," *Southwest Review* 74, no. 2 (Spring 1989): 233.

13. Atkinson, *Day of Battle*, 255.

14. David Hapgood and David Richardson, *Monte Cassino* (New York: Congdon & Weed, 1984), 43.

15. "The Way Is Cruel," Dec. 14, 1943, in Nichols, ed., *Ernie's War*, 172.

16. Atkinson, *Day of Battle*, 281–82.

17. Before the Germans arrived in San Pietro to construct their rocklike defenses, the fourteen hundred Italians who lived in pale pink and yellow houses and who had called that part of the valley home for generations had lived simple lives. Most years they subsisted by tending to their olive groves, planting wheat and corn, and harvesting grapes from ancient vines. But because the year before the Allies arrived in Italy had been a miserable one for olives and grapes, the San Pietrans' orchards and fields were mostly fallow—perfect for the defensive forces dug into the mountains around the village. See John Huston's World War II documentary *The Battle of San Pietro*, www.youtube.com/watch?v=3OLJZvgIx5w.

18. U.S. Army Center for Military History, "The Battles for San Pietro," https://history.army .mil/books/wwii/winterline/winter-II.htm.

19. Atkinson, *Day of Battle*, 292.

20. Huston, *The Battle of San Pietro*.

21. "The Way Is Cruel," in Nichols, ed., *Ernie's War*, 173.

22. Riley Tidwell called it a goat shed in his interview with James Tobin. Pyle called it a cowshed in his article about the death of Captain Waskow.

23. Atkinson, *Day of Battle*, 289.

24. James Tobin interview with Riley Tidwell, May 25, 1994, LL.

25. Michael S. Sweeney, "Appointment at Hill 1205: Ernie Pyle and Captain Henry T. Waskow," Texas Military Forces Museum, www.texasmilitaryforcesmuseum.org/36division/archives /waskow/sect9.htm.

26. James Tobin interview with W. B. "Buck" Slaughter, June 15, 1994, LL.

27. Sweeney, "Appointment at Hill 1205."

28. Sweeney, "Appointment at Hill 1205."

29. Sweeney, "Appointment at Hill 1205."

30. Sweeney, "Appointment at Hill 1205."

31. "Monte Sambucaro," Peakery, https://peakery.com/monte-sambucaro-italy.

32. Atkinson, *Day of Battle*, 279.

33. Bertelsen, "San Pietro and the 'Art' of War," 243.

34. Atkinson, *Day of Battle*, 288–89.

35. Bigart, "San Pietro a Village of the Dead," in *Reporting World War II*, 378.

36. U.S. Army Center for Military History, "The Battles for San Pietro."

37. James Tobin interview with Riley Tidwell, May 25, 1994, LL. See also Atkinson, *Day of Battle*, 288–89.

38. James Tobin interview with Riley Tidwell, May 25, 1994, LL.

39. U.S. Army Center for Military History, "The Battles for San Pietro."

40. James Tobin interview with Riley Tidwell, May 25, 1994, LL. "You couldn't see too much of him 'cause we had so many clothes on at that time," Tidwell said, "but you could see a huge hole in the overcoat, and whatever clothing he had on, and it went right into his chest. . . . He was layin' on his back, it had knocked him straight back."

41. James Tobin interview with Riley Tidwell, May 25, 1994, LL.

42. Bigart, "San Pietro a Village of the Dead," in *Reporting World War II*, 378.

43. James Tobin interview with Riley Tidwell, May 25, 1994, LL, LMC 2625, Indiana University.

44. James Tobin interview with Riley Tidwell, May 25, 1994, LL, LMC 2625, Indiana University.

45. "The Death of Captain Waskow," Jan. 10, 1944, in Nichols, ed., *Ernie's War*, 196–97.

46. James Tobin interview with Riley Tidwell, May 25, 1994, LL, LMC 2625, Indiana University.

47. James Tobin interview with Zeb Sunday, June 16, 1994, LL, LMC 2625, Indiana University.

48. "The Death of Captain Waskow," in Nichols, ed., *Ernie's War*, 196–97.

49. Lee G. Miller, *The Story of Ernie Pyle* (New York: Viking Press, 1950), 62.

50. Atkinson, *Day of Battle*, 373–74.

51. Miller, *Story of Ernie Pyle*, 296.

52. Miller, *Story of Ernie Pyle*, 297.

53. Miller, *Story of Ernie Pyle*, 297.

54. Miller, *Story of Ernie Pyle*, 297.

55. LM letter to EP, Letter No. 10, ISMA.

56. Bertelsen, "San Pietro and the 'Art' of War," 249.

57. LM letter to EP, Letter No. 10, ISMA.

58. Miller, *Story of Ernie Pyle*, 305.

59. Tim Brady, *A Death in San Pietro: The Untold Story of Ernie Pyle, John Huston, and the Fight for Purple Heart Valley* (New York: Hachette Books, 2013), 223.

60. Sweeney, "Appointment at Hill 1205."

CHAPTER 6: THE GHASTLY BROTHERHOOD OF WAR

1. "Buck Eversole: One of the Great Men of the War," Feb. 21, 1944, in David Nichols, ed., *Ernie's War: The Best of Ernie Pyle's World War II Dispatches* (New York: Random House, 1986), 212.

2. Lee G. Miller, *The Story of Ernie Pyle* (New York: Viking Press, 1950), 300–301.

3. EP letter to JP, Jan. 1, 1944, LL.

4. EP letter to JP, Jan. 12, 1944, LL.

5. Miller, *Story of Ernie Pyle*, 300–301.

6. Miller, *Story of Ernie Pyle*, 303.

7. Miller, *Story of Ernie Pyle*, 311.

8. EP letter to PC, Jan. 6, 1944, LL.

9. EP letter to JP, Jan. 1, 1944, LL.

10. EP letter to JP, Jan. 12, 1944, LL.

11. David Nichols, ed., *Ernie's War: The Best of Ernie Pyle's World War II Dispatches* (New York: Random House, 1986), 199.

12. "With the Air Force," Jan. 18, 1944, in Nichols, ed., *Ernie's War*, 200.

13. "With the Air Force," in Nichols, ed., *Ernie's War*, 201.

14. "With the Air Force," in Nichols, ed., *Ernie's War*, 201.

15. "Army Battle Casualties and Nonbattle Deaths in World War II, Final Report 7 December 1941–31 December 1946," Statistical and Accounting Branch Office of the Adjutant General, www.ibiblio.org/hyperwar/USA/ref/Casualties/index.html.

16. David Hapgood and David Richardson, *Monte Cassino* (New York: Congdon & Weed, 1984), 4.

17. Hapgood and Richardson, *Monte Cassino*, 4.

18. Hapgood and Richardson, *Monte Cassino*, 4.

19. Hapgood and Richardson, *Monte Cassino*, 78, 238.

20. Hapgood and Richardson, *Monte Cassino*, 9.

21. The monks' names were Eusebio Grossetti and Matronola. All but a few pages of the diary survived the war, and after the war, Matronola reconstructed the missing entries from memory. The "I" in any of the diary entries refers to Matronola. See Hapgood and Richardson, *Monte Cassino*, 58.

22. Hapgood and Richardson, *Monte Cassino*, 98.

23. Hapgood and Richardson, *Monte Cassino*, 90.

24. Hapgood and Richardson, *Monte Cassino*, 77, 238.

25. Hapgood and Richardson, *Monte Cassino*, 99.

26. Rick Atkinson, *The Day of Battle: The War in Sicily and Italy, 1943–1944* (New York: Henry Holt, 2007), 400.

27. Hapgood and Richardson, *Monte Cassino*, 37.

28. John Sheehy letter to LM, Sept. 17, 1945, ISMA.

29. Miller, *Story of Ernie Pyle*, 305. In addition, the associate editor at *Collier's Weekly*, Quentin Reynolds, said this of Pyle: "Three great discoveries of this war are the jeep, the Red Cross girl, and Ernie Pyle." Fred Painton reported to the *Saturday Evening Post* that Ernie Pyle "was probably the most prayed-for man with the American troops." *Life* wrote that Ernie "now occupied a place in American journalistic letters which no other correspondent in this war has achieved." See also EP letter to Shirley Mount, Nov. 13, 1943, LL: "Holt's are starting a second printing of 50,000 on the book next week, which will make a total of 200,000. Keerist!"

30. "Back to the 34th Division," Feb. 14, 1944, in Nichols, ed., *Ernie's War*, 207. See also Atkinson, *Day of Battle*, 406.

31. "Buck Eversole: One of the Great Men of the War," in Nichols, ed., *Ernie's War*, 212.

32. "Buck Eversole," in Nichols, ed., *Ernie's War*, 213–14.

33. Miller, *Story of Ernie Pyle*, 307.

34. Atkinson, *Day of Battle*, 328–29.

35. "Buck Eversole," in Nichols, ed., *Ernie's War*, 213.

36. Atkinson, *Day of Battle*, 406.

37. "Buck Eversole," in Nichols, ed., *Ernie's War*, 213–14. Sergeant Eversole was eventually mustered out after developing arthritis from having his feet frozen, according to Lee Miller. After the war, he and Eversole wrote letters to each other, and Eversole told Miller that he was "living on a small farm that he rented for ten dollars a month." See Miller, *Story of Ernie Pyle*, 310. Eversole eventually became a police officer in Walters, Oklahoma. On Feb. 4, 1967, he died suddenly from a heart attack at the age of fifty-one. He was survived by a wife, a daughter, and three grandchildren.

38. Atkinson, *Day of Battle*, 406.

39. Atkinson, *Day of Battle*, 405.

40. Atkinson, *Day of Battle*, 406.

41. Ernie Pyle, *Brave Men* (Lincoln: University of Nebraska Press, 2001 [1944]), 197.

42. Pyle, *Brave Men*, 285–86.

43. EP letter to LM, July 1, 1944, MD.

44. Column from Feb. 22, 1944, in Nichols, ed., *Ernie's War*, 216.

45. John Sheehy letter to LM, Sept. 17, 1945, ISMA.

46. James Tobin interview with Vince "Pete" Connors of Company E, Sept. 5, 1994, LL, LMC 2625, Indiana University.

47. John Sheehy letter to LM, Sept. 17, 1945, ISMA.

48. "A Lull in the Lines," Feb. 16, 1944, in Nichols, ed., *Ernie's War*, 209.

49. EP letter to JP, Jan. 27, 1944, ISMA.

50. Atkinson, *Day of Battle*, 328–29.

51. James Tobin interview with Vince "Pete" Connors of Company E, Sept. 5, 1994, LL, LMC 2625, Indiana University.

52. Atkinson, *Day of Battle*, 404.

53. Hapgood and Richardson, *Monte Cassino*, 156.

54. John Sheehy letter to LM, Sept. 17, 1945, ISMA.

55. Hapgood and Richardson, *Monte Cassino*, 156.

56. Atkinson, *Day of Battle*, 405.

57. James Tobin interview with Ed Bland, June 15, 1994, LL, LMC 2625, Indiana University. Bland was a squadron commander stationed at the Pomigliano Airbase near Naples—the home of the Twelfth Air Force. He and Ernie spent time together after Ernie came off the front lines near Cassino.

58. Hapgood and Richardson, *Monte Cassino*, 166–67.

59. Hapgood and Richardson, *Monte Cassino*, 168.

60. Hapgood and Richardson, *Monte Cassino*, 169.

61. Atkinson, *Day of Battle*, 433–34.
62. Hapgood and Richardson, *Monte Cassino*, 185.
63. Hapgood and Richardson, *Monte Cassino*, 186.
64. Atkinson, *Day of Battle*, 434.
65. Hapgood and Richardson, *Monte Cassino*, 191.
66. Hapgood and Richardson, *Monte Cassino*, 192.
67. Hapgood and Richardson, *Monte Cassino*, 198–99.
68. Hapgood and Richardson, *Monte Cassino*, 206.
69. Hapgood and Richardson, *Monte Cassino*, 200–201.
70. Hapgood and Richardson, *Monte Cassino*, 201.
71. Hapgood and Richardson, *Monte Cassino*, 199.
72. Hapgood and Richardson, *Monte Cassino*, 201.
73. Hapgood and Richardson, *Monte Cassino*, 202.
74. Atkinson, *Day of Battle*, 437.
75. Atkinson, *Day of Battle*, 438.
76. Hapgood and Richardson, *Monte Cassino*, 207.
77. Hapgood and Richardson, *Monte Cassino*, 208, 211.
78. Atkinson, *Day of Battle*, 438.
79. Atkinson, *Day of Battle*, 440.
80. Hapgood and Richardson, *Monte Cassino*, 211.
81. Atkinson, *Day of Battle*, 438.
82. Atkinson, *Day of Battle*, 438.
83. Hapgood and Richardson, *Monte Cassino*, 230.
84. Atkinson, *Day of Battle*, 439.
85. Hapgood and Richardson, *Monte Cassino*, 230.
86. Hapgood and Richardson, *Monte Cassino*, 75, 243.
87. Atkinson, *Day of Battle*, 439.
88. Hapgood and Richardson, *Monte Cassino*, 241.
89. Ray Moseley, *Reporting War: How Foreign Correspondents Risked Capture, Torture and Death to Cover World War II* (New Haven: Yale University Press, 2017), 226.
90. Moseley, *Reporting War*, 226.
91. Hapgood and Richardson, *Monte Cassino*, 230.
92. John Sheehy letter to LM, Sept. 17, 1945, ISMA.
93. Miller, *Story of Ernie Pyle*, 309–10.
94. Helen Scherer to James Tobin, date unknown, LL, LMC 2625, Indiana University.
95. Miller, *Story of Ernie Pyle*, 303.
96. Miller, *Story of Ernie Pyle*, 309–10.
97. EP letter to JP, Feb. 11, 1944, LL.
98. Miller, *Story of Ernie Pyle*, 303–4.
99. EP letter to JP, Feb. 11, 1944, LL. Ernie writes that his hemoglobin level was "only 50."
100. EP letter to JP, Feb. 11, 1944, LL.
101. EP letter to PC, Feb. 16, 1944, LL.
102. EP letter to JP, Feb. 11, 1944, LL.

CHAPTER 7: THE BITCHHEAD AT ANZIO

1. Ernie Pyle, "No Area Is Immune," Mar. 28, 1944, https://erniepyle.iu.edu/wartime-columns/area-immune.html.
2. Column from Apr. 25, 1944, in David Nichols, ed., *Ernie's War: The Best of Ernie Pyle's World War II Dispatches* (New York: Random House, 1986), 266.
3. Rick Atkinson, *The Day of Battle: The War in Sicily and Italy, 1943–1944* (New York: Henry Holt, 2007), 485.

4. "A Flat, Lethal Beachhead," Mar. 30, 1944, in Nichols, ed., *Ernie's War*, 244.

5. Atkinson, *Day of Battle*, 366.

6. Atkinson, *Day of Battle*, 412–13.

7. "A Flat, Lethal Beachhead," in Nichols, ed., *Ernie's War*, 245.

8. EP letter to JP, Mar. 15, 1944, LL.

9. EP letter to PC, Feb. 16, 1944, LL.

10. EP letter to JP, Mar. 15, 1944, LL.

11. Atkinson, *Day of Battle*, 351.

12. Alex Kershaw, *The Liberator: One World War II Soldier's 500-Day Odyssey from the Beaches of Sicily to the Gates of Dachau* (New York: Crown Publishers, 2012), 80. See also Clayton D. Laurie, "Anzio: The U.S. Army Campaign of World War II," United States Army Center of Military History, 1994, 9, https://history.army.mil/brochures/anzio/72-19.htm.

13. John B. Romeiser, ed., *Beachhead Don: Reporting the War from the European Theater, 1943–1945* (New York: Fordham University Press, 2004), 96–97.

14. Harvey Broadbent, *Gallipoli: The Fatal Shore* (Camberwell, Australia: Viking/Penguin, 2005), 27–28.

15. Atkinson, *Day of Battle*, 321.

16. Lloyd Clark, *Anzio: The Friction of War: Italy and the Battle for Rome 1944* (London: Headline Publishing Group, 2006), 69.

17. Clark, *Anzio*, 70–71, 76. See also John Keegan, *The Second World War* (New York: Penguin Books, 2005), 357, and Flint Whitlock, *Desperate Valour: Triumph at Anzio* (New York: Da Capo Press, 2018), 19.

18. Romeiser, ed., *Beachhead Don*, 98–99.

19. Romeiser, ed., *Beachhead Don*, 97.

20. "With the Fifth Army South of Rome, January 25," in Romeiser, ed., *Beachhead Don*, 103.

21. Atkinson, *Day of Battle*, 415.

22. Whitlock, *Desperate Valour*, 312.

23. Keegan, *Second World War*, 357.

24. Whitlock, *Desperate Valour*, 63. See also John Colville, *The Fringes of Power: Downing Street Diaries 1939–1945* (London: Weidenfeld & Nicolson, 2004), 456.

25. Lee G. Miller, *The Story of Ernie Pyle* (New York: Viking Press, 1950), 304.

26. EP letter to JP, Jan. 27, 1944, LL.

27. Lyle C. Wilson, "Raymond Clapper Killed in Plane Crash in Marshall Isle Invasion," *Santa Cruz Sentinel*, Feb. 3, 1944, www.newspapers.com/clip/4489269/santa-cruz-sentinel.

28. Miller, *Story of Ernie Pyle*, 98.

29. Miller, *Story of Ernie Pyle*, 311.

30. Miller, *Story of Ernie Pyle*, 311. To Jerry, Ernie wrote that "Ray Clapper's death sort of knocked the props out from under me too. It had just never occurred to me that anything would ever happen to him." See EP letter to JP, Feb. 11, 1944, LL.

31. EP letter to LM, Feb. 4, 1944, Ernie Pyle State Historic Site, https://sites.mediaschool.indiana.edu/erniepyle/1944/02/04/ive-had-it.

32. Whitlock, *Desperate Valour*, 32.

33. Clark, *Anzio*, 101.

34. Whitlock, *Desperate Valour*, 36.

35. Clark, *Anzio*, 123.

36. Atkinson, *Day of Battle*, 370.

37. Whitlock, *Desperate Valour*, 162.

38. Atkinson, *Day of Battle*, 485.

39. Atkinson, *Day of Battle*, 415.

40. Atkinson, *Day of Battle*, 370, 365.

41. EP letter to JP, Mar. 15, 1944, LL.

42. Whitlock, *Desperate Valour*, 171.

43. Phillip Knightley, *The First Casualty: From the Crimea to Vietnam: The War Correspondent as Hero, Propagandist, and Myth Maker* (New York: Harcourt Brace Jovanovich, 1975), 330.

44. Knightley, *The First Casualty*, 330.

45. Whitlock, *Desperate Valour*, 241. See also Karl-Heinz Frieser, *The Blitzkrieg Legend: The 1940 Campaign in the West* (Annapolis, MD: Naval Institute Press, 2005), 291–92.

46. Knightley, *The First Casualty*, 330.

47. Timothy M. Gay, *Assignment to Hell: The War Against Nazi Germany with Correspondents Walter Cronkite, Andy Rooney, A. J. Liebling, Homer Bigart, and Hal Boyle* (New York: The Penguin Group, 2013), 218.

48. Atkinson, *Day of Battle*, 486–87.

49. "'I Thought It Was the End,'" Mar. 20, 1944, in Nichols, ed., *Ernie's War*, 239.

50. "'I Thought It Was the End,'" in Nichols, ed., *Ernie's War*, 238.

51. EP letter to JP, Mar. 15, 1944, LL. See also "'I Thought It Was the End,'" in Nichols, ed., *Ernie's War*, 238.

52. "'I Thought It Was the End,'" in Nichols, ed., *Ernie's War*, 239.

53. Column from Mar. 21, 1944, in Nichols, ed., *Ernie's War*, 240. See also Atkinson, *Day of Battle*, 486–87.

54. EP letter to his father and aunt Mary, Mar. 30, 1944, https://erniepyle.iu.edu/wartime-columns/had-it.html. See also "'I Thought It Was the End,'" in Nichols, ed., *Ernie's War*, 239.

55. EP letter to JP, Mar. 30, 1944, LL.

56. Column from Mar. 21, 1944, in Nichols, ed., *Ernie's War*, 240.

57. Pyle, "No Area Is Immune."

58. EP letter to JP, Mar. 30, 1944, LL.

59. Pyle, "No Area Is Immune."

60. EP letter to JP, March 15, 1944, LL.

61. EP letter to JP, March 30, 1944, LL.

62. EP letter to his father and aunt Mary, Mar. 30, 1944, https://erniepyle.iu.edu/wartime-columns/had-it.html. See also "'I Thought It Was the End,'" in Nichols, ed., *Ernie's War*, 240.

63. EP letter to PC, Apr. 30, 1944, LL.

64. Column from Mar. 21, 1944, in Nichols, ed., *Ernie's War*, 240.

65. Column from Mar. 21, 1944, in Nichols, ed., *Ernie's War*, 241.

66. "Supplying the Beachhead," Apr. 18, 1944, in Nichols, ed., *Ernie's War*, 258.

67. "'They Don't Have That Stare,'" Apr. 5, 1944, in Nichols, ed., *Ernie's War*, 249. When used selectively, this poetic device—known as anaphora—gives an artistic effect to prose and creates a rhythm that sticks with a reader.

68. "'They Don't Have That Stare,'" in Nichols, ed., *Ernie's War*, 249.

69. "Hospital Ship," Apr. 28, 1944, in Nichols, ed., *Ernie's War*, 268.

70. "Anzio-Nettuno Described," Mar. 29, 1944, in Nichols, ed., *Ernie's War*, 242. See also Atkinson, *Day of Battle*, 366, 359.

71. "'They Don't Have That Stare,'" in Nichols, ed., *Ernie's War*, 250.

72. C. V. Wedgwood, *William the Silent: William of Nassau, Prince of Orange, 1533–1584* (New Haven: Yale University Press, 1944), as quoted in J. Atlas, "Pinpointing a Moment on the Map of History," *New York Times*, Mar. 19, 1955.

73. EP letter to PC, Mar. 24, 1944, LL.

74. EP letter to JP, Mar. 15, 1944, LL.

75. EP letter to PC, Mar. 24, 1944, LL. "There wasn't much to drink on the beachhead—that might have had something to do with my returning health."

76. EP letter to PC, Mar. 24, 1944, LL. In a letter to Jerry, Ernie gave a more accurate report on his health. "The last blood count showed my hemoglobin up to 90, and my red count at 4,810,000, which is pretty good. And actually I feel much better." See EP letter to JP, Mar. 30, 1944, LL.

77. EP letter to PC, Mar. 24, 1944, LL.
78. EP letter to JP, Mar. 30, 1944, LL.
79. EP letter to PC, Mar. 24, 1944, LL.
80. EP letter to JP, Feb. 11, 1944, LL.
81. Miller, *Story of Ernie Pyle*, 105. Poe previously worked as a nurse.
82. EP letter to PC, Feb. 16, 1944, LL. See also EP letter to PC, Mar. 24, 1944, LL.
83. EP letter to PC, Feb. 16, 1944, LL.
84. EP letter to PC, March 24, 1944, LL.
85. www.drugs.com/cons/bromo-seltzer.html.
86. EP letter to PC, Mar. 24, 1944, LL.
87. EP letter to JP, Mar. 30, 1944, LL. See also Miller, *Story of Ernie Pyle*, 317.
88. EP letter to PC, Mar. 24, 1944, LL.
89. Atkinson, *Day of Battle*, 486–87.
90. Ray Moseley, *Reporting War: How Foreign Correspondents Risked Capture, Torture and Death to Cover World War II* (New Haven: Yale University Press, 2017), 226–27.
91. EP letter to JP, Mar. 30, 1944, LL.
92. Column from Jan. 8, 1944, in Nichols, ed., *Ernie's War*, 194–95.
93. William D. Hassett, *Off the Record with F.D.R.* (New Brunswick, NJ: Rutgers University Press, 1958), 192.
94. Atkinson, *Day of Battle*, 582.
95. W. G. F. Jackson, *The Battle for Italy* (New York: Harper & Row, 1967), 291.
96. Winston S. Churchill, *Triumph and Tragedy* (New York: RosettaBooks, 2014), 531.
97. B. H. Liddell Hart, *The Other Side of the Hill* (London: Cassell, 1951), 373.
98. John Ellis, *Brute Force: Allied Strategy and Tactics in the Second World War* (New York: Viking, 1990), xx.
99. Douglas Porch, *The Path to Victory* (New York: Farrar, Straus and Giroux, 2004), xi.
100. Robert W. Love, *History of the U.S. Navy: 1942–1991*, vol. 2 (Harrisburg, PA: Stackpole Books, 1992), 87.
101. David M. Kennedy, *Freedom from Fear* (New York: Oxford University Press, 1999), 596.
102. Column from May 4, 1944, in Nichols, ed., *Ernie's War*, 271.
103. Column from May 4, 1944, in Nichols, ed., *Ernie's War*, 271.
104. Atkinson, *Day of Battle*, 581.
105. Column from May 4, 1944, in Nichols, ed., *Ernie's War*, 271.
106. EP letter to JP, Apr. 14, 1944.
107. John Sheehy letter to LM, Sept. 17, 1945, MD.
108. EP letter to William Pyle and Mary Bales, Apr. 14, 1944, MD.
109. EP letter to LM, Feb. 9, 1944, MD.
110. EP letter to William Pyle and Mary Bales, Apr. 14, 1944, MD. See also EP letter to JP, Apr. 14, 1944, LL.
111. EP letter to William Pyle and Mary Bales, Apr. 14, 1944, MD.
112. Column from May 5, 1944, in Nichols, ed., *Ernie's War*, 272.
113. Column from May 5, 1944, in Nichols, ed., *Ernie's War*, 271–72.
114. Column from May 5, 1944, in Nichols, ed., *Ernie's War*, 272.
115. EP letter to JP, Mar. 30, 1944, LL. See also Miller, *Story of Ernie Pyle*, 317.
116. EP letter to William Pyle and Mary Bales, Apr. 14, 1944, MD.

CHAPTER 8: WALKING THE LONG THIN LINE OF PERSONAL ANGUISH

1. "A Pure Miracle," June 12, 1944, in David Nichols, ed., *Ernie's War: The Best of Ernie Pyle's World War II Dispatches* (New York: Random House, 1986), 277–80.
2. They vomited bacon and eggs, pancakes and sausage, or pork chops and ice cream, according to Rick Atkinson, *The Guns at Last Light* (New York: Henry Holt, 2013), 37, 53. According

to Antony Beevor, "the cooks gave them 'as much steak, pork, chicken, ice cream, and candy' as they could eat. Other ships provided 'wieners, beans, coffee and doughnuts.'" See Antony Beevor, *D-Day: The Battle for Normandy* (New York: Penguin Books, 2019), 80.

3. Atkinson, *Guns at Last Light*, 57.

4. Stephen E. Ambrose, *D-Day: June 6, 1944: The Climactic Battle of World War II* (New York: Simon & Schuster, 2013), Kindle location 1697.

5. Alex Kershaw, *Blood and Champagne: The Life and Times of Robert Capa* (New York: Da Capo Press, 2002), 124.

6. Atkinson, *Guns at Last Light*, 65 (Kindle location, 1414–1418–1422).

7. Alex Kershaw, *The First Wave: The D-Day Warriors Who Led the Way to Victory in World War II* (New York: Dutton Caliber, 2019), 140. See also Ambrose, *D-Day*, Kindle location 5437.

8. Ambrose, *D-Day*, Kindle location 5437.

9. Ambrose, *D-Day*, Kindle location 5516.

10. Ambrose, *D-Day*, Kindle location 7137.

11. Atkinson, *Guns at Last Light*, 75 (Kindle location 1610–1611).

12. Ambrose, *D-Day*, Kindle location 7201.

13. Ambrose, *D-Day*, Kindle location 7697.

14. Ambrose, *D-Day*, Kindle location 7888.

15. Kershaw, *The First Wave*, 224.

16. Ambrose, *D-Day*, Kindle location 7156.

17. EP letter to JP, Apr. 14, 1944, LL.

18. EP letter to LM, Apr. 13, 1944, MD.

19. EP letter to LM, Nov. 7, 1944, MD.

20. EP letter to LM, Apr. 13, 1944, MD.

21. EP letter to JP, Apr. 14, 1944, LL.

22. EP letter to LM, Apr. 13, 1944, MD.

23. EP letter to LM, Apr. 13, 1944, MD.

24. EP letter to JP, Apr. 14, 1944, LL.

25. EP letter to LM, Apr. 28, 1944, MD.

26. EP letter to JP, Apr. 27, 1944, LL.

27. EP letter to JP, Apr. 14, 1944, LL.

28. EP letter to LM, Apr. 28, 1944, MD.

29. EP letter to JP, Apr. 27, 1944, LL.

30. John Mason Brown, "Brave Men" (essay date 1946), in Jennifer Gariepy, ed., *Twentieth-Century Literary Criticism* 75 (Farmington Hills, MI: Gale Cengage, 1998).

31. Ernie Pyle, *Brave Men* (Lincoln: University of Nebraska Press, 2001 [1944]), 339.

32. Pyle, *Brave Men*, 350.

33. Atkinson, *Guns at Last Light*, 1.

34. Pyle, *Brave Men*, 339.

35. Forrest C. Pogue, *Pogue's War: Diaries of a WWII Combat Historian* (Lexington: University of Kentucky Press, 2006), Kindle location 384.

36. Atkinson, *Guns at Last Light*, 2.

37. EP letter to JP, May 7, 1944, LL.

38. EP letter to JP, May 7, 1944, LL.

39. EP letter to LM, May 2, 1944, MD.

40. Pyle, *Brave Men*, 339.

41. Pyle, *Brave Men*, 340.

42. Pyle, *Brave Men*, 343.

43. Pyle, *Brave Men*, 349.

44. Mary Louise Roberts, *D-Day Through French Eyes: Normandy 1944* (Chicago: University of Chicago Press, 2014), 69. See also Ambrose, *D-Day*, Kindle location 1425.

45. Atkinson, *Guns at Last Light*, 5 (Kindle location 224–226).

46. Ambrose, *D-Day*, Kindle location 1491, 1496.

47. Ambrose, *D-Day*, Kindle location 1505, 1513.

48. According to Stephen E. Ambrose, "Churchill wanted the French consulted. Eisenhower's chief of staff, Gen. Walter B. Smith, then talked to Gen. Pierre-Joseph Koenig, the representative of Gen. Charles de Gaulle's Algiers-based French Committee of National Liberation. 'To my surprise,' Smith reported, 'Koenig takes a much more cold-blooded view than we do. His remark was, "This is war, and it must be expected that people will be killed. We would take the anticipated loss to be rid of the Germans."'" See Ambrose, *D-Day*, Kindle location 1476.

49. Roberts, *D-Day Through French Eyes*, 75.

50. Atkinson, *Guns at Last Light*, 85 (Kindle location 1827–1829). According to Mary Louise Roberts, "Most [French civilian] deaths occurred as a result of bombing. The Allies dropped 550,000 tons of bombs onto France in the years 1942–1944." See Roberts, *D-Day Through French Eyes*, 69.

51. Roberts, *D-Day Through French Eyes*, 5. See also Atkinson, *Guns at Last Light*, 55 (Kindle location 1209–1211).

52. Ambrose, *D-Day*, Kindle location 490.

53. Beevor, *D-Day*, 31.

54. Alex Kershaw, *The Bedford Boys: One American Town's Ultimate D-Day Sacrifice* (New York: MJF Books, 2003), 103–4. See also Atkinson, *Guns at Last Light*, 82.

55. Pyle, *Brave Men*, 341.

56. Pyle, *Brave Men*, 340.

57. Pyle, *Brave Men*, 350.

58. "I suspected it might be merely the nervous tension causing them, like that time I went to the clinic in Memphis." See EP letter to JP, May 7, 1944, LL.

59. EP letter to JP, May 7, 1944, LL.

60. EP letter to JP, July 1, 1944, LL.

61. LM letter to EP, May 1, 1944, LL.

62. EP letter to JP, July 1, 1944, LL.

63. James Holland, *Normandy '44: D-Day and the Epic 77-Day Battle for France—A New History* (New York: Atlantic Monthly Press, 2019), 91–92.

64. Ernie Pyle, pooled column, June 10, 1944, MCBL.

65. Holland, *Normandy '44*, 92.

66. EP letter to LM, May 21, 1944, MD.

67. Kershaw, *Blood and Champagne*, 118.

68. Pogue, *Pogue's War*, Kindle location 639.

69. Atkinson, *Guns at Last Light*, 15 (Kindle location 422–24).

70. EP letter to PC, Apr. 30, 1944, LL.

71. Liz Shaffer to LM, Apr. 9, 1944, MD.

72. EP letter to PC, Apr. 30, 1944, LL.

73. Liz Shaffer to LM, Apr. 9, 1944, MD.

74. Liz Shaffer to LM, Apr. 9, 1944, MD.

75. LM letter to EP, Apr. 12, 1944, MD. See also LM letter to EP, May 5, 1944.

76. EP letter to JP, Apr. 27, 1944, LL.

77. EP letter to LM, Apr. 28, 1944, MD.

78. EP letter to JP, Apr. 27, 1944, LL.

79. EP letter to PC, May 26, 1944, LL.

80. EP letter to JP, May 16, 1944, MD.

81. Sister Margaret Jane to LM, May 19, 1944, MD.

82. EP letter to PC, May 26, 1944, LL.

83. Sister Margaret Jane to LM, May 19, 1944, MD.

84. EP letter to PC, Apr. 30, 1944, LL.

85. EP letter to JP, Apr. 27, 1944, LL.

86. EP letter to JP, Apr. 27, 1944, LL.

87. EP letter to PC, Apr. 30, 1944, LL.

88. EP letter to LM, May 2, 1944, MD. A couple of weeks later, Lee wrote to Ernie: "I figure you will get another [Pulitzer] next year, maybe. The St. Louis Star-Times took a poll among Washington correspondents to see whether they agreed with the Pulitzer awards, and there was considerable dissent indeed, except that those polled were unanimous for Pyle." See LM letter to EP, May 14, 1944.

89. EP letter to JP, May 16, 1944, MD.

90. EP letter to LM, May 14, 1944, MD.

91. EP letter to PC, Apr. 30, 1944, LL.

92. Ernie agreed with Lee Miller that putting out another book in the fall of 1944 would be possible, assuming the European war was over by then. "But that seems doubtful to me," Ernie wrote to Lee, "and I'm inclined to feel it would be 'pressing' the market to put out another that soon if the war weren't over." See EP letter to LM, May 2, 1944, MD. Three days later, Lee wrote: "Holt's continue to feel strongly in favor of a fall book, and I think it should be done.... Unless you have violent ideas to the contrary, I will not discourage them. Of course they figure on a third book eventually." See also LM letter to EP, May 5, 1944.

93. LM letter to EP, May 14, 1944, MD.

94. EP letter to PC, May 26, 1944, LL.

95. EP letter to PC, May 26, 1944, LL.

96. Probably Monday, May 22, 1944, because the troops moved out on Tuesday, May 23, according to Atkinson, *Guns at Last Light*, 25.

97. Atkinson, *Guns at Last Light*, 2.

98. Jack Stenbuck, ed., *Typewriter Battalion: Dramatic Front-Line Dispatches from World War II* (New York: William Morrow, 1995), 179. This wasn't the first time Ernie had expressed such fears since arriving in pre-invasion London. In a June 15, 1944, letter to Jerry, Ernie wrote that he had "worried terribly about myself before we started over, but that was all gone the moment we actually started," ISMA. On June 29, 1944, Ernie wrote to Lee Miller, "Before the invasion I was depressed almost to the unbearable stage by feeling I wouldn't live through the invasion," MD.

99. Ernie Pyle, pooled column, June 10, 1944, MCBL.

100. Pyle, *Brave Men*, 375–76.

101. Ernie Pyle, pooled column, June 10, 1944, MCBL.

102. Stenbuck, ed., *Typewriter Battalion*, 179.

103. Ernie Pyle, pooled column, June 10, 1944, MCBL.

104. Kershaw, *The Bedford Boys*, 110. There were, according to Rick Atkinson, "cutters, corvettes, frigates, freighters, ferries, trawlers, tankers, subchasers; ships for channel marking, for cable-laying, for smoke-making; ships for refrigerating, towing, victualing." See Atkinson, *Guns at Last Light*, 36.

105. Atkinson, *Guns at Last Light*, 29.

106. "The Ocean Was Infested with Ships," June 15, 1944, in Nichols, ed., *Ernie's War*, 276.

107. Atkinson, *Guns at Last Light*, 30.

108. Holland, *Normandy '44*, 92.

109. EP letter to JP, July 1, 1944, LL.

110. Atkinson, *Guns at Last Light*, 37 (Kindle location: 897–899). See also Ambrose, *D-Day*, Kindle location 575.

111. Holland, *Normandy '44*, 92.

112. Pyle, *Brave Men*, 379.

113. EP letter to PC, May 26, 1944, LL; Pyle, *Brave Men*, 364; and EP letter to JP, Apr. 14, 1944, LL.

114. Atkinson, *Guns at Last Light*, 31.

115. Beevor, *D-Day*, 53.

116. Pyle, *Brave Men*, 379.

117. Pyle, *Brave Men*, 379.

118. Pyle, *Brave Men*, 380.

119. Pyle, *Brave Men*, 379.

120. Richard Collier, *Fighting Words: The War Correspondents of World War Two* (New York: St. Martin's Press, 1989), 159.

121. Pyle, *Brave Men*, 379.

122. "The Ocean Was Infested with Ships," in Nichols, ed., *Ernie's War*, 276; and "A Pure Miracle," June 12, 1944, in Nichols, ed., *Ernie's War*, 277–80.

123. Pyle, *Brave Men*, 381.

124. "The Ocean Was Infested with Ships," in Nichols, ed., *Ernie's War*, 277. See also Ambrose, *D-Day*, Kindle location 4496.

125. Ambrose, *D-Day*, Kindle location 4645.

126. Ambrose, *D-Day*, Kindle location 1899. See also Kershaw, *Blood and Champagne*, 123.

127. "The Ocean Was Infested with Ships," in Nichols, ed., *Ernie's War*, 277.

128. John McNamara, *EXTRA! U.S. War Correspondents in Action* (Boston: Houghton Mifflin Company, 1945), 192. See also Pyle, *Brave Men*, 395.

129. Pyle, *Brave Men*, 394.

130. Pyle, *Brave Men*, 387.

131. Pyle, *Brave Men*, 388.

132. Pyle, *Brave Men*, 389.

133. Pyle, *Brave Men*, 389.

134. Pyle, *Brave Men*, 389. See also Ray Moseley, *Reporting War: How Foreign Correspondents Risked Capture, Torture and Death to Cover World War II* (New Haven: Yale University Press, 2017), 231.

135. Pyle, *Brave Men*, 389.

136. Pyle, *Brave Men*, 389.

137. Pyle, *Brave Men*, 388.

138. Moseley, *Reporting War*, 231.

139. Pyle, *Brave Men*, 388.

140. Pogue, *Pogue's War*, Kindle location 1063, 1084.

141. Antony Beevor, *D-Day: The Battle for Normandy* (New York: Penguin Books, 2019), 153.

142. Alex Kershaw, *The First Wave: The D-Day Warriors Who Led the Way to Victory in World War II* (New York: Dutton Caliber, 2019), 242.

143. Atkinson, *Guns at Last Light*, 30.

144. "A Pure Miracle," June 12, 1944, in Nichols, ed., *Ernie's War*, 277–80. See also Ambrose, *D-Day*, Kindle location 6102.

145. Atkinson, *Guns at Last Light*, 65. See also Ambrose, *D-Day*, Kindle location 8123.

146. Beevor, *D-Day*, 110.

147. Atkinson, *Guns at Last Light*, 75.

148. Ambrose, *D-Day*, Kindle location 2264.

149. "The European Campaign Clarified," June 22, 1944, in Nichols, ed., *Ernie's War*, 287.

150. Beevor, *D-Day*, 111.

151. Beevor, *D-Day*, 111.

152. Beevor, *D-Day*, 153. See also Kershaw, *The First Wave*, 242.

153. "A Pure Miracle," in Nichols, ed., *Ernie's War*, 277–80.

154. Pyle, *Brave Men*, 395.

155. Pyle, *Brave Men*, 395.

156. Pyle, *Brave Men*, 395.

157. Pyle, *Brave Men*, 397.

158. Pyle, *Brave Men*, 397.

159. Pyle, *Brave Men*, 397.

160. Pyle, *Brave Men*, 397.

161. "On the Lighter Side," June 21, 1944, in Nichols, ed., *Ernie's War*, 284.

162. Pyle, *Brave Men*, 397.

163. Ambrose, *D-Day*, Kindle location 8365.

164. In a letter to Lee Miller, Ernie explained, "I can't go into any of our very well-laid plans for covering the invasion, but I can say that all preparations are finished and we are ready. Censorship will be very strict at first, so some of my first columns may arrive pretty badly butchered up. I won't be able to get stuff out right away, so don't expect to hear from me for several days after the landings." See EP letter to LM, May 21, 1944, MD.

165. Beevor, *D-Day*, 87.

166. Ambrose, *D-Day*, Kindle location 8347.

167. Ambrose, *D-Day*, Kindle location 8345, 8357. See also Marc Lancaster, "D-Day: Ernie Pyle's Struggle to Tell the Invasion Story," ww2ondeadline.com, June 10, 2020, https://ww2ondeadline.com/2020/06/10/d-day-ernie-pyle-columns-invasion-omaha-beach.

168. EP letter to LM, June 16, 1944, LL.

169. Brown, "Brave Men," in Gariepy, ed., *Twentieth-Century Literary Criticism* 75.

170. "A Pure Miracle," in Nichols, ed., *Ernie's War*, 277–80.

171. "The Horrible Waste of War," June 16, 1944, in Nichols, ed., *Ernie's War*, 280-82.

172. "A Long Thin Line of Personal Anguish," June 17, 1944, in Nichols, ed., *Ernie's War*, 282–84.

173. "A Long Thin Line of Personal Anguish," in Nichols, ed., *Ernie's War*, 282–84.

174. "A Long Thin Line of Personal Anguish," in Nichols, ed., *Ernie's War*, 282–84.

175. EP letter to LM, June 29, 1944, LL.

176. LM letter to EP, June 19, 1944, LL.

177. LM letter to EP, June 19, 1944, LL.

178. Lancaster, "D-Day: Ernie Pyle's Struggle to Tell the Invasion Story."

179. LM letter to EP, June 19, 1944, LL.

180. LM letter to EP, July 3, 1944, LL. Lee and Ernie liked the title *The Muddy Queen* best. In an Apr. 17, 1944, letter to Ernie, Lee wrote: "I have provided Holt's [*sic*] with all the columns issued since 'Here Is Your War' was closed up, and they are supposed to be having them shaped up so as to be ready to go ahead fast with a new book when, as and if it seems advisable." Toward the end of July, the presale numbers jumped to thirty thousand. According to Lee Miller, Holt expected "a sale as big, if not bigger, than the last book." See LM letter to EP, July 20, 1944, MD.

181. EP letter to LM, July 1, 1944, LL. See also July 1, 1944, letter from EP to JP, LL, and June 29, 1944, letter from EP to LM, LL.

182. EP letter to JP, June 15, 1944, LL.

183. EP letter to LM, June 16, 1944, LL.

184. EP letter to LM, June 29, 1944, LL.

185. EP letter to JP, June 15, 1944, LL.

186. Pyle, *Brave Men*, 406.

187. EP letter to LM, June 29, 1944, LL.

188. Ernie Pyle, Column No. 26, July 12, 1944, MCBL.

189. EP letter to JP, June 15, 1944, LL.

190. EP letter to LM, June 16, 1944, LL.

191. EP letter to LM, June 29, 1944, LL.

192. EP letter to JP, July 1, 1944, LL.

193. EP letter to JP, June 15, 1944, LL.
194. EP letter to LM, June 16, 1944, LL.

CHAPTER 9: WINNING THEIR BATTLES

1. Ernie Pyle, *Brave Men* (Lincoln: University of Nebraska Press, 2001 [1944]), 448.
2. Rick Atkinson, *The Guns at Last Light* (New York: Henry Holt, 2013), 123 (Kindle location 2606–2608).
3. Atkinson, *Guns at Last Light*, 120 (Kindle location 2558–2562).
4. Ernie Pyle, Column No. 26, July 11, 1944, MCBL.
5. Atkinson, *Guns at Last Light*, 111 (Kindle location 2352–2356).
6. Timothy M. Gay, *Assignment to Hell: The War Against Nazi Germany with Correspondents Walter Cronkite, Andy Rooney, A. J. Liebling, Homer Bigart, and Hal Boyle* (New York: The Penguin Group, 2013), 297.
7. Atkinson, *Guns at Last Light*, 111 (Kindle location 2358–2360).
8. Antony Beevor, *D-Day: The Battle for Normandy* (New York: Penguin Books, 2019), 252.
9. Atkinson, *Guns at Last Light*, 112 (Kindle location 2371–2373).
10. Stephen E. Ambrose, *D-Day: June 6, 1944: The Climactic Battle of World War II* (New York: Simon & Schuster, 2013), Kindle location 7722–7725. See also James Holland, *Normandy '44: D-Day and the Epic 77-Day Battle for France—A New History* (New York: Atlantic Monthly Press, 2019), 381–82.
11. Pyle, *Brave Men*, 467.
12. Pyle, *Brave Men*, 467–68.
13. Pyle, *Brave Men*, 468.
14. David Vergun, "'C-Rats' Fueled Troops During and After World War II," U.S. Department of Defense, www.defense.gov/News/Feature-Stories/story/Article/1933268/c-rats-fueled-troops-during-and-after-world-war-ii.
15. Ernie Pyle, Column No. 32, July 18, 1944, MCBL.
16. Ernie Pyle, Column No. 33, July 19, 1944, MCBL.
17. Ernie Pyle, Column No. 32, July 18, 1944, MCBL.
18. Ernie Pyle, Column No. 33, July 19, 1944, MCBL.
19. Mary Louise Roberts, *What Soldiers Do: Sex and the American GI in World War II France* (Chicago: University of Chicago Press, 2014), 78.
20. "A Tour of the Peninsula," June 23, 1944, in David Nichols, ed., *Ernie's War: The Best of Ernie Pyle's World War II Dispatches* (New York: Random House, 1986), 289.
21. Holland, *Normandy '44*, 345.
22. Ernie Pyle, Column No. 27, July 12, 1944, MCBL.
23. Holland, *Normandy '44*, 345.
24. Ernie Pyle, Column No. 28, July 13, 1944, MCBL.
25. Ernie Pyle, Column No. 27, July 12, 1944, MCBL.
26. Ernie Pyle, Column No. 28, July 13, 1944, MCBL.
27. Ernie Pyle, Column No. 28, July 13, 1944, MCBL.
28. Mary Louise Roberts, *D-Day Through French Eyes: Normandy 1944* (Chicago: University of Chicago Press, 2014), 102.
29. Ernie Pyle, Column No. 28, July 13, 1944, MCBL.
30. Beevor, *D-Day*, 258.
31. Ernie Pyle, Column No. 28, July 13, 1944, MCBL.
32. Ernie Pyle, Column No. 28, July 13, 1944, MCBL.
33. Ernie Pyle, Column No. 31, July 17, 1944, MCBL.
34. Ernie Pyle, Column No. 30, July 15, 1944, MCBL.
35. Ernie Pyle, Column No. 29, July 14, 1944, MCBL.

36. Alex Kershaw, *Blood and Champagne: The Life and Times of Robert Capa* (New York: Da Capo Press, 2002), 135–36.
37. Ernie Pyle, Column No. 27, July 12, 1944, MCBL.
38. Ernie Pyle, Column No. 27, July 12, 1944, MCBL.
39. Ernie Pyle, Column No. 29, July 14, 1944, MCBL.
40. Ernie Pyle, Column No. 30, July 15, 1944, MCBL.
41. Antony Beevor writes, "As the Americans closed in on Cherbourg they encountered a greater density of pillboxes and weapon pits." See Beevor, *D-Day*, 218.
42. Ernie Pyle, Column No. 30, July 15, 1944, MCBL.
43. Kershaw, *Blood and Champagne*, 137–38.
44. Ernie Pyle, Column No. 31, July 17, 1944, MCBL.
45. Kershaw, *Blood and Champagne*, 137–38.
46. Ernie Pyle, Column No. 31, July 17, 1944, MCBL.
47. Marc Lancaster, "Cy Peterman and the Liberation of Cherbourg," ww2ondeadline.com, June 27, 2021, https://ww2ondeadline.substack.com/p/cherbourg-liberation-cy-peterman-correspondent.
48. Ernie Pyle, Column No. 35, July 21, 1944, MCBL.
49. Holland, *Normandy '44*, 348.
50. EP letter to PC, June 30, 1944.
51. Gay, *Assignment to Hell*, 291.
52. EP letter to LM, July 1, 1944, LL.
53. EP letter to PC, June 30, 1944, LL. See also EP letter to JP, July 1, 1944, LL.
54. EP letter to JP, July 1, 1944, LL.
55. EP letter to JP, July 1, 1944, LL. See also EP letter to LM, July 1, 1944, LL.
56. EP letter to JP, July 1, 1944, LL.
57. EP letter to JP, July 1, 1944, LL.
58. Raymond Sokolov, *Wayward Reporter: The Life of A. J. Liebling* (New York: Harper & Row, Publishers, 1980), 167.
59. EP letter to LM, July 1, 1944, LL. See also A. J. Liebling, "Pictures of Ernie: An Intimate Reminiscence on Ernie Pyle, Who Fled Blindly from Personal Fears to Become the Hero and the Victim of War," *Esquire*, May 1, 1947.
60. Liebling, "Pictures of Ernie."
61. Liebling, "Pictures of Ernie."
62. Gay, *Assignment to Hell*, 292.
63. Gay, *Assignment to Hell*, 293. See also A. J. Liebling, "REVISITED Normandy: In Quest of a Gray Granite House," *New Yorker*, Nov. 16, 1957.
64. EP letter to JP, July 1, 1944, LL.
65. EP letter to LM, June 29, 1944, MD.
66. "Beachhead Breakout," in Nichols, ed., *Ernie's War*, 328–29.
67. Beevor, *D-Day*, 342.
68. "Beachhead Breakout," in Nichols, ed., *Ernie's War*, 328–29.
69. Beevor, *D-Day*, 344.
70. "Beachhead Breakout," in Nichols, ed., *Ernie's War*, 328–29.
71. "Beachhead Breakout," in Nichols, ed., *Ernie's War*, 328–29.
72. EP letter to JP, Aug. 1, 1944, LL.
73. Atkinson, *Guns at Last Light*, 140 (Kindle location 2957–2960).
74. Atkinson, *Guns at Last Light*, 140 (Kindle location 2960–2964).
75. Atkinson, *Guns at Last Light*, 139 (Kindle location 2951–2955).
76. "Attack at Midday," Aug. 7, 1944, in Nichols, ed., *Ernie's War*, 332.
77. Beevor, *D-Day*, 346.
78. "A Surge of Doom-Life Sound," Aug. 8, 1944, in Nichols, ed., *Ernie's War*, 332.

79. Beevor, *D-Day*, 344, 346. See also Pyle, *Brave Men*, 460.

80. Pyle, *Brave Men*, 460.

81. "A Surge of Doom-Life Sound," in Nichols, ed., *Ernie's War*, 332–33.

82. "A Surge of Doom-Life Sound," in Nichols, ed., *Ernie's War*, 334–35. See also Atkinson, *Guns at Last Light*, 143 (Kindle location 3016–3019).

83. "A Surge of Doom-Life Sound," in Nichols, ed., *Ernie's War*, 334–35.

84. Pyle, *Brave Men*, 463.

85. "A Surge of Doom-Life Sound," in Nichols, ed., *Ernie's War*, 336. See also Pyle, *Brave Men*, 463.

86. Column from Aug. 10, 1944, in Nichols, ed., *Ernie's War*, 337.

87. Holland, *Normandy '44*, 478.

88. Beevor, *D-Day*, 348.

89. Atkinson, *Guns at Last Light*, 145 (Kindle location 3042–3044).

90. Paul Fussell, *The Boys' Crusade: The American Infantry in Northwestern Europe* (New York: Random House Publishing Group, 2005), 51.

91. Beevor, *D-Day*, 349. Bayerlein had been ordered not to yield even a foot of ground to the Americans. See Holland, *Normandy '44*, 475.

92. Beevor, *D-Day*, 182.

93. Alex Kershaw, *The First Wave: The D-Day Warriors Who Led the Way to Victory in World War II* (New York: Dutton Caliber, 2019), 272.

94. Marc Lancaster, "Killed by Friendly Fire: Lesley J. McNair and Bede Irvin," ww2ondeadline .com, July 25, 2020, https://ww2ondeadline.com/2020/07/25/operation-cobra-gen-lesley-j -mcnair-george-bede-irvin-saint-lo.

95. Ernie wrote that he learned of McNair's death three days later, back at camp. "A Surge of Doom-Life Sound," in Nichols, ed., *Ernie's War*, 336. See also Pyle, *Brave Men*, 463–64.

96. Holland, *Normandy '44*, 478.

97. Atkinson, *Guns at Last Light*, 143 (Kindle location 3008–3009).

98. Martin Blumenson, *United States Army in World War II: The European Theater of Operations—Breakout and Pursuit* (Atlanta: Whitman Publishing, 2012), 241.

99. Column from Aug. 10, 1944, in Nichols, ed., *Ernie's War*, 337.

100. Beevor, *D-Day*, 347.

101. Atkinson, *Guns at Last Light*, 113 (Kindle location 2396–2398). See also Beevor, *D-Day*, 294, 260, 261.

102. Pyle, *Brave Men*, 465.

103. Column from Aug. 10, 1944, in Nichols, ed., *Ernie's War*, 338. See also Beevor, *D-Day*, 353.

104. EP letter to LM, Aug. 9, 1944, LL.

105. EP letter to JP, Aug. 1, 1944, LL. See also EP letter to JP, Aug. 9, 1944.

106. EP letter to LM, Aug. 9, 1944, LL.

107. EP letter to JP, Aug. 9, 1944, LL.

108. EP letter to LM, July 16, 1944, LL.

109. EP letter to LM, Aug. 11, 1944, LL.

110. EP letter to JP, Aug. 24, 1944, LL.

111. EP letter to JP, Aug. 9, 1944, LL.

112. EP letter to JP, Aug. 9, 1944, LL. See also EP letter to JP, Aug. 24, 1944.

113. EP letter to JP, Aug. 9, 1944, LL.

114. EP letter to JP, Aug. 24, 1944, LL.

115. Pyle, *Brave Men*, 477.

116. Pyle, *Brave Men*, 479.

117. Pyle, *Brave Men*, 478.

118. Pyle, *Brave Men*, 469.

119. Pyle, *Brave Men*, 478.

120. Ernie Pyle, No. 15, Aug. 22, 1944, MCBL.

121. Ernie Pyle, "Wounded British Flier Fights Death Eight Days," *The Steamboat Pilot* (Steamboat Springs, CO), Oct. 5, 1944, 2.

122. Pyle, *Brave Men*, 479.

123. Pyle, *Brave Men*, 480.

124. Pyle, *Brave Men*, 480.

125. Pyle, "Wounded British Flier Fights Death Eight Days."

126. Pyle, "Wounded British Flier Fights Death Eight Days."

127. Pyle, "Wounded British Flier Fights Death Eight Days."

128. Pyle, *Brave Men*, 480.

129. Pyle, *Brave Men*, 480.

130. Pyle, "Wounded British Flier Fights Death Eight Days."

131. Pyle, *Brave Men*, 481.

132. Pyle, "Wounded British Flier Fights Death Eight Days."

133. Willard Largent and Tod Roberts, *RAF Wings over Florida: Memories of World War II British Air Cadets* (Lafayette, IN: Purdue University Press, 2011), 95.

134. Atkinson, *Guns at Last Light*, 183.

135. Pyle, *Brave Men*, 491.

136. Atkinson, *Guns at Last Light*, 183.

137. Moseley, *Reporting War*, 261. See also Richard Collier, *Fighting Words: The War Correspondents of World War Two* (New York: St. Martin's Press, 1989), 196.

138. Pyle, *Brave Men*, 491.

139. According to a historical marker outside the château, "Between 10–12 June and 2 August 1944, the Château de Vouilly became the American press camp headquarters. For another two months, General Bradley, 42 journalists and their technicians shared this residence with the owners."

140. Pyle, *Brave Men*, 491.

141. Pyle, *Brave Men*, 493.

CHAPTER 10: NOTHING LEFT TO DO

1. "Europe This Is Not," Feb. 16, 1945, in David Nichols, ed., *Ernie's War: The Best of Ernie Pyle's World War II Dispatches* (New York: Random House, 1986), 366.

2. EP letter to LM, Oct. 1, 1944, MD. On Oct. 8, 1944, Ernie wrote to Lee Miller: "Lester phoned Friday that the Army was going to release Meredith entirely, then he would be free to make the picture, but I haven't heard from him since." See EP letter to LM, Oct. 8, 1944, MD. On Oct. 26, 1944, Lee wrote to Ernie: "The Burgess Meredith business is being announced for tomorrow." See also EP letter to LM, Oct. 31, 1944, MD.

3. EP letter to LM, Oct. 17, 1944, MD. See also EP letter to LM, Oct. 8, 1944, MD.

4. EP letter to LM, Oct. 8, 1944, MD.

5. EP letter to LM, Oct. 31, 1944, MD.

6. EP letter to LM, Oct. 8, 1944, MD.

7. EP letter to LM, Oct. 8, 1944, MD. See also EP letter to LM, Oct. 31, 1944, MD.

8. LM letter to EP, Oct. 11, 1944, MD.

9. EP letter to LM, Oct. 17, 1944, MD.

10. A close second came from the city of Albuquerque, which "produced the best method yet of 'honoring the leading citizen,'" Ernie joked, "by sending up a case of Old GrandDad"—one of his very favorite bourbon whiskeys. See EP letter to LM, Oct. 8, 1944, MD.

11. EP letter to LM, Oct. 8, 1944, MD.

12. EP letter to LM, Oct. 31, 1944, MD.

13. EP letter to LM, Oct. 31, 1944, MD.

14. Nichols, ed., *Ernie's War*, 363.

15. LM letter to EP, Oct. 12, 1944, MD. See also LM letter to EP, Oct. 26, 1944, MD.

16. LM letter to EP, Oct. 12, 1944, MD.
17. LM letter to EP, Oct. 4, 1944, MD.
18. LM letter to EP, Oct. 4, 1944, MD.
19. LM letter to EP, Oct. 4, 1944, MD.
20. LM letter to EP, Oct. 17, 1944, MD.
21. LM letter to EP, Oct. 26, 1944, MD.
22. LM letter to EP, Oct. 26, 1944, MD.
23. EP letter to LM, Oct. 8, 1944, MD.
24. EP letter to LM, Oct. 17, 1944, MD.
25. EP letter to LM, Oct. 17, 1944, MD.
26. EP letter to LM, Oct. 31, 1944, MD.
27. EP letter to LM, Nov. 7, 1944, MD.
28. EP letter to LM, Oct. 31, 1944, MD.
29. EP letter to JP, June 22, 1943, MD.
30. EP letter to LM, Oct. 8, 1944, MD.
31. EP letter to LM, Oct. 31, 1944, MD.
32. EP letter to LM, Oct. 31, 1944, MD. See also EP letter to LM, Nov. 7, 1944.
33. EP letter to LM, Oct. 31, 1944, MD.
34. EP letter to LM, Oct. 31, 1944, MD.
35. EP letter to PC, Oct. 31, 1944, LL.
36. EP letter to LM, Oct. 31, 1944, MD. See also EP letter to PC, Oct. 31, 1944, LL.
37. EP letter to LM, Oct. 31, 1944, MD.
38. EP letter to LM, Oct. 31, 1944, MD.
39. EP letter to LM, Oct. 31, 1944, MD.
40. EP letter to LM, Oct. 31, 1944, MD. See also EP letter to PC, Oct. 31, 1944, LL.
41. EP letter to LM, Oct. 8, 1944, LL.
42. EP letter to LM, Oct. 17, 1944, MD.
43. EP letter to LM, Oct. 31, 1944, MD.
44. EP letter to PC, Oct. 29, 1944, LL.
45. EP letter to LM, Oct. 31, 1944, MD.
46. EP letter to LM, Oct. 31, 1944, MD.
47. EP letter to PC, Oct. 31, 1944, LL. See also EP letter to LM, Oct. 31, 1944, MD.
48. EP letter to PC, Oct. 31, 1944, LL. See also EP letter to LM, Oct. 31, 1944, MD.
49. EP letter to LM, Oct. 31, 1944, MD.
50. EP letter to LM, Oct. 8, 1944, MD.
51. EP letter to PC, Oct. 31, 1944, LL.
52. EP letter to LM, Oct. 31, 1944, MD.
53. EP letter to LM, Nov. 7, 1944, MD.
54. EP letter to PC, Nov. 12, 1944, LL.
55. EP letter to LM, Dec. 3, 1944, MD.
56. EP letter to LM, Dec. 11, 1944, MD.
57. Richard Collier, *Fighting Words: The War Correspondents of World War Two* (New York: St. Martin's Press, 1989), 197.
58. EP letter to LM, Dec. 11, 1944, MD.
59. EP letter to JP, Jan. 10, 1945, LL.
60. EP letter to JP, Jan. 10, 1945, LL.
61. EP letter to JP, Jan. 10, 1945, LL.
62. EP letter to JP, Jan. 10, 1945, LL.
63. EP letter to JP, Jan. 13, 1945, LL.
64. EP letter to JP, Jan. 10, 1945, LL.
65. EP letter to JP, Jan. 13, 1945, LL.
66. EP letter to JP, Jan. 10, 1945, LL.

67. EP letter to JP, Jan. 13, 1945, LL.

68. EP letter to JP, Jan. 13, 1945, LL.

69. EP letter to JP, Jan. 13, 1945, LL.

70. Steve Newman, "John Steinbeck & Ernie Pyle: War Correspondents," stevenewmanwriter .medium.com, https://stevenewmanwriter.medium.com/john-steinbeck-ernie-pyle-war -correspondent-a555d0d62b6a.

71. Newman, "John Steinbeck & Ernie Pyle: War Correspondents."

72. From Ernie's final handwritten column, which belongs to the Albuquerque Public Library but was on loan to Santa Fe in Apr. 2022. Also published on the front page of *The Pittsburgh Press*, Sept. 24, 1945, https://erniepyle.iu.edu/wartime-columns/on-victory.html.

73. "Ernie Pyle Is Killed on Ie Island; Foe Fired When All Seemed Safe," *New York Times*, Apr. 19, 1945, www.nytimes.com/1945/04/19/archives/ernie-pyle-is-killed-on-ie-island-foe-fired -when-all-seemed-safe.html.

74. EP letter to JP, Jan. 13, 1945, LL.

75. EP letter to PC, Feb. 27, 1945, LL.

76. EP letter to JP, Jan. 19, 1945, LL.

77. EP letter to JP, Feb. 2, 1945, LL.

78. EP letter to JP, Feb. 2, 1945, LL.

79. EP letter to JP, March 4, 1945, LL.

80. EP letter to JP, Feb. 2, 1945, LL.

81. "Europe This Is Not," Feb. 16, 1945, in Nichols, ed., *Ernie's War*, 366.

82. "Europe This Is Not," in Nichols, ed., *Ernie's War*, 367.

83. Ernie Pyle, "The Illogical Japs," Feb. 26, 1945, Indiana University, https://erniepyle.iu.edu /wartime-columns/illogical-japs.html.

84. "A Finger on the Wide Web of the War," Feb. 22, 1945, Indiana University, https://erniepyle .iu.edu/wartime-columns/finger-wide-web.html.

85. "Aboard a Fighting Ship," Mar. 15, 1945, in Nichols, ed., *Ernie's War*, 386–88.

86. EP letter to PC, Feb. 27, 1945, LL.

87. "Aboard a Fighting Ship," in Nichols, ed., *Ernie's War*, 386–88.

88. Nichols, ed., *Ernie's War*, 385.

89. "Aboard a Fighting Ship," in Nichols, ed., *Ernie's War*, 386–88.

90. "Aboard a Fighting Ship," in Nichols, ed., *Ernie's War*, 386–88. "Yet she has never even re-turned to Pearl Harbor to patch her wounds. She slaps on some patches on the run, and is ready for the next battle. The crew in semi-jocularity cuss her chief engineer for keeping her in such good shape they have no excuse to go back to Honolulu or America for overhaul."

91. "Their Lives Are Pretty Good," Mar. 17, 1945, in Nichols, ed., *Ernie's War*, 390.

92. "Their Lives Are Pretty Good," in Nichols, ed., *Ernie's War*, 390.

93. Ernie Pyle, "A Finger on the Wide Web of the War," and "Their Lives Are Pretty Good," Western Pacific, Mar. 17, 1945, in Nichols, ed., *Ernie's War*, 369–71, 389–91.

94. EP letter to JP, Feb. 9, 1945, LL. See also EP letter to PC, Feb. 27, 1945, LL.

95. EP letter to PC, Mar. 14, 1945, LL.

96. EP letter to JP, Mar. 4, 1945, LL.

97. EP letter to JP, Feb. 9, 1945, LL.

98. EP letter to PC, Feb. 27, 1945, LL.

99. EP letter to JP, Mar. 4, 1945, LL.

100. EP letter to JP, Feb. 9, 1945, LL.

CHAPTER 11: AN END TO ALL THAT WANDERING

1. From Ernie's final handwritten column, which belongs to the Albuquerque Public Library but was on loan to Santa Fe in Apr. 2022. Also published on the front page of *The Pittsburgh Press*, Sept. 24, 1945. See https://erniepyle.iu.edu/wartime-columns/on-victory.html.

2. EP letter to PC, Mar. 14, 1945, LL.

3. "Waiting for Tomorrow," Apr. 3, 1945, in David Nichols, ed., *Ernie's War: The Best of Ernie Pyle's World War II Dispatches* (New York: Random House, 1986), 401.

4. "Waiting for Tomorrow," in Nichols, ed., *Ernie's War*, 402.

5. EP letter to JP, Mar. 26, 1945, LL.

6. "Waiting for Tomorrow," in Nichols, ed., *Ernie's War*, 403.

7. EP letter to JP, Apr. 8, 1945, LL.

8. Saul David, *Crucible of Hell: The Heroism and Tragedy of Okinawa, 1945* (New York: Hachette Books, 2020), 8.

9. David, *Crucible of Hell*, 8–9.

10. David, *Crucible of Hell*, 83.

11. "It Looks Like America," Apr. 10, 1945, in Nichols, ed., *Ernie's War*, 408.

12. Ernie Pyle, *Last Chapter* (New York: Henry Holt, 1946), 85.

13. "War Sounds," Apr. 12, 1945, in Nichols, ed., *Ernie's War*, 411.

14. David, *Crucible of Hell*, 100.

15. EP letter to JP, Apr. 8, 1945, LL. See also "They Just Lay There, Blinking," Apr. 21, 1945, in Nichols, ed., *Ernie's War*, 412.

16. EP letter to JP, Apr. 8, 1945, LL.

17. EP letter to JP, Apr. 8, 1945, LL.

18. Brian Best, *Reporting the Second World War: The Battle for Truth* (South Yorkshire, UK: Pen and Sword Military, 2015), 131.

19. David, *Crucible of Hell*, 155.

20. Rudy Faircloth and W. Horace Carter, *"Buddy," Ernie Pyle, World War II's Most Beloved Typewriter Soldier* (Tabor City, NC: Atlantic Publishing Company, 1982), 59–60.

21. David, *Crucible of Hell*, 154.

22. Ray E. Boomhower, "The Last Assignment: Ernie Pyle on Okinawa," Indiana Historical Society, Aug. 2020, https://indianahistory.org/blog/the-last-assignment-ernie-pyle-on-okinawa.

23. Evans Wylie, "The Quiet Little Man Traveled Half the World Following GIs to War Before a Jap Bullet Caught Up with His Luck on Ie Island," *Yank*, May 18, 1945, 11.

24. "Ernie Pyle Is Killed on Ie Island; Foe Fired When All Seemed Safe," *New York Times*, Apr. 19, 1945, www.nytimes.com/1945/04/19/archives/ernie-pyle-is-killed-on-ie-island-foe-fired-when-all-seemed-safe.html.

25. Boomhower, "The Last Assignment."

26. Joining Pyle and Coolidge on the trip were Major George H. Pratt and two enlisted men, Dale W. Bassett and John L. Barnes. See Boomhower, "The Last Assignment."

27. David, *Crucible of Hell*, 156.

28. "Ernie Pyle Is Killed on Ie Island; Foe Fired When All Seemed Safe."

29. Marc Lancaster, "Ernie Pyle Killed on Ie Shima," ww2ondeadline.com, Apr. 18, 2021, https://ww2ondeadline.com/2021/04/18/ernie-pyle-killed-ww2-correspondent.

30. Lancaster, "Ernie Pyle Killed on Ie Shima."

31. Boomhower, "The Last Assignment: Ernie Pyle on Okinawa."

32. Grant MacDonald, "Ernie Pyle Dies at Ie Front, Shot by Machine Gun," *New York Herald Tribune*, Apr. 19, 1945. See also Grant MacDonald, "GI and General, All Mourn Pyle," *Daily Boston Globe*, Apr. 19, 1945.

33. Lancaster, "Ernie Pyle Killed on Ie Shima."

34. "Pyle Will Rest Alongside G.I.s Who Loved Him," *New York Herald Tribune*, Apr. 20, 1945. See also "Reporter Who Saw Too Much of Death Finds His Own on Ie Jima," *Washington Post*, Apr. 19, 1945.

35. Late in the afternoon, Chaplain N. B. Saucier of Coffeeville, Mississippi, received permission to try to recover Ernie Pyle's body. Litter bearers T-S Paul Shapiro of Passaic, New Jersey; Sgt. Minter Moore of Elkins, West Virginia; Cpl. Robert Toaz of Huntington, New

York; and Sgt. Arthur Austin of Tekamah, Nebraska, volunteered to go with him. See Wylie, "The Quiet Little Man," 11.

36. Lancaster, "Ernie Pyle Killed on Ie Shima."

37. Ernie Pyle Eye Witness Death Account—Letter, Jan. 1999 (Indiana Historical Society). The letter is written by Brigadier General William G. King Jr., in reply to a request from E. M. Nathanson regarding his recollections of the death of Ernie Pyle.

38. David, *Crucible of Hell*, 156.

39. "Army & Navy—Operations: Curtain Raisers," *Time*, Nov. 27, 1944.

40. "Death Photo of War Reporter Pyle Found," Associated Press, Feb. 3, 2008.

41. "On Dec. 14, 1979, the *Daily Times-News* of Burlington, NC, ran the picture with a story about B. F. Coleman Jr., a local resident who, as a navy chief petty officer in 1945, had acquired a copy from a naval photographer aboard USS *Panamint*, a command ship in the Okinawa campaign. See also "No Scoop: Pyle's Death Photo Already Published," Associated Press, Feb. 13, 2008.

42. Lancaster, "Ernie Pyle Killed on Ie Shima."

43. Lancaster, "Ernie Pyle Killed on Ie Shima."

44. "Ernie Pyle Buried in Hand Made Coffin as Mortars Bark," *Chicago Daily Tribune*, Apr. 21, 1945.

45. "Ernie Pyle Laid to Rest Under Fire," *New York Times*, Apr. 21, 1945.

46. Boomhower, "The Last Assignment."

47. Lancaster, "Ernie Pyle Killed on Ie Shima."

48. Lee G. Miller, *The Story of Ernie Pyle* (New York: Viking Press, 1950), 42.

49. Rebecca Maksel, "Byline: Ernie Pyle," *Smithsonian Magazine*, Nov. 2011, www.airspacemag.com/history-of-flight/byline-ernie-pyle-76396157.

50. Lancaster, "Ernie Pyle Killed on Ie Shima."

51. "Ernie Pyle Is Killed on Ie Island; Foe Fired When All Seemed Safe."

52. MacDonald, "Ernie Pyle Dies at Ie Front, Shot by Machine Gun."

53. Lancaster, "Ernie Pyle Killed on Ie Shima."

54. Lancaster, "Ernie Pyle Killed on Ie Shima."

55. Alex Kershaw, *Blood and Champagne: The Life and Times of Robert Capa* (New York: Da Capo Press, 2002), 156.

56. MacDonald, "Ernie Pyle Dies at Ie Front, Shot by Machine Gun."

57. "Ernie Pyle Is Killed on Ie Island; Foe Fired When All Seemed Safe."

58. Lancaster, "Ernie Pyle Killed on Ie Shima."

59. Ray Boomhower, *The Soldier's Friend: A Life of Ernie Pyle* (Indianapolis: Indiana Historical Society, 2006), 106–7.

60. Richard Harwood, "Ernie Pyle: The Journalist as Hero," *Washington Post*, Sept. 28, 1986, www.washingtonpost.com/archive/entertainment/books/1986/09/28/ernie-pyle-the-journalist-as-hero/95f53055-0cee-4db2-a77b-e6e48e51d6d1. See also James Tobin, *Ernie Pyle's War: America's Eyewitness to World War II* (New York: The Free Press, 1997), 2.

61. "Statement by the President on the Death of Ernie Pyle," Apr. 18, 1945, Public Papers of Harry S. Truman, 1945–1953, Harry S. Truman Library and Museum, www.trumanlibrary.gov/library/public-papers/6/statement-president-death-ernie-pyle. See also "Ernie Pyle Is Killed on Ie Island; Foe Fired When All Seemed Safe."

62. Eleanor Roosevelt, "My Day by Eleanor Roosevelt, Apr. 19, 1945," Eleanor Roosevelt Papers Project, George Washington University, www2.gwu.edu/~erpapers/myday/displaydoc.cfm?_y=1945&_f=md000003.

63. "Ernie Pyle Laid to Rest Under Fire."

64. "GI's Urge Top Honor for Pyle," *New York Times*, Apr. 28, 1945.

65. "Medal for Ernie Pyle Favored by Truman," *Daily Boston Globe*, May 29, 1945.

66. The unpublished holograph draft of Steinbeck's obituary of Ernie Pyle is archived at the Steinbeck Research Center at San Jose State University.

67. Steve Newman, "John Steinbeck & Ernie Pyle: War Correspondents," stevenewmanwriter .medium.com, https://stevenewmanwriter.medium.com/john-steinbeck-ernie-pyle-war -correspondent-a555d0d62b6a.

68. Newman, "John Steinbeck & Ernie Pyle: War Correspondents."

69. John J. Contreni, "'A Story That Can't Be Printed': Ernie Pyle's Ie Shima Memorial Dedication, Dealing with Men, and Military Journalism in the Mid-Pacific During World War II," *Indiana Magazine of History* 111, no. 3 (Sept. 2015): 286–322, www.jstor.org/stable/pdf/10.5378 /indimagahist.111.3.0286.pdf?refreqid=excelsior%3A3084d1d2494859ccecf036fdaae8bec0.

70. Jack Briggs rose through the ranks in the pages of the *Midpacifican*, where he started as a "Makeup Editor, Reporter" in January 1944 and became the managing editor by September of that year. See Contreni, "'A Story That Can't Be Printed.'"

71. Jack Briggs, who went by the pen name "John Pacific," knew his version of events would never be published, so he ran off copies of it on a mimeograph machine and distributed it to four friends, one of whom was John J. Contreni's father, who arrived on Okinawa on April 26 and on Ie Shima on May 13, 1945. According to Contreni, "John Pacific's account of the Ernie Pyle memorial dedication survives today only on four mimeographed sheets. If there are any other copies, they have not come to light. The story adds a new piece to the emergent posthumous legend of Ernie Pyle." See Contreni, "'A Story That Can't Be Printed.'"

72. Contreni, "'A Story That Can't Be Printed.'"

73. "Remembering Ernie Pyle," *Newsweek*, Sept. 3, 1945, 67.

74. "Washington Merry-Go-Round," *Advocate* (Baton Rouge, LA), Aug. 3, 1945, 9A; "Pyle Memorial Goal Mushrooms," *Omaha World-Herald*, Aug. 11, 1945, 11; "Mrs. Pyle Rejects Plans for Elaborate Memorial to Ernie," *Canton* (OH) *Repository*, Aug. 21, 1945, page 15. Pyle, the sixteenth American casualty on Ie Shima, was buried there on April 20, 1945, a few hundred yards from the roadside memorial. His body was later moved to the army cemetery on Okinawa and finally to the National Memorial Cemetery of the Pacific on Oahu, Hawaii.

75. "The Pyle Memorial," *Omaha World-Herald*, Aug. 28, 1945, 10.

76. Boomhower, "The Last Assignment."

77. From Ernie's final handwritten column, which belongs to the Albuquerque Public Library but was on loan to Santa Fe in Apr. 2022. Also published on the front page of *The Pittsburgh Press*, Sept. 24, 1945. See https://erniepyle.iu.edu/wartime-columns/on-victory.html.

78. Tobin, *Ernie Pyle's War*, 4.

BIBLIOGRAPHY

Ambrose, Stephen E. *D-Day: June 6, 1944: The Climactic Battle of World War II*. New York: Simon & Schuster, 2013.

Appelbaum, Yoni. "Publishers Gave Away 122,951,031 Books During World War II." *Atlantic*, Sept. 10, 2014.

Appleman, Roy E., James M. Burns, Russell A. Gugeler, and John Stevens. *Okinawa: The Last Battle*. New York: Skyhorse Publishing, 2011.

Atkinson, Rick. *An Army at Dawn: The War in North Africa, 1942–1943*. New York: Henry Holt, 2002.

———. *The Day of Battle: The War in Sicily and Italy, 1943–1944*. New York: Henry Holt, 2007.

———. *The Guns at Last Light*. New York: Henry Holt, 2013.

Avagliano, Faustino. *Monte Cassino Under Fire: War Diaries from the Abbey*. Monte Cassino, 2018.

Barnett, Lincoln. "Ernie Pyle." *Life* 18, no. 14 (Apr. 2, 1945), 95–98, 101–102, 105–108. Reprinted in Lincoln Barnett, *Writing on Life: Sixteen Close-Ups*. New York: Sloane, 1951.

Bartov, Omer. *Mirrors of Destruction: War, Genocide, and Modern Identity*. New York: Oxford University Press, 2000.

Beevor, Antony. *D-Day: The Battle for Normandy*. New York: Penguin Books, 2019.

Beevor, Antony, and Luba Vinogradova. *A Writer at War: Vasily Grossman with the Red Army, 1941–1945*. New York: Pantheon Books, 2005.

Bell, Don. "I Met Ernie Pyle in a Foxhole." *Guideposts* 40, no. 40 (June 1985), 24–27.

Benson, Jackson J. *The True Adventures of John Steinbeck, Writer*. New York: Viking Press, 1984.

Bertelsen, Lance. "San Pietro and the 'Art' of War." *Southwest Review* 74, no. 2 (Spring 1989).

Best, Brian. *Reporting the Second World War: The Battle for Truth*. Barnsley, UK: Pen and Sword Military, 2015.

Bigart, Homer. "San Pietro a Village of the Dead; Victory Cost Americans Dearly." In *Reporting World War II: American Journalism 1938–1946*. New York: Library of America, 2001.

Blumenson, Martin. *Kasserine Pass: Where America Lost Her Military Innocence*. Boston: Houghton Mifflin, 1966.

——. *United States Army in World War II: The European Theater of Operations—Breakout and Pursuit*. Atlanta: Whitman Publishing, 2012.

Boomhower, Ray E. *Dispatches from the Pacific: The World War II Reporting of Robert L. Sherrod*. Bloomington: Indiana University Press, 2017.

——. "The Last Assignment: Ernie Pyle on Okinawa." Indiana Historical Society, Aug. 2020.

——. *The Soldier's Friend: A Life of Ernie Pyle*, Indianapolis: Indiana Historical Society, 2006.

Bradley, Omar N. *A Soldier's Story*. New York: Holt, 1951.

Brady, Tim. *A Death in San Pietro: The Untold Story of Ernie Pyle, John Huston, and the Fight for Purple Heart Valley*. New York: Hachette Books, 2013.

Brewer, Susan A. *Why America Fights: Patriotism and War Propaganda from the Philippines to Iraq*. New York: Oxford University Press, 2009.

Brock, Rita Nakashima, and Gabriella Lettini. *Soul Repair: Recovering from Moral Injury after War*. Boston: Beacon Press, 2012.

Burns, John Horne. *The Gallery*. New York: New York Review Books, 2004.

Caddick-Adams, Peter. *Sand & Steel: The D-Day Invasion and the Liberation of France*. New York: Oxford University Press, 2019.

Capa, Robert. *Slightly Out of Focus: The Legendary Photojournalist's Illustrated Memoir of World War II*. New York: Modern Library, 2001.

Carlson, Peter. "Ernie Pyle Stumps Arthur Miller." *American History* 49, no. 5 (Dec. 2014).

Carpenter, John R. *Bearing Witness: How Writers Brought the Brutality of World War II to Light*. New York: Skyhorse Publishing, 2014.

Carroll, Andrew, ed. *War Letters: Extraordinary Correspondence from American Wars*. New York: Scribner, 2001.

Cawthon, Charles R. *Other Clay: A Remembrance of the World War II Infantry*. Lincoln: Nebraska University Press, 2004.

Childers, Thomas. *Soldier from the War Returning: The Greatest Generation's Troubled Homecoming from World War II*. New York: Houghton Mifflin Harcourt, 2009.

Churchill, Winston S. *Triumph and Tragedy*. New York: RosettaBooks, 2014.

Clapper, Raymond, and Olive Ewing Clapper. *Watching the World, 1934–1944*. New York: Whittlesey House, 1944.

Clark, Lloyd. *Anzio: The Friction of War: Italy and the Battle for Rome 1944*. London: Headline Publishing Group, 2006.

Collier, Richard. *Fighting Words: The War Correspondents of World War Two*. New York: St. Martin's Press, 1989.

Colville, John. *The Fringes of Power: Downing Street Diaries 1939–1945*. London: Weidenfeld & Nicolson, 2004.

Contreni, John J. "'A Story That Can't Be Printed': Ernie Pyle's Ie Shima Memorial Dedication, Dealing with Men, and Military Journalism in the Mid-Pacific During World War II." *Indiana Magazine of History* 111, no. 3 (Sept. 2015).

Cook, Haruko Taya, and Theodore F. Cook. *Japan at War: An Oral History*. New York: New Press, 1992.

Cronkite, Walter. *A Reporter's Life*. New York: Ballantine Books, 1996.

David, Saul. *Crucible of Hell: The Heroism and Tragedy of Okinawa, 1945*. New York: Hachette Books, 2020.

Davidson, Jo. *Between Sittings: An Informal Autobiography of Jo Davidson*. New York: Dial, 1951.

Desmond, Robert W. *Tides of War: World News Reporting 1931–1945*. Ames: Iowa State University Press, 1982.

D'Este, Carlo. *Bitter Victory: The Battle for Sicily, 1943*. New York: Harper Perennial, 1988.

Doherty, Richard. *Monte Cassino: Opening the Road to Rome*. Barnsley, UK: Pen & Sword Military, 2018.

Dower, John W. *War Without Mercy: Race & Power in the Pacific War*. New York: Pantheon Books, 1986.

Ellis, John. *Brute Force: Allied Strategy and Tactics in the Second World War.* New York: Viking, 1990.

Evangelista, Matthew. "Manipulation and Memory in John Huston's *The Battle of San Pietro.*" *Film & History: An Interdisciplinary Journal* 46, no. 1 (Summer 2016), 4–20.

Evans, Richard J. *The Coming of the Third Reich.* New York: Penguin Press, 2004.

———. *The Third Reich in Power.* New York: Penguin Press, 2005.

———. *The Third Reich at War.* New York: Penguin Press, 2009.

Faircloth, Rudy, and W. Horace Carter. *"Buddy," Ernie Pyle, World War II's Most Beloved Typewriter Soldier.* Tabor City, NC: Atlantic Publishing Company, 1982.

Feinstein, Anthony. *Dangerous Lives: War and the Men and Women Who Report It.* Toronto: Thomas Allen Publishers, 2003.

Fine, Richard. "The Development of the 'Pyle Style' of War Reporting French North Africa, 1942–1943." *Media History* 23, no. 3–4 (2017): 376–90.

Fritz, Stephen G. *Frontsoldaten: The German Soldier in World War II.* Lexington: University of Kentucky Press, 1995.

Fussell, Paul. *The Boys' Crusade: The American Infantry in Northwestern Europe.* New York: Random House Publishing Group, 2005.

———. *Doing Battle: The Making of a Skeptic.* Boston: Little, Brown and Company, 1996.

———. *Wartime: Understanding and Behavior in the Second World War.* New York: Oxford University Press, 1989.

Gay, Timothy M. *Assignment to Hell: The War Against Nazi Germany with Correspondents Walter Cronkite, Andy Rooney, A. J. Liebling, Homer Bigart, and Hal Boyle.* New York: The Penguin Group, 2013.

Goodman, Rosamond. "The Ernie Pyle I Knew." *Pageant* 1, no. 8 (Aug.–Sept. 1945).

Gray, J. Glenn. *The Warriors: Reflections on Men in Battle.* Lincoln: University of Nebraska Press, 1998.

Hamill, Pete, ed. *A. J. Liebling: World War II Writings.* New York: Library of America, 2008.

Hapgood, David, and David Richardson. *Monte Cassino.* New York: Congdon & Weed, 1984.

Harden, Mike, and Evelyn Hobson. *On a Wing and a Prayer: The Aviation Columns of Ernie Pyle.* Friends of Ernie Pyle, 1995.

Harris, Mark. *Five Came Back: A Story of Hollywood and the Second World War.* New York: Penguin Books, 2014.

Harwood, Richard. "Ernie Pyle: The Journalist as Hero." *Washington Post,* Sept. 28, 1986.

Hassett, William D. *Off the Record with F.D.R.* New Brunswick, NJ: Rutgers University Press, 1958.

Hedges, Chris. *War Is a Force That Gives Us Meaning.* New York: PublicAffairs, 2002.

Herman, Judith L. *Trauma and Recovery: The Aftermath of Violence—from Domestic Abuse to Political Terror.* New York: Basic Books, 1992.

Hockensmith, Steve. "The Home Front." *Chicago Tribune,* Aug. 6, 2000.

Holland, James. *Normandy '44: D-Day and the Epic 77-Day Battle for France—A New History.* New York: Atlantic Monthly Press, 2019.

Hynes, Samuel. *The Soldiers' Tale: Bearing Witness to Modern War.* New York: Penguin Press, 1997.

Jackson, W. G. F. *The Battle for Italy.* New York: Harper & Row, 1967.

Johnson, Owen V., ed. *At Home with Ernie Pyle.* Bloomington: Indiana University Press, 2016.

———. "Darling Jerry, Darling Mabel, Darling Moran: Ernie Pyle and the Women Behind Him." Paper prepared for presentation to the History Division, Association for Education in Journalism & Mass Communication, San Francisco, Aug. 2–5, 2006.

Keegan, John. *The Second World War.* New York: Penguin Books, 2005.

———. *Six Armies in Normandy: From D-Day to the Liberation of Paris, June 6th–August 25th, 1944.* New York: Viking Press, 1982.

Kennedy, David M. *Freedom from Fear.* New York: Oxford University Press, 1999.

Kershaw, Alex. *The Bedford Boys: One American Town's Ultimate D-Day Sacrifice*. New York: MJF Books, 2003.

———. *Blood and Champagne: The Life and Times of Robert Capa*. New York: Da Capo Press, 2002.

———. *The First Wave: The D-Day Warriors Who Led the Way to Victory in World War II*. New York: Dutton Caliber, 2019.

———. *The Liberator: One World War II Soldier's 500-Day Odyssey from the Beaches of Sicily to the Gates of Dachau*. New York: Crown Publishers, 2012.

Knightley, Phillip. *The First Casualty: From the Crimea to Vietnam: The War Correspondent as Hero, Propagandist, and Myth Maker*. New York: Harcourt Brace Jovanovich, 1975.

Knott, Richard. *The Trio: Three War Correspondents of World War Two*. Stroud, UK: The History Press, 2015.

Lancaster, Marc. "Cy Peterman and the Liberation of Cherbourg." ww2ondeadline.com, June 27, 2021.

———. "D-Day: Ernie Pyle's Struggle to Tell the Invasion Story." ww2ondeadline.com, June 10, 2020.

———. "Ernie Pyle Killed on Ie Shima." ww2ondeadline.com, Apr. 18, 2021.

———. "Killed by Friendly Fire: Lesley J. McNair and Bede Irvin." ww2ondeadline.com, July 25, 2020.

———. "Liberation Day: When Paris Went Mad." ww2ondeadline.com, Aug. 25, 2020.

Lancaster, Paul. "Ernie Pyle: Chronicler of 'The Men Who Do the Dying.'" *American Heritage* 32, no. 2 (Feb.–Mar. 1981).

Largent, Willard, and Tod Roberts. *RAF Wings over Florida: Memories of World War II British Air Cadets*. Lafayette, IN: Purdue University Press, 2011.

Laurie, Clayton D. "Anzio: The U.S. Army Campaign of World War II." United States Army Center of Military History, 1994.

Lee, David. *Up Close and Personal: The Reality of Close-Quarter Fighting in World War II*. Barnsley, UK: Frontline Books, 2006.

Lewis, Norman. *Naples '44: A World War II Diary of Occupied Italy*. New York: Carroll & Graf Publishers, 2005.

Lidden Hart, B. H. *The Other Side of the Hill*. London: Cassell, 1951.

Liebling, A. J. "Pictures of Ernie: An Intimate Reminiscence on Ernie Pyle, Who Fled Blindly from Personal Fears to Become the Hero and the Victim of War." *Esquire*, May 1, 1947.

———. "Pyle Set the Style." *New Yorker*, Sept. 2, 1950.

———. "REVISITED Normandy: In Quest of a Gray Granite House." *New Yorker*, Nov. 16, 1957.

Liggett, Lila N. "That Girl of Ernie Pyle's." *Woman with Woman's Digest*, July 1945.

Love, Robert W. *History of the U.S. Navy: 1942–1991*, vol. 2. Harrisburg, PA: Stackpole Books, 1992.

MacDonald, Grant. "Ernie Pyle Dies at Ie Front, Shot by Machine Gun." *New York Herald Tribune*, Apr. 19, 1945.

MacMillan, Margaret. *War: How Conflict Shapes Us*. New York: Random House, 2020.

Maksel, Rebecca. "Byline: Ernie Pyle." *Smithsonian Magazine*, Nov. 2011.

Malaparte, Curzio. *The Skin*. New York: New York Review Books, 2013.

Manchester, William. *Goodbye Darkness: A Memoir of the Pacific War*. Boston: Little, Brown and Company, 1979.

Marlantes, Karl. *What It Is Like to Go to War*. New York: Atlantic Monthly Press, 2011.

Martin, Ralph G. *The GI War: 1941–1945*. Boston: Little, Brown, 1967.

Mauldin, Bill. *Back Home: Text and Pictures by Bill Mauldin*. New York: William Sloane Associates, 1947.

———. *Up Front: Text and Pictures by Bill Mauldin*. New York: Henry Holt, 1945.

Mazower, Mark. *Dark Continent: Europe's Twentieth Century*. New York: Vintage Books, 1998.

McNamara, John. *EXTRA! U.S. War Correspondents in Action*. Boston: Houghton Mifflin Company, 1945.

Melzer, Richard. *Ernie Pyle in the American Southwest*. Santa Fe, NM: Sunstone Press, 1995.

Miller, Arthur. *Situation Normal*. New York: Reynal & Hitchcock, 1944.

Miller, Lee G. *An Ernie Pyle Album*. New York: William Sloane Associates, 1946.

———. *The Story of Ernie Pyle*, New York: Viking Press, 1950.

Moen, Margaret. "Ernie Pyle: Travel Writer." *Elks Magazine* 92, no. 10 (May 2014).

Morriss, Mack. "Pyle Goes Home." *Yank,* Oct. 6, 1944; reprinted as "Friend of the GIs," *New York World-Telegram*, Oct. 30, 1944, and in *Publishers' Auxiliary* 79, no. 45 (Nov. 4, 1944).

Moseley, Ray. *Reporting War: How Foreign Correspondents Risked Capture, Torture and Death to Cover World War II*. New Haven: Yale University Press, 2017.

Mosse, George L. *Fallen Soldiers: Reshaping the Memory of the World Wars*. New York: Oxford University Press, 1990.

Neiberg, Michael. *The Blood of Free Men: The Liberation of Paris, 1944*. New York: Basic Books, 2012.

Newman, Steve. "John Steinbeck & Ernie Pyle: War Correspondents." stevenewmanwriter.medium.com.

Nguyen, Viet Thanh. *Nothing Ever Dies: Vietnam and the Memory of War*. Cambridge, MA: Harvard University Press, 2016.

Nichols, David, ed. *The Best of Ernie Pyle's 1930s Travel Dispatches*. New York: Random House, 1989.

———, ed. *Ernie's War: The Best of Ernie Pyle's World War II Dispatches*. New York: Random House, 1986.

O'Neill, Robert, ed. *I Am Soldier: War Stories from the Ancient World to the 20th Century*. New York: Osprey Publishing, 2009.

Painton, Frederick C. "The Hoosier Letter Writer." *Saturday Evening Post*, Oct. 2, 1943.

Piehler, G. Kurt. *Remembering War the American Way*. Washington, DC: Smithsonian Books, 1995.

Pillsbury, Dorothy. "A Little White House on a Hilltop Where People Stop a While." *Christian Science Monitor*, Nov. 16, 1949.

Plan, Rebecca Jo. "Preventing the Inevitable: John Appel and the Problem of Psychiatric Casualties in the US Army during World War II." In Frank Biess and Daniel M. Gross, ed., *Science and Emotions after 1945: A Transatlantic Perspective*, published to Chicago Scholarship Online.

Playfair, Major General I. S. O., et al. *The Mediterranean and Middle East: The Destruction of the Axis Forces in Africa*. History of the Second World War United Kingdom Military Series. Uckfield, UK: Naval & Military Press, 2004.

Plumb, Charlie. "Ernie Pyle's Ulithi Interlude." *VFW Magazine* 61, no. 8 (Apr. 1974).

Pogue, Forrest C. *Pogue's War: Diaries of a WWII Combat Historian*. Lexington: University of Kentucky Press, 2006.

Porch, Douglas. *The Path to Victory*. New York: Farrar, Straus and Giroux, 2004.

Pratt, Fletcher. "How the Censors Rigged the News." *Harper's* 192, no. 1149 (Feb. 1946).

Pratt, Henry. "Remembering Ernie Pyle." *Retired Officer* 47, no. 2 (Feb. 1991).

Pyle, Ernie. *Brave Men*. Lincoln: University of Nebraska Press, 2001. First published 1944 by Grosset & Dunlap.

———. *Here Is Your War*. New York: Henry Holt, 1943.

———. *Home Country*. New York: William Sloane Associates, 1947.

———. *Last Chapter*. New York: Henry Holt, 1946, Uncommon Valor Reprint Series, 1947.

———. "Why Albuquerque?" *New Mexico Magazine*, Jan. 1942.

Randle, Edwin H. *Ernie Pyle Comes Ashore and Other Stories*. Clearwater, FL: Eldnar Press, 1972.

Rice, William. "A Journey through 1930s America with Ernie Pyle." *Chicago Tribune*, Aug. 27, 1989.

Redman, Clarence E. "That Girl." *Bombsight*, Christmas 1943.

Robb, Edwin G. "Jerry Pyle: Ernie's Afton Connection." *Afton Paper* (MN), Apr. 1994.

Robb, Esther C. "Jerry, His Wife: Here Is a Story Never Told Before About 'That Girl'—Ernie Pyle's Wife." *Golfer & Sportsman* 20, no. 4 (Apr. 1947).

Roberts, Mary Louise. *D-Day Through French Eyes: Normandy 1944.* Chicago: University of Chicago Press, 2014.

———. *What Soldiers Do: Sex and the American GI in World War II France.* Chicago: University of Chicago Press, 2014.

Robertson, Stewart. "Ernie Pyle." *Family Circle* 23, no. 19 (Nov. 5, 1943).

Romeiser, John B., ed. *Beachhead Don: Reporting the War from the European Theater, 1943–1945.* New York: Fordham University Press, 2004.

———, ed. *Combat Reporter: Don Whitehead's World War II Diary and Memoirs.* New York: Fordham University Press, 2006.

Rooney, Andy. *My War.* New York: PublicAffairs, 1995.

Roosevelt, Eleanor. "My Day," June 21, 1943, and Nov. 5, 1943, in *My Day by Eleanor Roosevelt,* George Washington University.

Rose, Alexander. *Men of War: The American Soldier in Combat at Bunker Hill, Gettysburg, and Iwo Jima.* New York: Random House, 2015.

Rose, Sarah. *D-Day Girls: The Spies Who Armed the Resistance, Sabotaged the Nazis, and Helped Win World War II.* New York: Broadway Books, 2019.

Rubin Suleiman, Susan. *Crises of Memory and the Second World War.* Cambridge, MA: Harvard University Press, 2006.

Salecker, Gene Eric. *Rolling Thunder Against the Rising Sun: The Combat History of U.S. Army Tank Battalions in the Pacific in World War II.* Mechanicsburg, PA: Stackpole Books, 2008.

Sarantakes, Nicholas Evan. *Seven Stars: The Okinawa Battle Diaries of Simon Bolivar Buckner, Jr., and Joseph Stilwell.* College Station: Texas A&M University Press, 2004.

Scranton, Roy. *Total Mobilization: World War II and American Literature.* Chicago: University of Chicago Press, 2019.

Seethaler, Josef, Matthias Karmasin, Gabriele Melischek, and Romy Wöhlert, eds. *Selling War: The Role of the Mass Media in Hostile Conflicts from World War I to the "War on Terror."* Bristol, UK: Intellect, 2013.

Sevareid, Eric. *Not So Wild a Dream: A Personal Story of Youth and War and the American Faith.* New York: Atheneum, 1976.

Shephard, Ben. *A War of Nerves: Soldiers and Psychiatrists in the Twentieth Century.* Cambridge, MA: Harvard University Press, 2001.

Sherrod, Robert. *Tarawa: The Incredible Story of One of World War II's Bloodiest Battles.* New York: Skyhorse Publishing, 2013.

Shimpo, Ryukyu. *Descent into Hell: Civilian Memories of the Battle of Okinawa.* Portland, ME: MerwinAsia, 2014.

Shomon, Joseph. *Crosses in the Wind: Graves Registration Service in the Second World War.* New York: Stratford House, 1947.

Simmonds, Roy. *John Steinbeck: The War Years, 1939–1945.* Lewisburg, PA: Bucknell University Press, 1996.

Sloan, Bill. *The Ultimate Battle: Okinawa 1945—The Last Epic Struggle of World War II.* New York: Simon & Schuster, 2007.

Sokolov, Raymond. *Wayward Reporter: The Life of A. J. Liebling.* New York: Harper & Row, Publishers, 1980.

Sorel, Nancy Caldwell. *The Women Who Wrote the War: The Riveting Saga of World War II's Daredevil Women Correspondents.* New York: Arcade Publishing, 1999.

Stargardt, Nicholas. *The German War: A National Under Arms, 1939–1945.* New York: Basic Books, 2015.

Stenbuck, Jack, ed. *Typewriter Battalion: Dramatic Front-Line Dispatches from World War II.* New York: William Morrow, 1995.

Stephenson, Michael. *The Last Full Measure: How Soldiers Die in Battle*. New York: Broadway Paperbacks, 2012.

Stewart, Ollie. "The Ernie Pyle I Knew." *American Legion Magazine* 70, no. 2 (Feb. 1961).

Stoddard, Ruth. "Ernie Pyle." *Outdoor Indiana* 32, no. 2 (Nov. 1966).

Stoler, Mark A., and Melanie S. Gustafson, eds. *Major Problems in the History of World War II*. Boston: Houghton Mifflin Harcourt, 2003.

Sweeney, Michael S. "Appointment at Hill 1205: Ernie Pyle and Captain Henry T. Waskow." Texas Military Forces Museum, 36th Infantry Division Association.

———. *The Military and the Press: An Uneasy Truce*. Evanston, IL: Northwestern University Press, 2006.

Tick, Edward. *War and the Soul: Healing Our Nation's Veterans from Post-Traumatic Stress Disorder*. Wheaton, IL: Quest Books, 2005.

Tobin, James. *Ernie Pyle's War: America's Eyewitness to World War II*. New York: The Free Press, 1997.

Treanor, Tom. "What Did You See, Tom?" *Vogue* 104 (Oct. 1, 1944).

Tregaskis, Richard. *Guadalcanal Diary*. New York: Modern Library, 2000.

———. *Invasion Diary*. Lincoln: University of Nebraska Press, 2004.

Trimmer, Maurice. "Ernie Pyle Called Albuquerque 'Home.'" *New Mexico Magazine* 38 (Oct. 1960).

Waller, Willard W. *The Veteran Comes Back*. New York: Dryden Press, 1944.

Watson, Bruce Allen. *Exit Rommel: The Tunisian Campaign, 1942–43*. Mechanicsburg, PA: Stackpole Books, 2007.

Weber, Ronald. *Dateline—Liberated Paris: The Hotel Scribe and the Invasion of the Press*. New York: Rowman & Littlefield, 2019.

Wheelan, Joseph. *Bloody Okinawa: The Last Great Battle of World War II*. New York: Hachette Books, 2020.

White, William L. *Journey for Margaret*. New York: Harcourt, Brace & Company, 1941.

Whitlock, Flint. *Desperate Valour: Triumph at Anzio*. New York: Da Capo Press, 2018.

Wood, David. *What Have We Done: The Moral Injury of Our Longest Wars*. New York: Little, Brown and Company, 2016.

Wright, James. *Those Who Have Borne the Battle: A History of America's Wars and Those Who Fought Them*. New York: PublicAffairs, 2012.

Wylie, Evans. "The Quiet Little Man Traveled Half the World Following GIs to War Before a Jap Bullet Caught up with His Luck on Ie Island." *Yank*, May 18, 1945; reprinted in Debs Myers, Jonathan Kilbourn, and Richard Harrity, eds., *Yank—the GI Story of the War*. New York: Duell, Sloan & Pearce, 1947.

Yahara, Hiromichi. *The Battle of Okinawa: A Japanese Officer's Eyewitness Account of the Last Great Campaign of World War II*. New York: John Wiley & Sons, 1995.

INDEX